2311A: Advanced Web Application Development Using ASP.NET

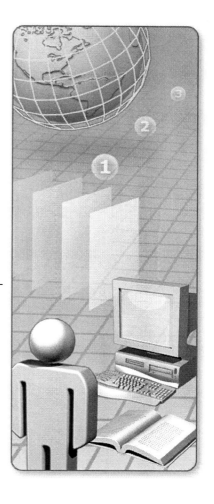

Information in this document, including URL and other Internet Web site references, is subject to change without notice. Unless otherwise noted, the example companies, products, domain names, e-mail addresses, logos, people, places, and events depicted herein are fictitious, and no association with any real company, organization, product, domain name, e-mail address, logo, person, places or events is intended or should be inferred. Complying with all applicable copyright laws is the responsibility of the user. Without limiting the rights under copyright, no part of this document may be reproduced, stored in or introduced into a retrieval system, or transmitted in any form or by any means (electronic, mechanical, photocopying, recording, or otherwise), or for any purpose, without express written permission of Hilton Computer Strategies.

Hilton Computer Strategies or Microsoft may have patents, patent applications, trademarks, copyrights, or other intellectual property rights covering subject matter in this document. Except as expressly provided in any written license agreement from Hilton Computer Strategies or Microsoft, respectively, the furnishing of this document does not give you any license to these patents, trademarks, copyrights, or other intellectual property.

© 2003-2004 Hilton Computer Strategies. All rights reserved.

Hilton Computer Strategies
6001 Savoy, Suite 207
Houston, TX 77036
713.782.6665
800.324.7415
Fax 713.782.0630
www.hiltoncomputer.com

Microsoft, MS-DOS, Windows, Windows NT, ActiveX, BizTalk, IntelliSense, Jscript, MSDN, PowerPoint, SQL Server, Visual Basic, Visual C++, Visual C#, Visual J#, Visual Studio, and Win32, are either registered trademarks or trademarks of Microsoft Corporation in the USA and/or other countries.

The names of actual companies and products mentioned herein may be the trademarks of their respective owners.

This course was developed by Hilton Computer Strategies in association with Microsoft Learning. Thank you to everyone at Hilton Computer Strategies and Microsoft Learning who helped make this book possible.

Clinic: 2311A
Part Number: X10-81641
Released: 09/2004

END-USER LICENSE AGREEMENT FOR MICROSOFT LEARNING PRODUCTS – STUDENT EDITION

PLEASE READ THIS END-USER LICENSE AGREEMENT ("EULA") CAREFULLY. BY USING THE MATERIALS AND/OR USING OR INSTALLING THE SOFTWARE THAT ACCOMPANIES THIS EULA (COLLECTIVELY, THE "LICENSED CONTENT"), YOU AGREE TO THE TERMS OF THIS EULA. IF YOU DO NOT AGREE, DO NOT USE THE LICENSED CONTENT.

1. **GENERAL.** This EULA is a legal agreement between you (either an individual or a single entity) and Microsoft Corporation ("Microsoft"). This EULA governs the Licensed Content, which includes computer software (including online and electronic documentation), training materials, and any other associated media and printed materials. This EULA applies to updates, supplements, add-on components, and Internet-based services components of the Licensed Content that Microsoft may provide or make available to you unless Microsoft provides other terms with the update, supplement, add-on component, or Internet-based services component. Microsoft reserves the right to discontinue any Internet-based services provided to you or made available to you through the use of the Licensed Content. This EULA also governs any product support services relating to the Licensed Content except as may be included in another agreement between you and Microsoft. An amendment or addendum to this EULA may accompany the Licensed Content.

2. **GENERAL GRANT OF LICENSE.** Microsoft grants you the following rights, conditioned on your compliance with all the terms and conditions of this EULA. Microsoft grants you a limited, non-exclusive, royalty-free license to install and use the Licensed Content solely in conjunction with your participation as a student in an Authorized Training Session (as defined below). You may install and use one copy of the software on a single computer, device, workstation, terminal, or other digital electronic or analog device ("Device"). You may make a second copy of the software and install it on a portable Device for the exclusive use of the person who is the primary user of the first copy of the software. A license for the software may not be shared for use by multiple end users. An "Authorized Training Session" means a training session conducted at a Microsoft Certified Technical Education Center, an IT Academy, via a Microsoft Certified Partner, or such other entity as Microsoft may designate from time to time in writing, by a Microsoft Certified Trainer (for more information on these entities, please visit www.microsoft.com). WITHOUT LIMITING THE FOREGOING, COPYING OR REPRODUCTION OF THE LICENSED CONTENT TO ANY SERVER OR LOCATION FOR FURTHER REPRODUCTION OR REDISTRIBUTION IS EXPRESSLY PROHIBITED.

3. **DESCRIPTION OF OTHER RIGHTS AND LICENSE LIMITATIONS**

    3.1 *Use of Documentation and Printed Training Materials.*

    3.1.1 The documents and related graphics included in the Licensed Content may include technical inaccuracies or typographical errors. Changes are periodically made to the content. Microsoft may make improvements and/or changes in any of the components of the Licensed Content at any time without notice. The names of companies, products, people, characters and/or data mentioned in the Licensed Content may be fictitious and are in no way intended to represent any real individual, company, product or event, unless otherwise noted.

    3.1.2 Microsoft grants you the right to reproduce portions of documents (such as student workbooks, white papers, press releases, datasheets and FAQs) (the "Documents") provided with the Licensed Content. You may not print any book (either electronic or print version) in its entirety. If you choose to reproduce Documents, you agree that: (a) use of such printed Documents will be solely in conjunction with your personal training use; (b) the Documents will not republished or posted on any network computer or broadcast in any media; (c) any reproduction will include either the Document's original copyright notice or a copyright notice to Microsoft's benefit substantially in the format provided below; and (d) to comply with all terms and conditions of this EULA. In addition, no modifications may made to any Document.

    Form of Notice:

    Copyright undefined.

    © 2004. Reprinted with permission by Microsoft Corporation. All rights reserved.

    Microsoft and Windows are either registered trademarks or trademarks of Microsoft Corporation in the US and/or other countries. Other product and company names mentioned herein may be the trademarks of their respective owners.

    3.2 *Use of Media Elements.* The Licensed Content may include certain photographs, clip art, animations, sounds, music, and video clips (together "Media Elements"). You may not modify these Media Elements.

    3.3 *Use of Sample Code.* In the event that the Licensed Content include sample source code ("Sample Code"), Microsoft grants you a limited, non-exclusive, royalty-free license to use, copy and modify the Sample Code; if you elect to exercise the foregoing rights, you agree to comply with all other terms and conditions of this EULA, including without limitation Sections 3.4, 3.5, and 6.

    3.4 *Permitted Modifications.* In the event that you exercise any rights provided under this EULA to create modifications of the Licensed Content, you agree that any such modifications: (a) will not be used for providing training where a fee is charged in public or private classes; (b) indemnify, hold harmless, and defend Microsoft from and against any claims or lawsuits, including attorneys' fees, which arise from or result from your use of any modified version of the Licensed Content; and (c) not to transfer or assign any rights to any modified version of the Licensed Content to any third party without the express written permission of Microsoft.

3.5   *Reproduction/Redistribution Licensed Content.* Except as expressly provided in this EULA, you may not reproduce or distribute the Licensed Content or any portion thereof (including any permitted modifications) to any third parties without the express written permission of Microsoft.

4.   **RESERVATION OF RIGHTS AND OWNERSHIP.** Microsoft reserves all rights not expressly granted to you in this EULA. The Licensed Content is protected by copyright and other intellectual property laws and treaties. Microsoft or its suppliers own the title, copyright, and other intellectual property rights in the Licensed Content. You may not remove or obscure any copyright, trademark or patent notices that appear on the Licensed Content, or any components thereof, as delivered to you. **The Licensed Content is licensed, not sold.**

5.   **LIMITATIONS ON REVERSE ENGINEERING, DECOMPILATION, AND DISASSEMBLY.** You may not reverse engineer, decompile, or disassemble the Software or Media Elements, except and only to the extent that such activity is expressly permitted by applicable law notwithstanding this limitation.

6.   **LIMITATIONS ON SALE, RENTAL, ETC. AND CERTAIN ASSIGNMENTS.** You may not provide commercial hosting services with, sell, rent, lease, lend, sublicense, or assign copies of the Licensed Content, or any portion thereof (including any permitted modifications thereof) on a stand-alone basis or as part of any collection, product or service.

7.   **CONSENT TO USE OF DATA.** You agree that Microsoft and its affiliates may collect and use technical information gathered as part of the product support services provided to you, if any, related to the Licensed Content. Microsoft may use this information solely to improve our products or to provide customized services or technologies to you and will not disclose this information in a form that personally identifies you.

8.   **LINKS TO THIRD PARTY SITES.** You may link to third party sites through the use of the Licensed Content. The third party sites are not under the control of Microsoft, and Microsoft is not responsible for the contents of any third party sites, any links contained in third party sites, or any changes or updates to third party sites. Microsoft is not responsible for webcasting or any other form of transmission received from any third party sites. Microsoft is providing these links to third party sites to you only as a convenience, and the inclusion of any link does not imply an endorsement by Microsoft of the third party site.

9.   **ADDITIONAL LICENSED CONTENT/SERVICES.** This EULA applies to updates, supplements, add-on components, or Internet-based services components, of the Licensed Content that Microsoft may provide to you or make available to you after the date you obtain your initial copy of the Licensed Content, unless we provide other terms along with the update, supplement, add-on component, or Internet-based services component. Microsoft reserves the right to discontinue any Internet-based services provided to you or made available to you through the use of the Licensed Content.

10.   **U.S. GOVERNMENT LICENSE RIGHTS**. All software provided to the U.S. Government pursuant to solicitations issued on or after December 1, 1995 is provided with the commercial license rights and restrictions described elsewhere herein. All software provided to the U.S. Government pursuant to solicitations issued prior to December 1, 1995 is provided with "Restricted Rights" as provided for in FAR, 48 CFR 52.227-14 (JUNE 1987) or DFAR, 48 CFR 252.227-7013 (OCT 1988), as applicable.

11.   **EXPORT RESTRICTIONS.** You acknowledge that the Licensed Content is subject to U.S. export jurisdiction. You agree to comply with all applicable international and national laws that apply to the Licensed Content, including the U.S. Export Administration Regulations, as well as end-user, end-use, and destination restrictions issued by U.S. and other governments. For additional information see <http://www.microsoft.com/exporting/>.

12.   **TRANSFER.** The initial user of the Licensed Content may make a one-time permanent transfer of this EULA and Licensed Content to another end user, provided the initial user retains no copies of the Licensed Content. The transfer may not be an indirect transfer, such as a consignment. Prior to the transfer, the end user receiving the Licensed Content must agree to all the EULA terms.

13.   **"NOT FOR RESALE" LICENSED CONTENT.** Licensed Content identified as "Not For Resale" or "NFR," may not be sold or otherwise transferred for value, or used for any purpose other than demonstration, test or evaluation.

14.   **TERMINATION.** Without prejudice to any other rights, Microsoft may terminate this EULA if you fail to comply with the terms and conditions of this EULA. In such event, you must destroy all copies of the Licensed Content and all of its component parts.

15.   <u>**DISCLAIMER OF WARRANTIES.**</u> **TO THE MAXIMUM EXTENT PERMITTED BY APPLICABLE LAW, MICROSOFT AND ITS SUPPLIERS PROVIDE THE LICENSED CONTENT AND SUPPORT SERVICES (IF ANY)** *AS IS AND WITH ALL FAULTS,* **AND MICROSOFT AND ITS SUPPLIERS HEREBY DISCLAIM ALL OTHER WARRANTIES AND CONDITIONS, WHETHER EXPRESS, IMPLIED OR STATUTORY, INCLUDING, BUT NOT LIMITED TO, ANY (IF ANY) IMPLIED WARRANTIES, DUTIES OR CONDITIONS OF MERCHANTABILITY, OF FITNESS FOR A PARTICULAR PURPOSE, OF RELIABILITY OR AVAILABILITY, OF ACCURACY OR COMPLETENESS OF RESPONSES, OF RESULTS, OF WORKMANLIKE EFFORT, OF LACK OF VIRUSES, AND OF LACK OF NEGLIGENCE, ALL WITH REGARD TO THE LICENSED CONTENT, AND THE PROVISION OF OR FAILURE TO PROVIDE SUPPORT OR OTHER SERVICES, INFORMATION, SOFTWARE, AND RELATED CONTENT THROUGH THE LICENSED CONTENT, OR OTHERWISE ARISING OUT OF THE USE OF THE LICENSED CONTENT. ALSO, THERE IS NO WARRANTY OR CONDITION OF TITLE, QUIET ENJOYMENT, QUIET POSSESSION, CORRESPONDENCE TO DESCRIPTION OR NON-INFRINGEMENT WITH REGARD TO THE LICENSED CONTENT. THE ENTIRE RISK AS TO THE QUALITY, OR ARISING OUT OF THE USE OR PERFORMANCE OF THE LICENSED CONTENT, AND ANY SUPPORT SERVICES, REMAINS WITH YOU.**

16.   <u>**EXCLUSION OF INCIDENTAL, CONSEQUENTIAL AND CERTAIN OTHER DAMAGES.**</u> **TO THE MAXIMUM EXTENT PERMITTED BY APPLICABLE LAW, IN NO EVENT SHALL MICROSOFT OR ITS SUPPLIERS BE LIABLE FOR ANY SPECIAL, INCIDENTAL, PUNITIVE, INDIRECT, OR CONSEQUENTIAL DAMAGES WHATSOEVER (INCLUDING, BUT NOT**

LIMITED TO, DAMAGES FOR LOSS OF PROFITS OR CONFIDENTIAL OR OTHER INFORMATION, FOR BUSINESS INTERRUPTION, FOR PERSONAL INJURY, FOR LOSS OF PRIVACY, FOR FAILURE TO MEET ANY DUTY INCLUDING OF GOOD FAITH OR OF REASONABLE CARE, FOR NEGLIGENCE, AND FOR ANY OTHER PECUNIARY OR OTHER LOSS WHATSOEVER) ARISING OUT OF OR IN ANY WAY RELATED TO THE USE OF OR INABILITY TO USE THE LICENSED CONTENT, THE PROVISION OF OR FAILURE TO PROVIDE SUPPORT OR OTHER SERVICES, INFORMATION, SOFTWARE, AND RELATED CONTENT THROUGH THE LICENSED CONTENT, OR OTHERWISE ARISING OUT OF THE USE OF THE LICENSED CONTENT, OR OTHERWISE UNDER OR IN CONNECTION WITH ANY PROVISION OF THIS EULA, EVEN IN THE EVENT OF THE FAULT, TORT (INCLUDING NEGLIGENCE), MISREPRESENTATION, STRICT LIABILITY, BREACH OF CONTRACT OR BREACH OF WARRANTY OF MICROSOFT OR ANY SUPPLIER, AND EVEN IF MICROSOFT OR ANY SUPPLIER HAS BEEN ADVISED OF THE POSSIBILITY OF SUCH DAMAGES. BECAUSE SOME STATES/JURISDICTIONS DO NOT ALLOW THE EXCLUSION OR LIMITATION OF LIABILITY FOR CONSEQUENTIAL OR INCIDENTAL DAMAGES, THE ABOVE LIMITATION MAY NOT APPLY TO YOU.

17. **LIMITATION OF LIABILITY AND REMEDIES.** NOTWITHSTANDING ANY DAMAGES THAT YOU MIGHT INCUR FOR ANY REASON WHATSOEVER (INCLUDING, WITHOUT LIMITATION, ALL DAMAGES REFERENCED HEREIN AND ALL DIRECT OR GENERAL DAMAGES IN CONTRACT OR ANYTHING ELSE), THE ENTIRE LIABILITY OF MICROSOFT AND ANY OF ITS SUPPLIERS UNDER ANY PROVISION OF THIS EULA AND YOUR EXCLUSIVE REMEDY HEREUNDER SHALL BE LIMITED TO THE GREATER OF THE ACTUAL DAMAGES YOU INCUR IN REASONABLE RELIANCE ON THE LICENSED CONTENT UP TO THE AMOUNT ACTUALLY PAID BY YOU FOR THE LICENSED CONTENT OR US$5.00. THE FOREGOING LIMITATIONS, EXCLUSIONS AND DISCLAIMERS SHALL APPLY TO THE MAXIMUM EXTENT PERMITTED BY APPLICABLE LAW, EVEN IF ANY REMEDY FAILS ITS ESSENTIAL PURPOSE.

18. **APPLICABLE LAW.** If you acquired this Licensed Content in the United States, this EULA is governed by the laws of the State of Washington. If you acquired this Licensed Content in Canada, unless expressly prohibited by local law, this EULA is governed by the laws in force in the Province of Ontario, Canada; and, in respect of any dispute which may arise hereunder, you consent to the jurisdiction of the federal and provincial courts sitting in Toronto, Ontario. If you acquired this Licensed Content in the European Union, Iceland, Norway, or Switzerland, then local law applies. If you acquired this Licensed Content in any other country, then local law may apply.

19. **ENTIRE AGREEMENT; SEVERABILITY.** This EULA (including any addendum or amendment to this EULA which is included with the Licensed Content) are the entire agreement between you and Microsoft relating to the Licensed Content and the support services (if any) and they supersede all prior or contemporaneous oral or written communications, proposals and representations with respect to the Licensed Content or any other subject matter covered by this EULA. To the extent the terms of any Microsoft policies or programs for support services conflict with the terms of this EULA, the terms of this EULA shall control. If any provision of this EULA is held to be void, invalid, unenforceable or illegal, the other provisions shall continue in full force and effect.

Should you have any questions concerning this EULA, or if you desire to contact Microsoft for any reason, please use the address information enclosed in this Licensed Content to contact the Microsoft subsidiary serving your country or visit Microsoft on the World Wide Web at http://www.microsoft.com.

Si vous avez acquis votre Contenu Sous Licence Microsoft au CANADA :

DÉNI DE GARANTIES. Dans la mesure maximale permise par les lois applicables, le Contenu Sous Licence et les services de soutien technique (le cas échéant) sont fournis *TELS QUELS ET AVEC TOUS LES DÉFAUTS* par Microsoft et ses fournisseurs, lesquels par les présentes dénient toutes autres garanties et conditions expresses, implicites ou en vertu de la loi, notamment, mais sans limitation, (le cas échéant) les garanties, devoirs ou conditions implicites de qualité marchande, d'adaptation à une fin usage particulière, de fiabilité ou de disponibilité, d'exactitude ou d'exhaustivité des réponses, des résultats, des efforts déployés selon les règles de l'art, d'absence de virus et d'absence de négligence, le tout à l'égard du Contenu Sous Licence et de la prestation des services de soutien technique ou de l'omission de la 'une telle prestation des services de soutien technique ou à l'égard de la fourniture ou de l'omission de la fourniture de tous autres services, renseignements, Contenus Sous Licence, et contenu qui s'y rapporte grâce au Contenu Sous Licence ou provenant autrement de l'utilisation du Contenu Sous Licence. PAR AILLEURS, IL N'Y A AUCUNE GARANTIE OU CONDITION QUANT AU TITRE DE PROPRIÉTÉ, À LA JOUISSANCE OU LA POSSESSION PAISIBLE, À LA CONCORDANCE À UNE DESCRIPTION NI QUANT À UNE ABSENCE DE CONTREFAÇON CONCERNANT LE CONTENU SOUS LICENCE.

EXCLUSION DES DOMMAGES ACCESSOIRES, INDIRECTS ET DE CERTAINS AUTRES DOMMAGES. DANS LA MESURE MAXIMALE PERMISE PAR LES LOIS APPLICABLES, EN AUCUN CAS MICROSOFT OU SES FOURNISSEURS NE SERONT RESPONSABLES DES DOMMAGES SPÉCIAUX, CONSÉCUTIFS, ACCESSOIRES OU INDIRECTS DE QUELQUE NATURE QUE CE SOIT (NOTAMMENT, LES DOMMAGES À L'ÉGARD DU MANQUE À GAGNER OU DE LA DIVULGATION DE RENSEIGNEMENTS CONFIDENTIELS OU AUTRES, DE LA PERTE D'EXPLOITATION, DE BLESSURES CORPORELLES, DE LA VIOLATION DE LA VIE PRIVÉE, DE L'OMISSION DE REMPLIR TOUT DEVOIR, Y COMPRIS D'AGIR DE BONNE FOI OU D'EXERCER UN SOIN RAISONNABLE, DE LA NÉGLIGENCE ET DE TOUTE AUTRE PERTE PÉCUNIAIRE OU AUTRE PERTE

DE QUELQUE NATURE QUE CE SOIT) SE RAPPORTANT DE QUELQUE MANIÈRE QUE CE SOIT À L'UTILISATION DU CONTENU SOUS LICENCE OU À L'INCAPACITÉ DE S'EN SERVIR, À LA PRESTATION OU À L'OMISSION DE LA 'UNE TELLE PRESTATION DE SERVICES DE SOUTIEN TECHNIQUE OU À LA FOURNITURE OU À L'OMISSION DE LA FOURNITURE DE TOUS AUTRES SERVICES, RENSEIGNEMENTS, CONTENUS SOUS LICENCE, ET CONTENU QUI S'Y RAPPORTE GRÂCE AU CONTENU SOUS LICENCE OU PROVENANT AUTREMENT DE L'UTILISATION DU CONTENU SOUS LICENCE OU AUTREMENT AUX TERMES DE TOUTE DISPOSITION DE LA U PRÉSENTE CONVENTION EULA OU RELATIVEMENT À UNE TELLE DISPOSITION, MÊME EN CAS DE FAUTE, DE DÉLIT CIVIL (Y COMPRIS LA NÉGLIGENCE), DE RESPONSABILITÉ STRICTE, DE VIOLATION DE CONTRAT OU DE VIOLATION DE GARANTIE DE MICROSOFT OU DE TOUT FOURNISSEUR ET MÊME SI MICROSOFT OU TOUT FOURNISSEUR A ÉTÉ AVISÉ DE LA POSSIBILITÉ DE TELS DOMMAGES.

<u>LIMITATION DE RESPONSABILITÉ ET RECOURS.</u>   MALGRÉ LES DOMMAGES QUE VOUS PUISSIEZ SUBIR POUR QUELQUE MOTIF QUE CE SOIT (NOTAMMENT, MAIS SANS LIMITATION, TOUS LES DOMMAGES SUSMENTIONNÉS ET TOUS LES DOMMAGES DIRECTS OU GÉNÉRAUX OU AUTRES), LA SEULE RESPONSABILITÉ 'OBLIGATION INTÉGRALE DE MICROSOFT ET DE L'UN OU L'AUTRE DE SES FOURNISSEURS AUX TERMES DE TOUTE DISPOSITION DEU LA PRÉSENTE CONVENTION EULA ET VOTRE RECOURS EXCLUSIF À L'ÉGARD DE TOUT CE QUI PRÉCÈDE SE LIMITE AU PLUS ÉLEVÉ ENTRE LES MONTANTS SUIVANTS : LE MONTANT QUE VOUS AVEZ RÉELLEMENT PAYÉ POUR LE CONTENU SOUS LICENCE OU 5,00 $US. LES LIMITES, EXCLUSIONS ET DÉNIS QUI PRÉCÈDENT (Y COMPRIS LES CLAUSES CI-DESSUS), S'APPLIQUENT DANS LA MESURE MAXIMALE PERMISE PAR LES LOIS APPLICABLES, MÊME SI TOUT RECOURS N'ATTEINT PAS SON BUT ESSENTIEL.

À moins que cela ne soit prohibé par le droit local applicable, la présente Convention est régie par les lois de la province d'Ontario, Canada. Vous consentez Chacune des parties à la présente reconnaît irrévocablement à la compétence des tribunaux fédéraux et provinciaux siégeant à Toronto, dans de la province d'Ontario et consent à instituer tout litige qui pourrait découler de la présente auprès des tribunaux situés dans le district judiciaire de York, province d'Ontario.

Au cas où vous auriez des questions concernant cette licence ou que vous désiriez vous mettre en rapport avec Microsoft pour quelque raison que ce soit, veuillez utiliser l'information contenue dans le Contenu Sous Licence pour contacter la filiale de succursale Microsoft desservant votre pays, dont l'adresse est fournie dans ce produit, ou visitez écrivez à : Microsoft sur le World Wide Web à http://www.microsoft.com

Contents

Introduction	About this Course	
Module 1	Considerations for Building Advanced ASP.NET Applications	
Lab 1	Understanding Application Structure	19
Module 2	Designing Data Tier Components	
Lab 2	Using Data Access Components	68
Module 3	Web Presentation Patterns	
Lab 3	Implementing Databound Presentations	63
Module 4	Building Custom Controls	
Lab 4	Building Custom Controls	33
Module 5	Using Graphics Classes to Generate Images	
Lab 5	Generating Data-Driven Graphics	25
Module 6	Creating a Secure Infrastructure	
Lab 6	Creating a Security Infrastructure	42
Module 7	Caching Patterns and Practices	
Lab 7	Caching in the Portal Application	47
Module 8	Diagnostics and Exception Handling	
Lab 8	Using the Exception Manager	22
Module 9	Interoperability with COM	
Lab 9	Interoperability with COM	23
Module 10	ASP.NET Configuration	
Lab 10	Configuration Management	33
Module 11	Administering and Extending the Portal	
Lab 11	Extending the Portal with New Modules	20

About This Course

This section provides you with a brief description of the course, audience, suggested prerequisites, and course objectives.

Description

The course provides the information that developers need to know to successfully extend their ASP.NET Web development skills. The material that comprises this course deals with advanced topics in ASP.NET for those who have already had significant exposure to the basics. This course also contains information about ASP.NET best practices and guidelines for architecting ASP.NET applications. It draws extensively on the Microsoft Patterns and Practices material, which is included as part of the courseware. Rather than introducing students to the fundamental features of ASP.NET, it is intended to provide depth in specific topics such as data access, databinding, custom controls, graphics, security, caching, debugging, performance measurement and tuning, configuration settings, and COM interop. To illustrate the concepts presented, the ASP.NET Starter Kits, particularly the Portal and Time Tracker applications, furnish many of the examples. The main lab application is derived from the ASP.NET Starter Kit Portal application, enhanced to illustrate best practices which have been discovered in the developer community.

Audience

This course is intended for existing Web developers who have written ASP Web applications. This course requires that students meet the following prerequisites:

- Ability to create Hypertext Markup Language (HTML) pages with tables, images, and forms.
- Experience using a scripting language, such as Microsoft Visual Basic® Scripting Edition or JavaScript.
- Experience using ASP.NET to create Web applications.
- Ability to retrieve data from a relational database by using ADO.NET.
- Familiarity with a Microsoft .NET-based programming language.

Course Objectives

After completing this course, students will be able to:

- Explain the major architectural choices in designing and building ASP.NET applications.
- Use databinding to create sophisticated data reports.
- Create bound and unbound custom controls.
- Generate graphics dynamically using GDI+.
- Describe the tradeoffs in designing a security strategy.
- Implement advanced caching techniques.
- Carry out production debugging procedures.
- Measure and tune ASP.NET application performance.

Introduction

Contents

Introduction	1
Course Materials	2
Prerequisites	3
Course Outline	4
Setup	6
Facilities	7

Information in this document, including URL and other Internet Web site references, is subject to change without notice. Unless otherwise noted, the example companies, products, domain names, e-mail addresses, logos, people, places, and events depicted herein are fictitious, and no association with any real company, organization, product, domain name, e-mail address, logo, person, places or events is intended or should be inferred. Complying with all applicable copyright laws is the responsibility of the user. Without limiting the rights under copyright, no part of this document may be reproduced, stored in or introduced into a retrieval system, or transmitted in any form or by any means (electronic, mechanical, photocopying, recording, or otherwise), or for any purpose, without express written permission of Hilton Computer Strategies.

Hilton Computer Strategies or Microsoft may have patents, patent applications, trademarks, copyrights, or other intellectual property rights covering subject matter in this document. Except as expressly provided in any written license agreement from Hilton Computer Strategies or Microsoft, respectively, the furnishing of this document does not give you any license to these patents, trademarks, copyrights, or other intellectual property.

© 2003-2004 Hilton Computer Strategies. All rights reserved.

Hilton Computer Strategies
6001 Savoy, Suite 207
Houston, TX 77036
713.782.6665
800.324.7415
Fax 713.782.0630
www.hiltoncomputer.com

Microsoft, MS-DOS, Windows, Windows NT, ActiveX, BizTalk, IntelliSense, Jscript, MSDN, PowerPoint, SQL Server, Visual Basic, Visual C++, Visual C#, Visual J#, Visual Studio, and Win32, are either registered trademarks or trademarks of Microsoft Corporation in the USA and/or other countries.

The names of actual companies and products mentioned herein may be the trademarks of their respective owners.

Course Number: 2311
Released: 09/2004

Introduction

- Name
- Company affiliation
- Title and function
- Job responsibility
- Programming, networking, and database experience
- Product experience
- Expectations for the course

Course Materials

- Name card
- Student workbook
- Student Materials compact disc
- Assessments
- Course evaluation

The following materials are included with your kit:

- *Name card*. Write your name on both sides of the name card.
- *Student workbook*. The student workbook contains the materials covered in class, in addition to the hands-on lab exercises.
- *Student Materials compact disc*. The Student Materials compact disc contains the Web page that provides you with links to resources pertaining to this course, including additional readings, review and lab answers, lab files, multimedia presentations, and course-related Web sites.

   Note To open the Web page, insert the Student Materials compact disc into the CD-ROM drive, and then, in the root directory of the compact disc, double-click **StartCD.exe**.

- *Assessments*. There are assessments for each lesson, located on the Student Materials compact disc. You can use them as pre-assessments to identify areas of difficulty, or you can use them as post-assessments to validate learning.
- *Course evaluation*. To provide feedback on the course, training facility, and instructor, you will have the opportunity to complete an online evaluation near the end of the course.

  To provide additional comments or feedback about the course, send e-mail to support@mscourseware.com. To inquire about the Microsoft Certified Professional program, send e-mail to mcphelp@microsoft.com.

Prerequisites

> - Ability to create HTML pages with tables, images, and forms
> - Experience using a scripting language, such as Microsoft Visual Basic Scripting Edition or JavaScript
> - Experience using Microsoft ASP.NET to create Web applications
> - Ability to retrieve data from a relational database by using Microsoft ADO.NET
> - Familiarity with a Microsoft .NET–based programming language

This course requires that you have experience in the following areas:

- Ability to create Hypertext Markup Language (HTML) pages with tables, images, and forms.
- Experience using a scripting language, such as Microsoft® Visual Basic® Scripting Edition or JavaScript.
- Experience using Microsoft ASP.NET to create Web applications.
- Ability to retrieve data from a relational database by using ADO.NET.
- Familiarity with a Microsoft .NET–based programming language.

Course Outline

> - Module 1: Considerations for Building Advanced ASP.NET Applications
> - Module 2: Designing Data Tier Components
> - Module 3: Web Presentation Patterns
> - Module 4: Building Custom Controls OR Module 5: Using Graphics Classes to Generate Images
> - Module 6: Creating a Secure Infrastructure
> - Module 7: Caching Patterns and Practices
> - Module 8: Diagnostics and Exception Handling
> - Module 9: Interoperability with COM
> - Module 10: ASP.NET Configuration
> - Module 11: Administering and Extending the Portal

Module 1, "Considerations for Building Advanced ASP .NET Applications," describes the architecture of IBuySpy Portal, a Microsoft® ASP.NET Web application based on a fictitious company, and relates it to the Microsoft recommended practices for building such applications.

Module 2, "Designing Data Tier Components," instructs you on how to enable scalable, high-performance data retrieval, persistence, and transfer in a multi-tiered Web application. By building from the data tier to the user interface tier, the architect can ensure that one of the fundamental pillars of the application is stable, well-factored, and extensible.

Module 3, "Web Presentation Patterns," teaches you how user interface elements can be built by using proven design patterns for ASP.NET applications. A pattern describes a recurring problem that occurs in a given context and, based on a set of guiding forces, recommends a solution.

Module 4, "Building Custom Controls," teaches you how to implement custom controls to extend the user interface of your ASP.NET application. Developers can either derive from an existing control or create their own control by deriving it from the **Control** or **WebControl** classes.

Module 5, "Using Graphics Classes to Generate Images," introduces how to use the classes in the System.Drawing namespace to generate images in ASP.NET pages. The classes included in Microsoft Windows® Graphics Device Interface (GDI+) provide a powerful and flexible set of tools to produce such images. This module demonstrates best practices for implementing user data to populate such commonly used business graphics as bar charts and pie charts using 3-D effects.

Module 6, "Creating a Secure Infrastructure," discusses the security of your Web applications. This module presents scenarios to help you identify the factors involved in effectively authenticating and authorizing clients to ASP.NET Web applications. The module also examines how to build secure communication channels so that clients can interact without fear of privileged information being compromised. You will learn about some of the major risks and common pitfalls faced by developers when designing a security infrastructure. Finally, you will learn how a portal implements a flexible and extensible security system.

Module 7, "Caching Patterns and Practices," describes how the cache object works and how it can be used with the portal module object model to optimize caching capabilities.

Module 8, "Diagnostics and Exception Handling," teaches you how to choose appropriate debugging techniques for Web applications, implement logging and diagnostics frameworks, stress-test Web applications, and use performance counters to measure application performance.

Module 9, "Interoperability with COM," describes the usefulness of COM components and how to integrate their functionality into .NET applications.

Module 10, "ASP.NET Configuration," teaches you the .NET configuration architecture, how to read and write custom configuration sections, and how to abstract configuration information so that it can be stored in different types of storage mediums.

Module 11, "Administering and Extending the Portal," presents an extensible administrative infrastructure for managing the portal application. You will explore the major features of the administrative interface and add new modules to the portal.

Setup

- Microsoft Windows Server 2003, Enterprise Edition
- Microsoft SQL Server 2000
- Microsoft Visual Studio 2003

The following software will be used in the classroom:

- Microsoft Windows Server™ 2003 Enterprise Edition
- Microsoft SQL Server™ 2000
- Microsoft Visual Studio® 2003

Course files

There are files associated with the labs in this course. The lab files are located in the folder D:\2311\Labfiles\LabXX on the student computers.

Facilities

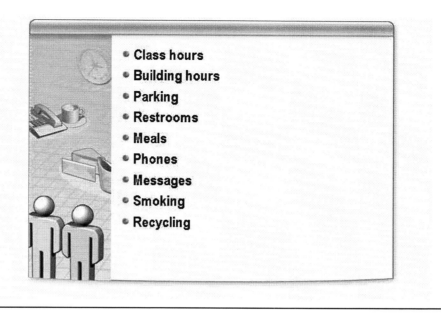

Module 1: Considerations for Building Advanced ASP.NET Applications

Overview

- ASP.NET Architecture
- Guiding Principles for Designing Web Applications
- Portal Architecture

Overview

This module describes the architecture of IBuySpy Portal, a Microsoft® ASP.NET Web application based on a fictitious company, and relates it to the Microsoft recommended practices for building such applications.

Since its release in January 2002, the IBuySpy Portal and its more recent ASP.NET Starter Kit version have been embraced by the Microsoft .NET development community as an essential reference application for building ASP.NET applications. This module uses the example of a custom-built version of IBuySpy Portal to identify best practices for enterprise-class Web applications and explore the unique features of ASP.NET that support these practices. The module also explains the use of two ASP.NET Starter Kit applications: the TimeTracker and Portal applications. You can freely download these applications in both C# and Microsoft Visual Basic® .NET versions by going to http://www.asp.net. They are also included as part of the course materials and have been pre-installed in the Microsoft Virtual PC image for this course.

The application that is contained in this course is a portal application that is used to share information within the organization. Many businesses have the need to share information with employees on a regular basis. A portal is a great way to accomplish this. Employees may want to look for information that is relevant to their particular interests or needs, and the design of this portal categorizes information under topic-based tabs at the top of the portal home page.

Two requirements affect the architecture and design of the application. One requirement is for the application to be extensible. This means that additional tabs for new topics can be added to the application easily. In addition, modules (as described later in the course) can be added to portal pages easily.

The second requirement is that the look of the portal can be changed and administered by a portal administrator without the need for development skills. This requirement leads to an administration page that allows non-developers to add additional tabs and configure page content.

Objectives

After completing this module, you will be able to:

- Describe an ASP.NET Web application architecture that is easy to maintain and extend.
- Explain the use of the object-oriented features of .NET in constructing a portal application.
- Describe the data access and storage architecture of the application.
- Explain application configuration settings and the tradeoffs involved in creating a configuration strategy.

Lesson: General Considerations for Application Architecture

> **Lesson: General Considerations for Application Architecture**
> - ASP.NET Architecture
> - Guiding Principles for Web Applications
> - Portal Architecture

Introduction

This lesson introduces important concepts that you need to understand before building an ASP.NET Web application, including the essential components of ASP.NET architecture and fundamental guidelines for designing a Web application.

The Web application to be created in this course will be divided into presentation, business, and data tiers to isolate each major part from changes in the others, following current standards for loosely coupled design.

Lesson Objectives

After completing this lesson, you will be able to:

- Describe the basic components of ASP.NET architecture.
- Understand important considerations for designing Web applications.

ASP.NET Architecture

> **ASP.NET Architecture**
>
> **Client requests in ASP.NET**
> - HttpRuntime delegates request processing to a Page class instance
> - IIS transfers request to the worker process and then sends the response back to the client

Introduction

Microsoft ASP.NET offers a fundamentally different approach to handling client requests than previous versions of Active Server Pages (ASP). This section outlines two of the most important differences between the architecture of ASP.NET and its predecessor.

Page Processing in ASP.NET

Instead of all page processing taking place in a single process (Inetinfo.exe), the **HttpRuntime** service delegates request processing to a **Page** class instance that is responsible for responding to a specific request.

ASP.NET and IIS

In ASP.NET, the Internet Information Services (IIS) Web server performs security authentication. However, the primary function of IIS in ASP.NET is simply to transfer the request to the worker process and then send the response back to the client. This makes ASP.NET an ideal framework for developing component-oriented architectures.

Guiding Principles for Designing Web Applications

> **Guiding Principles for Designing Web Applications**
> - Ensure component consistency
> - Keep data formats to a minimum
> - Maximize use of attributes
> - Choose an appropriate layering strategy

Introduction

When designing a Web application, you should keep in mind the following design principles:

- Ensure that components are consistent in their design by centralizing configurations and establishing base classes for components.
- Keep data formats to a minimum.
- Maximize use of attributes.
- Choose an appropriate layering strategy.

Ensure Component Consistency

The most important principle of Web application architecture is to design all components of a particular type to be as consistent as possible by using one design model or a limited set of design models. This not only ensures predictability and maintainability, but it also allows Web applications to be more easily changed and extended. By encapsulating site functionality into a few consistently designed components and keeping configurations centralized in a small number of files, upgrading the site and adding new units of content can be easily managed.

It is a good practice to establish base classes for all components that follow a similar pattern. For example, in the portal application that will be developed in this module, a **PortalModuleControl** acts as the base class for all modules added to the site.

Keep Data Formats to a Minimum

It is also recommended that you use a small set of data formats rather than blending a collection of Extensible Markup Language (XML) documents, strings, arrays, and data objects. In most Web applications, the display functionality is serviced by **DataReaders**. In some cases, for example where data needs to be transferred between components, **DataSets** are the preferred choice. As a general rule, the fewer the formats, the more efficient and effective data access will be. The more data formats that need to be supported, the more difficult it will be to extend the application.

Maximize Use of Attributes

Policy code such as configuration, security, exception handling, and instrumentation should be abstracted from the business logic as much as possible. Attributes allow many such features to be declaratively programmed, so it is good practice to make maximum use of them for enforcing policy. Utility components that are reused across a range of applications are another good choice for this type of functionality.

Choose an Appropriate Layering Strategy

You should choose your layering strategy early in the course of application design. If the multitier model is strictly followed, every call from upstream components in the presentation layer should pass through a middle layer before being received and processed by the data layer. In real applications, this may lead to code that has no other purpose than to enforce this model. Many Web applications fall into this category. In cases where business logic requirements can be satisfied in code-behind pages without the risk of excessive redundancy, it is acceptable to call directly from the presentation to the data tier. However, calls from downstream to upstream components should be avoided in most scenarios.

Portal Architecture

> **Portal Architecture**
>
> - The portal comprises a data access layer, a business logic layer, and user interface components
> - Application layers
>   - The Configuration class provides access to configuration information
>   - The SiteConfiguration class provides data structure for working with configuration details
>   - The PortalSecurity class provides methods for managing users and roles
> - User interface
>   - Built from user controls and custom controls
>   - Primary unit of content is the *module*

Introduction

The portal uses a *data access layer*, a *business logic layer*, and user interface components. A set of data layer components provides access to the data stores. This layer is optimized for common operations across deployment patterns. It allows the application to scale easily as usage increases while providing reusable functionality to support a wide array of application needs. This layer is built on a standard pattern that allows new content modules to be easily added by following a few basic steps. Many components in the data access layer correspond to modules that provide a certain type of content for the user.

Data Access Layer

Access to configuration information is provided by a **Configuration** class that provides methods for retrieving configuration data. Other components control what content is available, how it is laid out, and who has access to it. An extensible library of business objects directs the management and use of portal information. The **SiteConfiguration** class is a typed **DataSet** that provides the main data structure for working with configuration details. Common data access functions are abstracted through the use of a data factory known as the *Data Access Application Block*.

Business Logic Layer

The business logic layer includes a **PortalSecurity** class that provides methods to allow the role of the current user to be easily checked, along with the ability to manage users and roles. Roles are also controlled and edited through a Roles user control.

User Interface

The user interface is built from user controls and custom controls. The primary unit of content is the *module*, whose main characteristics are defined in the **PortalModuleControl** base class, which derives from **UserControl**, thus creating a single custom control which provides the base functionality for all modules. The combination of the classes derived from this control and from Web forms using common server controls such as **DataGrids** and **DataLists** makes up the primary user interface functionality.

The Web application centralizes exception handling through the use of a flexible exception management component which extends the Microsoft Exception Management Application Block for .NET.

Lesson: Web Application Design

> **Lesson: Web Application Design**
> - General Design Practices
> - User Interface Design
> - Application Data Storage and Business Logic
> - Best Practices for Application Design

Introduction

Building a Web portal application requires an understanding of the key elements of Web application design. In addition to general design considerations, you will need to be familiar with practices specific to Web application and user interface design, as well as application data storage and business logic.

Objectives

After completing this lesson, you will be able to:

- Identify general design best practices.
- Understand user interface and Web application design considerations.
- Explain the role of application data storage and business logic in a Web application.

General Design Practices

> **General Design Practices**
> - Keep components that perform a similar role consistent
> - Keep data exchange formats consistent

Introduction

When designing a Web application, it is important to ensure that the application can be easily maintained. You can achieve this by making sure that your Web application's components and data exchange formats are consistent with one another.

Keep Components Consistent

The first principle of maintainability is to keep components that perform a similar role consistent. For this purpose, all of the portal modules use a single design model. Through inheritance, the base properties and methods for each unit of display (for example, Announcements, Task Tracking, and so on) are defined uniformly. Each module can be extended by using its own associated classes and stored procedures. Because these classes and stored procedures are modeled on a consistent pattern, they can be easily extended.

Keep Data Exchange Formats Consistent

Another area where coherent design pays off is with respect to data exchange formats. When displaying data in modules, a **DataReader** provides the best performance for read-only reporting. When consuming data in business processes, a strongly typed **DataSet** is often the best choice. Site configuration information is required by many parts of the portal. By defining a **SiteConfiguration** class as a typed **DataSet**, you can retrieve configuration data and use it across the application in a dependable and reusable format. Strongly typed collection classes can enhance performance, as well as provide an abstraction that maps closely to user interface requirements. The **ModuleItem** class represents the basic attributes of a module while providing methods to support object-specific behavior, such as sorting rules.

User Interface Design

> **User Interface Design**
> - Web forms facilitate editing and administration of user and module information
> - ASP.NET Cache object enhances application performance by reducing contention for database resources
> - User process components control access to business entities such as User objects
> - CurrentCulture enables customized localization

Introduction

The user interface for this portal consists primarily of dynamically loaded user controls. Data display is accomplished by using lightweight **DataList** or **Repeater** controls and, when necessary, **DataGrid** controls. Data is retrieved by using each module's associated data access component and is bound to a server control.

Editing and Administration

Another important aspect of Web application design is editing and administration of user and module information. A set of Web forms provides the editing interface for all properties that can be administered in each module. Where appropriate, validation controls have been used for client and server-side validation. The administrator can use these Web forms to customize the appearance and content of the portal by selecting modules and choosing which modules will be displayed to which roles.

One of the most significant aspects of user interface design, particularly from the user's perspective, is the speed at which the content is rendered. ASP.NET provides major enhancements in this area over previous versions of Microsoft Web technologies. ASP.NET furnishes a **Cache** object that can dramatically improve the performance of the application by reducing contention for database resources. Instead of making more round-trips to the database, data or user interface elements can be cached on the Web server. In contrast to previous types of ASP caching, the **Cache** object permits control over expiration length and allows stored data to have dependencies. The portal application takes advantage of this through the use of a **CachedPortalModuleControl** object that derives from the base class **PortalModuleControl**. This custom server control stores the content of a module in the **Cache** object so that it can be quickly retrieved in the **Page_Init** event and used to populate user interface controls. A key goal of user interface design is achieved: to avoid reconstructing elements. The pattern used here can be replicated in many situations where infrequently changed user content needs to be delivered.

User process components control access to business entities such as **User** objects. To display attributes and collections of business entities, the portal databinds controls to collections of entity components. Because the data-bound Web controls can bind to any object that implements the **ICollection** interface, displaying the attributes of business entities is straightforward and extensible.

Localization

Localization must be addressed in applications that will be accessed internationally. The portal responds with appropriate date, number, and currency formats according to user locale by detecting the **CurrentCulture** in the Global.asax file.

Application Data Storage and Business Logic

> **Application Data Storage and Business Logic**
>
> - Configuration files
>   - Web.config
>   - PortalCfg.xml
> - Business logic
> - Database schema
> - Configuration DataSet schema

Introduction

Portal applications use data for the creation of site content and use configuration files to determine how the site operates. These two distinct roles call for distinct data-management strategies. Content-oriented data must be stored for quick retrieval of potentially large quantities of information. A relational database provides the most favorable performance and manageability for this type of data. Configuration data is likely to be relatively small in quantity but needs to be easily accessed and edited, and should be cached for quick retrieval. For this purpose, an XML-formatted configuration file at the root of the Web application makes an effective choice.

Configuration File

In the IBuySpy example Web application, application configuration information will be stored in the Web.config file and a separate PortalCfg.xml file. The PortalCfg.xml file will contain definitions of the major content sections of the site, divided into tabs and modules. Tabs constitute the major sections of the site; for example, "Defect Tracking," "Task Tracking," and "Manage Files." Modules display the content when a given part of the site is accessed. The PortalCfg.xml file also determines who can access which tabs and modules. This file is read at run time and is used to populate the typed **DataSet SiteConfiguration**. This **DataSet** has been enhanced with methods to provide access to the configuration information.

Business Logic

In a portal application, business rules need to be enforced when changes are made to the content, layout, or accessibility of the site. To support these administrative services, a series of components have been created that encapsulate the methods needed to carry out editing. These components map to the types of data managed by the application. They are built by using the *Table Data Gateway* pattern, which prescribes a standard relationship between the class and its underlying data. In order to streamline the application, much of the business logic (mainly enforcing the correct roles and validating the input) is located in either the stored procedures or the code-behind pages.

Database Schema

The following illustration shows the table structure that supports the example site. Note the one-to-one correspondence between the types of information displayed in modules and the tables. The security structure is supported through the Users, UserRoles, and Roles tables.

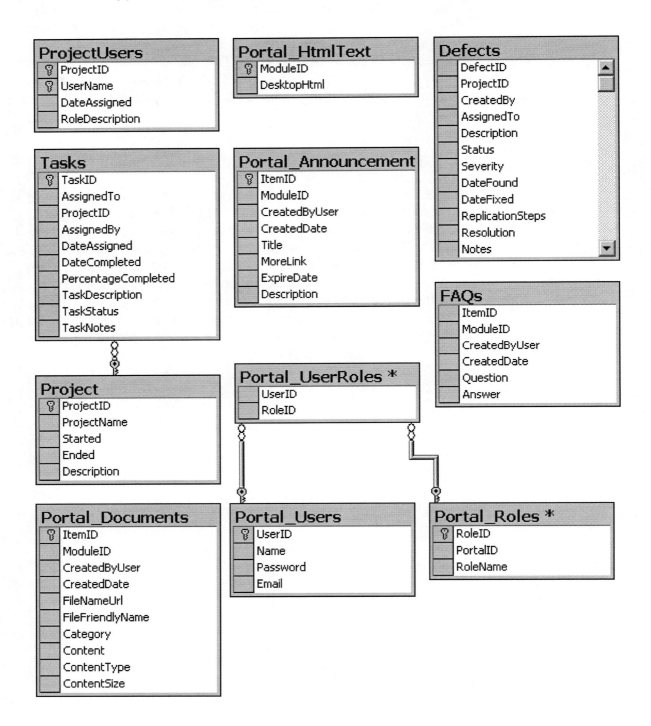

Configuration DataSet Schema

The schema for the configuration file displays the major types of information stored in the configuration file, as illustrated below:

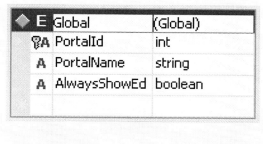

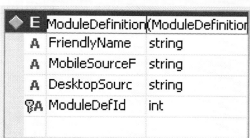

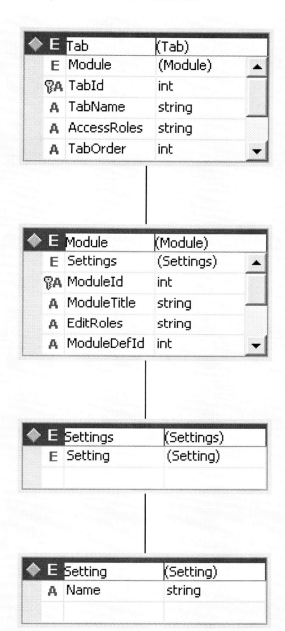

Best Practices for Application Design

> **Best Practices for Application Design**
> - Be consistent: Use a limited set of design models for components
> - Establish base classes
> - Use a limited set of data formats
> - Abstract policy code into its own reusable classes
> - Choose an appropriate layering strategy

Consider the following recommended best practices when designing your Web application:

- Be as consistent as possible by using one design model or a limited set of design models for components. This enables easy site upgrades and allows new units of content or functionality to be quickly added.

- Establish base classes for all components that follow a similar pattern.

- Rather than blending XML documents, strings, arrays, and data objects, use the minimum number of data formats necessary, erring on the side of caution. The example portal will use business entities and DataSets.

- Policy code such as configuration, security, exception handling, and instrumentation should be abstracted from the business logic as much as possible.

- Choose a sensible layering strategy. In cases where business logic requirements can be satisfied in code-behind pages without the risk of excessive redundancy, it is acceptable to call directly from the presentation to the data tier. However, calls from downstream to upstream components should be avoided in most scenarios.

Lab 1: Understanding Application Structure

> **Lab 1: Understanding Application Structure**
> - Exercise 1: Examining the Structure of the Application
> - Exercise 2: Building Utility Controls

Introduction

After completing this lab, you will have demonstrated your ability to:

- Use the Class Viewer to understand the basic structure of an application.
- Implement a user control that uses configuration settings.
- Check user roles by using the PortalSecurity class.
- Employ the user role to selectively add tabs to the display control.

Prerequisites

Before working on this lab, you must have the knowledge and skills necessary to develop a simple Web Forms application by using a Microsoft Visual Studio® .NET–compatible programming language. The DesktopDefault.aspx file provides a common access point to portal features. Each page, or tab, requires certain layout elements: a tab strip to display the available tabs and a title for each of the modules. Rather than duplicate the code on each page or in each module, the portal employs user controls for these common purposes. In this lab, you will implement code-behind pages for the **DesktopModuleTitle** and **DesktopPortalBanner** user controls to create this functionality.

Estimated time to complete this lab: 75 minutes

Starting a virtual machine

1. On the **Start** menu, point to **All Programs**, and then click **Microsoft Virtual PC**. If the Virtual PC console window does not appear, right-click the **Virtual PC** icon in the notification area (system tray), and then click **Show Virtual PC Console**.
2. In the Virtual PC console window, select the virtual machine that you would like to open, and then click **Start**.

NOTE: Depending on your time zone, the first time you start each of the virtual machines, you may receive an error message that the parent virtual hard disk appears to have been modified. You can ignore this message.

3. The virtual machine will start up in a new window.

Closing a virtual machine

1. In the virtual machine window, on the **Action** menu, click **Close**.

NOTE: To avoid accidentally closing the virtual machine during the lab, the **Close** button in the top right corner of the virtual machine is disabled.

2. The virtual machine window will close. All changes to the virtual hard disk are discarded.

Exercise 1: Examining the Structure of the Application

In this exercise, you will examine the structure of the solution to the portal application that you will build in this class. In the following instructions, Visual Basic .NET solution code will be followed by C# solution code. The formatting of the code displayed in the labs will not necessarily reflect the formatting of the code in the actual application. Also note that the Solution folder in each lab will contain the completed solution files.

■ Open the lab starter project

1. Open the ASPProjectVB or ASPProjectCS project in Visual Studio .NET by browsing to D:\2311\Labfiles\Lab01\Starter\VB or D:\2311\Labfiles\Lab01\Starter\CS.

2. Start the project by double-clicking **ASPProjectVB.sln** or **ASPProjectCS.sln** in the lab starter folder.

■ Examine the portal class structure

1. Open the Class Viewer by using the **Visual Studio** toolbar or by pressing CTRL+SHIFT+C.

2. Examine the following classes in the ASPProject namespace:

    a. **Configuration class**: This class encapsulates all the data logic necessary to modify the configuration settings, module configuration settings, and module definitions. In many ways, this class contains the site's core functionality because almost every aspect of the site is controlled through the configuration file that is read by this class.

    b. Examine the following methods:
    - **GetSiteSettings**
    - **GetModuleDefinitions**
    - **GetSingleModuleDefinition**
    - **GetModuleSettings**

    c. Note in particular the typed **DataSet** that is used in these methods: **SiteConfiguration**. Also, observe where the configuration settings are stored.

    d. **PortalSettings class**: This class encapsulates all the settings for the portal, in addition to the configuration settings required to execute the current tab view within the portal. Examine the constructor. All logic needed to render a portal tab is encapsulated here.

e. **PortalModuleControl class**: This class defines a custom base class inherited by all the desktop portal modules within the portal. Examine each property. Familiarize yourself with the **CachedPortalModuleControl** class and note the differences in how the two module classes are implemented.

f. **Announcements class**: Examine this class as a typical example of how the modules are constructed. This class displays announcements using the **AnnouncementsDB** class.

g. **AnnouncementsDB class**: This class performs the data access logic necessary to manage the information in the Announcements table.

h. **EditAnnouncements class**. This class enables authorized users to update and delete announcement information. It illustrates how to use the methods of the **AnnouncementsDB** class and how the individual units of information are edited. The same pattern is repeated across all of the modules.

i. **PortalSecurity class**: This class encapsulates helper methods to determine user security status. Examine the following methods:
   - **IsInRole**
   - **IsInRoles**
   - **HasEditPermissions**
   - **GetProjectRole**

j. **Project class**: This class encapsulates the methods needed to manage projects.

k. **Task class**: This class encapsulates the methods needed to manage tasks in projects.

Exercise 2: Building Utility Controls

The portal requires two services on each displayed page. The available tabs should be displayed in a tab strip across the top of each page. Each module should also have a title. To illustrate some of the site's basic structures, you will create two utility controls to encapsulate these services. The first, DesktopPortalBanner.ascx, will display the tabs at the top of each page by using a data-bound control. The second, DesktopModuleTitle.ascx, displays the title for each module. The code-behind files for each user control illustrate how the **PortalSettings** class provides the basic information needed to populate the different elements of the portal.

- **Add code to implement the DesktopModuleTitle control**

1. The **DesktopModuleTitle** control is a user control that is registered in each portal module. It displays the module title as it is configured in the PortalCfg.xml file. As a commonly used feature of the application, it illustrates how the configuration information is referenced and used by reusable components. See the Announcements.ascx file for an example of how this control is used in a module.

2. Open DesktopModuleTitle.ascx, which can be found in the application root, in design view. Note that it consists of a table labeled with the ID "ModuleTitle" and a hyperlink with the ID of "EditButton."

3. Open DesktopModuleTitle.ascx.vb or DesktopModuleTitle.ascx.cs in code view.

4. Locate the comment "TODO Obtain the PortalSettings from the current context." Declare a variable named "portalSettings" of type PortalSettings and instantiate it by setting it equal to the current value of the "PortalSettings" value in the **HttpContext** object. Your code should resemble the following:

Visual Basic .NET
```
Dim portalSettings As portalSettings =
    CType(HttpContext.Current.Items("PortalSettings"), portalSettings)
```

C#
```
PortalSettings portalSettings = (PortalSettings)
    HttpContext.Current.Items["PortalSettings"];
```

5. Locate the comment "TODO Obtain reference to parent portal module." Declare and instantiate a variable named "portalModule" of type PortalModuleControl and set it equal to the parent of the current module. This will be the module that contains the **DesktopModuleTitle** control being referenced. You will use the title of this module to provide the title for the control. Your code should resemble the following:

   Visual Basic .NET

   ```
   Dim portalModule As PortalModuleControl = CType(Me.Parent, PortalModuleControl)
   ```

   C#

   ```
   PortalModuleControl portalModule = (PortalModuleControl) this.Parent;
   ```

6. Locate the comment "TODO Display Modular Title Text and Edit Buttons." Set the Text property of the ModuleTitle label to the ModuleTitle property of the ModuleConfiguration property of the parent module. Your code should resemble the following:

   Visual Basic .NET

   ```
   ModuleTitle.Text = portalModule.ModuleConfiguration.ModuleTitle
   ```

   C#

   ```
   ModuleTitle.Text = portalModule.ModuleConfiguration.ModuleTitle;
   ```

6. Locate the comment "TODO Display the Edit button if the parent portalmodule has configured the PortalModuleTitle User Control to display it." Use an **If** statement to check the **AlwaysShowEditButton** property of the **portalSettings** object, and to make sure that the user is in one of the authorized editing roles and that the **EditText** property has been set to a value in the user control:

   Visual Basic .NET

   ```
   If portalSettings.AlwaysShowEditButton = True Or _
   (PortalSecurity.IsInRoles(portalModule.ModuleConfiguration.AuthorizedEditRoles) _
       And Not (EditText Is Nothing)) Then

       EditButton.Text = EditText
       EditButton.NavigateUrl = EditUrl + "?mid=" +
           portalModule.ModuleId.ToString()
       EditButton.Target = EditTarget

   End If
   ```

C#

```csharp
if ((portalSettings.AlwaysShowEditButton == true) ||
    (PortalSecurity.IsInRoles(portalModule.ModuleConfiguration.AuthorizedEditRoles)
    )
    && (EditText != null))
{

    EditButton.Text = EditText;
    EditButton.NavigateUrl = EditUrl + "?mid=" +
     portalModule.ModuleId.ToString();
    EditButton.Target = EditTarget;
}
```

7. The **EditText**, **EditUrl**, and **EditTarget** properties are set in the attributes of the user control. The **EditText** property will be displayed when the control is in edit mode. The **EditUrl** property will be used for editing the module contents. The **EditTarget** property determines where the edit page will be displayed if the portal uses frames, which this implementation does not use.

- **Add code to implement the DesktopPortalBanner control**

The **DesktopPortalBanner** control is a user control that is used to display the tab strip along the top of each page. The strip is rendered by a **DataList** that binds to an **ArrayList** of the tabs to be displayed. The implementation of this class illustrates a number of good practices for building flexible data-driven interface controls.

1. Open DesktopPortalBanner.ascx in the application root in design view. Note that the **DataList** consists of two templates: one for the unselected tabs and the other for the selected tab. The root path of the application is obtained from the **GetApplicationPath** method of the **Global** class. This method returns the correct relative path when installing the portal on a root Web site instead of a virtual directory.

2. Open DesktopPortalBanner.ascx.vb or DesktopPortalBanner.ascx.cs in code view. Locate the comment "Obtain PortalSettings from Current Context." Note that the code is the same as that used in the **DesktopModuleTitle** control to obtain the **portalSettings** object.

3. Locate the comment "TODO Dynamically Populate the Portal Site Name." Use the **PortalName** property of the **portalSettings** object to populate the **Text** property of the **siteName** label:

Visual Basic .NET
```
siteName.Text = portalSettings.PortalName
```

C#
```
siteName.Text = portalSettings.PortalName;
```

4. Locate the comment "TODO If user logged in, customize welcome message." Use the **IsAuthenticated** property of the **Request** object to ensure that the user is logged in. Use the **Identity** property of the current user to present a welcome message with the user's name.

Check the authentication mode currently being used. If forms authentication is being used, provide a logoff link. Your code should resemble the following:

Visual Basic .NET
```
If Request.IsAuthenticated = True Then

    WelcomeMessage.Text = "Welcome " + Context.User.Identity.Name + _
        "! <" + "span class=Accent" + ">|<" + "/span" + ">"

    If Context.User.Identity.AuthenticationType = "Forms" Then
        LogoffLink = "<" + "span class=""Accent"">|</span>" + _
        ControlChars.Lf + "<" + "a href=" + _
        Global.GetApplicationPath(Request) + "/Admin/Logoff.aspx" + _
        "class=SiteLink> Logoff" + "<" + "/a>"
    End If
End If
```

C#
```csharp
if (Request.IsAuthenticated == true)
{
    WelcomeMessage.Text = "Welcome " + Context.User.Identity.Name + "! <" +
    "span class=Accent" + ">|<" + "/span" + ">";

    // if authentication mode is Forms, provide a logoff link
    if (Context.User.Identity.AuthenticationType == "Forms")
    {
        LogoffLink = "<" + "span class=\"Accent\">|</span>\n" + "<" + "a
            href=" + Global.GetApplicationPath(Request) +
            "/Admin/Logoff.aspx class=SiteLink> Logoff" + "<" + "/a>";
    }
}
```

5. Locate the comment "TODO Dynamically render the portal tab strip." After the **If** statement, set the **tabIndex** property to the **TabIndex** property of the **portalSettings ActiveTab** property. Your code should resemble the following:

Visual Basic .NET
```
tabIndex = portalSettings.ActiveTab.TabIndex
```

C#
```csharp
tabIndex = portalSettings.ActiveTab.TabIndex;
```

6. Locate the comment "TODO Build a list of tabs to be shown to the user." Note the three variables that have been declared. The **ArrayList** named **authorizedTabs** will be used to bind the **DataList**. Create a For loop that loops through each of the tabs in the **DesktopTabs** collection of the **portalSettings**. Start the loop by declaring a variable named **tab** of type **TabStripDetails** to hold the properties for each tab. Use the **IsInRoles** method of the **PortalSecurity** class to check that the user is authorized for a particular tab. If so, add the tab to the **authorizedTabs ArrayList**. Check to see whether the current tab has the selected **tabIndex**. If so, set the **SelectedIndex** property for the **DataList** (tabs) to that index. Increment the **addedTabs** in each loop. Your code should resemble the following:

Visual Basic .NET

```
For i = 0 To portalSettings.DesktopTabs.Count - 1

    Dim tab As TabStripDetails = CType(portalSettings.DesktopTabs(i), _
        TabStripDetails)

    If PortalSecurity.IsInRoles(tab.AuthorizedRoles) Then
        authorizedTabs.Add(tab)
    End If

    If addedTabs = tabIndex Then
        tabs.SelectedIndex = addedTabs
    End If
    addedTabs += 1
Next i
```

C#

```
for (int i=0; i < portalSettings.DesktopTabs.Count; i++)
{

    TabStripDetails tab =
        (TabStripDetails)portalSettings.DesktopTabs[i];

    if (PortalSecurity.IsInRoles(tab.AuthorizedRoles))
    {
        authorizedTabs.Add(tab);
    }

    if (addedTabs == tabIndex)
    {
        tabs.SelectedIndex = addedTabs;
    }
    addedTabs++;
}
```

7. Locate the comment "TODO Populate Tab List at Top of the Page with authorized tabs." Bind the DataList to the ArrayList **authorizedTabs**. Your code should resemble the following:

Visual Basic .NET

```
tabs.DataSource = authorizedTabs
tabs.DataBind()
```

C#

```
tabs.DataSource = authorizedTabs;
tabs.DataBind();
```

8. Build the application and test by executing the DesktopDefault.aspx page using the **View in Browser** selection from the popup menu on the Solution Explorer. Ensure that the tab strip works properly, and examine the links for each tab to verify that the **tabIndex** and **tabId** properties are being set correctly.

9. Use the built-in administrator account admin@contoso.com to log in with a password of **P@ssw0rd**. Confirm that the title of each module appears correctly and that the **Edit** button appears and has a valid Uniform Resource Locator (URL).

Module 2: Designing Data Tier Components

> **Module 2: Designing Data Tier Components**
> - Implementing Data Access Logic Components
> - Designing a Data Abstraction Layer
> - Performance Tuning for Data Access
> - Managing Portal Settings

Overview

You will need to make several important decisions when deciding how to construct the data access layer for an ASP.NET application. Because providing access to data is the primary purpose of portal applications, constructing a well-designed data access layer must be your first priority. By building from the data tier to the user interface tier, the architect can ensure that one of the fundamental pillars of the application is stable, well-factored, and extensible. In this module, you will learn how to enable scalable, high-performance data retrieval, persistence, and transfer in a multitiered Web application.

Objectives

After completing this module, you will be able to:

- Design and implement effective data access logic components for Web applications.
- Describe the purpose and function of a data abstraction layer.
- Understand the benefits of performance tuning for data access.
- Manage portal settings.

Lesson: Implementing Data Access Logic Components

> **Lesson: Implementing Data Access Logic Components**
> - Defining Business Entities
> - Implementing Data Access Logic Components
> - Using Stored Procedures Effectively
> - Representing Business Entities as DataSets
> - Custom Business Entity Components
> - Summary of Recommendations for Presenting Data

Introduction

Efficient and effective data access is a key aspect of developing a Web application that results in user satisfaction. This lesson provides an introduction to the major design decisions you must make when creating a data access logic layer for an ASP.NET Web application.

Lesson Objectives

After completing this lesson, you will be able to:

- Define business entities to represent real-world data.
- Implement data access logic components to avoid code duplication.
- Use stored procedures in data access components to perform regular data routines.
- Explain the options for representing business entity data, and the trade-offs that these options entail.

Defining Business Entities

> **Defining Business Entities**
>
> - Business entities
>   - Represent real-world business data
>   - Map to tables in the relational database structure
>   - Should support data binding
> - Database tables
>   - Should be modeled to maximize efficient data access and distribution
>   - May or may not map directly to business entities
> - All data access methods and properties related to a business entity should be encapsulated in the corresponding data access component

Introduction

Business entities represent the real-world business data that an application works with. For example, in a portal application, an announcement represents a unit of content that the application must manage and to which it must offer access. Business entities often map to tables in the relational database structure that underlies the site. It is important to distinguish between database objects and the business entities that make up the structural units that the application will manage.

Database Tables

Database tables must be modeled in ways that maximize efficient access and distribution of data, including normalization rules and other considerations. The resulting tables may or may not map directly to business entities. In most cases, data access logic components will encapsulate data operations for a single database and a table or set of tables within that database. The architect must create appropriate abstractions based on the underlying data.

In the announcements example, you can readily identify an entity and its corresponding table, **Announcements**, which contains all the details for each announcement. However, in the case of more sophisticated objects, this one-to-one correspondence may not exist. For example, an Order component may contain data from both the **Order** table and the **Order Details** table.

Data Display and Performance

Many factors enter into the design of business entities. In ASP.NET applications, you must consider how the data represented by entities will be displayed. Some form of data binding will usually furnish a user-friendly presentation. Therefore, create a type, that directly supports data binding and exposes the attributes corresponding to the information to be displayed. These components must also support sorting or other ordering mechanisms.

Performance is also a key consideration in any Web-based application, as is scalability and maintainability. The architect must define entities in a way that optimizes performance for the Web environment, while making the addition of new entities to the structure as straightforward as possible.

Corresponding Data Access Components

All the data access and manipulation methods and properties related to a business entity must be encapsulated in the corresponding data access component. For example, the **AnnoucementDB** component has the following methods: **DeleteAnnouncement**, **AddAnnouncement**, **UpdateAnnouncement**, **GetAnnouncements**, and **GetSingleAnnouncement**. The same principle applies when working with an e-commerce application in which a Customer and Order might represent business entities.

In general, methods that return a particular type of business entity should be placed in the data access component of that type. Consequently, the methods for retrieving customers should be placed in the **Customer** class, while methods for retrieving orders for a particular customer should be placed in the **Order** class.

Implementing Data Access Logic Components

> **Implementing Data Access Logic Components**
> - Avoid code duplication
>   - Use the Data Access Application Block
>   - Create base classes
> - Four ways to pass data into and out of data access components
>   - Scalar values
>   - XML strings
>   - DataSets
>   - Custom entity components

Introduction

Developers who have experience with data-driven Web applications soon notice patterns in their data access code. Most developers find themselves repeating the same set of data access functions. By distilling these functions into their essential elements, a set of helper classes can be defined that encapsulate data access in a reusable way. This is the purpose of the Data Access Application Block (available from Microsoft at http://msdn.microsoft.com/library/default.asp?url=/library/en-us/dnbda/html/daab-rm.asp) that forms the data abstraction layer for the portal. By creating a centralized data access API, code duplication is avoided.

Another technique for reducing code duplication is to define common functionality in a base class. Derived classes that represent business entities can implement methods specific to their types while taking advantage of common utility functions defined in the base class.

Passing Data into and Out of Components

The main choices for passing data into and out of data access components are scalar values, XML strings, **DataSets**, and custom entity components. Each has its advantages and disadvantages.

The most common practice is to pass scalar values into and out of methods. The scalar values correspond to the data attributes of a business entity. In this case, the caller does not need to know the structure of the entity, but only the acceptable data types for the input parameters. This approach allows the most efficient input because only the necessary data is passed. The main disadvantage of this approach is that changes in the underlying data structure may require a corresponding change in the method signature, with possible effects on other methods. If the method signature needs to be altered to take account of a new field, all uses of that method must be tracked down and changed.

XML Strings

The necessity of changing the method signature when passing scalar values often leads developers to find a way to pass data by using a single data structure. In environments where data is being passed over a network to application components, XML strings allow all of the data to be consolidated into a single document. By gathering all of the data for a business entity, exchanges between application parts become much more efficient because data is not broken into multiple discrete units.

An added advantage is that after the data is in XML format, it can be used within a wide variety of application types and platforms. The disadvantage of this technique is also inherent to the XML format: tagged data introduces redundant information. This option makes sense mainly in scenarios where applications must collaborate over network connections, such as when using Web services. Even then, it often can be more efficient to use .NET remoting, so long as both sides of the exchange can execute .NET components.

DataSets

If you prefer to pass data by using a more compact and functional format, the **DataSet** object offers a natural choice. One of the main purposes of the **DataSet** is to provide a class that has methods reserved for handling optimistic concurrency issues. Previous versions of Microsoft® ActiveX Data Objects (ADO) required the developer to build a mechanism for handling concurrency violations, but the **DataSet** has such a mechanism built in.

DataSets can hold collections of data corresponding to individual business entities and are well-adapted to hierarchical data. Typed **DataSets** contain the metadata necessary for type validation on data fields. When a method accepts a **DataSet** as an input type, changes to the **DataSet** schema do not require changes to the method signature. **DataSets** incorporate the advantages of XML formats because they can be quickly serialized and deserialized.

The primary disadvantage of this approach is that the **DataSet** is a large and complex object specialized for holding sets of data. If the application is primarily working with discrete values rather than collections of entities, it will perform better by directly manipulating those values than by incurring the overhead of a **DataSet** without using the extra functionality it offers.

Custom Entity Components

Custom entity components offer a variation on the **DataSet** approach. This is a particularly advantageous approach for Web applications because the entities can correspond to the user interface elements. In the portal, the tabs that coincide with the major parts of the site must be populated with sets of data attributes that are the properties of each tab. The **TabSettings** class encapsulates the detailed settings for each tab, including the name of the tab, the tab order, and the modules to be displayed within the tab. Similarly, in the portal application, the **Project** class is used to represent all of the properties and methods of a project: **ProjectName**, **ProjectStarted**, **ProjectEnded**, and so on.

By using custom components of this type, collections of entities can be passed into and out of functions. You can also use such components in integration scenarios in a way similar to **DataSets**. Data contained in the custom object can be serialized into XML for transfer between applications.

Using Stored Procedures Effectively

> **Using Stored Procedures Effectively**
> - Keep business logic in business components
> - Avoid redundancy by associating each stored procedure with a single data access component
> - Use **Parameter** objects to enhance performance benefits and protect against SQL injection attacks

Introduction

Most creators of data-driven Web applications are familiar with the advantages of stored procedures. The advantages that stored procedures offer in terms of performance and modular design make them the optimal choice in scenarios where an application needs to perform regular data routines. However, developers should beware of placing too much business logic in stored procedures because database resources are inherently less scalable than business components. Placing too much business logic in stored procedures can overburden a server. Maintenance issues could arise when business logic must be propagated across the relational database management system (RDBMS).

Best Practices for Stored Procedures

As a general rule, each stored procedure should be associated with a single data access component. The component that encapsulates the **Discussion** object in a Forums module should be the only class that has methods that call the **AddMessage** stored procedure. This class, rather than a **Participant** class, would be the correct location for the procedure.

Parameters should not be passed to stored procedures by concatenating strings. Instead, parameter objects should be used, both for their performance benefits and to protect against SQL injection attacks. Strings passed as values of **Parameter** objects are treated as literals. Any attempt to pass strings containing database commands to the **IDataParameter** object will be neutralized.

Representing Business Entities as DataSets

> **Representing Business Entities as DataSets**
> - Two types of **DataSets**
>   - Generic
>   - Typed
> - Generic **DataSets**
>   - Represent business entities
>   - Adequate for most data representation needs
>   - Slower than typed **DataSets**
>   - Lack type checking capability
> - Typed **DataSets**
>   - Contain a schema that defines tables, columns, and rows
>   - Faster than generic **DataSets** due to early binding
>   - Schema changes require regeneration
>   - Support relational-to-object mapping

Introduction

DataSets come in two varieties, *generic* and *typed*. A generic **DataSet** contains data in its collection of **DataTables**, but the data is accessed by indexing into the **DataTables** and **DataRows**. A typed **DataSet** is a class that derives from the **DataSet** class and provides methods, events, and properties that correspond to the data it contains. Typed **DataSets** allow access to tables and rows as strongly typed properties of the **DataSet**, rather than using collection-based methods. They offer compile-time type checking for the data types of the values inserted into columns, as well as spelling checks on all the names used to access tables and fields.

Both varieties support the functionality needed to represent common business entities. **DataSets** are large and complex objects that contain several sub-objects that incur high startup costs when compared with representing data as XML strings or as custom business objects. They are best used when large amounts of data must be structured according to the requirements of an application's business entities. The ratio of the startup costs versus the amount of data to be loaded improves as data increases.

Generic DataSets

A **DataSet** can represent a business entity. **DataSets** are designed to hold collections of data, so entities can be represented as **DataRows** in a **DataTable** object. Because **DataTables** can have relations with other **DataTables**, hierarchies of entities can also be represented. In the portal, you will need to place a collection of **Module** objects in each **Tab** object. This relation could be represented by creating a Tab **DataTable** and a Module **DataTable**, and then setting up a **DataRelation** between the two.

Another example is the **LoadProject** method of the **Project** class. Because it is necessary to retrieve both the project information and the project members, the following stored procedure is used:

```
ALTER PROCEDURE GetProject
(
     @ProjectID int
)
AS

SELECT
     ProjectID, ProjectName, Started, Ended, Description

FROM
     Project

WHERE
     ProjectID = @ProjectID

exec GetProjectUsers @ProjectID
```

Notice that after the project information is retrieved, user information is retrieved in a separate procedure. The following function creates a **DataSet** that contains two **DataTables**. (This code is from the **Project** class in the lab portal application.)

Microsoft Visual Basic® .NET

```vbnet
Public Function LoadProject() As Boolean
    Dim ds As DataSet =
        SqlHelper.ExecuteDataset( _
            ConfigurationSettings.AppSettings("connectionstring"), _
            "GetProject", _
            Me.ProjectID)

    If ds.Tables(0).Rows.Count < 1 Then
        Return False
    End If
    Me.mName = ds.Tables(0).Rows(0)("ProjectName").ToString()
    Me.mDescription = ds.Tables(0).Rows(0)("Description").ToString()
    Me.mStarted = CType(ds.Tables(0).Rows(0)("Started"), DateTime)
    Me.mEnded = CType(ds.Tables(0).Rows(0)("Ended"), DateTime)
    Me.members = New ProjectMemberList()
    If ds.Tables.Count > 1 Then
        Dim r As DataRow
        For Each r In ds.Tables(1).Rows
            Dim m As ProjectMember = New ProjectMember()
            m.UserName = r("UserName").ToString()
            m.DateAssigned = CType(r("DateAssigned"), DateTime)
            m.ProjectRole =
            CType([Enum].Parse(GetType(EnumProjectRole), _
            r("RoleDescription").ToString()), _
            EnumProjectRole)
                members.Add(m)
        Next
    End If
    Return True
End Function
```

C#

```csharp
public bool LoadProject()
{
    DataSet ds = SqlHelper.ExecuteDataset(
        ConfigurationSettings.AppSettings["connectionstring"],
        "GetProject", this.projectID);

    if (ds.Tables[0].Rows.Count < 1)
        return false;

    this.mName = ds.Tables[0].Rows[0]["ProjectName"].ToString();
    this.mDescription = ds.Tables[0].Rows[0]["Description"].ToString();
    this.mStarted = (DateTime) ds.Tables[0].Rows[0]["Started"];
    this.mEnded = (DateTime)ds.Tables[0].Rows[0]["Ended"];

    this.members = new ProjectMemberList();
    if (ds.Tables.Count > 1 )
    {
        foreach(DataRow r in ds.Tables[1].Rows)
        {
            ProjectMember m = new ProjectMember();
            m.UserName = r["UserName"].ToString();
            m.DateAssigned = (DateTime)r["DateAssigned"];
            m.ProjectRole = (EnumProjectRole)Enum.Parse(
       typeof(ASPProject.EnumProjectRole),
        r["RoleDescription"].ToString(), true);
            members.Add(m);
        }
    }
}
```

The second **DataTable** contains the project members. These values are used to populate the **ProjectMemberList** collection class.

DataSets can also support portal management. **DataSets** can be bound to more than one data-bound control on a form, acting as the single source for data to be displayed in multiple configurations. Through the use of a **DataView**, sorting, filtering, finding, and editing capabilities are built into the data representation.

Because generic **DataSets** can only access data by indexing into collections, they are inherently slower than typed **DataSets**. They also lack the compile-time type checking capability. This means that if the developer misspells the name of a table or column, the error will not be detected until run-time. In addition, there is no Microsoft® IntelliSense® support for typed data objects in generic **DataSets**. Another deficiency is the inability to hide data in private fields.

Typed DataSets

Typed **DataSets** contain a schema that defines their tables, columns, and rows. Because all of the data objects are typed, access is faster due to early binding, which enables Intellisense support. Microsoft Visual Studio® provides tools to automatically generate and manipulate a typed **DataSet**. Despite these advantages, typed **DataSets** incur the same overhead as the generic variety.

Another advantage of typed objects is improved code readability. In the portal, it is frequently necessary to access a business entity that represents the configuration settings for the site. A **SiteConfiguration** object, which is a typed **DataSet**, is used for this purpose. If a generic **DataSet** were used, it would be necessary to write the following to reference the **DataTable** that contains tab information:

Visual Basic .NET

```
Dim tabTable As SiteConfiguration.Tables("Tab")
```

C#

```
DataTable tabTable = SiteConfiguration.Tables("Tab");
```

Using a typed **SiteConfiguration DataSet** makes it possible to access the **Tab** table in this way. This code is from the **PortalSettings** class in the lab portal application.)

Visual Basic .NET

```
Dim tabTable As SiteConfiguration.TabDataTable
```

C#

```
SiteConfiguration.TabDataTable tabTable = siteSettings.Tab;
```

In a similar way, you can directly access the methods of the Tab table to retrieve the data for a particular tab. (This code is from the **PortalSettings** class in the lab portal application.)

Visual Basic .NET

```
Dim tabRow As SiteConfiguration.TabRow =
    siteSettings.Tab.FindByTabId(tabId)
```

C#

```
SiteConfiguration.TabRow tabRow = siteSettings.Tab.FindByTabId(tabId);
```

However, this convenience comes at a price. If the underlying database schema changes, the **DataSet** will need to be regenerated. If the **DataSet** is regenerated automatically by using Visual Studio tools, any customization added to the typed **DataSet** will be lost. It is a common practice to set up expression columns in such **DataSets** to represent calculated data and return it in a type-safe manner. Such expression columns will be removed if Visual Studio tools are used to regenerate the typed **DataSet** automatically.

Relational-to-Object Mapping

The most important advantage of using a typed **DataSet** is that it can already contain the mapping between the relational and the object model that the developer would otherwise have to create. In the past, one approach to creating this mapping was to create multiple table joins. The resulting rowset contained an object graph representing the relationships between the tables. The attributes of the business object were then mapped to this data. With typed **DataSets**, you can create these relationships more efficiently. Rather than using joins, **DataRelation** objects relate **DataTables**. When navigating these relationships, you are navigating related rows in tables without the duplication produced by table joins. The relational-to-object mapping is inherent in the way a **DataSet** works.

This leaves the developer with two major tasks: getting the data and writing business rules. Because much of the data manipulation code is already contained in the **DataSet**, getting the data is mainly a matter of writing stored procedures or parameterized SQL statements that can be associated with the **DataAdapter** that is used to fill the **DataSet** and update the data store.

The business logic must be added. At a minimum, this mandates that the data type rules for the underlying data store be enforced. You have seen that using typed **DataSets** means that type checking is automatically performed as data is added to the fields.

Using RowChanging and RowChanged Events

For more sophisticated validation, you can use the **RowChanging** and **RowChanged** events, which are automatically added to the typed **DataSet**. To add this logic, you derive from your typed **DataSet** and provide implementations for the event handlers. If you wanted to ensure that only users in valid access roles (represented by the **AccessRole** property of the **TabRow** object) could access tabs, you could use the **TabRowChangeEventHandler** as shown below:

Visual Basic .NET

```
Private Sub TabRowChanging(ByVal source As Object, ByVal args as
TabRowChangeEventargs)
        If (args.Action = DataRowAction.Add || args.Action = _
            DataRowAction.Change) Then
            If (args.Row.AccessRole <> "Admin") Then
                Throw new Exception _
                ("Only Admins are allowed access to this tab!")
            End If
        End If
    End Sub
```

C#

```csharp
private void TabRowChanging(object source, TabRowChangeEventargs args)
    {
        if (args.Action == DataRowAction.Add || args.Action ==
            DataRowAction.Change)
        {
            if (args.Row.AccessRole != "Admin")
            {
                    throw new System.Exception("Only Admins are allowed
                    access to this tab!");
            }

        }
    }
```

When using the **AddTabRow** method of the **TabDataTable**, you can ensure that only Admins will be added as a role for that tab. This code should be placed in a class that derives from your typed **DataSet** rather than the typed **DataSet** itself. Using a derived class segments your additions, leaving the base class available for other application purposes.

Demonstration: Using Typed DataSets

Introduction

The purpose of this demonstration is to provide a practical example of the advantage of using typed **DataSets**. The instructor will first demonstrate how a **DataRelation** is created with a generic **DataSet**, and will then show how a typed **DataSet** can automatically create the **DataRelation**. The typed **DataSet** code is already referenced in the code-behind file, but is commented out at the beginning of the demonstration.

- **To create a DataRelation**
1. Open the project by double-clicking the Mod02.sln file under D:\2311\Democode\Mod02\CS or D:\2311\Democode\Mod02\VB.
2. Right-click UseRelations.aspx and then select **View in Browser**.
3. Demonstrate how the parent and child records are displayed in each **DataGrid**.
4. Open the code-behind file and point out the following code:
   a. Note that three methods are called in the **Page_Load** method.
   b. In the **CreateDataSet** method, note that **dsCustomerOrders DataSet** is a generic **DataSet**.
   c. Note that **MakeDataRelation** creates a **DataRelation** between the two **DataTables** in the **DataSet**.
   d. Point out the **dgParent_SelectedIndexChanged** method. This method is executed whenever the user makes a selection in the parent **DataGrid**. Note how the current row index is determined. Show the **GetChildRows** and **CreateChildView** method calls.
5. Show the **CustomerOrders DataSet**. This typed **DataSet** has already been created. You might want to demonstrate how to create it by using the **DataSet** item template. Note the following:
   a. The schema is described in an xsd file. Open the designer for the xsd file and note the data fields and the relation. Briefly show the xsd code and how it is structured.
   b. Open the CustomerOrders.cs or CustomerOrders.vb file. Show that it derives from the **DataSet** class. Point out the **CustomersDataTable** and **OrdersDataTable** classes, showing that each column is a defined property of the table.
   c. Show where the **DataRelation** between the customers and orders tables is defined in the **InitClass** method.
   d. Show the **FindByCustomerID** method to illustrate the extra functionality that has been added.
6. Return to the UseRelations.aspx code-behind page.
7. At the top of the class, uncomment the **DataSet** declaration for a typed **DataSet CustomerOrders**. Comment the generic **DataSet** declaration.
8. In the **CreateDataSet** method, uncomment the instantiation of the typed **DataSet**. Comment the generic **DataSet** instantiation.

9. In **MakeDataRelation**, uncomment the statements defining the parent and child column objects using the typed **DataSet**. Comment the statements which use the generic **DataSet**. Show how the syntax has changed. Demonstrate how Intellisense now gives access to the column objects.

10. In the **dgParent_SelectedIndexChanged** method, uncomment the statement that retrieves the **currentParentRow DataRow** object by using the typed **DataSet**. Comment the statement by using the generic **DataSet**. Do the same with the **parentTableView**.

11. Uncomment the **For** loop that uses the **DataRelation** "CustomersOrders" in the **GetChildRows** method, and then comment the loop that uses "CustOrders." Do the same for the statement that uses the **CreateChildView** method.

12. Comment out the **MakeDataRelation** call in the **Page_Load** method and in the **dgParent_PageIndexChanged** method.

13. Build the project and ensure that there are no errors. Right-click the page and select **View in Browser**. Note that the page still works the same way as before by using the automatically generated **DataRelation**.

Custom Business Entity Components

> **Custom Business Entity Components**
>
> - Benefits of using custom business entity components
>   - Code readability
>   - Low overhead
>   - Encapsulated business rules
> - Disadvantages
>   - Developer must implement custom collection classes
>   - Relationships must be implemented programmatically

Introduction

Despite the advantages offered by the built-in functionality of **DataSets**, there is one major disadvantage—high instantiation and marshaling costs. Creating custom business entity components is a way of avoiding these costs while gaining the advantages of strong typing. These classes generally feature private fields for local data caching, public properties for storing object state, methods for performing localized processing, and events to capture changes in object state. The properties can reflect the logical structure of the business entity, rather than the underlying database object as would be the case with the **DataSet**. In the Web applications, minimizing overhead is usually a key requirement. The portal site makes extensive use of custom business entities and user interface components.

Business Entities

A good example can be found in the project management section of the portal. The **Project** class contains all members and categories needed to work with projects. When the user needs to retrieve a collection of projects, the following code is used in the **GetProjects** method of the **Project** class. (This code comes from the **Project** class in the lab portal application.)

Visual Basic .NET

```vb
Public Shared Function GetProjects() As ProjectList
    Dim ds As DataSet = _
        SqlHelper.ExecuteDataset( _
            ConfigurationSettings.AppSettings("connectionString"), _
            "GetProjectListByUser", _
            PortalSecurity.UserName)

    Dim pl As ProjectList = New ProjectList()
    Dim r As DataRow
    For Each r In ds.Tables(0).Rows
        Dim p As ProjectInfo = New ProjectInfo()

        p.ProjectID = CType(r("ProjectID"), Integer)
        p.ProjectName = CType(r("ProjectName"), String)
        p.DateStarted = CType(r("Started"), DateTime)
        pl.Add(p)

    Next
    Return pl
End Function
```

C#

```csharp
public static ProjectList GetProjects()
{
    DataSet ds = SqlHelper.ExecuteDataset(
            ConfigurationSettings.AppSettings["connectionString"],
            "GetProjectListByUser", PortalSecurity.UserName);
    ProjectList pl= new ProjectList();
    foreach(DataRow r in ds.Tables[0].Rows)
    {
            ProjectInfo p = new ProjectInfo();
            p.ProjectID = (int)r["ProjectID"];
            p.ProjectName = (string)r["ProjectName"];
            p.DateStarted = (DateTime)r["Started"];
            pl.Add(p);
    }
    return pl;
}
```

The **SqlHelper** class, part of the Data Access Application Block, supplies the data access functionality. After the **DataSet** is retrieved, it is used to populate a strongly typed **ProjectList** object, which is returned from the function. This is the typical pattern for business entities and data access logic components. In the case of the portal, many of the objects have no complex business rules associated with them. These rules have been incorporated directly into the DAL (Data Access Logic) component. This approach leads to greater performance and less overhead by eliminating an unnecessary middle-tier component.

Performance and Scalability Considerations

You need to make a number of decisions when designing custom entities that have a direct impact on the performance and scalability of the application. When creating lightweight objects such as a **TabSetting**, the object used to encapsulate the details for a tab, either a class or a *struct* (**Structure** in Visual Basic .NET) can be used. Because the data is only a series of properties, with no hierarchy and no methods, developers will find that they get better performance by using a struct.

A struct is a value type and therefore makes no use of the managed heap. Because the data it contains is allocated on the stack, it is quickly released. It is quite possible that as the application grows, it might be desirable to extend the **TabSetting** object to include more functionality, such as a set of subsettings corresponding to a set of subtabs. If you choose a struct to hold this information, you will not be able to extend it later by deriving a new subclass because structs cannot inherit. All of the objects that represent either business data or user interface elements have been created as classes.

Representing Data in Collections

Internal data will often be represented in the form of collections of similar items. The **PortalSettings** class encapsulates all of the settings set up in the configuration file for the site. The collection of tabs that might be displayed is contained in the **DesktopTabs** property, which is an **ArrayList**. An **ArrayList** is a lightweight object that automatically resizes itself as more elements are added, making it more efficient than the **Array**.

DataSets are also used to hold collections of similar items, but their main advantage over **ArrayLists** is that they can easily represent hierarchies of data. They also provide sorting, filtering, and finding capabilities that are more convenient than those found in **ArrayLists**. Their main disadvantage is higher overhead. Rather than using **DataSets**, the portal uses custom classes that represent the data fields for an object, such as the **TabSettings** class.

As an illustration, consider the definition of the **PortalSettings** class, which is used to hold all of the portal and configuration settings. (This code is from the **PortalSettings** class in the lab portal application.)

Visual Basic .NET

```
Public Class PortalSettings

    Public PortalId As Integer
    Public PortalName As String
    Public AlwaysShowEditButton As Boolean
    Public DesktopTabs As New ArrayList()
    Public MobileTabs As New ArrayList()
    Public ActiveTab As New TabSettings()
```

C#

```
public class PortalSettings
{
    public int         PortalId;
    public String      PortalName;
    public bool        AlwaysShowEditButton;
    public ArrayList   DesktopTabs = new ArrayList();
    public TabSettings ActiveTab = new TabSettings();
```

Binding Data to Web Form Controls

It is often necessary to bind data from custom entity components to controls on a Web Form. Only components that implement the **ICollection** interface can be bound. The developer will not need to implement this directly, but will derive it from a base class that implements the interface. In the TimeTracker application, the **DataGrid** that displays project details is populated with the following code. (This code is from the ASP.NET Starter Kit Time Tracker project in the TimeEntry.aspx code-behind file.)

Visual Basic .NET

```vb
Private Sub BindProjectList()
    If Not (ProjectList.SelectedItem Is Nothing) Then
        _userInput.ProjectID = _
        Convert.ToInt32(ProjectList.SelectedItem.Value)
    End If

    ProjectList.DataSource = ListUserProjects()
    ProjectList.DataTextField = "Name"
    ProjectList.DataValueField = "ProjectID"
    ProjectList.DataBind()

    ' Select the correct item from ProjectList.
    If Not (ProjectList.Items.FindByValue(_userInput.ProjectID.ToString()) _
        Is Nothing) Then
        ProjectList.Items.FindByValue(_userInput.ProjectID.ToString()).Selected _
            = True
    End If
End Sub
```

C#

```csharp
private void BindProjectList()
{
    // Preserve the selected value so information is still there after
    // postback.
    if (ProjectList.SelectedItem != null)
        _userInput.ProjectID =
    Convert.ToInt32(ProjectList.SelectedItem.Value);

            ProjectList.DataSource = ListUserProjects();
            ProjectList.DataTextField = "Name";
            ProjectList.DataValueField = "ProjectID";
            ProjectList.DataBind();

    // Select the correct item from ProjectList.
    if (ProjectList.Items.FindByValue(_userInput.ProjectID.ToString())
       != null)

  ProjectList.Items.FindByValue(_userInput.ProjectID.ToString()).Selected
       = true;
}
```

Notice that the data is obtained from the method **ListUserProjects()**. This function returns an object of type **ProjectsCollection** using the following implementation. (This code is from the ASP.NET Starter Kit Time Tracker project in the TimeEntry.aspx code-behind file.)

Visual Basic .NET

```vbnet
Return BusinessLogicLayer.Project.GetProjects(_user.UserID, _
    Convert.ToInt32(UserList.SelectedItem.Value))
```

C#

```csharp
return BusinessLogicLayer.Project.GetProjects(_user.UserID,
    Convert.ToInt32(UserList.SelectedItem.Value));
```

The **ProjectsCollection** object inherits from the **ArrayList**, which implements the **ICollection** interface. This class overrides the **Sort** method of the **ArrayList** so that it can provide its own sorting methods for the different types of sorts that are needed. This makes flexible data display very straightforward. You will use a similar method in the Task Tracking tab of the portal application.

Summary of Benefits and Disadvantages

To summarize, using custom business entities offers the following benefits:

- **Code readability**. Data in custom business entities is contained in strongly typed properties or subclasses. Just as in a typed DataSet, you benefit from compile-time type checking, early binding, and Intellisense aid in writing code.

- **Low overhead**. Because the custom entity includes only the properties, methods, and events needed to represent its object, the developer does not incur the overhead penalty of a DataSet object.

- **Encapsulated business rules**. Methods can access data cached in the entity component, rather than making expensive trips to the database.

The principal disadvantage of this approach is that if collections of business entities are required, the developer must implement custom collection classes, as the TimeTracker did with the **UserCollection**. With the **DataSet**, this behavior is built-in. The same applies to representation of complex or hierarchical relationships between business entities. These relationships must be implemented programmatically when using a custom entity. The **DataSet** has a **DataRelations** collection that can represent hierarchical relationships easily. When using typed **DataSets**, the classes corresponding to these relationships can be automatically generated.

The need to provide custom implementations also applies to sorting mechanisms, though it is often desirable to provide sorting methods that correspond to the needs of the user interface. To extend the **ProjectsCollection** example, the following code overrides the **Sort** method of the base **ArrayList** class. (This code is from the ASP.NET Starter Kit Time Tracker project in the **ProjectsCollection** class.)

Visual Basic .NET

```vbnet
Public Overloads Sub Sort(ByVal sortField As ProjectFields, ByVal _
    isAscending As Boolean)
    Select Case sortField
        Case ProjectFields.Name
            MyBase.Sort(New NameComparer())
        Case ProjectFields.ManagerUserName
            MyBase.Sort(New ManagerUserNameComparer())
        Case ProjectFields.CompletionDate
            MyBase.Sort(New CompletionDateComparer())
        Case ProjectFields.Duration
            MyBase.Sort(New DurationComparer())
    End Select

    If Not isAscending Then
        MyBase.Reverse()
    End If
End Sub
```

C#

```csharp
public void Sort(ProjectFields sortField, bool isAscending)
{
    switch (sortField)
    {
        case ProjectFields.Name:
            base.Sort(new NameComparer());
            break;
        case ProjectFields.ManagerUserName:
            base.Sort(new ManagerUserNameComparer());
            break;
        case ProjectFields.CompletionDate:
            base.Sort(new CompletionDateComparer());
            break;
        case ProjectFields.Duration:
            base.Sort(new DurationComparer());
            break;
    }

    if (!isAscending) base.Reverse();
}
```

Each type of sort is defined by the **ProjectFields** property that is passed to the procedure. All that is necessary to enable the sort is to provide classes that implement the **IComparer** interface. (This code is from the ASP.NET Starter Kit Time Tracker project in the **ProjectsCollection** class.)

Visual Basic .NET

```
Private NotInheritable Class NameComparer
    Implements IComparer

        Public Function Compare(ByVal x As Object, ByVal y As Object) As _
        Integer Implements IComparer.Compare
            Dim first As Project = CType(x, Project)
            Dim second As Project = CType(y, Project)
            Return first.Name.CompareTo(second.Name)
    End Function 'Compare
End Class
```

C#

```
private sealed class NameComparer : IComparer
{
        public int Compare(object x, object y)
        {
                Project first = (Project) x;
                Project second = (Project) y;
                return first.Name.CompareTo(second.Name);
        }
}
```

Using this interface makes several different sorting options available. This method of creating optional sorting routines will be explored in detail when data binding is discussed.

Code Walkthrough: Passing Data with Collection Classes

> **Code Walkthrough: Passing Data with Collection Classes**
> - In this presentation, your instructor will demonstrate how data is passed between application layers by using collection classes

Introduction

In this code walkthrough, the instructor will demonstrate how data can be passed between application layers by using collection classes. The code is taken from the ASP.NET Starter Kit Time Tracker application. The Time Tracker application is installed in its default installation location of D:\2311\ASP.NET Starter Kits\ASP.NET TimeTracker (CSVS) or D:\2311\ASP.NET Starter Kits\ASP.NET TimeTracker (VBVS), depending on the language that is used. To demonstrate the application, double-click on the ASP.NET Time Tracker Starter Kit (VBVS).sln or ASP.NET Time Tracker Starter Kit (CSVS).sln file which will be found at the path above according to language preference. When the application opens, right-click on the Default.aspx page in the TTWebVBVS or TTWebCSVS project and select "View in Browser" from the popup menu for the Solution Explorer. You should be at the logon page. Click the **Register** button and register with your preferred credentials. Click the **Register and Sign In Now** link, and you will be taken to the **Log** tab of the Time Tracker Starter Kit.

- **To pass data between application layers using collection classes**
    1. Open the code-behind file for the TimeEntry.aspx page.
    2. Briefly describe and demonstrate the application. It is a practical time and project management application with reporting features.
    3. Go to the **BindTimeSheet** method, which has four parameters. Show the call to the **GetEntries** method of the **TimeEntry** object and explain that it returns a collection of **TimeEntry** objects that will be bound to a **DataGrid**.
    4. Go to the method definition for **GetEntries**, located in the TimeEntry file under the the \Components\BLL folder, and briefly show the major parts of the class where it resides.
    5. Note the following points about the method:
        a. It requires no object instantiation because it is marked "static" (Shared in Visual Basic .NET).
        b. It uses a data abstraction class named **SqlHelper** to populate a **DataSet**. This class will be explained in detail later.
        c. It creates an object of type **TimeEntriesCollection** and uses the **DataSet** to populate it and return it from the function.
    6. Go the definition for the **TimeEntriesCollection** class. Note the following:
        a. It derives from **ArrayList**. This allows the **Sort** method to be overridden so that business objects can be given sorting rules.
        b. Explain how the **Sort** method uses the implementation of the **IComparer** interface.
        c. Show the **IComparer** classes and explain the comparison rules.
    7. Return to the code-behind page for TimeEntry.aspx.
    8. Show how the **SortGridData** method chooses the appropriate column for sorting.
    9. Return to the **BindTimeSheet** method. Show how the same data is used to bind to the **DataGrid** and to produce the chart.
    10. Leave Visual Studio open for later demonstrations.

Summary of Recommendations for Representing Data

> **Summary of Recommendations for Representing Data**
> - Use **DataSets** if the data includes hierarchical relationships
> - Use custom classes for applications that use instance data
> - Carefully examine **DataSet** functionality before choosing custom classes

To summarize, you should consider the following recommendations for representing data when designing your Web application:

- **DataSets** are recommended if the application is primarily working with large collections of items and needs standard sorting, filtering, and searching capabilities. This is especially true if the data needs to incorporate complex or hierarchical relationships.

- If the application mainly works with instance data (for example, a single **Tab** or **Project** object), custom business entities will normally be the better choice. There is no need to incur the overhead of **DataSets** when only one row of data is sufficient for most purposes.

- In many cases, the time and effort of creating custom business entities will not be worth the effort because the **DataSet** can meet most common needs.

Lesson: Designing a Data Abstraction Layer

> **Lesson: Designing a Data Abstraction Layer**
> - What Is Data Abstraction?
> - Data Access Application Block Design
> - Retrieving Multiple Rows Using a **SqlDataReader**

Introduction

This lesson provides an introduction to the considerations involved in designing a data access layer for an ASP.NET application.

Lesson Objectives

After completing this lesson, you will be able to:

- Describe the purpose and function of a data abstraction layer.
- Explain the purpose and benefits of creating a data factory.
- Identify the methods which should be included in a data abstraction layer.
- Use caching functions to increase data access performance.

What Is Data Abstraction?

> **What Is Data Abstraction?**
> - Encapsulating Common Access
> - Abstracting the Provider

Introduction

Developers who write database-driven applications often find themselves duplicating sets of similar code. Studies that analyze how most applications use data have identified patterns that can be used to consolidate much of this duplicate coding. According to the design documents for the Microsoft Data Access Application Block (DAAB), the two main candidates for consolidation are executing commands and parameter caching. The DAAB addresses these two areas through the **SqlHelper** class for executing commands, and the **SqlHelperParameterCache** class for caching parameters.

Encapsulating Common Access

The general purpose of classes such as **SqlHelper** and **SqlHelperParameterCache** is to create methods and properties that abstract common operations such as the instantiation of connection objects, the execution of commands with various types of return values, and managing parameters. A reusable data access layer can speed development in a number of scenarios. To be as widely applicable as possible, this layer should also allow the provider to be abstracted, rather than using only a single provider as the DAAB does. Such a class might also abstract all database-specific syntax, to make application code more portable.

Another task that tends to cause high overhead is managing parameters. ADO.NET requires that parameter objects be created for each parameter passed to a stored procedure or SQL statement. Rather than having to create and add each parameter individually, it would be convenient to add all parameters by supplying an array of values at execution time. Because such procedures are often executed many times during the lifetime of the application, caching the parameters could lead to significant improvements in performance. A complete data abstraction layer will address these needs.

Abstracting the Provider

One of the goals of the creators of ADO.NET was to allow data classes to take advantage of the special features of specific databases. Oracle offers a set of features that are best exploited in one way, while Microsoft SQL Server™ offers a different set that requires a different approach. One of the weaknesses of ADO was the fact that its objects did not offer much specialization for the specific features of different RDBMS. ADO.NET offers specialized classes known as Managed Providers that utilize the attributes of specific databases.

When using the SQL Server provider to create a connection, the **SqlClient** class constructs a series of Tabular Data Stream (TDS) messages corresponding to the correct protocol sequence for SQL Server. Client and server exchange data by using this provider-specific protocol that optimizes access by avoiding the need to pass through OLEDB or Open Database Connectivity (ODBC) layers. The major disadvantage of this approach is that it can only be used with one type of database.

A data abstraction layer can overcome this limitation by dynamically loading the appropriate types when the DAL (Data Abstraction Layer class, or data factory) is instantiated. For example, you might want to add a method such as the following to be called during object creation:

Visual Basic .NET

```
Private Sub SetProviderType()
  ` Provider is a public property of the class

  Select Case Me.Provider
    Case "SqlClient"
      mConnectionType = GetType(SqlConnection)
      mCommandType = GetType(SqlCommand)
      mDataReaderType = GetType(SqlDataReader)
      mDataAdapterType = GetType(SqlDataAdapter)
      mParameterType = GetType(SqlParameter)
      mDatatypes = mSqlDataTypes

    Case "OleDb"
      mConType = GetType(OleDbConnection)
      mComType = GetType(OleDbCommand)
      mDrType = GetType(OleDbDataReader)
      mDaType = GetType(OleDbDataAdapter)
      mParmType = GetType(OleDbParameter)
      mDatatypes = mOledbDataTypes
    Case Else
```

C#

```csharp
private void SetProviderType()
{
    switch (this.Provider)
    {
        case "SqlClient":
            mConnectionType = GetType(SqlConnection);
            mCommandType = GetType(SqlCommand);
            mDataReaderType = GetType(SqlDataReader);
            mDataAdapterType = GetType(SqlDataAdapter);
            mConType = GetType(OleDbConnection);
            mComType = GetType(OleDbCommand);
            mDrType = GetType(OleDbDataReader);
            mDaType = GetType(OleDbDataAdapter);
            mParmType = GetType(OleDbParameter);
            mDatatypes = mSqlDataTypes;
        case "OleDb":
            mConType = GetType(OleDbConnection);
            mComType = GetType(OleDbCommand);
            mDrType = GetType(OleDbDataReader);
            mDaType = GetType(OleDbDataAdapter);
            mParmType = GetType(OleDbParameter);
            mDatatypes = mOledbDataTypes;

            // Case "Oracle" add other providers here

        default:
    }
```

After the specific objects are set, the procedure might go on to create a connection by using the **Activator.CreatInstance** method to instantiate the **Connection** class and then casting it to the **IDbConnection** interface as follows:

Visual Basic .NET

```vbnet
_connection = CType(Activator.CreateInstance(_connectionType), IDbConnection)
```

C#

```csharp
_connection = (IDbConnection)Activator.CreateInstance(_connectionType)
```

An alternative approach is to use common interfaces for the data objects. Instead of creating a **SqlConnection** object, a factory class could supply an **IDbConnection** object that could also be used to connect to the database. By coding to the interfaces instead of the class, a certain measure of database independence could be gained. The disadvantage of this approach is that it restricts functionality to the lowest common denominator, losing database-specific features and optimizations. The better approach is the one suggested above. This can be extended by supplying the application with a configuration file that contains settings for additional providers. This file can be read at run time to furnish application-specific managed provider information.

A similar approach could be taken to provide database-specific data types. A **_sqlDatatypes** variable holds a **HashTable** of types, as shown below:

Visual Basic .NET

```
mSqlDataTypes.Add("bigint", SqlDbType.BigInt)
mSqlDataTypes.Add("binary", SqlDbType.Binary)
mSqlDataTypes.Add("bit", SqlDbType.Bit)
mSqlDataTypes.Add("varchar", SqlDbType.VarChar)
mSqlDataTypes.Add("char", SqlDbType.Char)
mSqlDataTypes.Add("datetime", SqlDbType.DateTime)   ...
```

C#

```
mSqlDataTypes.Add("bigint", SqlDbType.BigInt);
mSqlDataTypes.Add("binary", SqlDbType.Binary);
mSqlDataTypes.Add("bit", SqlDbType.Bit);
mSqlDataTypes.Add("varchar", SqlDbType.VarChar);
mSqlDataTypes.Add("char", SqlDbType.Char);
mSqlDataTypes.Add("datetime", SqlDbType.DateTime);   ...
```

This **HashTable** can be used when types need to be supplied for **SqlParameter** objects.

Data Access Application Block Design

> **Data Access Application Block Design**
> - Encapsulates common data access tasks
> - Supplies consistent methods
> - Stored procedures and SQL statements use the same methods
> - Parameters can be provided
>   - As arrays
>   - As single values
>   - As **SqlParameter** objects
> - Transactions can be added

Introduction

The DAAB from Microsoft contains optimized data access code. Now that you have seen how to make a DAL database-independent, you will learn about the features of the DAAB that are particularly helpful to portal applications.

DAAB Design Goals

The design goals of the DAAB were as follows:

- The class should leverage best practices for high-performance and scalable data access.

- The class should encapsulate the most common data access tasks, requiring as little custom code as possible.

- Client applications should be able to execute commands to perform database updates, or retrieve values, **SqlDataReader** objects, **DataSet** objects, or XML streams (**XmlReader** objects), by using a consistent set of methods.

- Client applications should be able to execute either **Transact-SQL** statements or stored procedures by using the same method.

- Client applications should be able to specify either a connection string or a **SqlConnection** object to determine the data source.
- If parameters are required, the client application should be able to supply them as an array of **SqlParameter** objects or as a list of parameter values for stored procedures.
- Clients should be able to specify an ADO.NET transaction and have a command participate in it.

You will learn how to use the DAAB according to the best practices described in the ".NET Data AccessArchitecture Guide" (http://msdn.microsoft.com/library/default.asp?url=/library/en-us/dnbda/html/daag.asp).

Retrieving Multiple Rows Using a SqlDataReader

> **Retrieving Multiple Rows Using a SqlDataReader**
> - Using **ExecuteReader**
> - Assigning Parameter Values

Introduction

One of the most frequent tasks performed by Web applications is to retrieve multiple rows from a database and display them in a table. Much of the functionality of a portal consists in retrieving rows and formatting them for readable display. If there is no need to hold the data in a cache for later retrieval, or to pass the data to another part of the application, the overhead of a **DataSet** adds no value. The application merely creates an unnecessary duplicate copy of the data. To avoid wasting resources, you use the **DataReader**, which also supports data binding without some of the overhead of **DataSet** data binding.

Using ExecuteReader

The DAAB provides a series of overloads for an **ExecuteReader** method that returns a **SqlDataReader**. Consider a case where you need to populate the **Announcements** user control with "News and Features." The user control contains a **DataList**, whose **DataSrc** property retrieves data from the **GetAnnouncements** method of the **AnnouncementsDB** class. Rather than fill a **DataSet** that will be immediately discarded, the **GetAnnouncements** method can be written as follows. (This code is from the **AnnouncementsDB** class in the lab portal application.)

Visual Basic .NET

```
Dim reader As SqlDataReader = SqlHelper.ExecuteReader( _
    ConfigurationSettings.AppSettings("connectionString"), _
    "GetAnnouncements", _
    moduleId)
  Return reader
```

C#

```
SqlDataReader reader = SqlHelper.ExecuteReader(
    ConfigurationSettings.AppSettings["connectionString"],
    "Portal_GetAnnouncements",
    moduleId);
return reader;
```

This overload of the **ExecuteReader** method accepts three parameters: a connection string, the name of a command (in this case a stored procedure), and an array of one or more parameter values. This overloaded method in **SqlHelper** reveals the flexibility this allows. (This code is from the **SqlHelper** class included in the Democode folder for this modu

Visual Basic .NET

```vbnet
Public Overloads Shared Function ExecuteReader _
    (ByVal connectionString As String, _
    ByVal spName As String, _
    ByVal ParamArray parameterValues() As Object) As SqlDataReader

    Dim commandParameters As SqlParameter()
    ' First check for parameter values
    If Not (parameterValues Is Nothing) And parameterValues.Length > 0 Then
        ' Retrieve the parameters from the parameter cache (or discover
        ' them & populate the cache)
        commandParameters = _
        SqlHelperParameterCache.GetSpParameterSet( _
            connectionString, _
                spName)

        ' Assign the provided values to these parameters based on
        'parameter order
        AssignParameterValues(commandParameters, parameterValues)

    ' Call the overload that takes an array of SqlParameters
        Return ExecuteReader( _
        connectionString, _
        CommandType.StoredProcedure, _
        spName, _
            commandParameters)

    'otherwise we can just call the SP without params
    Else
        Return ExecuteReader( _
            connectionString, _
                CommandType.StoredProcedure, _
            spName)
    End If
End Function 'ExecuteReader
```

C#

```csharp
public static SqlDataReader ExecuteReader(string connectionString, string spName, params object[] parameterValues)
{
    //if we receive parameter values, we need to figure out where they go
    if ((parameterValues != null) && (parameterValues.Length > 0))
    {
        //pull the parameters for this stored procedure from the
        //parameter cache (or discover them & populate the cache)
        SqlParameter[] commandParameters = SqlHelperParameterCache.GetSpParameterSet(
            connectionString,
            spName);

        //assign the provided values to these parameters based on
        //parameter order
        AssignParameterValues(commandParameters, parameterValues);

        //call the overload that takes an array of SqlParameters
        return ExecuteReader(connectionString,
            CommandType.StoredProcedure, spName, commandParameters);
    }
        //otherwise we can just call the SP without params
    else
    {
        return ExecuteReader(connectionString,
            CommandType.StoredProcedure, spName);
    }
}
```

Because the parameter values are defined as an array of values, you can pass in any number of parameter values without concern about creating **SqlParameter** objects for each one. Notice on the third line of the function that the parameters are looked up through the **SqlHelpParameterCache** object. This class provides methods to cache and retrieve parameters. The **GetSpParameterSet** method retrieves the parameter details for a stored procedure and caches them for future accesses. The connection string and stored procedure name are used as the key for the **HashTable** used to cache the **SqlParameter** objects.

Assigning Parameter Values

AssignParameterValues is a utility procedure that assigns the values in **parameterValues** to the **commandParameters** array that was retrieved from the **GetSpParameterSet** function. This requires that the parameters be passed in the order they are assigned in the stored procedure because **AssignParameterValues** simply loops through the **commandParameter** array and assigns each parameter the corresponding value in **parameterValues**.

You create the **SqlDataReader** by calling an overload that accepts the array of **SqlParameter** objects that have been generated. You can then bind the **SqlDataReader** to the **DataList** in the Announcements.ascx user control and display "News and Features" data to your users.

Lesson: Performance Tuning for Data Access

> **Lesson: Performance Tuning for Data Access**
> - Options for Storing Connection Strings
> - Performance Tuning Single Value Retrieval

Introduction

Data access is the area of development that potentially can benefit most from performance tuning. In this lesson, you will learn about some of the most effective strategies for achieving this tuning.

Lesson Objectives

After completing this lesson, you will be able to:

- Evaluate the options for storing database connection information.
- Explain the strategic alternatives for retrieving single values and single rows.

Options for Storing Connection Strings

> **Options for Storing Connection Strings**
> - Web.config
> - Machine.config
> - Registry Settings

Introduction

One issue that can have a large impact on maintenance and code size is storing connection information for use by data access logic. Most of the data retrieval overloads in the DAAB require either a connection string or a connection object to be passed to the method.

Web.config

In the previous example, the strings were stored in the Web.config file for the site, from which they can be quickly retrieved by using the **AppSettings** property of the **ConfigurationSettings** class. A useful enhancement would be to add an extra layer of abstraction to wrap the call in a class that would provide methods to retrieve settings and create connection objects from these settings.

There are a number of options for storing this type of setting. For Web applications, the usual choice is to put connection strings in the Web.config file and optionally encrypt them if security is an issue. The appSettings section of the file can be used as follows:

```xml
<configuration>
    <appSettings>
        <add key="ConnectionString"
            value="server=localhost;Trusted_Connection=true;database=Portal" />
    </appSettings>
</configuration>
```

The primary advantage of this approach is ease of deployment. With this approach, the connection string will now be deployed with the rest of the project when the Web.config is copied.

In most deployments, the connection string or strings will have to be changed to correspond to the production database. To make the configuration change as simple as possible, many developers provide a management utility that allows the appSettings and other sections of Web.config to be easily updated. Despite the fact that the settings are stored in a file, access is fast because the data is cached at run time. Any changes made to the file are immediately recached without an application restart, so the new settings are immediately available.

The main disadvantage to this approach is lack of security because the connection string details are stored in clear text. You will learn how to use classes in the System.Security.Cryptography namespace to hash string values in the module on security.

Machine.config

A popular variation on this approach is to store configuration settings in the Machine.config file, which is the global configuration file for the server. In this way, settings for different stages (for example, development, staging, and production) can be established one time only, eliminating the need to change the Web.config file each time the application is moved to a different stage. Although there is an appSettings section in the Machine.config, the creation of separate names or prefixes for each application on the server in this section would be a maintenance issue. Creating a custom configuration section is an effective alternative that can be used in many different application configuration scenarios.

To create a custom configuration section in the Machine.config file, you should add an additional section to the configuration section of the Machine.config file. The appSettings section is defined by the following XML code, located in the <configSections> element at the beginning of the Machine.config file:

```xml
<section
         name="appSettings"
             type="System.Configuration.NameValueFileSectionHandler,
             System />
```

The **type** attribute designates which class will be used to handle the values stored in the configuration section. The **NameValueFileSectionHandler** allows the values in the section to be accessed as name/value pairs in the same way as you observed above in the appSettings section of the Web.config file; that is, by using <add> elements with **key** and **value** attributes. By adding new section elements to the configuration section, you can define new areas in the Machine.config file to store settings. Because it is likely that custom sections will contain subsections, it is convenient to group the settings as follows:

```xml
<sectionGroup name="SpectrumPortal">
    <sectionGroup name="Settings">
        <section name="PortalVBVS"
                type="System.Configuration. NameValueFileSectionHandler,,
                System "/>
    </sectionGroup>
        </sectionGroup>
```

A new section can be inserted into the configuration section in this way. Note the correspondence between the sections in the <sectionGroup> element and the sections in the <SpectrumPortal> element:

```xml
<SpectrumPortal>
    <Settings>
        <PortalVBVS>
            <add key= "DevelopConnectionString"
                 value="devServer;Trusted_Connection=true;database=DevPortal"
            />
            <add key="StagingConnectionString"
                 value="
stagingServer;Trusted_Connection=true;database=StagingPortal"/>
            <add key= "ProdConnectionString"
                 value="
prodServer;Trusted_Connection=true;database=ProdPortal" />
        </PortalVBVS>
    </Settings>
</SpectrumPortal>
```

To retrieve settings, which will be returned as a **HashTable**, a class could be created to access the values by using the **ConfigurationSettings** class:

Visual Basic .NET

```vb
Imports System
Imports System.Collections
Imports System.Configuration

Namespace SpectrumPortal
    Public Class CustomConfiguration

  Public Shared ReadOnly Property ProdSettings() As Hashtable
        Get
            Return _
                CType(ConfigurationSettings.GetConfig( _
                    ConfigurationSettings.AppSettings( _
                        "SpectrumPortal/Settings/PortalVBVS") _
                                    ("ProdConnectionString"), _
                    Hashtable)
        End Get
    End Property
   End Class 'CustomConfiguration
End Namespace
```

C#

```csharp
using System;
using System.Collections;
using System.Configuration;

namespace SpectrumPortal
{
    public class CustomConfiguration
    {
      public static readonly Hashtable ProdSettings()
      {
         get
         {
             return (Hashtable)
             ConfigurationSettings.GetConfig(
             ConfigurationSettings.AppSettings(
             "SpectrumPortal/Settings/PortalVBVS")
             ("ProdConnectionString"));
         }
      }
    }
}
```

This class can be used to retrieve settings in a convenient and easy-to-change format, allowing configuration information to be centrally stored and managed.

Registry Settings

To ensure limited access to production database strings, registry settings are often used. Access control lists (ACLs) can ensure that only selected groups have access to specific keys. You can combine this approach with encryption for a still higher security level. The .NET Framework supplies classes that provide easy access to registry keys. The principal disadvantage is that the deployment project will be required to create registry entries on the target server. This process is made straightforward through the use of the Registry Editor utility in the Web Deployment project.

Performance Tuning Single Value Retrieval

> **Performance Tuning Single Value Retrieval**
>
> **Three methods for retrieving single values**
> - **ExecuteScalar**
>   - Specialized for returning single values
>   - Requires less code than the alternatives
> - Output parameters of stored procedures
>   - Works well across a range of stress levels
> - **DataReader**
>   - Provides more speed under similar stress conditions

Introduction

You have examined the best practices for returning a **SqlDataReader** by using the DAAB. In this section, you will learn about some of the options for retrieving single values from stored procedures.

ExecuteScalar

Very often it is necessary to retrieve single values from stored procedures. The developer may need to check whether a user has already been added to a User table, in which case a Boolean return value is usually sufficient. In another scenario, you may want to retrieve the ID field for a project that has just been added. The **Insert** method of the **Project** class inserts a project into the database. The following code is used to accomplish this. (This code is from the **Project** class in the lab portal application.)

Visual Basic .NET

```
SqlHelper.ExecuteScalar( _
    ConfigurationSettings.AppSettings("connectionString"), _
    "AddProject", _
    Me.mName, _
    Me.mStarted, _
    Me.mEnded, _
    Me.mDescription, _
    selectedMembers.ToString())
```

C#

```
SqlHelper.ExecuteScalar(
    ConfigurationSettings.AppSettings[ "connectionString"],
    "AddProject",
    this.mName,
    this.mStarted,
    this.mEnded,
    this.mDescription,
    selectedMembers.ToString());
```

Similar to the **ExecuteReader** method, the **ExecuteScalar** method of the DAAB provides an overload that accepts a variable-length array of parameter values to be passed to a stored procedure. **ExecuteScalar** also performs parameter caching. Although this is an acceptable solution, there are several options that need to be considered when returning a single value. Three methods have been provided to retrieve single values: the **ExecuteScalar** method of the **Command** object, output parameters from stored procedures, and a **DataReader** object.

Output Parameters from Stored Procedures

The advantage of the **ExecuteScalar** method is that it is specialized for returning single values and requires less code than either of the alternatives. However, if maximum performance is the goal, using the output parameter of a stored procedure has been found to be the optimal approach.

To retrieve a single item, you can use a stored procedure output parameter or return value, together with the **ExecuteNonQuery** method. This approach works well across a range of stress levels. For more information about choosing an appropriate approach for looking up a single item, see the DAAB Help file.

The DataReader Object

If connection pooling is enabled, a **DataReader** will often provide more speed under similar stress conditions. Under conditions of low stress, the **ExecuteScalar** method will provide very similar performance.

When you need to retrieve a single row of data, such as the details for an event, the **DataReader** will provide acceptable performance and is the preferred method when metadata is required. The **GetSingleEvent** method of the **EventsDB** class in the ASP.NET Portal Starter Kit illustrates the how the **SqlHelper** class could optimize the data retrieval in this method by using the **ExecuteReader** method of the **SqlHelper** class:

Visual Basic .NET

```
Public Function GetSingleEvent(ByVal itemId As Integer) As SqlDataReader

    Dim reader As SqlDataReader = SqlHelper.ExecuteReader( _
        ConfigurationSettings.AppSettings("connectionString"), _
        "GetSingleEvent", _
        itemId)

    Return reader
End Function
```

C#

```
public SqlDataReader GetSingleEvent(int itemId) {

    SqlDataReader reader = SqlHelper.ExecuteReader(
      ConfigurationSettings.AppSettings("connectionString"),
     "GetSingleEvent", _
      itemId);

    return reader;
}
```

Lesson: Managing Portal Settings

Lesson: Managing Portal Settings
- Managing Settings and Configuration
- Data Access Logic Best Practices

Introduction

One of the most important factors in creating manageable Web applications is a well-planned configuration-management strategy. This section provides a detailed description of a primary aspect of site functionality: the management of portal configurations to define the tabs and modules that are available on a page.

Lesson Objectives

After completing this lesson, you will be able to:

- Describe the advantages of using a typed **DataSet** as the repository for configuration settings.

- Trace the execution pattern for rendering each tab and module to be displayed.

- Explain how the object structure of the portal provides a manageable framework for content development.

Managing Settings and Configuration

> **Managing Settings and Configuration**
>
> - Managing Configuration
>   - **PortalSettings** class determines what content to display to which user
>   - PortalCfg.xml file defines available tabs and modules and determines which roles have access
> - Managing Settings
>   - **ModuleSettings** object contains all properties necessary to set up modules for display
>   - **AuthorizedEditRoles** property controls which users have the right to edit the module
> - Setting Module Properties
>   - **ModuleConfiguration** property allows modules access to properties necessary for their user controls to be populated

Introduction

You have already been introduced to the fundamental management tool for configuring a site, the typed **DataSet** named **SiteConfiguration**. In this section, you will learn about the portal settings framework that is used to manage this configuration.

Managing Configuration

In order to determine what content to display to which user, the **PortalSettings** class is populated at each Web request. This operation takes place in the global.asax **Application_BeginRequest** event where a new **PortalSettings** object is instantiated and stored in the **HttpContext** object for the duration of the request. This object is defined in the Configuration component and contains the following properties:

- Public **PortalId** As Integer.
- Public **PortalName** As String.
- Public **AlwaysShowEditButton** As Boolean.
- Public **DesktopTabs** As New **ArrayList**().
- Public **ActiveTab** As New **TabSettings**().

Note in particular the **DesktopTabs** and **ActiveTab** properties. **DesktopTabs** corresponds to the tabs that should be available for a particular user. These tabs are configured in the PortalCfg.xml file, which defines all available tabs and modules and determines which roles have access. This file is read whenever a new **PortalSettings** object is created and defines the features of each tab. The constructor of the **PortalSettings** class illustrates how the configurations are set up. (This code is from the **PortalSettings** class of the lab portal application.)

Visual Basic .NET

```vbnet
Public Sub New(ByVal tabIndex As Integer, ByVal tabId As Integer)
    ' Get the configuration data
    Dim siteSettings As SiteConfiguration = _
        Configuration.GetSiteSettings()

    ' Read the Desktop Tab Information, and sort by Tab Order
    Dim tRow As SiteConfiguration.TabRow
    For Each tRow In siteSettings.Tab.Select("", "TabOrder")
        Dim tabDetails As New TabStripDetails()

        With tabDetails
            .TabId = tRow.TabId
            .TabName = tRow.TabName
            .TabOrder = tRow.TabOrder
            .AuthorizedRoles = tRow.AccessRoles
        End With

        Me.DesktopTabs.Add(tabDetails)
    Next
```

C#

```csharp
public PortalSettings(int tabIndex, int tabId)
{
        // Get the configuration data
        SiteConfiguration siteSettings = Configuration.GetSiteSettings();

        // Read the Desktop Tab Information, and sort by Tab Order
        foreach(SiteConfiguration.TabRow tRow in
siteSettings.Tab.Select("",
        "TabOrder"))
        {
                TabStripDetails tabDetails = new TabStripDetails();

                tabDetails.TabId = tRow.TabId;
                tabDetails.TabName = tRow.TabName;
                tabDetails.TabOrder = tRow.TabOrder;
                tabDetails.AuthorizedRoles = tRow.AccessRoles;

                this.DesktopTabs.Add(tabDetails);
        }
```

Understanding this code is critical to understanding how the site operates. This code segment populates the tab array that will be bound to the **DataList** on the DesktopPortalBanner.aspx page. The tab settings are retrieved from the PortalCfg.xml file through the **GetSiteSettings** method of the **Configuration** class. This method returns a typed **DataSet** (**SiteConfiguration**) that corresponds to these settings. This object is populated by using the **ReadXml** method, demonstrating the XML support provided by ADO.NET. It is cached in the **Cache** property of the current Context so that it will be available throughout the request. An initial sort is given to the tab array by using the **Select** method of the **DataTable** object. The properties of each tab are set by using a **TabStripDetails** object. Each instance of **TabStripDetails** is then added to the **DesktopTabs** array.

The tab array is populated, so the modules for each tab must be assigned. The pattern for this is similar to the one for retrieving tabs. (This code is from the **PortalSettings** class in the lab portal application.)

Visual Basic .NET

```vbnet
' Read the Module Information for the current (Active) tab
Dim activeTab As SiteConfiguration.TabRow = _
    siteSettings.Tab.FindByTabId(tabId)
Dim moduleRow As SiteConfiguration._ModuleRow

' Get Modules for this Tab based on the Data Relation
For Each moduleRow In activeTab.GetModuleRows()
    Dim moduleSettings As New moduleSettings()

    With moduleSettings
        .ModuleTitle = moduleRow.ModuleTitle
        .ModuleId = moduleRow.ModuleId
        .ModuleDefId = moduleRow.ModuleDefId
        .ModuleOrder = moduleRow.ModuleOrder
        .TabId = tabId
        .PaneName = moduleRow.PaneName
        .AuthorizedEditRoles = moduleRow.EditRoles
        .CacheTime = moduleRow.CacheTimeout

        ' ModuleDefinition data
        Dim modDefRow As SiteConfiguration.ModuleDefinitionRow = _
        siteSettings.ModuleDefinition.FindByModuleDefId(.ModuleDefId)

        .DesktopSrc = modDefRow.DesktopSourceFile
    End With

    Me.ActiveTab.Modules.Add(moduleSettings)
Next
```

C#

```csharp
// Read the Module Information for the current (Active) tab
SiteConfiguration.TabRow activeTab =
    siteSettings.Tab.FindByTabId(tabId);

// Get Modules for this Tab based on the Data Relation
foreach(SiteConfiguration.ModuleRow moduleRow in
    activeTab.GetModuleRows())
{
        ModuleSettings moduleSettings = new ModuleSettings();

        moduleSettings.ModuleTitle = moduleRow.ModuleTitle;
        moduleSettings.ModuleId = moduleRow.ModuleId;
        moduleSettings.ModuleDefId = moduleRow.ModuleDefId;
        moduleSettings.ModuleOrder = moduleRow.ModuleOrder;
        moduleSettings.TabId = tabId;
        moduleSettings.PaneName = moduleRow.PaneName;
        moduleSettings.AuthorizedEditRoles = moduleRow.EditRoles;
        moduleSettings.CacheTime = moduleRow.CacheTimeout;

        // ModuleDefinition data
        SiteConfiguration.ModuleDefinitionRow modDefRow =
          siteSettings.ModuleDefinition.FindByModuleDefId(
    moduleSettings.ModuleDefId);

        moduleSettings.DesktopSrc = modDefRow.DesktopSourceFile;

        this.ActiveTab.Modules.Add(moduleSettings);
}
```

Once again, you use the **siteSettings DataSet** to identify the modules for a tab. The **FindByTabId** method that has been added to the typed **DataSet** retrieves the **TabDataTable** object that contains the module settings. The **activeTab** is determined by the **tabId**, which is passed to the constructor when the **PortalSettings** object is initialized in the global.asax file. When the user clicks a tab, the **tabIndex** and **tabId** properties of the tab are used to populate a new **PortalSettings** object. The modules corresponding to this tab are used to populate the page.

Managing Settings

The modules provide the content that the portal displays. Each module is a user control that inherits the **PortalModuleControl** base class. Each module has a corresponding a **ModuleSettings** object that contains all properties necessary to set up the modules for display, including properties that define which tab the module belongs to and in which pane (right, middle, or left) the module will be displayed. The **AuthorizedEditRoles** property controls which users have the right to edit the module. You will learn how these roles are constructed in the security module.

The Settings subelement contains Setting elements for extra elements, such as image files for Image type modules or xml and xsl files for the XML type modules.

The PortalCfg.xml file has two sections in which module properties are defined. The display information needed for each module is contained in Module elements that are nested within their corresponding Tab elements. Other module features are defined in the ModuleDefinition section. These features include the DesktopSourceFile used to identify the user control for a module, and the ModuleDefId that creates the relationship between the Module elements and the ModuleDefinition elements. All of this information becomes available through the **SiteConfiguration** typed **DataSet**, along with the methods needed to access it. After the **ModuleSettings** object is completely populated, it is added to the Modules collection of the **ActiveTab** property of the **PortalSettings** object.

Each page servicing the request has access to the **PortalSettings object** through **HttpContext**. The DesktopDefault.aspx page will normally be the first page accessed by users. In the **Page_Init** event of this page, the **PortalSettings** object is retrieved with the following code:

Visual Basic .NET

```
Dim _portalSettings As PortalSettings =
    CType(HttpContext.Current.Items("PortalSettings"), PortalSettings)
```

C#

```
PortalSettings portalSettings = (PortalSettings)
    HttpContext.Current.Items["PortalSettings"];
```

The Modules collection of the **ActiveTab** property now provides direct access to all of the modules and module settings needed to create the page. All that is necessary to display the modules is to loop through the modules collection for this tab, load the user controls corresponding to the modules, and then add them to the appropriate pane. (This code is from the **Page_Init** method in the DefaultDesktop.aspx code-behind file.)

Visual Basic .NET

```
For Each _moduleSettings In _portalSettings.ActiveTab.Modules

    Dim parent As Control = Page.FindControl(_moduleSettings.PaneName)

    If _moduleSettings.CacheTime = 0 Then

        Dim portalModule As PortalModuleControl = _
        CType(Page.LoadControl(_moduleSettings.DesktopSrc), _
        PortalModuleControl)

        portalModule.PortalId = _portalSettings.PortalId
        portalModule.ModuleConfiguration = _moduleSettings

        parent.Controls.Add(portalModule)

    Else
      Dim portalModule As New CachedPortalModuleControl()
      portalModule.PortalId = _portalSettings.PortalId
      portalModule.ModuleConfiguration = _moduleSettings
      parent.Controls.Add(portalModule)

    End If

    parent.Controls.Add(New LiteralControl("<" + "br" + ">"))
    parent.Visible = True

Next _moduleSettings
```

C#

```csharp
foreach (ModuleSettings _moduleSettings in
    portalSettings.ActiveTab.Modules)
{
    Control parent = Page.FindControl(_moduleSettings.PaneName);

    // If no caching is specified, create the user control instance and
    // dynamically inject it into the page.  Otherwise, create a cached
    // module instance that may or may not optionally inject the module
    // into the tree

    if ((_moduleSettings.CacheTime) == 0)
    {
        PortalModuleControl portalModule = (PortalModuleControl)
        Page.LoadControl(_moduleSettings.DesktopSrc);

        portalModule.PortalId = portalSettings.PortalId;
        portalModule.ModuleConfiguration = _moduleSettings;

        parent.Controls.Add(portalModule);
    }
    else
    {
        CachedPortalModuleControl portalModule = new
            CachedPortalModuleControl();

        portalModule.PortalId = portalSettings.PortalId;
        portalModule.ModuleConfiguration = _moduleSettings;

        parent.Controls.Add(portalModule);
    }

    // Dynamically inject separator break between portal modules
    parent.Controls.Add(new LiteralControl("<" + "br" + ">"));
    parent.Visible = true;
}
```

The **CacheTime** property defined in the configuration file determines the way each module is loaded. If the **CacheTime** property is set to 0, no caching takes place for that module. The **PortalModuleControl** is used as the class definition for the module, and is loaded by using the **LoadControl** method of the **Page** object. The module is then placed in the correct pane (table cell objects defined in the main table for the page) in the order defined for that module. If caching is defined for the module, the **CachedPortalModuleControl** object is instantiated. Details of how caching works in the portal are covered in the Caching module. Note that the **CachedPortalModuleControl** wraps a **PortalModuleControl** object. In the **Render** method of the **CachedPortalModuleControl** class, the portal module user control object is stored in a **Cache** object for later retrieval.

Setting Module Properties

The properties of the module are set through the **ModuleConfiguration** property of the **portalModule** object. The **ModuleConfiguration** property allows the modules access to the properties necessary for their corresponding user controls to be populated. The **Announcements** control needs the **ModuleId** property so that the **GetAnnouncements** method can retrieve the announcements for that module.

Data Access Logic Best Practices

Managing Settings and Configuration

- Managing Configuration
  - **PortalSettings** class determines what content to display to which user
  - PortalCfg.xml file defines available tabs and modules and determines which roles have access
- Managing Settings
  - **ModuleSettings** object contains all properties necessary to set up modules for display
  - **AuthorizedEditRoles** property controls which users have the right to edit the module
- Setting Module Properties
  - **ModuleConfiguration** property allows modules access to properties necessary for their user controls to be populated

Consider the following best practices when designing the data access logic for your Web application:

- Use a **DataReader** for optimized data reporting. This object returns a forward-only stream of data while making use of minimum memory resources.

- If there is no need to hold the data in a cache for later retrieval, or to pass the data to another part of the application, incurring the overhead of a **DataSet** may not add value. The application merely creates an unnecessary duplicate copy of the data. To avoid wasting resources, you should use the **DataReader**.

- As a general rule, each stored procedure should be associated with a single data access component. Business logic components should have no database schema dependencies.

- **DataSets** are best used with large amounts of data. The ratio of startup costs to the amount of data loaded improves as data increases.

- **DataSets** are recommended if the application is primarily working with collections of items and needs standard sorting, filtering, and searching capabilities. This is especially true if the data needs to incorporate complex or hierarchical relationships.

- Consider the advantages of custom collection objects:
    - **Code Readability**. Data in custom business entities is contained in strongly typed properties or subclasses. Just as in a typed **DataSet**, you get compile-time type checking, early binding, and Intellisense aid in writing code.
    - **Low Overhead**. The custom entity includes only the properties, methods, and events needed to represent its entity, rather than the overhead penalty of a **DataSet** object.
    - **Flexibility**. Creating a custom configuration section in the Machine.config file can be used in many different application scenarios to centralize access to configuration settings.

Lab 2: Using Data Access Components

Lab 2: Using Data Access Components
- Exercise 1: Using Data Access Components for Data Binding
- Exercise 2: Creating Collection Classes for Data Display

Introduction

After completing this lab, you will have demonstrated your ability to:
- Implement reusable data access logic components.
- Use custom business entities.
- Create collection classes to display business entity data.

Prerequisites

Before working on this lab, you must have the knowledge and skills necessary to develop ADO.NET data components. One of the most important content areas for the portal site is the tab that manages project and task tracking. Two major classes are used to manage this information, the **Project** and **Task** classes. Each of these classes has corresponding collection classes that are used to access and display information for collections of these items. The student will implement selected portions of this functionality.

Estimated time to complete this lab: 60 minutes

Starting a Virtual Machine

1. On the student computer, on the **Start** menu, point to **All Programs**, and then click **Microsoft Virtual PC**. If the Virtual PC console window does not appear, then right-click the **Virtual PC icon** in the notification area (system tray), and click **Show Virtual PC Console**.
2. In the Virtual PC console window, select the virtual machine that you would like to open and then click **Start**.

   NOTE: Depending on your time zone, the first time you start each of the virtual machines, you may receive an error message that the parent virtual hard disk appears to have been modified. You can ignore this message.
3. The virtual machine will start up in a new window.

Closing a Virtual Machine

1. On the student computer, in the virtual machine window, on the **Action** menu, click **Close**.

   NOTE: To avoid accidentally closing the virtual machine during the lab, the Close button in the top right corner of the virtual machine is disabled.
2. The virtual machine window will close. All changes to the virtual hard disk are discarded.

Exercise 1: Creating a Project Data Access Component

In this exercise, you will examine the structure of the **Project** class and implement functionality that illustrates best practices for data access.

▪ Open the lab starter project

1. Open the ASPProjectVB or ASPProjectCS project in Visual Studio .NET by browsing to D:\2311\Labfiles\Lab02\Starter\VB or D:\2311\Labfiles\ Lab02\Starter\CS.
2. Launch the project by double-clicking the ASPProjectVB.sln or ASPProjectCS.sln file in the lab starter folder.

Examine the Project class

1. The **Project** class is used for all management and display tasks for project information. Find this class in the Project.vb or Project.cs file in the Project folder under the Components folder.

2. Note the properties and methods implemented in this class. In particular, note the **ProjectMembers** property that will be used to track the members of a particular project. Members are stored and accessed by using the **ProjectMemberList** collection class.

3. Study the **Insert** method to familiarize yourself with how the members of a project are added when a new project is added. The **selectedMembers** property is populated when the **LoadProjects** method is called. This is done on the EditProjects.aspx page, which you will examine when implementing the management infrastructure.

Implement the GetAllProjects method

1. This method of the **Project** class is used by the ProjectModule.ascx user control to display a drop-down list of project information on the Admin tab. Open the Project.vb or Project.cs file in the Project folder. Locate the comment "TODO Use the SqlHelper class to retrieve a DataSet." Examine the overloads in the SqlHelper.vb or SqlHelper.cs file to identify a suitable overload to retrieve a **DataSet** by using the **GetAllProjects** stored procedure.

2. Write a call to an **ExecuteDataSet** overload to retrieve information about all the projects:

Visual Basic .NET

```
Dim ds As DataSet = SqlHelper.ExecuteDataset( _
    ConfigurationSettings.AppSettings("connectionString"), _
    "GetAllProjects")
```

C#

```
DataSet ds = SqlHelper.ExecuteDataset(
    ConfigurationSettings.AppSettings[ "connectionString"],
    "GetAllProjects");
```

3. Locate the comment "TODO Populate a ProjectList object with project information." Open the ProjectCollections file and examine the **ProjectList** class. Note that it contains **ProjectInfo** objects. **ProjectInfo** is a structure that contains project information.

4. Declare and instantiate a **ProjectList** object.
5. Declare and instantiate a **DataRow** object.
6. Use a **For** loop to loop through the rows in the **DataSet** that contains project information.
7. Declare and instantiate a **ProjectInfo** object.
8. Store the project information in the properties of the **ProjectInfo** object according to the following table:

ProjectInfo property	DataRow column
ProjectID	ProjectID
ProjectName	ProjectName
DateStarted	Started

9. Add each **ProjectInfo** object to the **ProjectList**.
10. Return the **ProjectList** from the function.
11. Your code should resemble the following:

Visual Basic .NET

```vb
Dim pl As ProjectList = New ProjectList()
Dim r As DataRow
For Each r In ds.Tables(0).Rows
    Dim p As ProjectInfo = New ProjectInfo()

    p.ProjectID = CType(r("ProjectID"), Integer)
    p.ProjectName = CType(r("ProjectName"), String)
    p.DateStarted = CType(r("Started"), DateTime)
    pl.Add(p)

Next
Return pl
```

C#

```
ProjectList pl= new ProjectList();
foreach(DataRow r in ds.Tables[0].Rows)
{
    ProjectInfo p = new ProjectInfo();

    p.ProjectID =   (int)r["ProjectID"];
    p.ProjectName = (string)r["ProjectName"];
    p.DateStarted = (DateTime)r["Started"];
    pl.Add(p);

}
return pl;
```

12. Build the project.

13. Test the new method by clicking the **Admin** tab. You must first log in with an administrator account. In the **Manage Projects** section in the right-hand pane, ensure that the **Projects** drop-down list box is populated.

- **Implement the GetMembers method**

    This method of the **Project** class is used by the TaskModule.ascx user control to display a drop-down list of user information.

1. Locate the comment "TODO Use the SqlHelper class to retrieve a DataSet of project members."

2. Examine the overloads in the SqlHelper.vb or SqlHelper.cs file to identify a suitable overload to retrieve a **DataSet** by using the **GetProjectUsers** stored procedure, which accepts a projectID parameter.

3. Write a call to an **ExecuteDataSet** overload to retrieve information about all users for a specific project:

Visual Basic .NET

```
Dim ds As DataSet = SqlHelper.ExecuteDataset( _
    ConfigurationSettings.AppSettings("connectionstring"), _
    "GetProjectUsers", _
    projectID)
```

C#

```
DataSet ds = SqlHelper.ExecuteDataset(
    ConfigurationSettings.AppSettings["connectionstring"],
    "GetProjectUsers",
    projectID);
```

4. Locate the comment "TODO Populate a ProjectMemberList object with member information." Open the ProjectCollections file and examine the **ProjectMemberList** class. It contains **ProjectMember** objects. **ProjectMember** is a class that is used to manage member information.

5. Open the ProjectMember.vb or ProjectMember.cs file. Note in particular the **GetProjectRoles** method. This method enables project security by returning the roles of a particular member.

6. Declare and instantiate a **ProjectMemberList** object. **Note**: This code has been provided in the C# version of the lab starter files to ensure that the project would compile before the student has completed the lab.

7. Declare and instantiate a **DataRow** object.

8. Use a **For** loop to loop through the rows in the **DataSet** that contains member information.

9. Declare and instantiate a **ProjectMember** object.

10. Store the project information in the properties of the **ProjectMember** object according to the following table:

ProjectInfo property	DataRow column
UserName	UserName
DateAssigned	N/A (see code below)
ProjectRole	RoleDescription (see code below)

11. The **DateAssigned** property should be assigned today's date.

12. The **ProjectRole** should use the enumeration **EnumProjectRole** to assign the value from the RoleDescription column. Use the **GetType** method and the **Parse** method of the **Enum** class to convert the RoleDescription into the correct enumerated value.

13. Add each **ProjectMember** object to the **ProjectMemberList**.

14. Return the **ProjectMemberList** from the function. **Note**: This code has been provided in the C# version of the lab starter files to ensure that the project would compile before the student has completed the lab.

15. Your code should resemble the following:

Visual Basic .NET

```
Dim members As ProjectMemberList = New ProjectMemberList()
Dim r As DataRow
For Each r In ds.Tables(0).Rows
    Dim member As ProjectMember = New ProjectMember()

    member.UserName = CType(r("UserName"), String)
    member.DateAssigned = CType(member.DateAssigned, DateTime)
    member.ProjectRole = CType( _
        [Enum].Parse(GetType(EnumProjectRole), _
        r("RoleDescription").ToString()), _
        EnumProjectRole)
    members.Add(member)
Next
Return members
```

C#

```
ProjectMemberList members = new ProjectMemberList();
foreach(DataRow r in ds.Tables[0].Rows)
{
    ProjectMember member = new ProjectMember();

    member.UserName = (string)r["UserName"];
    member.DateAssigned = (DateTime)member.DateAssigned;
    member.ProjectRole = (EnumProjectRole)Enum.Parse(
        typeof(ASPProject.EnumProjectRole),
    r["RoleDescription"].ToString(), true);
    members.Add(member);

}

return members;
```

16. Build the project.
17. Test the function by clicking the **Task Tracking** tab. Ensure that the users drop-down list (**UserSelection**) on the Tasks module is populated.

Exercise 2: Creating a Task Data Access Component

In this exercise, you will examine the structure of the **Task** class and implement functionality that illustrates data access for tasks that are managed within projects.

- **Open the portal application project and study the Task display functionality**

    1. In Visual Studio .NET, open the ASPProjectVB or ASPProjectCS project.

    2. In the Module directory, open the TaskModule.ascx file. The user control will display information about a specific task. Note that a **Repeater** control is used to display task data.

    3. In the Module directory, open the TaskModule.ascx.vb or TaskModule.ascx.cs file. Note the properties and methods implemented in this class, in particular the **BindProjectList**, **BindUserList**, and **BindTaskList** methods. The **BindTaskList** method will populate the **Repeater** control for this user control.

    4. In the **TaskTracking** directory, open the Task.vb or Task.cs file. Study the properties defined in the PUBLIC PROPERTIES region.

    5. Open the ADD UPDATE DELETE region. Note the use of **SqlHelper** methods for the three tasks.

- **Implement the GetTask method**

    1. Locate the comment "TODO Implement the Shared GetTask function."

    2. Inside the function, declare and instantiate a **DataSet** by using the **SqlHelper ExecuteDataSet** method. Use the overload that accepts three parameters: a connection string, the name of a stored procedure, and a parameter array. Assign the values of these parameters according to the following table:

Parameter	Value
Connection String	ConfigurationSettings.AppSettings("ConnectionString")
Stored Procedure	"GetTask"
Parameter Array	taskId

3. Declare and instantiate a **DataRow** object and assign it to the first row object in the first **DataTable** in the **DataSet** created in step 2 above. Note that a new **Task** object has been declared and instantiated.
4. Assign the taskId to the mtaskID property of the Task object. Note: the C# version of the code uses taskID for this property.
5. Assign the other properties of the **Task** object by using the **DataRow** according to the values in the following table:

Visual Basic .NET

Task property	DataRow column
mAssignedTo	AssignedTo
mProjectID	ProjectID
mAssignedBy	AssignedBy
mDateAssigned	DateAssigned
mDateCompleted	DateCompleted
mPercentageCompleted	PercentageCompleted
mTaskDescription	TaskDescription
mTaskStatus	TaskStatus
mTaskNotes	TaskNotes

C#

Task property	DataRow column
assignedTo	AssignedTo
projectID	ProjectID
assignedBy	AssignedBy
dateAssigned	DateAssigned
dateCompleted	DateCompleted
percentageCompleted	PercentageCompleted
taskDescription	TaskDescription
taskStatus	TaskStatus
taskNotes	TaskNotes

6. Note that the **Task** object is returned from the function. Your code should resemble the following:

Visual Basic .NET

```vb
Dim ds As DataSet = _
 SqlHelper.ExecuteDataset( _
     ConfigurationSettings.AppSettings("connectionstring"), _
     "GetTask", _
     taskId)

Dim r As DataRow = ds.Tables(0).Rows(0)
Dim t As New Task()

t.mTaskID = taskId
t.mAssignedTo = r("AssignedTo").ToString()
t.mProjectID = CInt(r("ProjectID"))
t.mAssignedBy = r("AssignedBy").ToString()

t.mDateAssigned = CType(r("DateAssigned"), DateTime)
t.mDateCompleted = CType(r("DateCompleted"), DateTime)
t.mPercentageCompleted = CInt(r("PercentageCompleted"))
t.mTaskDescription = CStr(r("TaskDescription"))
t.mTaskStatus = CStr(r("TaskStatus"))
t.mTaskNotes = CStr(r("TaskNotes"))

Return t
```

C#

```csharp
DataSet ds = SqlHelper.ExecuteDataset(
        ConfigurationSettings.AppSettings[ "connectionstring"],
        "GetTask",
        taskId);
DataRow r = ds.Tables[ 0] .Rows[ 0] ;
Task t = new Task();

t.taskID = taskId;
t.assignedTo = r[ "AssignedTo"] .ToString();
t.projectID = (int)r[ "ProjectID"] ;
t.assignedBy = r[ "AssignedBy"] .ToString();

t.dateAssigned = (DateTime)r[ "DateAssigned"] ;
t.dateCompleted = (DateTime)r[ "DateCompleted"] ;
t.percentageCompleted = (int)r[ "PercentageCompleted"] ;
t.taskDescription = (string)r[ "TaskDescription"] ;
t.taskStatus = (string)r[ "TaskStatus"] ;
t.taskNotes = (string)r[ "TaskNotes"] ;

return t;
```

- **Implement the GetTasks overloads**

    1. Locate the comment "TODO Implement the first GetTasks overload." This method accepts a userName and projectID and returns a **TaskCollection** object.

    2. Open the TaskCollection.vb or TaskCollection.cs file. Study the properties of the **TaskInfo** structure. The **TaskCollection** inherits the **CollectionBase** class and implements an **Add** method that adds a **TaskInfo** item to the **List** property and returns the position of the object. The method implemented here will use a **DataSet** to populate a **TaskCollection** object with **TaskInfo** objects.

    3. Go back to the Tasks.vb or Tasks.cs file. Inside the first **GetTasks** overload, declare and instantiate a **DataSet** by using the **SqlHelper ExecuteDataSet** method. Use the overload that accepts three parameters: a connection string, the name of a stored procedure, and a parameter array. Assign the values of these parameters according to the following table:

Parameter	Value
Connection String	ConfigurationSettings.AppSettings("ConnectionString")
Stored Procedure	"GetTasks"
Parameter Array	userName, projectID

    4. Note that a new **TaskCollection** object has been declared and instantiated.

    5. Declare and instantiate a **DataRow** object.

    6. Use a **For** loop to loop through the rows in the first **DataTable** of the **DataSet**.

    7. Inside the loop, declare and instantiate a **TaskInfo** object.

    8. Populate the property values of the **TaskInfo** object according to the following table:

TaskInfo property	DataRow column
TaskID	taskId
DateAssigned	DateAssigned
TaskDescription	TaskDescription
TaskStatus	TaskStatus

9. Inside the loop, add the **TaskInfo** object to the **TaskCollection** object.
10. Note that the **TaskCollection** object is returned from the function.
11. Your code should resemble the following:

Visual Basic .NET

```
Dim ds As DataSet = _
 SqlHelper.ExecuteDataset( _
    ConfigurationSettings.AppSettings("connectionstring"), _
    "GetTasks", _
    userName, _
    projectID)

Dim tc As New TaskCollection()
Dim r As DataRow
For Each r In ds.Tables(0).Rows
    Dim t As New TaskInfo()

    t.TaskID = CInt(r("taskId"))

    t.DateAssigned = CType(r("DateAssigned"), DateTime)
    t.TaskDescription = CStr(r("TaskDescription"))
    t.TaskStatus = CStr(r("TaskStatus"))
    tc.Add(t)
Next r

Return tc
```

C#

```
public static TaskCollection GetTasks(string userName, int projectID)
{
    DataSet ds = SqlHelper.ExecuteDataset(
        ConfigurationSettings.AppSettings["connectionstring"],
        "GetTasks",
        userName,
        projectID);
    TaskCollection tc = new TaskCollection();
    foreach(DataRow r in ds.Tables[0].Rows)
    {
        TaskInfo t = new TaskInfo();

        t.TaskID = (int)r["taskId"];

        t.DateAssigned = (DateTime)r["DateAssigned"];
        t.TaskDescription = (string)r["TaskDescription"];
        t.TaskStatus = (string)r["TaskStatus"];
        tc.Add(t);
    }
    return tc;
}
```

12. Locate the comment "TODO Implement the second GetTasks overload." This method accepts a userName, projectID, pageNumber, pageSize, sortOrder, and numberOfRecords and returns a **TaskCollection** object.

13. Create an array of **SqlParameter** objects that can hold six elements named **arParms**.

14. Populate the array by creating **SqlParameters** with the properties from the following table:

Array Element	Name	Data Type	Size	Value	Direction
0	@UserName	SqlDbType.NVarChar	50	userName	Input
1	@ProjectID	SqlDbType.Int	N/A	projectID	Input
2	@PageNumber	SqlDbType.Int	N/A	pageNumber	Input
3	@PageSize	SqlDbType.Int	N/A	pageSize	Input
4	@SortOrder	SqlDbType.NVarChar	30	sortOrder	Input
5	@NumberOfRecords	SqlDbType.Int	N/A	numberOfRecords	Output

15. Inside the function, declare and instantiate a **DataSet** by using the **SqlHelper ExecuteDataSet** method. Use the overload that accepts four parameters: a connection string, a command type, the name of a stored procedure, and a parameter array. Assign the values of these parameters according to the following table:

Parameter	Value
Connection String	ConfigurationSettings.AppSettings("ConnectionString")
CommandType	StoredProcedure
Stored Procedure	"GetTasksByPage"
Parameter Array	arParms

16. A new **TaskCollection** object has been declared and instantiated.
17. Declare and instantiate a **DataRow** object.
18. Use a **For** loop to loop through the rows in the **DataSet**.
19. Inside the loop, declare and instantiate a **TaskInfo** object.
20. Populate the property values of the **TaskInfo** object according to the following table:

TaskInfo property	DataRow column
TaskID	taskId
DateAssigned	DateAssigned
TaskDescription	TaskDescription
TaskStatus	TaskStatus

21. Inside the loop, add the **TaskInfo** object to the **TaskCollection** object.
22. After the loop, retrieve the output parameter numberOfRecords by accessing the element of the array.
23. The **TaskCollection** object is returned from the function.
24. Your code should resemble the following:

Visual Basic .NET

```vbnet
Dim arParms(6) As SqlParameter
arParms(0) = New SqlParameter("@UserName", SqlDbType.NVarChar, 50)
arParms(0).Value = userName
arParms(1) = New SqlParameter("@ProjectID", SqlDbType.Int)
arParms(1).Value = projectID
arParms(2) = New SqlParameter("@PageNumber", SqlDbType.Int)
arParms(2).Value = pageNumber
arParms(3) = New SqlParameter("@PageSize", SqlDbType.Int)
arParms(3).Value = pageSize
arParms(4) = New SqlParameter("@SortOrder", SqlDbType.NVarChar, 30)
arParms(4).Value = sortOrder
arParms(5) = New SqlParameter("@NumberOfRecords", SqlDbType.Int)
arParms(5).Value = numberOfRecords
arParms(5).Direction = ParameterDirection.Output

Dim ds As DataSet = SqlHelper.ExecuteDataset( _
    ConfigurationSettings.AppSettings("connectionstring"), _
    CommandType.StoredProcedure, _
    "GetTasksByPage", _
    arParms)
Dim tc As New TaskCollection()
Dim r As DataRow
For Each r In ds.Tables(0).Rows
    Dim t As New TaskInfo()

    t.TaskID = CInt(r("taskId"))

    t.DateAssigned = CType(r("DateAssigned"), DateTime)
    t.TaskDescription = CStr(r("TaskDescription"))
    t.TaskStatus = CStr(r("TaskStatus"))
    tc.Add(t)
Next r
numberOfRecords = CInt(arParms(5).Value)

Return tc
```

C#

```csharp
SqlParameter [] arParms = new SqlParameter[ 6] ;
arParms[ 0] = new SqlParameter("@UserName", SqlDbType.NVarChar, 50 );
arParms[ 0] .Value = userName;
arParms[ 1] = new SqlParameter("@ProjectID", SqlDbType.Int);
arParms[ 1] .Value = projectID;
arParms[ 2] = new SqlParameter("@PageNumber", SqlDbType.Int);
arParms[ 2] .Value = pageNumber;
arParms[ 3] = new SqlParameter("@PageSize", SqlDbType.Int);
arParms[ 3] .Value = pageSize;
arParms[ 4] = new SqlParameter("@SortOrder", SqlDbType.NVarChar, 30 );
arParms[ 4] .Value = sortOrder;
arParms[ 5] = new SqlParameter("@NumberOfRecords", SqlDbType.Int);
arParms[ 5] .Value = numberOfRecords;
arParms[ 5] .Direction = ParameterDirection.Output;

DataSet ds = SqlHelper.ExecuteDataset(
    ConfigurationSettings.AppSettings[ "connectionstring"] ,
    CommandType.StoredProcedure,
    "GetTasksByPage",
     arParms);
TaskCollection tc = new TaskCollection();
foreach(DataRow r in ds.Tables[ 0] .Rows)
{
    TaskInfo t = new TaskInfo();

    t.TaskID = (int)r[ "taskId"] ;

    t.DateAssigned = (DateTime)r[ "DateAssigned"] ;
    t.TaskDescription = (string)r[ "TaskDescription"] ;
    t.TaskStatus = (string)r[ "TaskStatus"] ;
    tc.Add(t);

}
numberOfRecords = (int)arParms[ 5] .Value;

return tc;
```

25. Build the application and test by clicking the **Task Tracking** tab. Add some tasks by using the **Add Task** link. Make sure that the tasks appear correctly.

Module 3: Web Presentation Patterns

> **Module 3: Web Presentation Patterns**
> - .NET Design Patterns
> - Exploring the DataGrid

Overview

A great deal of portal functionality is focused on providing an easy-to-manipulate and high-performance user interface. In this module, you will learn how user interface elements can be built by using the following design patterns that have been found particularly useful for ASP.NET applications.

After completing this module, you will be able to:

- Design patterns for .NET.
- Describe the DataGrid and apply data-binding techniques.

Lesson: .NET Design Patterns

Lesson: .NET Design Patterns
- **Defining Presentation Patterns**
- **Implementing the Pattern**
- **Page Template Patterns**

Introduction

The book *Patterns for Building Enterprise Solutions*, published by Microsoft Press (April, 2003), defines a pattern as follows: "A pattern describes a recurring problem that occurs in a given context and, based on a set of guiding forces, recommends a solution. The solution is usually a simple mechanism, a collaboration between two or more classes, objects, services, processes, threads, components, or nodes that work together to resolve the problem identified in the pattern." This lesson introduces the concept of patterns as they apply to ASP.NET Web application design.

Lesson Objectives

After completing this lesson, you will be able to:

- Define patterns as they apply to Web application design.
- Describe common ASP.NET user interface problems and associated solutions achieved by using patterns.
- Describe the Page Controller and how to create a base page controller class to avoid code duplication, increase consistency, and make testing easier.

Defining Presentation Patterns

> **Defining Presentation Patterns**
>
> - A *pattern* is a description of a recurring problem that occurs in a particular application context and its associated solution
> - ASP.NET encourages separation of business logic from presentation
> - The Model-View-Controller pattern separates the modeling of the domain, the presentation, and user interactivity into Model, View, and Controller classes
> - Benefits of separation:
>   - The model can be built and tested independently of the presentation
>   - Support for multiple design views
> - Disadvantage is increased complexity

Introduction

A *pattern* is a description of a recurring problem that occurs in a particular application context and its associated solution. The portal application that you are building in this class is primarily focused on effectively organizing content for a specific audience. In support of this goal, the object-oriented features of ASP.NET are fully exploited, resulting in architectural efficiencies that were not possible with the previous version of ASP. In order to understand the rationale behind many of these decisions, it is necessary to understand design patterns, a well-established object-oriented tool that enables ASP.NET developers to make informed choices in the new environment.

Patterns of Interaction

One feature that distinguishes ASP.NET from its predecessor is the way it encourages separation of business logic from presentation. This section explains what drives this separation by examining the architectural choices in the context of a typical Web application.

Most Web applications retrieve information from a data store and present it to the user. The user makes changes to the information and the application then validates the user input and stores it in the database. Because the key flow of information is between the user interface and the data store, the developer might suppose that the best approach would be to tie these two components together, thus reducing the amount of code and improving performance. Although this approach is simple to implement, it soon becomes apparent that the user interface is likely to change far more often than the data store. Business logic is likely to add a changing set of rules to the data retrieval process.

Therefore the problem lies in how to modularize the user interface so that the individual parts are easily modified. You first need to consider the forces that influence a typical Web application. User interfaces must be constantly upgraded in most Web applications, including styles, navigation layouts, page layouts, and interactive elements such as form fields. If presentation code and business logic are combined in a single object, each change in interface design could require a change in business logic, which must then be retested.

The application may require that the same information be displayed differently either according to user choice or by design. Sales statistics could be displayed in a grid structure or as an exploded pie chart. If the user interacts with the data, data changes must be updated in all display formats.

Presentation vs. Business Logic

Web developer skill sets tend to be divided between designers who understand how to lay out page elements for the optimal graphical effect and programmers who excel at devising business logic. Application architecture should capitalize on this natural division so that each group can make the best use of its specific expertise. This is best accomplished by the clean separation of these tasks.

User interface code tends to be much more device-dependent than business logic. If new requirements demand that additional browsers be supported, or if the application must be accessible on handheld devices, new interface code must be written while the business logic might remain unaffected. Testing user interfaces is usually much more involved, requiring many more use cases than those needed for business logic. Separating user interface from business logic leads to better written and more maintainable designs.

The solution is suggested by the **Model-View-Controller** pattern. This pattern separates the modeling of the domain, the presentation, and user interactivity into three separate classes:

- **Model**. The model manages the behavior and data of the application, responds to information requests (usually from the presentation layer), and responds to requests from the controller (usually in response to state changes).
- **View**. The view class manages the presentation of information.
- **Controller**. The controller adds the interactivity by interpreting user input (mouse clicks, keyboard input) to send messages to the **View** or **Model** to make changes as needed.

This diagram illustrates the relationship:

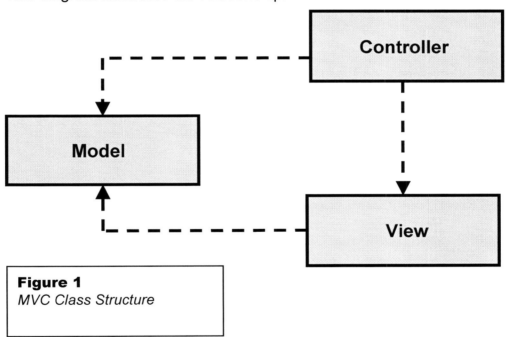

Figure 1
MVC Class Structure

Benefits and Disadvantages of Separation

The first benefit of this separation is that the model can be built and tested independently of the presentation because it does not depend on the view. The more interdependent components there are, the more difficult they are to test. Web applications involve so many elements that even simple interactions require complicated setups. With so many elements interacting, isolating the cause of a particular problem can also be challenging. This pattern breaks storing, displaying, and updating data into independently testable units.

Other benefits include support for multiple views. In the TimeTracker application, the main display (TimeTracker.aspx) presents project data in the form of a **DataGrid** and as a chart. In the portal, the administrator can configure each Tab to display different modules or allow different Tabs to display the same modules. Due to the separation, adding new views, in the case of the portal, new modules, can be done without entailing changes to business or data logic.

The major disadvantage is increased complexity. Interaction between the parts, and the event-driven nature of the interface, constitute a less straightforward model than most traditional ASP applications would involve. You will see that the improved functionality outweighs this drawback.

Implementing the Pattern

> **Implementing the Pattern**
>
> - **The *View* is code that renders the HTML to the browser**
>   - In the portal, the View is represented by the aspx pages and user controls
> - **The *Model* is the logic that reacts to the events**
> - **Benefits of implementing the pattern**
>   - Reduced code duplication
>   - Functionality can be tested independently of the HTML interface
>   - Optimization is easier because data access is encapsulated in a single component

Introduction

In Web applications, the *View* is code that renders the Hypertext Markup Language (HTML) to the browser. In the portal, the **View** is represented by the aspx pages and user controls, which are files with an ascx extension. The **Controller** in this case is ASP.NET, which raises the events that take place when the user interacts with a form; for example, the **SaveButton_Click** event. The *Model* is the logic that reacts to the events; for example, by populating a drop-down list with city names. This logic can be contained in the event handlers or in separate components.

Pattern Example

As an illustration of the pattern, consider the Announcements.ascx user control that is used to display news items. The HTML elements and server controls, such as the **DataList**, constitute the View. The Model role is implemented in the **Page_Load** event. ASP.NET supplies the role of **Controller** by raising the events to which the Model responds. By separating the Model into the code-behind page, changes in the **DataList** can be made independently of changes in the data access logic. Another level of separation and reusability is obtained by encapsulating the data logic in the **AnnouncementsDB** component.

The pattern referenced by the separation of data access logic is known as the *Table Data Gateway* pattern. A Table Data Gateway pattern is a class that contains all of the data operations for accessing, inserting, updating,

or deleting data from a single table. By rigorously adhering to this pattern for each module's corresponding data component, the portal establishes a framework for easily adding new modules. The **AnnouncementsDB** component displays the basic structure. (This code is from the **AnnouncementsDB** class in the lab portal application.)

Visual Basic .NET

```
Public Class AnnouncementsDB

    Public Function GetAnnouncements(ByVal moduleId As Integer) As _
        SqlDataReader

    Public Function GetSingleAnnouncement(ByVal ItemId As Integer, _
        ByVal ModuleId As Integer) As SqlDataReader

    Public Function GetSingleAnnouncement(ByVal itemId As Integer) As _
        SqlDataReader

    Public Sub DeleteAnnouncement(ByVal itemID As Integer)

    Public Function AddAnnouncement(ByVal moduleId As Integer, ByVal _
        itemId As Integer, ByVal userName As String, ByVal title As _
        String, ByVal expireDate As DateTime, ByVal description As _
        String, ByVal moreLink As String, ByVal mobileMoreLink As _
        String) As Integer

    Public Sub UpdateAnnouncement(ByVal moduleId As Integer, ByVal _
        itemId As Integer, ByVal userName As String, ByVal title As _
        String, ByVal expireDate As DateTime, ByVal description As _
        String, ByVal moreLink As String, ByVal mobileMoreLink As _
        String)
End Class
```

C#

```csharp
public class AnnouncementsDB
{
    public SqlDataReader GetAnnouncements(int moduleId)

    public SqlDataReader GetSingleAnnouncement(int itemId)

    public void DeleteAnnouncement(int itemID)

    public int AddAnnouncement(int moduleId, int itemId, String userName,
        String title, DateTime expireDate, String description, String
        moreLink)

    public void UpdateAnnouncement(int moduleId, int itemId, String userName,
        String title, DateTime expireDate, String description, String
        moreLink)
}
```

By using this class, the model code is adapted to the **DataList** control on the page. The code-behind page maps the events that the controller forwards to the specific action methods. Because the model returns a bindable **SqlDataReader** object, the task of the **AnnouncementsDB** class is straightforward. The following code, similar to the **View** code, does not depend on how data is retrieved from the database. (This code is from the code-behind file for the Announcements.ascx control in the lab portal application.)

Visual Basic .NET

```vb
Private Sub Page_Load(ByVal sender As System.Object, _
    ByVal e As System.EventArgs) Handles MyBase.Load

    Dim announcements As New ASPNET.StarterKit.Portal.AnnouncementsDB()

    myDataList.DataSource = announcements.GetAnnouncements(ModuleId)
    myDataList.DataBind()

End Sub
```

C#

```csharp
private void Page_Load(object sender, System.EventArgs e)
{
    // Obtain announcement information from Announcements table
    // and bind to the datalist control
    ASPProject.AnnouncementsDB announcements = new
        ASPProject.AnnouncementsDB();

    // DataBind Announcements to DataList Control
    myDataList.DataSource = announcements.GetAnnouncements(ModuleId);
    myDataList.DataBind();
}
```

The component can now be independently tested by using a unit testing tool such as NUnit (http://nunit.org), built for .NET component testing.

Benefits Summary

The most immediate benefit of implementing the pattern is reduced code duplication. The **AnnouncementsDB** class can also be used by other pages or other interface types. An implementation using the Mobile Internet Toolkit uses the same component to provide data to mobile devices. It is now possible to test functionality independently of the HTML interface, meaning that designers and programmers can now work in parallel on the same part of the application without interfering with each other's work. Optimization is also easier because data access is encapsulated in a single component.

Page Template Patterns

> **Page Template Patterns**
>
> - **The Page Controller pattern enforces separation between dispatching logic and view-related code**
> - **Advantages**
>   - **Reduces code duplication**
>   - **Increases consistency**
>   - **Facilitates testing**
> - **Disadvantages**
>   - **Introduces additional overhead that could impede performance**
>   - **Can lead to inflexible designs unless base class functionality is kept to the minimum**

Introduction

One of the more common and useful patterns for ASP.NET applications is known as the *Page Controller*. Because ASP.NET is object-oriented, the classes that create the user interface for each page can contain many of the graphical elements common to the whole site, such as banners and menu bars. The Page Controller pattern enforces further separation between the dispatching logic and view-related code. It includes the creation of a base page controller class to avoid code duplication, increase consistency, and make testing easier.

The following diagram shows the relationship between the Page Controller and the Model and View:

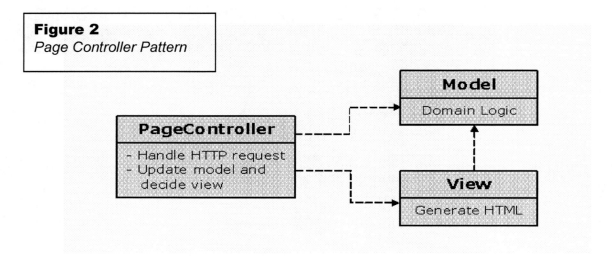

Figure 2
Page Controller Pattern

Elements of the Pattern

In addition to display elements, much other functionality of a Web site is duplicated from page to page, such as validation. Following this pattern involves consolidating such functionality into a single base class. Each individual **Page** object can then inherit from this base class and avoid code duplication and excessive maintenance.

This approach works best if all of the pages have similar layout and interactivity. Otherwise, some fraction of the code in the base class will either be wasted or have to be overridden, thus counteracting a major purpose of this pattern. One way to deal with this issue is to create an inheritance tree with different levels corresponding to the needs of each group of pages. In many sites, all pages parse input parameters, such as those needed to highlight the correct item on the menu display, but only some of the pages display data retrieved from a database. Still other pages require the user to enter data that can be submitted to the Model for insertion into the database.

To support these different levels of functionality, a **BaseController** class could be created to supply the basic functionality for all the pages. Two derived classes, **ListController** and **DataEntryController**, could supply the special functions, with **ListController** supplying the pages that display lists and **DataEntryController** supplying the pages that require data entry and submission. Due to the number of variations that an application might be required to support, the developer might be tempted to add conditional logic into the base classes to accommodate these. However, this practice could lead to complex inheritance trees that could inhibit extensibility. Helper classes would furnish a more maintainable solution, such as a custom chart class, as in TimeTracker.

PortalModuleControl Class

By moving common code from individual pages into a base class, the site can be more easily maintained because changes and additions are stored in a central location. One way this pattern is implemented is in the portal through the use of the **PortalModuleControl** class. The portal's user interface is built from dynamically loaded user controls. The **PortalModuleControl** class defines the base properties required by each module. Each module requires an **IsEditable** property, which is a Boolean value that determines whether a module can be edited. The property definition performs the settings lookup to determine the value of the property. (This code is from the **PortalModuleControl** class in the lab portal application.)

Visual Basic .NET

```vbnet
Public ReadOnly Property IsEditable() As Boolean

    Get
        If _isEditable = 0 Then
            Dim _portalSettings As PortalSettings = _
                CType(HttpContext.Current.Items("PortalSettings"), _
                PortalSettings)

            If _portalSettings.AlwaysShowEditButton = True Or _
                PortalSecurity.IsInRoles
                    (_moduleConfiguration.AuthorizedEditRoles) _
                Then
                    _isEditable = 1
            Else
                    _isEditable = 2
            End If
        End If
    End Get

    Return (_isEditable = 1)

End Property
```

C#

```csharp
public bool IsEditable
{
    get
    {
        // Perform tri-state switch check to avoid having to perform a
        // security role lookup on every property access (instead caching
        // the result)
        if (_isEditable == 0)
        {
        // Obtain PortalSettings from Current Context
        PortalSettings portalSettings = (PortalSettings)
            HttpContext.Current.Items["PortalSettings"];
        }

        if (portalSettings.AlwaysShowEditButton == true ||
            PortalSecurity.IsInRoles
             (_moduleConfiguration.AuthorizedEditRoles))
        {
            _isEditable = 1;
        }
        else
        {
            _isEditable = 2;
        }
    }

    return (_isEditable == 1);
}
```

Because this property is defined in the base class, each individual module has direct access to a preset property and thus needs to provide no implementation. Sitewide changes can be made easily.

ModuleConfiguration and ModuleSettings

The **ModuleConfiguration** property encapsulates the detailed settings for a specific module in the portal. The type returned from the property is **ModuleSettings**. This class implements the **CompareTo** method of the **IComparable** interface so that custom sorting methods can be provided and overridden as needed by particular modules. This makes it easy to rearrange the order in which modules appear.

A similar mechanism is used to control the order of tabs. (This code is from the **ModuleSettings** class in the lab portal application.)

Visual Basic .NET

```vbnet
Public Property ModuleConfiguration() As ModuleSettings

    Get
        Return _moduleConfiguration
    End Get
    Set(ByVal Value As ModuleSettings)
        _moduleConfiguration = Value
    End Set

End Property

Public Class ModuleSettings
    Implements IComparable

    Public TabId As Integer
    Public CacheTime As Integer
    Public ModuleOrder As Integer
    Public PaneName As String
    Public ModuleTitle As String
    Public AuthorizedEditRoles As String
    Public ShowMobile As Boolean
    Public DesktopSrc As String
    Public MobileSrc As String

    Protected Overridable Function CompareTo(ByVal value As Object) _
        As Integer Implements IComparable.CompareTo

        If value Is Nothing Then
            Return 1
        End If

        Dim compareOrder As Integer = CType(value, _
            ModuleSettings).ModuleOrder

        If Me.ModuleOrder = compareOrder Then Return 0
        If Me.ModuleOrder < compareOrder Then Return -1
        If Me.ModuleOrder > compareOrder Then Return 1

        Return 0

    End Function
End Class
```

C#

```csharp
public ModuleSettings ModuleConfiguration
{
    get
    {
        return _moduleConfiguration;
    }
    set
    {
        _moduleConfiguration = value;
    }
}

public class ModuleSettings : IComparable
{
        public int          ModuleId;
        public int          ModuleDefId;
        public int          TabId;
        public int          CacheTime;
        public int          ModuleOrder;
        public String       PaneName;
        public String       ModuleTitle;
        public String       AuthorizedEditRoles;
                public String       DesktopSrc;

        public int CompareTo(object value)
        {

            if (value == null) return 1;
            int compareOrder = ((ModuleSettings)value).ModuleOrder;

            if (this.ModuleOrder == compareOrder) return 0;
            if (this.ModuleOrder < compareOrder) return -1;
            if (this.ModuleOrder > compareOrder) return 1;
            return 0;
        }
}
```

The **ModuleSettings** property is initially populated in the **PortalSettings** constructor, which is invoked from the global.asax file when a request is received. The site configuration file is read, and the module settings for each tab are used to populate the **_moduleSettings** field. This field is used to configure each module for display. If new properties need to be added to all the modules, they can be added to the **ModuleSettings** class; for example, a **ShowMobile** property to indicate that this module should be displayed on mobile devices. All of these settings are accessed through the **ModuleConfiguration** property that is inherited by each control.

To be able to extend the basic properties of a module without having to change the **ModuleSettings** class properties, a **Settings** property is defined. **Settings** represents an added element or set of elements to the Module element in the configuration file that can be used flexibly to augment the basic module configuration. It is accessed in the same way as the **ModuleConfiguration** property.

By using this inheritance structure, each module can rely on a base set of functionality while providing its own specific variations. You have already seen how the Announcements module implements the **PortalModuleControl**. The Links module inherits the same base class, but implements it quite differently as can be seen from one of the methods in its code-behind. In the **Page_Load** method, the **IsEditable** property is used to determine which image is displayed in the Links module. (This code is from the Links.ascx user control in the ASP.NET Portal Starter Kit application.)

Visual Basic .NET

```
Private Sub Page_Load(ByVal sender As System.Object, ByVal e As
    System.EventArgs) Handles MyBase.Load

    If IsEditable Then
        linkImage = "~/images/edit.gif"
    Else
        linkImage = "~/images/navlink.gif"
    End If

    Dim links As New ASPNET.StarterKit.Portal.LinkDB()
    myDataList.DataSource = links.GetLinks(ModuleId)
    myDataList.DataBind()

End Sub
```

C#

```csharp
private void Page_Load(object sender, System.EventArgs e)
{
    // Set the link image type
    if (IsEditable)
    {
        linkImage = "~/images/edit.gif";
    }
    else
    {
        linkImage = "~/images/navlink.gif";
    }

    // Obtain links information from the Links table
    // and bind to the datalist control
    ASPNET.StarterKit.Portal.LinkDB links = new
     ASPNET.StarterKit.Portal.LinkDB();

    myDataList.DataSource = links.GetLinks(ModuleId);
    myDataList.DataBind();
}
```

The display is produced in the same way as in most of the other modules: by binding a **DataList** to a **DataReader** returned from the component that implements the Table Data Gateway pattern for the underlying data table. A similar set of methods in the code-behind control different display options. **ChooseUrl** controls whether or not to display an editable Uniform Resource Locator (URL). **ChooseTip** controls whether to display the word "Edit" or a description of the link.

Disadvantages of Page Template Patterns

Implementing the Page Controller pattern does involve some liabilities. Each module must inherit from the base module class that inserts an intervening layer between the module classes and the underlying **UserControl** class from which **PortalModuleControl** inherits. This extra layer introduces additional overhead that could impede performance.

Using inheritance to share implementation can lead to inflexible, brittle designs unless base class functionality is kept to the minimum necessary. This may require the base class to be periodically refactored to ensure that only common behavior is included. As an alternative, the developer may wish to examine the Intercepting Filter pattern, which adds common functionality through a configuration file rather than making changes to the pages themselves. With the current application, both approaches are combined. The Portalcfg.xml file supplies the settings that are implemented by the properties and functions of the modules. By implementing this pattern, the resulting design permits all modules access to basic settings while affording scope for a wide range of variations.

Lesson: Exploring the DataGrid

> **Lesson: Exploring the DataGrid**
>
> - **Effective Data Binding**
> - **Elements of the DataGrid**
> - **Properties and Events of the DataGrid**
> - **Creating Master/Detail Reports**
> - **Using Templates in DataGrids**
> - **Data Paging Options**
> - **DataGrid Editing Techniques**
> - **Retrieving User Input from a DataGrid**
> - **Best Practices for Web Presentation Patterns**

Introduction

Effective data-binding is essential to Web application design. This lesson presents a valuable data-binding technique. One section provides a detailed overview of the **DataGrid** with many practical examples.

Lesson Objectives

After completing this lesson, you will be able to:

- Bind data controls by using custom business entities.
- Identify the elements, properties, and events of a **DataGrid**.
- Create master/detail reports by using several different techniques.
- Maximize data paging efficiency.
- Edit data in a **DataGrid**.
- Apply best practices when implementing Web presentation patterns in your Web application

Effective Data Binding

> **Effective Data Binding**
>
> - **DataReader**
>   - The most efficient way to display data on a Web page
>   - Prevents unnecessary duplication of data

Introduction

Any object that supports the **IEnumerable** interface can be data-bound. This includes objects such as **ArrayList**, **HashTable**, **SortedList**, and **StringCollection**. In most cases, data to be displayed in a bound control will be retrieved from a database. The most efficient way to display data on a Web page is to use a **DataReader**. This object provides forward-only, streaming access to the data and makes no copy of the data.

Data Source Tradeoffs

The main reason for this preference is to avoid creating an unnecessary duplicate of the data. When considering how data-binding works, the argument for using a **DataReader** is even more compelling. Data-bound controls must retain the data that is bound to them across page postbacks. If a **DataSet** is used to supply data to the control, the first time it is bound the data is copied into the **DataSet** object. When the binding process takes place, that data is copied again into an internal storage structure, which is used to create the rows for the table. If view state is enabled for the grid, the data is copied to the **ViewState** field so that it can be restored on subsequent postbacks. This data storage and retrieval may impede performance.

The **DataGrid** does not store its data source in view state. Instead, it caches its data in public properties. The **DataGrid** does store data in the child controls that make up the table, such as a **TableCell**. View state is also required to support operations such as paging and sorting, otherwise the paging and sorting event handlers will not be executed. By using a **DataReader** in place of a **DataSet**, the first copy (into the **DataSet**) is avoided. The data is copied from the **DataReader** into the internal data structure used by the **DataGrid**. If view state is disabled, a copy into view state is avoided as well.

Alternative Sorting Techniques

The most common type of data-binding is illustrated below using the code that binds the category drop-down list in the **DataGrid** that displays project data. (This code is from the ASP.NET Time Tracker application in the code-behind file for the TimeEntry page.)

Visual Basic .NET

```
Private Sub BindCategoryList()

    If Not (ProjectList.SelectedItem Is Nothing) Then
        CategoryList.DataSource = _
            Project.GetCategories(Convert.ToInt32(ProjectList.SelectedItem.Value))
        CategoryList.DataValueField = "CategoryID"
        CategoryList.DataTextField = "Abbreviation"
        CategoryList.DataBind()
    End If

End Sub
```

C#

```
private void BindCategoryList()
{
            if (ProjectList.SelectedItem != null)
            {
                    // CategoryList is different for each project,
        // Project.GetCategories gets a list of
                    // categories based on the project.
                    CategoryList.DataSource =
            Project.GetCategories(Convert.ToInt32(ProjectList.SelectedItem.Value));
                    CategoryList.DataValueField = "CategoryID";
                    CategoryList.DataTextField = "Abbreviation";
                    CategoryList.DataBind();
            }
}
```

The built-in properties distinguish between the field to display (**DataTextField**) and the field to return as the value attribute for the control (**DataValueField**). Another notable feature of this procedure is that

GetCategories returns a **CategoriesCollection**. This class is a custom collection class that inherits from **ArrayList**, which overrides the **Sort** method of **ArrayList**.

By using collection classes with data-binding, you can easily extend the information to be displayed as well as the sorting. As an example, you will examine how sorting works in the **DataGrid** in TimeTracker that displays project information. Whenever a user clicks on one of the headers on the **DataGrid**, the **SortGridData** subroutine is invoked. This chooses the correct field for sorting and calls the **Sort** method of the **TimeEntriesCollection** object. (This code is from the ASP.NET Time Tracker application in the **TimeEntriesCollection** class.)

Visual Basic .NET

```vb
Private Sub SortGridData(ByVal list As TimeEntriesCollection, ByVal _
    sortField As String, ByVal asc As Boolean)

    Dim sortCol As TimeEntriesCollection.TimeEntryFields = _
        TimeEntriesCollection.TimeEntryFields.InitValue

    Select Case sortField
        Case "EntryDate"
            sortCol = TimeEntriesCollection.TimeEntryFields.Day
        Case "ProjectName"
            sortCol = TimeEntriesCollection.TimeEntryFields.Project
        Case "CategoryName"
            sortCol = TimeEntriesCollection.TimeEntryFields.Category
        Case "Duration"
            sortCol = TimeEntriesCollection.TimeEntryFields.Hours
        Case "Description"
            sortCol = _
                TimeEntriesCollection.TimeEntryFields.Description
        Case Else
    End Select

    list.Sort(sortCol, asc)
End Sub 'SortGridData
```

C#

```csharp
private void SortGridData(TimeEntriesCollection list, string sortField,
    bool asc)
{
        TimeEntriesCollection.TimeEntryFields sortCol =
        TimeEntriesCollection.TimeEntryFields.InitValue;

        switch(sortField)
        {
          case "EntryDate":
                        sortCol =
TimeEntriesCollection.TimeEntryFields.Day;
                        break;
                    case "ProjectName":
                        sortCol =
TimeEntriesCollection.TimeEntryFields.Project;
                        break;
                    case "CategoryName":
                        sortCol =
TimeEntriesCollection.TimeEntryFields.Category;
                        break;
                    case "Duration":
                        sortCol =
TimeEntriesCollection.TimeEntryFields.Hours;
                        break;
                    case "Description":
                        sortCol =
TimeEntriesCollection.TimeEntryFields.Description;
                        break;
                    default:
                        break;
        }

    list.Sort(sortCol, asc);
}
```

The **sortCol** variable is assigned an enumerated value that corresponds to an implementation of the **IComparer** interface in the **TimeEntriesCollection** class. The **Sort** method in this class selects the implementation. **DayComparer** sets up a comparison by day. (This code is from the ASP.NET Time Tracker application in the **TimeEntriesCollection** class.)

Visual Basic .NET

```vbnet
Public Overloads Sub Sort(ByVal sortField As TimeEntryFields, ByVal _
    isAscending As Boolean)
    Select Case sortField
        Case TimeEntryFields.Day
            MyBase.Sort(New DayComparer())
        Case TimeEntryFields.Category
            MyBase.Sort(New CategoryComparer())
        Case TimeEntryFields.Description
            MyBase.Sort(New DescriptionComparer())
        Case TimeEntryFields.Hours
            MyBase.Sort(New HoursComparer())
        Case TimeEntryFields.Project
            MyBase.Sort(New ProjectComparer())
    End Select

    If Not isAscending Then
        MyBase.Reverse()
    End If
End Sub 'Sort

Private NotInheritable Class DayComparer
    Implements IComparer

    Public Function Compare(ByVal x As Object, ByVal y As Object) As _
        Integer Implements System.Collections.IComparer.Compare
        Dim first As TimeEntry = CType(x, TimeEntry)
        Dim second As TimeEntry = CType(y, TimeEntry)
        Return first.EntryDate.CompareTo(second.EntryDate)
    End Function 'Compare

End Class 'DayComparer
```

C#

```csharp
public void Sort(TimeEntryFields sortField, bool isAscending)
{
    switch (sortField)
        {
            case TimeEntryFields.Day:
                base.Sort(new DayComparer());
                break;
            case TimeEntryFields.Category:
                base.Sort(new CategoryComparer());
                break;
            case TimeEntryFields.Description:
                base.Sort(new DescriptionComparer());
                break;
            case TimeEntryFields.Hours:
                base.Sort(new HoursComparer());
                break;
            case TimeEntryFields.Project:
                base.Sort(new ProjectComparer());
                break;
        }

        if (!isAscending) base.Reverse();
}

    private sealed class DayComparer : IComparer
    {
        public int Compare(object x, object y)
        {
            TimeEntry first = (TimeEntry) x;
            TimeEntry second = (TimeEntry) y;
            return first.EntryDate.CompareTo(second.EntryDate);
        }
    }
```

In this way, all the logic needed for sorting can be placed into a single object. Because the class implements **IEnumerable**, each public property in the class will be exposed for binding. The **TimeEntriesCollection** consists of **TimeEntry** objects. The fields in the **TimeEntries** objects will furnish the values displayed in the DataGrid. These properties are:

- **CategoryID**
- **CategoryName**
- **CategoryShortName**
- **Day**
- **Description**
- **EntryDate**
- **EntryLogID**
- **ProjectID**
- **ProjectName**

Which fields are actually displayed is controlled by the use of data-binding tags contained in the columns defined in the **TemplateColumn** element of the **DataGrid**. One of the major advantages of this design is that adding a new field to be displayed is simply a matter of adding a new member to the **TimeEntry** class and then creating a new binding tag to display it.

Elements of the DataGrid

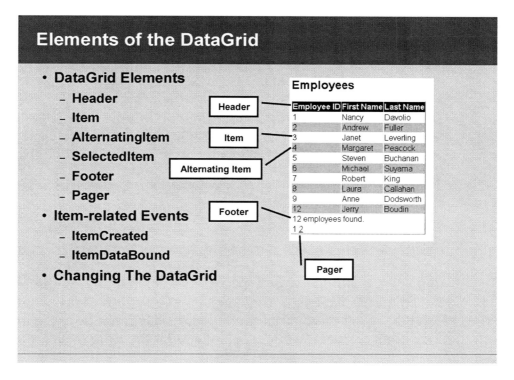

Introduction

The **DataGrid** control renders a data-bound grid similar to Microsoft® Excel. Each column is fully templated, allowing the developer to control the layout and appearance of the data to a high degree. The **DataGrid** includes features that allow paging, sorting, and editing. You will learn about the major properties of the **DataGrid** so that you can fully exploit its functionality to produce editable grids and effective master/detail views, and use advanced data paging techniques.

DataGrid Elements

The elements of a **DataGrid** are defined by the **ListItemType** enumeration. The properties of these elements can be controlled through style tags such as <AlternatingItemStyle>, <EditItemStyle>, <FooterItemStyle>, and so on. The attributes of these tags control the appearance of the corresponding item. In addition, each element has a **CssClass** attribute that can be used to assign the element to a cascading style sheet (CSS) class. These items are straightforward to apply, but the Footer and Pager elements often need to be structured differently from the others.

The Footer can act as a summary row. To serve this function, it must span all columns above it, although this is not its default behavior. The reason for this is that the Footer simply represents the bottom of each column. By default, any Footer output will only apply to that particular column. To create a summary column, all of the Footer elements must be merged into a single row by using the *ItemCreated* event. *ItemCreated* is part of the built-in event-handling infrastructure of the **DataGrid**. Each item that is added to a **DataGrid** is a **DataGridItem** that corresponds to a table row, whether the row currently being added is a header, footer, or data item. The collection of table rows is referred to as the **Items** collection and is available in many DataGrid event handlers. Each time an item is created, two events are raised: *ItemCreated* and *ItemDataBound*.

ItemCreated

The *ItemCreated* event is raised as soon as the **DataGridItem** is created, but before it is added to the table. This event is commonly used to control the appearance of the row as it is added. To change the rendering of the **Footer** row so that it displays a single cell that spans the width of the entire grid, the following event handler for *ItemCreated* illustrates how this might be done. (This code is from the code-behind file for the Employees.aspx page in the Democode for this module.)

Visual Basic .NET

```
Public Sub DataGrid1_ItemCreated(ByVal sender As Object, ByVal e As _
    DataGridItemEventArgs) Handles DataGrid1.ItemCreated
    Dim elementType As ListItemType = e.Item.ItemType
    If elementType = ListItemType.Footer Then

        Dim cellCollection As TableCellCollection = e.Item.Cells
        Dim columnCount As Integer = cellCollection.Count

        Dim i As Integer = 0
        While i < columnCount - 1
            e.Item.Cells.RemoveAt(0)
            i = i + 1
        End While

        Dim footerCell As TableCell = e.Item.Cells(0)
        footerCell.ColumnSpan = columnCount
        Dim dsEmployees As DataSet = CType(Session("dsEmployees"), _
            DataSet)
        Dim dvEmployees As DataView = _
            dsEmployees.Tables("Employees").DefaultView
        footerCell.Text = dvEmployees.Count.ToString() + _
            "</b> employees found."
    End If
End Sub
```

C#

```csharp
private void DataGrid1_ItemCreated(object sender,
    System.Web.UI.WebControls.DataGridItemEventArgs e)
{
    ListItemType elementType = e.Item.ItemType;

    if (elementType == ListItemType.Footer)
    {
        TableCellCollection cellCollection = e.Item.Cells;
        int columnCount = cellCollection.Count;

        int i = 0;
        while( i < columnCount - 1)
        {
        e.Item.Cells.RemoveAt(0);
        i = i + 1;
        }

        TableCell footerCell = e.Item.Cells[0];
        footerCell.ColumnSpan = columnCount;
        DataSet dsEmployees = (DataSet)(Session["dsEmployees"]);
        DataView dvEmployees =
            dsEmployees.Tables["Employees"].DefaultView;
        footerCell.Text = dvEmployees.Count.ToString() +
            "</b> employees found.";
    }
}
```

DataGridItemEventArgs contains an **Item** element that represents the newly created **DataGridItem**. You use the **ItemType** property to determine whether or not you have a reference to the Footer row. Next, you get a reference to all cells in the table row. You loop through each cell in the row and remove it until only a single cell remains. The **ColumnSpan** property on that cell is set to the number of columns in the table. The value you want to display is calculated by using the **DataView** that the **DataGrid** is using as its **DataSource**. Finally, you populate the footer cell text with the string to be displayed.

ItemDataBound

After this event and its handler have been processed, the *ItemDataBound* event is raised. The handler for this event provides you with the last opportunity to make changes to the item before it is displayed.

Properties and Events of the DataGrid

> **Properties and Events of the DataGrid**
>
> - **DataGrid columns**
>   - **BoundColumn** displays the field value from the data source
>   - **ButtonColumn** displays a user-configurable button for each row
>   - **EditCommandColumn** contains an Edit button for each row
>   - **HyperLinkColumn** contains a hyperlink for each row
>   - **TemplateColumn** allows customized control layouts

Introduction

A **DataGrid** is essentially a collection of columns. To gain maximum control over grid appearance, you should use the **Columns** collection. By default, the **DataGrid** will bind to all of the columns in its underlying data source. To choose which columns appear, turn off this default behavior by setting the **AutoGenerateColumns** property to false.

DataGrid Columns

You can choose the following types of columns:

- **BoundColumn**. Displays the value of the field in the data source that is designed by using the **DataField** property. This is the default column type. Items can be formatted by using the **DataFormatString** attribute. Header display is set by using the **HeaderText** property.
- **ButtonColumn**. Displays a user-configurable button for each row in the **DataGrid**. The name of each button can be bound to a field in the data source by using the **DataTextField** attribute. Whenever the button is clicked, it raises the **ItemCommand** event.

- **EditCommandColumn.** Contains an Edit button for each row in the **DataGrid.** When the Edit button is clicked, an Update button and a Cancel button appear. Clicking the Edit button raises the **EditCommand** event. Typically, you will write code for this event that opens the EditItemTemplate column by using the **EditItemIndex** property. The default behavior is to put the row in edit mode, which means that each column is redrawn using text boxes to display values.
- **HyperLinkColumn.** Contains a hyperlink for each row in the **DataGrid.** The URL of the hyperlink can be specified through the **NavigateUrl** property. Both the **Text** and **NavigateUrl** properties can be data-bound.
- **TemplateColumn.** Allows you to customize the layout of controls in a column. Different parts of the template can be customized by the use of the **HeaderTemplate, FooterTemplate,** and **ItemTemplate.** The EditItemTemplate controls the display appearance when the Edit button is clicked.

ItemCommand

Whenever a user clicks on a button in the **DataGrid,** an **ItemCommand** event is raised. Different button clicks can be distinguished by giving each button a separate **CommandName** attribute. A **Select Case** or switch statement can be used to execute the logic appropriate to that button. Command names are case-sensitive. For instance, an *ItemCommand* event handler might be implemented as follows:

Visual Basic .NET

```
Private Sub productGrid_ItemCommand(ByVal [ source] As Object, ByVal e As _
    System.Web.UI.WebControls.DataGridCommandEventArgs) Handles _
    productGrid.ItemCommand, shoppingCartGrid.ItemCommand
    Select Case e.CommandName
        Case "AddToShoppingCart"
            AddItemToCart(e.Item, e.Item.ItemIndex)
        Case "RemoveItemFromCart"
            RemoveItemFromCart(e.Item.ItemIndex)
        Case "SelectRow"
            currentSelectedIndex = e.Item.ItemIndex
            SelectItem()
    End Select
End Sub
```

C#

```csharp
private void productGrid_ItemCommand(object source,
    System.Web.UI.WebControls.DataGridCommandEventArgs e)
{
        switch(e.CommandName)
        {
            case "AddItemToCart":
                AddItemToCart(e.Item, e.Item.ItemIndex);
                break;
            case "RemoveItemFromCart":
                RemoveItemFromCart(e.Item.ItemIndex);
                break;
            case "SelectRow":
                currentSelectedIndex = e.Item.ItemIndex;
                SelectItem();
                break;
        }
}
```

Sorting

Another common task during the *ItemCreated* event is to create special styling for DataGrid elements depending on its current state. You may want to show the current sort direction by placing an arrow next to the label for the field being sorted. Another common use of the *ItemCreated* event is to format and populate a summary row.

The *ItemDataBound* event takes place as soon as the item is bound to data. This affords an opportunity to use column values to create effects such as adding a ToolTip with a data value.

Sorting is controlled through two attributes. **AllowSorting** is an attribute that must be set to true to display sorting hyperlinks in the **DataGrid** header row. Sorting can be turned on and off in each column by providing or omitting a **SortExpression** property that specifies which field is used for sorting the contents of the column. Multicolumn sorts can also be defined.

When an item in the **DataGrid** is selected, you can use the **ItemIndex** property of the **Item** to find out which row the user clicked. However, this will tell you nothing about the location of the underlying data for the Item. To translate between the location of an item in the **DataGrid** and a field (usually a key field) in the underlying data source, you use the **DataKeys** attribute. The key value will be extracted and stored when the item is data-bound. The following examples indicate how the **DataKeys** collection might be used:

Visual Basic .NET

```vb
Dim productKey As Integer = CInt(productGrid.DataKeys(rowIndex))
Dim productRows As DataRow() = dtProducts.Select((productGrid.DataKeyField _
    + "=" + productKey.ToString()))
Dim tableRow As DataRow = productRows(0)
```

C#

```csharp
int productKey = (int) productGrid.DataKeys[ rowIndex];
DataRow[] productRows = dtProducts.Select(productGrid.DataKeyField + "=" +
    productKey.ToString());
DataRow tableRow = productRows[ 0];
```

In these examples, **rowIndex** corresponds to the **ItemIndex** of the selected **Item**. By retrieving the **productKey** from the **DataGrid**, you can extract the information for that product from the **DataTable** that contains shopping cart items.

Creating Master/Detail Reports

Creating Master/Detail Reports

- **HyperLinkColumns**
  - Create a hyperlink for each row
  - Can be databound by using DataTextField
  - A data source value can be passed to a URL by using DataNavigateUrlFormatString
- **Creating DataGrids programmatically**
  - Allows creation of DataGrids with sub-elements corresponding to child data

Introduction

An iframe control is populated with details according to the row selected in the **DataGrid**. Although this is an efficient approach, more flexibility is often needed. This topic describes **DataGrid** properties that can be used to create detailed information in the form of master/detail reports for display within the **DataGrid**.

HyperLinkColumn

One way to create a link between **DataGrids** so that detail records can be displayed is to use a **HyperLinkColumn**, which creates a hyperlink for each row. The **HyperLinkColumn** can be data-bound by using the **DataTextField** property. The **DataNavigateUrlField** allows a value to be retrieved from the data source that can be passed to a URL by using the **DataNavigateUrlFormatString** attribute. To pass the name of a customer as the value of a query string on a URL, the following definition of a **HyperLinkColumn** could be used:

```
<asp:HyperLinkColumn
    DataTextField="CustomerID"
    DataNavigateUrlField="CustomerID"
    DataNavigateUrlFormatString="OrderDetails.aspx?customerid={0}"
    HeaderText="ID"
    Target="OrderView" />
```

The URL can be targeted through the use of the **Target** attribute which could display detail information in an iframe.

Creating Columns Programmatically

Columns can be created at design time or programmatically. Creating them programmatically allows **DataGrids** to be created with subelements corresponding to child data, such as order items for a customer. A **DataGrid** with order items could be inserted programmatically inside another **DataGrid**. To do this, you should use the *ItemDataBound* event so that the **DataItem** is available. This item is only available in the *ItemDataBound* event handler and allows access to the values of the **DataRowView**, a representation of the underlying **DataRow**.

The code below illustrates the basic elements of this concept. The pages in the Democode folder for this module named CustomerOrders.aspx and OrderDetails.aspx provide a complete example of this technique:

Visual Basic .NET

```vbnet
Dim OrdersDataGrid As DataGrid = New DataGrid()
' Set the style properties of the embedded DataGrid
Dim bc As BoundColumn = New BoundColumn()
bc.HeaderText = "Order ID"
bc.DataField = "OrderID"
bc.ItemStyle.Wrap = False
OrdersDataGrid.Columns.Add(bc)

' Create the rest of the columns using the same technique

' Use the DataItem to populate the RowFilter property
Dim drv As DataRowView = CType(e.Item.DataItem, DataRowView)
Dim dvOrders As DataView = dsCustomers.Tables("Orders").DefaultView
dvOrders.RowFilter = "CustomerID='" + drv("customerId") + "'"

OrdersDataGrid.DataSource = dvOrders
OrdersDataGrid.DataBind()

e.Item.Cells(3).Controls.Add(OrdersDataGrid)
```

C#

```csharp
DataGrid DetailDataGrid = new DataGrid();
// Set the style properties of the embedded DataGrid
BoundColumn bc = new BoundColumn();
bc.HeaderText = "ID";
bc.DataField = "ProductID";
bc.ItemStyle.Wrap = false;
DetailDataGrid.Columns.Add(bc);

// Create the rest of the columns using the same technique

// Use the DataItem to populate the RowFilter property
DataView dvDetail = dsOrderDetails.Tables["OrderDetail"].DefaultView;
DataRowView drv = (DataRowView) e.Item.DataItem;
dvDetail.RowFilter = "OrderID='" + drv["orderId"].ToString() +"'";

DetailDataGrid.DataSource = dvDetail;
DetailDataGrid.DataBind();
e.Item.Cells[1].Controls.Add(DetailDataGrid);
```

Note the final line of code, which adds the newly created **DataGrid** to the third cell in the current row. This is how a dynamically produced server control can be embedded in a **DataGrid**.

Establishing Parent-Child Relationships

Another method for producing master/detail views in a **DataGrid** begins by creating a **DataRelation** between a parent and child table in a **DataSet**. After the relationship is established, child controls on the **DataGrid** can be bound to the child **DataTable** to display details related to the parent. In the Democode for this module, you will find an example page, "GridDropDown.aspx," that illustrates this principle.

There are several ways of establishing this relationship visually, but one of the most efficient way is to use a data-bound control within the **DataGrid** and bind its **DataSource** property to a function that uses the relation. One of the typical ways to apply this is to insert a **DropDownList** within a row and populate it by using a function that retrieves a set of child records corresponding to the parent that supplies the data for that row.

In the example page GridDropDown.aspx, each row displays information for a particular employee and contains a **DropDownList** that displays territories for that employee. The **DropDownList** is populated by using a function as follows:

Visual Basic .NET

```
<asp:dropdownlist
  id="ddTerritories"
  runat="server"
  backcolor="white"
  width="120px"
  datasource=<%# GetTerritories(Container.DataItem) %> />
```

C#

```
<asp:dropdownlist
  id="ddTerritories"
  runat="server"
  backcolor="white"
  width="120px"
  datasource=<%# GetTerritories((DataRowView)Container.DataItem) %> />
```

Inside the **DataGrid**, the **Container** object refers to the **DataGrid** itself. The **DataItem** is the item that is currently being bound and is an instance of the **DataRowView** object. The function that is called within the data-binding tags must return an object that implements **ICollection** or **IEnumerable**. The method used in this example accepts a parameter of type **DataRowView** and returns an **ArrayList**. The **ArrayList** provides a light, efficient array of strings to bind in the **DropDownList**:

Visual Basic .NET

```
Protected Function GetTerritories(ByVal drv As DataRowView) As ArrayList
    Dim drEmp As DataRow = drv.Row

    Dim arrDataRows() As DataRow = _
        drEmp.GetChildRows("EmpTerr")

    Dim alTerritories As ArrayList = New ArrayList()
    Dim drTerritories As DataRow
    For Each drTerritories In arrDataRows
        alTerritories.Add(Trim(drTerritories("territorydescription")))
    Next

    Return alTerritories
End Function
```

C#

```
protected ArrayList GetTerritories(DataRowView drv)
{
        DataRow drEmp = drv.Row;

        DataRow[] arrDataRows = drEmp.GetChildRows("EmpTerr");

        ArrayList alTerritories = new ArrayList();
        foreach(DataRow drTerritories in arrDataRows)
                alTerritories.Add(drTerritories["territorydescription"]);
        return alTerritories;
}
```

The **DataRowView** object contains a **DataRow** that contains the information for the parent row. By using the **GetChildRows** method of the **DataRow**, you can retrieve an array of **DataRow** objects corresponding to the territory information. You can then translate the information in these rows to an **ArrayList** to return from the function.

Another often-required variation on master/detail views is to hide and show detail information on user demand. This type of view is often known as a *drill-down report* and it requires an understanding of how templates function in a **DataGrid**.

Using Templates in DataGrids

> **Using Templates in DataGrids**
>
> - Templates allow special layouts and functionality
> - Template types
>   - ItemTemplate: Creates a custom layout for a data item
>   - EditItemTemplate: Creates a custom layout for edit mode
>   - HeaderTemplate: Specifies header appearance
>   - FooterTemplate: Controls footer appearance
> - Steps to create a drill-down report
>   - Create A new DataGrid in the *ItemDataBound* event handler
>   - Populate the control with data
>   - Display the control when the *ItemCommand* event is raised

Introduction

Real-world reporting applications often require more flexible layout than the default **DataGrid** columns provide. Templates allow the developer to combine HTML and server controls to create custom layouts as needed. Through the use of data-binding tags, the data fields of the underlying source can be laid out in whatever order is necessary. Although the **Eval** method of the **DataBinder** class is often used for this purpose, more efficient alternatives will be presented in the topic DataGrid Editing Techniques below.

Template Types

Templates are defined within TemplateColumn tags, which can contain four types of templates:

- **ItemTemplate**. Creates a customized layout for a data item. Any combination of HTML and server controls can be used to create the template.

- **EditItemTemplate**. Specifies how the data item fields should be presented when the **DataGrid** is in edit mode. The fields shown here do not necessarily correspond to those presented in the noneditable column. Typically, the editable data will be presented in the form of text box controls.

- **HeaderTemplate**. Controls the heading section of the TemplateColumn. For example, ToolTips or graphical indicators could be inserted into the header.
- **FooterTemplate**. Controls the appearance of the footer section of the column. Just as with the **Footer** item in a **BoundColumn**, this content does not appear unless **ShowFooter** is set to true.

Combining Data into a Single Column

In the Democode for this module, an example page named "EditGrid.aspx" illustrates some of the basic points you should be aware of when using templates. **ItemTemplates** allow data from many fields to be combined into a single column as follows:

```
<ItemTemplate>
  <b>
        <%# DataBinder.Eval(Container.DataItem, "CompanyName") %>
  </b>
  <br>
  <%# DataBinder.Eval(Container.DataItem, "ContactName") %>
  -
  <%# DataBinder.Eval(Container.DataItem, "ContactTitle") %>
  <br>
  <%# DataBinder.Eval(Container.DataItem, "Address") %>
  <br>
  <%# DataBinder.Eval(Container.DataItem, "City") %>,
  <%# DataBinder.Eval(Container.DataItem, "Region") %>
  <%# DataBinder.Eval(Container.DataItem, "PostalCode") %>

</ItemTemplate>
```

Creating a Details View

One of the most commonly requested types of master/detail reports allows business users to begin the report view with a high-level overview that displays only the major data points and then lets them drill down into the details. By using templates and creating server controls in response to *ItemCommand* events, the **DataGrid** can support drill-down report functionality. This section describes one of the most common techniques used to create a details view in a **DataGrid**.

In order to create a details display, a control in a row of the parent **DataGrid** is created and populated with data in reaction to a user event. Because the **DataItem** becomes available at the time of the *ItemDataBound* event, the handler for this event forms the most natural location for creating a control to reveal details. Although a **ButtonColumn** could be used to respond to a user selection, a **LinkButton** in an **ItemTemplate** provides more flexibility in the button display while still raising the *ItemCommand* event.

The essence of this technique is to create a new **DataGrid** and add it to the parent grid whenever the user selects the row. In order to allow the row to be selected and unselected, a Boolean variable is used to signal when the row is to be displayed and when it should be hidden. After the inner **DataGrid** has been created, the row needs to be expanded so that the grid with the details can be viewed. Unlike the **DataList**, which has a **SelectedItemTemplate** that can be used for this purpose, the **DataGrid** has only one expandable template column type, the **EditItemTemplate**. The contents of this template are shown when the **EditItemIndex** property of the **DataGrid** is set to the index of a particular row, which can then be edited by the user. However, in this case no editable controls will be provided, but the contents of the newly created **DataGrid** will simply be displayed.

As each data item is bound, the *ItemDataBound* event handler will check to see if the row is in edit mode. If so, a call is made to the database to retrieve the order details for a particular customer. This data is then used to populate a **DataGrid**. (This code is from the code-behind file for the HierarchicalGrid.aspx page found in the Democode for this module.)

Visual Basic .NET

```vbnet
Dim dgOrdersGrid As New DataGrid()
' The style properties of the DataGrid are set

' AutoGenerateColumns set to false since are creating column objects
dgOrdersGrid.AutoGenerateColumns = False

' Four BoundColumn objects are created to hold order information
dgOrdersGrid.Columns.Add(SetStyles(New BoundColumn(), "Order", _
    "OrderID", ""))
dgOrdersGrid.Columns.Add(SetStyles(New BoundColumn(), "Order Date", _
    "OrderDate", "{0:D}"))
dgOrdersGrid.Columns.Add(SetStyles(New BoundColumn(), "Required Date", _
    "RequiredDate", "{0:D}"))
dgOrdersGrid.Columns.Add(SetStyles(New BoundColumn(), "Freight", _
    "Freight", ""))
dgOrdersGrid.DataSource = dsCustOrders
dgOrdersGrid.DataBind()
```

C#

```csharp
DataGrid dgOrdersGrid = new DataGrid();

// The style properties of the DataGrid are set
// AutoGenerateColumns set to false since are creating column objects
dgOrdersGrid.AutoGenerateColumns = false;

// Four BoundColumn objects are created to hold order information
dgOrdersGrid.Columns.Add(SetStyles(new BoundColumn(),"Order","OrderID",""));
dgOrdersGrid.Columns.Add(SetStyles(new BoundColumn(),
    "Order Date","OrderDate","{0:D}"));
dgOrdersGrid.Columns.Add(SetStyles(new BoundColumn(),
    "Required Date","RequiredDate","{0:D}"));
dgOrdersGrid.Columns.Add(SetStyles(new
    BoundColumn(),"Freight","Freight",""));

dgOrdersGrid.DataSource = dsCustOrders;
dgOrdersGrid.DataBind();
```

SetStyles is a built-in function that sets the properties for the **BoundColumn**. Next, you need to create an UnSelect button so that the user can unselect the current item and go on to the next. The previous **LinkButton** named Select must be hidden. This is done by setting its visible property to false. You then need to create a new **LinkButton** with a **Text** property of **UnSelect**, and to bind the *Click* event of this button to an event handler that will contain the code to unselect the row. Finally, you add the new **LinkButton** to the **DataGrid** and the new **DataGrid** is inserted into the row. (This code is from the code-behind file for the HierarchicalGrid.aspx page found in the Democode for this module.)

Visual Basic .NET

```vbnet
Dim lbSelect As LinkButton = _
    CType(e.Item.Cells(2).FindControl("LinkButton1"), LinkButton)
lbSelect.Visible = False
Dim lbUnSelect As New LinkButton()
lbUnSelect.ForeColor = Color.White
lbUnSelect.Font.Bold = True
lbUnSelect.Text = "Unselect"
AddHandler lbUnSelect.Click, AddressOf lbUnSelect_Click
dgOrdersGrid.Controls.Add(lbUnSelect)
e.Item.Cells(2).Controls.Add(dgOrdersGrid)
```

C#

```csharp
LinkButton lbSelect = (LinkButton)
e.Item.Cells[2].FindControl("LinkButton1");
lbSelect.Visible = false;
LinkButton lbUnSelect = new LinkButton();
lbUnSelect.ForeColor = Color.White;
lbUnSelect.Font.Bold = true;
lbUnSelect.Text = "Unselect";
lbUnSelect.Click += new EventHandler(this.lbUnSelect_Click);
dgOrdersGrid.Controls.Add(lbUnSelect);
e.Item.Cells[2].Controls.Add(dgOrdersGrid);
```

The completed code can be found in the Democode for this module.

Data Paging Options

> **Data Paging Options**
>
> - DataGrid offers built-in functionality such as paging, sorting, and editing
> - Custom paging options are available to optimize performance
>   - AllowCustomPaging attribute

Introduction

One of the most compelling features of the **DataGrid** is built-in functionality such as paging and sorting. However, in real-world scenarios, developers often find that built-in features must be considerably modified or abandoned altogether for optimal performance. This section describes custom paging options that are available for this purpose.

Custom Paging

To use the automatic paging mechanism, you set the **AllowPaging** attribute of the **DataGrid** to true and then add a handler for the **PageIndexChanged** event. What many developers do not realize is that when using the default mechanism, the **DataGrid** must be supplied with a complete set of records each time the **DataBind** method is called. This mechanism negates one of the primary benefits sought from paging – to avoid retrieving all of the records each time a new page is requested.

To avoid this overhead, the developer can implement a custom paging method when the **AllowCustomPaging** attribute is set to true. The *Microsoft .NET Data Access Architecture Guide* recommends a manual option for data paging due to its superior performance at many different stress levels. Instead of requiring that the number of pages be counted each time the DataGrid rebinds to its **DataSource**, the **VirtualItemCount** property is set when the grid is first populated, normally by using a stored procedure to count the number of records to be paged. When the grid is bound, a function must calculate the next batch of pages. This is straightforward if the underlying table has a linear indexer, such as an identity field in SQL Server. The index for the last record displayed is stored persistently (for instance, in a Session variable) and is used to calculate the next set of pages. The following is a sample stored procedure that could be used for this purpose:

```
CREATE PROCEDURE GetCustomersPaged
@lastCustomerID int,
@pageSize int
AS
SET ROWCOUNT @pageSize
SELECT *
FROM Customers
WHERE [ standard search criteria]
AND CustomerID > @lastCustomerID
ORDER BY [ Criteria that autoincrements CustomerID]
```

This approach avoids passing data over the network that will simply be discarded. It also puts more stress on the server than caching a data object between page refreshes, so applications that use data paging frequently must ensure sufficient server resources.

DataGrid Editing Techniques

> **DataGrid Editing Techniques**
>
> - **Limitations Of automatic DataGrid editing**
>   - Only visible fields are can be updated
>   - Display fields may need data from multiple columns
>   - No client-side validation can be performed
>   - Only text fields can be displayed
>   - Retrieving user input is difficult
> - **Using EditItemTemplate**
>   - Any combination of visible and invisible fields can be displayed for editing
>   - Any defined columns can be updated
>   - The item being edited can be directly accessed

Introduction

Another feature that is built into the **DataGrid** is editing. Simple editing can be enabled by setting the **EditItemIndex** property to the row that the user wants to edit. Instead of table cells, text boxes will be used to display the contents of that row for editing. The developer must then add logic to event handlers to update or insert the new information. However, most professional applications that allow user editing need to offer much more functionality than is provided by the built-in **DataGrid** editing feature. This section describes several tools and techniques that can enhance your editing capabilities.

Editing Control

The automatic editing mechanism in the **DataGrid** has several drawbacks. First, only the visible fields can be updated. However, by using templates, any combination of visible and invisible fields can be displayed for editing.

Note that the contents of the cells may not directly map to the columns in the underlying data table. By using templates, the developer can ensure a match between the data contents and the required field in the database. The contents of the **DataFormatString**, which is used to format the field for display, will appear as text. No client-side validation can be performed. It is recommended that you use a **RegularExpressionValidator** to ensure that a text box matches a given pattern.

With the automatic editing mechanism in the **DataGrid**, only text fields can be displayed. It is often desirable to use drop-down lists or calendars to aid user selections. Moreover, only the **BoundColumn** columns can be updated with the automatic editing mechanism, but with templates, any defined columns can be updated. In addition, with the automatic editing mechanism, retrieving user input is difficult because it is accessed by array index. **EditItemTemplate** allows direct access to the item being edited through the **EditItemIndex** property.

The TimeTracker application allows users to enter details about the projects that they are working on. This information is displayed in a **DataGrid**. The grid has two drop-down lists that are dependent on each other. When the user selects a project from one drop-down list, the categories list must be updated with the applicable categories in the other drop-down list. One of the primary goals in creating such a grid is to encapsulate as much of the display functionality as possible into a set of extensible objects. You will explore this grid by examining what is provided by the grid and what has to be added programmatically.

EditCommand, CancelCommand, and UpdateCommand

The **DataGrid** exposes three server-side events: **EditCommand**, **CancelCommand**, and **UpdateCommand**. These events can be wired by using the attributes **OnEditCommand**, **OnCancelCommand**, and **OnUpdateCommand**. By adding an **EditCommandColumn**, the links for the Edit, Cancel, and Delete commands can be automatically produced by setting the appropriate attributes. For more flexibility, a **TemplateColumn** can be created. If a command with a **CommandName** of Edit is placed in the column, it will raise the DataGrid's **EditCommand** event by default. The same applies to **Update** and **Delete** commands.

EditItemTemplate

To place the type and the layout of the fields to be edited under developer control, an **EditItemTemplate** should be defined. In the **EditCommand** event, the **EditItemIndex** of the grid is set to the index for a particular row, and the **EditItemTemplate** is displayed so that the fields can be edited. In the TimeTracker grid, the **ItemTemplate** displays the noneditable fields and the **EditItemTemplate** displays the editable layout. The **EditItemTemplate** fields must be read so that the data may be updated in the database. In both cases, the fields to be bound use data-binding tags for display as follows:

```
<%# DataBinder.Eval(Container, "DataItem.CategoryName") %>
```

DataBinder.Eval is a convenient method for retrieving values, but the grid will normally respond faster by using the **Container.DataItem** property and converting the field to appropriate type:

```
<%# CType(Container.DataItem, IDataRecord)("CategoryName") %>
```

In this case, the **IDataRecord** type is used because the underlying data source is a **DataReader**. The **DataBinder** class uses reflection to determine the data type of the source and retrieve the value for display. In spite of the extra overhead, using this class insulates the application from changes in the underlying data source. If the **DataGrid** was no longer bound to a **DataReader**, but used a **DataSet** instead, the first line of code would require no changes, but the second line would need to change **IDataRecord** to **DataRowView**.

DataGrid Population

The full benefits of using business entities for data display become apparent when you examine how the **DataGrid** is populated. The **Page_Load** event calls three procedures that add three types of information to the grid: **BindUserList**, **BindEntryFields**, and **BindTimeSheet**.

In order to display a list of users at the top of the form so that the projects for those users may be displayed, the **BindUserList** procedure is used. This subroutine makes use of a **TTUser** object to provide data for the binding. (This code is from the ASP.NET Time Tracker Starter Kit application in the code-behind file for the TimeEntry.aspx page.)

Visual Basic .NET

```
Private Sub BindUserList()
    UserList.DataSource = TTUser.GetUsers(_user.UserID, _user.Role)
    UserList.DataBind()

    UserList.Items.FindByValue(_user.UserID.ToString()).Selected = True
End Sub
```

C#

```
private void BindUserList()
{
        UserList.DataSource = TTUser.GetUsers(_user.UserID, _user.Role);
        UserList.DataBind();

        //Select User Drop Down to the correct value.
        UserList.Items.FindByValue(_user.UserID.ToString()).Selected=true;
}
```

The static **GetUsers** method retrieves a list of users according to the role and ID of the user. Administrators can see all users, but consultants can only see other consultants.

When a user is selected from the **UserList**, the **OnChange** event causes the **DataGrid** to be re-bound by using the **BindTimeSheet** subroutine. **BindTimeSheet** calls the **GetEntries** method of the **TimeEntry** object to retrieve a list of entries by passing in the user role, the user ID, and the time period. The **GetEntries** method calls a stored procedure by using the data abstraction layer, and retrieves information according to what should be visible to a particular user. (This code is from the ASP.NET Time Tracker Starter Kit application in the **TimeEntry** class.)

Visual Basic .NET

```vbnet
Public Shared Function GetEntries(ByVal queryUserID As Integer, ByVal _
    userID As Integer, ByVal startDate As DateTime, ByVal endDate As _
    DateTime) As TimeEntriesCollection

    Dim dsData As DataSet = SqlHelper.ExecuteDataset( _
        ConfigurationSettings.AppSettings(Web.Global.CfgKeyConnString), _
        "ListTimeEntries", _
        queryUserID, _
        userID, _
        startDate, _
        endDate)

    Dim entryList As New TimeEntriesCollection()

    Dim row As DataRow

    For Each row In dsData.Tables(0).Rows
        Dim time As New TimeEntry()
        time.EntryLogID = Convert.ToInt32(row("EntryLogID"))
        time.Description = row("Description").ToString()
        time.Duration = Convert.ToDecimal(row("Duration"))
        time.EntryDate = Convert.ToDateTime(row("EntryDate"))
        time.ProjectID = Convert.ToInt32(row("ProjectID"))
        time.CategoryID = Convert.ToInt32(row("CategoryID"))
        time.CategoryName = row("CategoryName").ToString()
        time.ProjectName = row("ProjectName").ToString()
        time.Day = time.EntryDate.ToString("dddd")
        time.CategoryShortName = row("CatShortName").ToString()

        entryList.Add(time)
    Next row

    Return entryList

End Function 'GetEntries
```

C#

```csharp
public static TimeEntriesCollection GetEntries(int queryUserID, int userID,
  DateTime startDate, DateTime endDate)
{
        DataSet dsData = SqlHelper.ExecuteDataset(
            ConfigurationSettings.AppSettings[ Web.Global.CfgKeyConnString] ,
            "TT_ListTimeEntries", queryUserID, userID, startDate, endDate);
        TimeEntriesCollection entryList = new TimeEntriesCollection();

        // Separate Data into a collection of TimeEntrys.
        foreach(DataRow row in dsData.Tables[ 0] .Rows)
        {
            TimeEntry time = new TimeEntry();
            time.EntryLogID = Convert.ToInt32(row[ "EntryLogID"] );
            time.Description = row[ "Description"] .ToString();
            time.Duration = Convert.ToDecimal(row[ "Duration"] );
            time.EntryDate = Convert.ToDateTime(row[ "EntryDate"] );
            time.ProjectID = Convert.ToInt32(row[ "ProjectID"] );
            time.CategoryID = Convert.ToInt32(row[ "CategoryID"] );
            time.CategoryName = row[ "CategoryName"] .ToString();
            time.ProjectName = row[ "ProjectName"] .ToString();
            time.Day = time.EntryDate.ToString("dddd");
            time.CategoryShortName = row[ "CatShortName"] .ToString();

            entryList.Add(time);
        }
        return entryList;
}
```

The properties of the **TimeEntry** objects are populated from the **DataSet** and are added to the **TimeEntriesCollection** and then passed back to **BindTimeSheet**. The collection of **TimeEntries** contained in **entryList** can then be used in a variety of ways to create display functionality. (This code is from the ASP.NET Time Tracker Starter Kit application in the code-behind file for the TimeEntry.aspx page.)

Visual Basic .NET

```
Private Overloads Sub BindTimeSheet(ByVal queryUserID As Integer, _
    ByVal userID As Integer, ByVal start As DateTime, ByVal [end]) As _
    DateTime

    Dim entryList As TimeEntriesCollection = _
        BusinessLogicLayer.TimeEntry.GetEntries( _
            queryUserID, _
            userID, _
            start, _
            [end])

    If Not (entryList Is Nothing) Then
        SortGridData(entryList, SortField, SortAscending)
    End If

    DrawTimeGraph(entryList, _dayListTable)

    TimeEntryGrid.DataSource = entryList
    TimeEntryGrid.DataBind()

End Sub 'BindTimeSheet
```

C#

```
private void BindTimeSheet(int queryUserID, int userID, DateTime start,
    DateTime end)
{
    TimeEntriesCollection entryList =
    BusinessLogicLayer.TimeEntry.GetEntries(queryUserID, userID, start, end);

    // Sort datagrid if it is not empty.
        if (entryList != null)
        {
            SortGridData(entryList, SortField, SortAscending);
        }
        // Draw time graph with new dataset.
        DrawTimeGraph(entryList, _dayListTable);

        TimeEntryGrid.DataSource = entryList;
        TimeEntryGrid.DataBind();
}
```

The same data is used to sort the grid, to generate the time graph, and to provide the fields for **DataGrid** display. These economies are the product of well-factored objects and collection classes.

When the user clicks the Edit button, the drop-down lists for the projects and categories are populated through the use of data-binding tags, as illustrated in the tag for the projects drop-down list. (This code is from the ASP.NET Time Tracker Starter Kit application in the TimeEntry.aspx page.)

```
<asp:dropdownlist
      Width="100px"
      ID="EntryProjects"
      AutoPostBack="True"
      CssClass="Standard-text"
      DataSource='<%# ListUserProjects() %>'
      DataTextField="Name"
      DataValueField="ProjectID"
      Runat="server"
      OnSelectedIndexChanged="UserProjects_OnChange"
/>
```

ListUserProjects() returns a **ProjectsCollection** that corresponds to the projects that should be visible to a particular user based on project membership. This is one of the easiest to implement and most efficient ways to bind a drop-down list in a **DataGrid**.

The **UserProjects_OnChange** method is executed whenever a user selects a project in the **EditItemTemplate**. This method allows the categories drop-down list to be repopulated according to the categories available for a particular project. The **_userInput** variable, a **TimeEntry** object, is used to collect information for the user-selected information. Because it holds the **ProjectID** for the selected project, the **ListGridCategories** method can use the **ProjectID** to display the appropriate categories. This method calls the **GetCategories** method of the **Project** object. (This code is from the ASP.NET Time Tracker Starter Kit application in the code-behind file for the TimeEntry .aspx page.)

Visual Basic .NET

```
Protected Function ListGridCategories(ByVal projectID As Integer) As _
    CategoriesCollection
        Return Project.GetCategories(projectID)
End Function 'ListGridCategories
```

C#

```
protected CategoriesCollection ListGridCategories(int projectID)
{
        return Project.GetCategories(projectID);
}
```

The **ListGridCategories** method is called in a data-binding tag in the **EntryCategories** drop-down list. The data is returned in the form of a **CategoriesCollection** object that is bound to the drop-down list. The categories in the categories drop-down list correspond to the projects in the projects drop-down list.

Retrieving User Input from a DataGrid

- Use the FindControl method to retrieve user input values from the DataGrid
- Use the ItemDataBound event to set selected values to the last selection made by the user, or according to the values selected in another drop-down list

Introduction

In order to retrieve user input values from the **DataGrid**, you use the **FindControl** method of the **TableCell** object that contains the data to be extracted. The values must be accessed through the **TableCell**, not at the **Page** or **DataGrid** level.

TimeEntryGrid_OnUpdate

In the TimeTracker application, the following update method, **TimeEntryGrid_OnUpdate** from the code-behind page for TimeEntry.aspx, uses the **e.Item** object that corresponds to the **TableCell**, which contains the text box with the user-inserted value. (This code is from the ASP.NET Time Tracker Starter Kit application in the code-behind file for the TimeEntry.aspx page.)

Visual Basic .NET

```vbnet
projectID = _
    Convert.ToInt32(CType(e.Item.FindControl("EntryProjects"), _
    DropDownList).SelectedItem.Value)

categoryID = Convert.ToInt32(CType(e.Item.FindControl("EntryCategories"), _
    DropDownList).SelectedItem.Value)

taskDate = Convert.ToDateTime(CType(e.Item.FindControl("EntryDays"), _
    DropDownList).SelectedItem.Value)

description = _
    TTSecurity.CleanStringRegex(CType(e.Item.FindControl("EntryDescription"), _
    TextBox).Text)

duration = Convert.ToDecimal(CType(e.Item.FindControl("EntryHours"), _
    TextBox).Text)

te = New BusinessLogicLayer.TimeEntry(entryLogID, userID, projectID, _
    categoryID, taskDate, description, duration)

te.Save()

TimeEntryGrid.EditItemIndex = -1

BindTimeSheet(_user.UserID, Convert.ToInt32(UserList.SelectedItem.Value), _
    _weekStartingDate, _weekEndingDate)
```

C#

```
projectID = Convert.ToInt32(CType(e.Item.FindControl("EntryProjects"),
    DropDownList).SelectedItem.Value);

categoryID = Convert.ToInt32(CType(e.Item.FindControl("EntryCategories"),
    DropDownList).SelectedItem.Value);

taskDate = Convert.ToDateTime(CType(e.Item.FindControl("EntryDays"),
    DropDownList).SelectedItem.Value);

description =
    TTSecurity.CleanStringRegex(CType(e.Item.FindControl("EntryDescription"),
    TextBox).Text);

duration = Convert.ToDecimal(CType(e.Item.FindControl("EntryHours"),
    TextBox).Text);

te = New BusinessLogicLayer.TimeEntry(entryLogID, userID, projectID,
    categoryID, taskDate, description, duration);

te.Save();

TimeEntryGrid.EditItemIndex = -1;

BindTimeSheet(_user.UserID, Convert.ToInt32(UserList.SelectedItem.Value),
    _weekStartingDate, _weekEndingDate);
```

The values retrieved are used to create a **TimeEntry** object, which can then be used for updating the database. As soon as the values are saved, the **DataGrid** is re-bound. The **EditItemIndex** cannot be used at the grid level. Any attempt to access the **EntryProjects** drop-down list directly would cause a compile-time error.

Initializing the values of drop-down lists can be accomplished in the **ItemDataBound** event of the **DataGrid**. By using this event, the selected values of the lists can be set to the last selection made by the user, or according to the values selected in another drop-down list, thus allowing for dependencies. (This code is from the ASP.NET Time Tracker Starter Kit application in the code-behind file for the TimeEntry.aspx page.)

Visual Basic .NET

```vbnet
Private Sub TimeEntryGrid_Itembound(ByVal sender As Object, ByVal e As _
    System.Web.UI.WebControls.DataGridItemEventArgs) Handles _
    TimeEntryGrid.ItemDataBound

    If e.Item.ItemType = ListItemType.EditItem Then

        Dim currentCbo As DropDownList = CType(e.Item.FindControl("EntryDays"), _
            DropDownList)

        currentCbo.SelectedIndex = _
            currentCbo.Items.IndexOf(currentCbo.Items.FindByText(_userInput.Day))

            currentCbo = CType(e.Item.FindControl("EntryProjects"), _
            DropDownList)

         currentCbo.SelectedIndex = _
            currentCbo.Items.IndexOf( _
            currentCbo.Items.FindByText(_userInput.ProjectName))

             currentCbo = CType(e.Item.FindControl("EntryCategories"), _
            DropDownList)

             currentCbo.SelectedIndex = _
            currentCbo.Items.IndexOf( _
            currentCbo.Items.FindByText(_userInput.CategoryName))
    End If
End Sub
```

C#

```csharp
private void TimeEntryGrid_Itembound(object sender,
    System.Web.UI.WebControls.DataGridItemEventArgs e)
{
    if (e.Item.ItemType == ListItemType.EditItem)
    {
        DropDownList currentCbo = (DropDownList)
        e.Item.FindControl("EntryDays");
            currentCbo.SelectedIndex =
        currentCbo.Items.IndexOf(
            currentCbo.Items.FindByText(_userInput.Day));

        currentCbo = (DropDownList) e.Item.FindControl("EntryProjects");
        currentCbo.SelectedIndex =
         currentCbo.Items.IndexOf(
         currentCbo.Items.FindByText(_userInput.ProjectName));

        currentCbo = (DropDownList) e.Item.FindControl("EntryCategories");
        currentCbo.SelectedIndex =
         currentCbo.Items.IndexOf(
         currentCbo.Items.FindByText(_userInput.CategoryName));

    }
}
```

In this code segment, **FindControl** is used to get references to each of the drop-down lists in the grid. The **SelectedIndex** of the list is set by an object that contains the user-selected values, **_userInput**, and a **TimeEntry** data type. The **EntryCategories** is not only re-bound to show the appropriate categories for a particular project, but the selected item also corresponds to the last item selected by the user.

Best Practices for Web Presentation Patterns

> **Best Practices for Web Presentation Patterns**
>
> - Use patterns such as Page Controller to reduce code duplication and facilitate easier testing
> - Page Controller pattern works best if all pages have similar layout and interactivity
> - Use collection classes with databinding to easily extend the information to be displayed and add custom sorting rules
> - Avoid the overhead of automatic paging by using the custom paging method
> - Maintaining a single data format allows the same object to be used to sort the grid, generate the time graph, and provide fields for DataGrid display

Consider the following recommended best practices when implementing Web presentation patterns in your Web application:

- Use patterns such as Page Controller to reduce code duplication. This enables device independence and easier testing.

- Optimizing data access is made easier by the Table Data Gateway pattern because data access is encapsulated in a single component.

- The Page Controller pattern works best if all pages have similar layout and interactivity. Otherwise, some fraction of the code in the base class will either be wasted or have to be overridden, thus working against the major purpose of this pattern.

- By using collection classes with data-binding, you can easily extend the information to be displayed and add custom sorting rules.

- Avoid the overhead of automatic paging by using the custom paging method recommended in the *Microsoft .NET Data Access Architecture Guide*.

- By maintaining a single data format, the same object can be used to sort the grid, to generate the time graph, and to provide the fields for **DataGrid** display. These economies are the product of well-factored objects and collection classes.

Lab 3: Implementing Data-Bound Presentations

Lab 3: Implementing Data Bound Presentations

Exercise 1: Implementing the Defect Class
Exercise 2: Implementing the Defect Module
Exercise 3: Creating a Master/Detail Report

Introduction

In this lab, you will examine the major aspects of the defect tracking functionality. One of the most important content areas for the portal site is the tab that manages defect tracking. The main class used in this lab to enable defect tracking is **Defect**. In order to display defects owned by a particular user, you will implement a display page that uses a **DataGrid**. The module that displays this information derives from a base **PortalModuleControl** class that provides functionality to all of the modules in the site. You will also deploy features of the Data Access Application Block to provide records for custom paging. When the user wishes to view the details of a defect, or edit information about the defect, the ViewDefect.aspx page is displayed.

After completing this lab, you will have demonstrated your ability to:

- Use user interface classes to define base functionality across a Web site.
- Implement low-overhead data-binding.
- Enable efficient data paging.

Prerequisites

Before working on this lab, you must have the knowledge and skills necessary to use data-bound list controls.

Estimated time to complete this lab: 60 minutes

Starting a Virtual Machine

1. On the student computer, on the **Start** menu, point to **All Programs**, and then click **Microsoft Virtual PC**. If the Virtual PC console window does not appear, then right-click the **Virtual PC icon** in the notification area (system tray), and click **Show Virtual PC Console**.

2. In the Virtual PC console window, select the virtual machine that you would like to open then click **Start**.

NOTE: Depending on your time zone, the first time you start each of the virtual machines, you may receive an error message that the parent virtual hard disk appears to have been modified. You can ignore this message.

3. The virtual machine will start up in a new window.

Closing a Virtual Machine

1. On the student computer, in the virtual machine window, on the **Action** menu, click **Close**.

NOTE: To avoid accidentally closing the virtual machine during the lab, the Close button in the top right corner of the virtual machine is disabled.

2. The virtual machine window will close. All changes to the virtual hard disk are discarded.

Exercise 1: Implementing the Defect Class

In this exercise, you will implement a **Defect** class that will be used to manage and display defect information.

- **Open the lab starter project**

    1. In Visual Studio .NET, open the ASPProjectVB or ASPProjectCS project by browsing to D:\2311\Labfiles\Lab03\Starter\VB or D:\2311\Labfiles\Lab03\Starter\CS.

    2. Launch the project by double-clicking the ASPProjectVB.sln or ASPProjectCS.sln file in the lab starter folder.

- **Open the portal application project and study the Defect class**

    1. In the **DefectTracking** folder (found under the Components folder in the application directory), find Defect.vb or Defect.cs and open it in the code window. Note the properties in the PUBLIC PROPERTIES region. These correspond to the properties that will be used for display. Open the ADD UPDATE DELETE region. Each method uses the **ExecuteNonQuery** method of the **SqlHelper** class.

    2. In the GET METHODS region, study the static (Shared in Visual Basic .NET) function **GetDefect**. For efficiency, the lab uses the **ExecuteReader** method of the **SqlHelper** class. This method will be used by the ViewDefect.aspx page to view details about a defect.

- **Implement the first GetDefects overload**

    1. Locate the comment "TODO Implement the first GetDefects overload." This method accepts a **userName** and **projectID** and returns a **DefectsDataSet** object. The use of the **DefectsDataSet** object illustrates how to use a typed **DataSet** for data access.

    2. A **DefectsDataSet** object named "ds" has already been declared and instantiated.

3. Use the **FillDataSet** overload of the **SqlHelper** class, which accepts the following parameters. Using the **FillDataSet** method has two principal advantages over the **ExecuteDataSet** method. First, it allows typed **DataSets** to be used. Second, it allows the **DataSet** to be reused.

Parameter order	Parameter value
1	VB: ConfigurationSettings.AppSettings("ConnectionString") C#: ConfigurationSettings.AppSettings["ConnectionString"]
2	"GetDefects"
3	ds
4	New String() {"Defects"}
5	userName
6	projectID

4. Note that the **DataSet** has been returned from the function. Your code should resemble the following:

Visual Basic .NET

```
Dim ds As New DefectsDataSet()
SqlHelper.FillDataset( _
    ConfigurationSettings.AppSettings("connectionString"), _
    "GetDefects", _
    ds, _
    New String() { "Defects"}, _
    userName, _
    projectID)
Return ds
```

C#

```
DefectsDataSet ds = new DefectsDataSet();
SqlHelper.FillDataset(
    ConfigurationSettings.AppSettings["connectionString"],
                "GetDefects",
                ds,
                new string[]{ "Defects"},
                userName,
                projectID);
return ds;
```

▪ Implement the second GetDefects overload

1. Locate the comment "TODO Implement the second GetDefects overload." This method accepts a **userName** and **projectID** as before, but also accepts pageNumber, pageSize, sortField, and totalRecords. It returns a **DefectsDataSet** object. The additional parameters are used to implement custom paging.

2. To implement custom paging, you will create three SQL statements. The first will select records for all pages up to the current page displayed in the grid. The second will select records up to the page before the page currently being displayed. The third will subtract the second set of records from the first. The result will be the records needed for a particular page sorted by any field. This method eliminates the overhead of saving key values and using them when the user selects a new page. It also allows custom paging by a user selected field.

3. Declare a string variable named **select1**. Use the **String.Format** method to create a select statement that includes the values in the following table:

Format item	Value to insert
0	pageNumber * pageSize
1	userName
2	projectID
3	sortField

4. The select statement should resemble the following:

Visual Basic .NET

```
Dim select1 As String = [String].Format("(select top {0} defectID, description, _
    assignedTo, status, severity, datefound from defects where assignedTo = _
    '{1}' and projectid ={2} order by {3}) as t1", _
        pageNumber * pageSize, _
        userName, _
        projectID, _
        sortField)
```

C#

```
string select1 = String.Format("(select top {0} defectID, description,
    assignedTo, status, severity, datefound from defects where assignedTo =
    '{1}' and projectid ={2} order by {3}) as t1",
                pageNumber * pageSize,
                userName,
                projectID,
                sortField);
```

5. Declare a string variable named **select2**. Use the **String.Format** method to create a select statement that includes the values in the following table:

Format item	Value to insert
0	(pageNumber-1) * pageSize
1	userName
2	projectID
3	sortField

6. The select statement should resemble the following:

Visual Basic .NET

```
Dim select2 As String = [String].Format("select top {0} defectID from defects
    where assignedTo = '{1}' and projectid ={2} order by {3}", _
            (pageNumber - 1) * pageSize, _
            userName, _
            projectID, _
            sortField)
```

C#

```
string select2 = String.Format("select top {0} defectID from defects where
    assignedTo = '{1}' and projectid ={2} order by {3}",
                (pageNumber-1) * pageSize,
                userName,
                projectID,
                            sortField);
```

7. Declare a string variable named **sql**. Use the **String.Format** method to create a select statement that includes the values in the following table:

Format item	Value to insert
0	select1
1	select2

8. The select statement should resemble the following:

Visual Basic .NET

```
Dim sql As String = [String].Format("select * from {0} where defectID not in
    ({1})", select1, select2)
```

C#

```
string sql = String.Format("select * from {0} where defectID not in ({1})",
    select1, select2);
```

9. Note that a **DefectsDataSet** object named "ds" has already been declared and instantiated.
10. Use the **FillDataSet** method of the **SqlHelper**, which accepts the parameters as illustrated in the following table:

Parameter order	Parameter value
1	ConfigurationSettings.AppSettings("ConnectionString")
2	CommandType.Text
3	sql
4	ds
5	New String() {"Defects"}

11. The **FillDataSet** call should resemble the following:

Visual Basic .NET

```
SqlHelper.FillDataset( _
    ConfigurationSettings.AppSettings("connectionString"), _
    CommandType.Text, _
    sql, _
    ds, _
    New String() {"Defects"})
```

C#

```
SqlHelper.FillDataset(
    ConfigurationSettings.AppSettings["connectionString"],
    CommandType.Text,
    sql,
    ds,
    new string[]{"Defects"});
```

12. Use the **ExecuteScalar** method of the **SqlHelper** to execute a **GetDefectCount** stored procedure. Use the overload that accepts the parameters as shown in the following table:

Parameter Order	Parameter Value
1	ConfigurationSettings.AppSettings("ConnectionString")
2	"GetDefectCount"
3	userName
4	projectID

13. The **ExecuteScalar** call should resemble the following:

Visual Basic .NET

```
totalRecords = CInt(SqlHelper.ExecuteScalar( _
    ConfigurationSettings.AppSettings("connectionString"), _
    "GetDefectCount", _
    userName, _
        projectID))
```

C#

```
totalRecords = (int)SqlHelper.ExecuteScalar(
    ConfigurationSettings.AppSettings["connectionString"],
    "GetDefectCount",
    userName,
    projectID);
```

14. Note that the **DataSet** has been returned from the function.
15. You will test the procedure after implementing the user control in the next exercise.

Exercise 2: Implementing the Defect Module

In this exercise, you will implement a DefectModule.ascx code-behind class that derives from the base **PortalModuleControl**.

- **Inherit from PortalModuleControl**

1. In Visual Studio .NET, open the ASPProjectVB or ASPProjectCS project if it is not already open.

2. In the **Modules** directory, find the DefectModule.ascx file and select it in the code window. At the top are two drop-down lists, one for project information and the other for users. The user list will contain only users who are members of a particular project. In the last lab, you implemented the **GetMembers** method of the **Project** class. This method looks up the members of a project. Note the **DataGrid** where the defects will be displayed.

3. You will begin by inheriting from the **PortalModuleControl** class. Note: If you try to execute this file or open it in Design view before implementing inheritance according to the following instructions, an error will be generated. Locate the comment "TODO Inherit from PortalModuleControl." Open the DesktopControls.vb or DesktopControls.cs file located in the MainPortal folder. The file inherits from **UserControl**, which allows it to be loaded by the **Page.LoadControl** method. Study each of the properties implemented by the control. These constitute the base functionality of the site. The code inherits from the **PortalModuleControl** using the Inherits keyword or C# syntax as displayed below:

Visual Basic .NET

```
Inherits PortalModuleControl
```

C#

```
public abstract class DefectModule: PortalModuleControl
```

- **Implement the BindDefectList method**

1. Open the DefectModule.ascx.vb or DefectModule.ascx.cs file. Locate the comment "TODO Implement the BindDefectList method."

2. The method has already been partially completed and contains an **If** statement that checks the user's security role. Place the **If** statement that you will build below before the included **If** statement. End your **If** statement after the included **If** statement.

3. Use an **If** statement to check that a project is selected in the **ProjectSelection** drop-down list and the **UserSelection** drop-down list. Defects can be displayed only for particular projects and users.

4. Declare and instantiate a **DefectsDataSet** object. This is a typed **DataSet** that contains properties for the defects.

5. Use the static (Shared in Visual Basic .NET) function **GetDefects** to retrieve a **DataSet** containing the data needed to bind to the **DataGrid**. The overload of **GetDefects** that is used here requires six parameters: the userName to whom the defect is assigned and a projectID for the defect tracking project, along with the parameters for retrieving the records for the specific page displayed in the **DataGrid**. The following table shows which parameters should be passed to the following table:

Parameter name	Parameter value
userName	UserSelection.SelectedItem.Text
projectID	Integer.Parse(ProjectSelection.SelectedItem.Value)
pageNumber	grid.CurrentPageIndex + 1
pageSize	4
sortField	ViewState("SortOrder").ToString()
totalRecords	totalRecords

6. Your code should resemble the following:

Visual Basic .NET

```
If Not (ProjectSelection.SelectedItem Is Nothing) And Not _
    (UserSelection.SelectedItem Is Nothing) Then
    Dim ds As DefectsDataSet = Defect.GetDefects( _
        UserSelection.SelectedItem.Text, _
        Integer.Parse(ProjectSelection.SelectedItem.Value), _
        grid.CurrentPageIndex + 1, _
        4, _
        ViewState("SortOrder").ToString(), _
            totalRecords)
```

C#

```
if((ProjectSelection.SelectedItem != null)&&(UserSelection.SelectedItem != null))
    DefectsDataSet ds = Defect.GetDefects(
        UserSelection.SelectedItem.Text,
        int.Parse(ProjectSelection.SelectedItem.Value),
        grid.CurrentPageIndex+1,
        4,
        ViewState["SortOrder"].ToString(),
        ref totalRecords);
```

7. Check the **Count** property of the **Defects DataTable** in the **DataSet** to see if it is greater than 0. If so, set the **VirtualItemCount** property of the **DataGrid** to the value of the totalRecords parameter returned from the **GetDefects** call. Bind the **DataGrid** to the **Defects** table.

8. In the **Else** clause, declare and instantiate a **LiteralControl**. Set the **Text** property of the **LiteralControl** to "There are no tasks assigned currently." Add the **LiteralControl** to the header **TableCell** at the first index location. Clear the **DataGrid** by using the **Clear** method of the DataGrid's **Controls** collection. End the **If** statement.

9. Your code should resemble the following. The provided code is security-related and will be explained in the security module.

Visual Basic .NET

```
If ds.Defects.Count > 0 Then
    grid.VirtualItemCount = totalRecords
    grid.DataSource = ds.Defects
    grid.DataBind()
Else
    Dim l As New Literal()
    l.Text = "There are no tasks assigned currently"
    header.Controls.AddAt(0, l)
    grid.Controls.Clear()
End If
```

C#

```
if(ds.Defects.Count > 0)
{
    grid.VirtualItemCount = totalRecords;
    grid.DataSource = ds.Defects;
    grid.DataBind();
}
else
{
    Literal l = new Literal();
    l.Text = "There are no tasks assigned currently";
    header.Controls.AddAt(0, l);
    grid.Controls.Clear();
}
```

10. End the first **If** statement.

- **(Optional) Implement the SetupHeader method**

1. Examine the beginning of the **SetupHeader** method in DefectModule.ascs.vb or DefectModule.ascs.vb. Note that the **DataGridItemEventArgs** are passed into the subroutine. The "SortOrder" is stored in the **ViewState** properties. One Boolean variable determines if the sort expression is descending. One String variable replaces the "DESC" string with an empty string to turn off a descending sort.

2. Locate the comment "TODO Show sort direction."

3. Create a loop that loops through each **Column** object of the **DataGrid**.

4. Inside the loop, declare a string variable named **colSortExpr** and set it equal to the **SortExpression** property of the current Column.

5. Check whether **pureSortExpr** is equal to **colSortExpr** and that **colSortExpr** is not an empty string.

6. If both conditions are true, declare a **TableCell** object by using the Cells collection of the DataGridItemEventArgs variable to refer to the current cell.

7. Declare and instantiate a **Label** object named **lblSorted**.

8. Set the **Font.Name** property of the **Label** object to **Webdings**.

9. Set the **Font.Size** property of the **Label** object to **FontUnit.XSmall**.

10. Check the **isDesc** variable. If it is true, set the **Text** property of the **Label** object to **6**. Otherwise, set it to **5**. These are the Webdings up and down arrows.

11. Add the **Label** object to the **Controls** collection for the current cell. End the **If** statement.

12. Your code should resemble the following:

Visual Basic .NET

```
For i = 0 To grid.Columns.Count - 1
    ' Draw the glyph to reflect sorting direction
    Dim colSortExpr As String = grid.Columns(i).SortExpression
    If pureSortExpr = colSortExpr And colSortExpr <> "" Then
        Dim cell As TableCell = e.Item.Cells(i)
        Dim lblSorted As New Label()
        lblSorted.Font.Name = "webdings"
        lblSorted.Font.Size = FontUnit.XSmall
        If isDesc = True Then
            lblSorted.Text = " 6"
        Else
            lblSorted.Text = " 5"
        End If
            cell.Controls.Add(lblSorted)
    End If
Next i
```

C#

```
for (int i=0; i<grid.Columns.Count; i++)
{
    // Draw the glyph to reflect sorting direction
    string colSortExpr = grid.Columns[i].SortExpression;
    if (pureSortExpr == colSortExpr && colSortExpr != "")
    {
        TableCell cell = e.Item.Cells[i];
        Label lblSorted = new Label();
        lblSorted.Font.Name = "Webdings";
        lblSorted.Font.Size = FontUnit.XSmall;
        lblSorted.Text = (isDesc ? " 6" :" 5");
        cell.Controls.Add(lblSorted);
    }
}
```

13. Build the project and view DesktopDefault.aspx in the browser.
14. Log in as administrator using admin@contoso.com with a password of **P@ssw0rd**.
15. Test your work by selecting the **Defect Tracking** tab by adding a new defect to your project. If you reassign a defect, you may have to log in again to see the reassigned defects.

Exercise 3: Creating a Master/Detail Report

In this exercise, you will create a Master/Detail report by using a **DataList**, a **DataGrid**, two business logic components, and a data access layer component. This lab uses a **DataList** to demonstrate a lightweight alternative to the **DataGrid**. One of its advantages for creating Master/Detail reports is that it contains a **SelectedItemTemplate** that can be used to create nested data layers in a straightforward way. It does not contain any built-in support for sorting as the **DataGrid** does. Therefore, you will create a custom collection class with **IComparer** implementations to add this functionality to the **DataList**.

■ Open the lab starter project

1. Browse to D:\2311\Labfiles\Lab03\Exercise03\Starter\VB\ or D:\2311\Labfiles\Lab03\Exercise03\Starter\CS\.

2. Double-click the DrillDownApp.sln file.

■ Implement the DrillDown.aspx user interface

1. Open the DrillDown.aspx page and study the user interface code.

2. Note that it contains data-bound controls:

    a. A **DataList** with an ID of "Customers."

    b. **Customers** contains a **SelectedItemTemplate** with an embedded **DataList** with an ID of "Orders."

    c. Note that the Orders **DataList** contains a **HeaderTemplate** with a table. In the first row of the table are a series of **LinkButtons**. These will be used to sort the **DataList** items according to an **IComparer** implementation in a custom collection class. Each has an **OnCommand** attribute set to the **Order_Sort** method.

    d. The **DataSource** attribute of **Orders** is set to the **GetOrders** method through a data-binding tag that passes the value of the **CustomerID** property to the method.

    e. **Orders** contains a **SelectedItemTemplate** with an outer table containing two nested tables. In the second nested table will be a **DataGrid** with an ID of "OrderDetails."

3. The three nested data controls represent the hierarchical relationship between the data items they contain. At the outer level are Customer items. The children of Customer items are Order items, and the children of Order items are OrderDetail items.

4. The **SelectedItemTemplate** elements contain customized layouts using table tags that will be shown when the user selects the row.

5. The Customers **DataList** has an **OnItemCommand** attribute that is set to the **Customers_ItemCommand** method. This method will be executed when the user makes a selection by clicking the **LinkButton** corresponding to a company name. The **Orders** DataList contains a similar attribute.

6. Implement the **ItemTemplate** for Customers by creating the following elements at the points indicated in the code by comments.

    a. Locate the comment "Insert a linkbutton that will bind to the CompanyName and select the row."

    b. Write code to create a **LinkButton** control according to the attributes in the following table:

Attribute	Value
id	btnSelect
runat	server
CommandName	"Select"
Text	<%# DataBinder.Eval(Container.DataItem, "CompanyName") %>

7. Your code should resemble the following:

```
<asp:linkbutton
       id="btnSelect"
       runat="server"
       CommandName="select"
       Text='<%# DataBinder.Eval(Container.DataItem, "CompanyName") %>'>
</asp:linkbutton>
```

8. Note that after the LinkButton control is a data-bound label. This label is used to hold the CustomerID so that it can be stored in the **ViewState**.

9. Identify the **SelectedItemTemplate** in the Orders **DataList**. In the second table inside this template, locate the comment "Create a DataGrid to display order details."

10. Create a **DataGrid** opening tag with the following attributes and values:

Attribute	Value
id	OrderDetails
runat	server
AutoGenerateColumns	False
DataSource	<%# GetOrderDetails((int)DataBinder.Eval(Container.DataItem, "OrderID")) %>
BorderWidth	0
Width	100%

11. Inside the **DataGrid**, create a **HeaderStyle** tag with an attribute of **BackColor** set to **#336666** and **ForeColor** set to **White**.

12. Create an **AlternatingItemStyle** with a **BackColor** attribute set to **LightGreen**.

13. Create an **ItemStyle** with a **BackColor** attribute set to **White**.

14. Open a tag to hold a **Columns** collection and create three **BoundColumns** according to the values below:

    a. **DataField="ProductName"**; **HeaderText="Product"**; **Itemstyle-Width="200"**

    b. **DataField=" UnitPrice"**; **HeaderText=" Unit Price"**; **DataFormatString="{0:c}"**; **Itemstyle-Width="70"**

    c. **DataField=" Quantity"**; **HeaderText=" Quantity"**; **Itemstyle-Width="100"**

15. Close the **DataGrid** tag. Your code should resemble the following:

```
<asp:datagrid
    id=OrderDetails
    runat="server"
    AutoGenerateColumns="false"
    DataSource=
        '<%# GetOrderDetails(CInt(DataBinder.Eval(Container.DataItem,
        "OrderID"))) %>' BorderWidth="0" Width="100%">
    <HeaderStyle BackColor="#336666" ForeColor="White" />
    <AlternatingItemStyle BackColor="LightGreen" />
    <ItemStyle BackColor="White" />
    <columns>
    <asp:boundcolumn DataField="ProductName" HeaderText="Product"
        Itemstyle-Width="200">
    </asp:boundcolumn>
    <asp:boundcolumn DataField="UnitPrice" HeaderText="Unit Price"
        DataFormatString="{0:c} " Itemstyle-Width="70">
    </asp:boundcolumn>
    <asp:boundcolumn DataField="Quantity" HeaderText="Quantity"
        Itemstyle-Width="100">
    </asp:boundcolumn>
    </columns>
</asp:datagrid>
```

Advanced Web Application Development Using Microsoft ASP .NET

- **Implement a code-behind page to DrillDown.aspx**

1. Two components form the business logic layer for this application: one named DrillDownReport.cs or DrillDownReport.vb, and another named DrillDownReportCollection.cs or DrillDownReportCollection.vb. Open DrillDownReport.cs or DrillDownReport.vb in the BLL folder. Study the methods and note the following:

    a. The static (Shared in Visual Basic .NET) methods **GetCustomers**, **GetOrders**, and **GetOrderDetails** return data in the form of a **DrillDownReportCollection**, a collection class that contains objects of type **DrillDownReport**.

    b. The **SqlHelper ExecuteDataSet** method is used to execute stored procedures to retrieve the data for each method.

2. Open DrillDownReportCollection.cs or DrillDownReportCollection.vb and study the code, noting the following:

    a. The class inherits from **ArrayList**. This allows access to the **Sort** method, which will be overridden to provide sorting rules.

    b. The three **IComparer** implementations define the sorting rules for **OrderDate**, **ShippedDate,** and **Freight** sorting.

    c. Note the call to the **base.Reverse** method to provide reversible sorting according to the value of a Boolean parameter.

3. Open the code-behind page for the DrillDown.aspx page. The **SortField** and **SortAscending** properties are defined at the beginning of the **DrillDown** class. These will persist sorting parameters in ViewState so reversible sorting can be supported.

4. Study the **SortDataGrid** method at the end of the class. This method is called whenever the data in the Orders **DataList** is re-bound. It accepts a set of data in the form of a **DrillDownReportCollection** and returns a sorted version of the list. Because the collection class implements the **IComparer** interface, the data can be re-sorted by calling the **Sort** method of the class and passing in an instance of the class that implements **IComparer**. This will allow the user to sort the **Orders** data by clicking **LinkButtons** at the top of each column.

5. The **Page_Load** method ensures that **SortField** has a value, and then calls **BindList**.

6. Locate the comment "TODO Implement the BindList method."

7. Declare a variable named "customerList" of type **DrillDownReportCollection**. Assign the return value from a call to the static **GetCustomers** method of the **DrillDownReport** class to this variable.

8. Set the **DataSource** property of **Customers** to **customerList** and then call **DataBind** on the **DataList**. Your code should resemble the following:

Visual Basic .NET
```
Dim customerList As DrillDownReportCollection = _
    DrillDownReport.GetCustomers()
Customers.DataSource = customerList
Customers.DataBind()
```

C#
```
DrillDownReportCollection customerList = DrillDownReport.GetCustomers();
Customers.DataSource = customerList;
Customers.DataBind();
```

9. Locate the comment "TODO Implement the Customers DataList ItemCommand event handler."

10. Create a string variable named **cmd**.

11. Write an expression that retrieves the **CommandSource** property of the **DataListCommandEventArgs** parameter and converts it to a **LinkButton** type. Retrieve the **CommandName** property from the **LinkButton** and assign it to **cmd**.

12. Check to see if **cmd** holds the string "select." If so, write an expression to convert the sender parameter to a **DataList** type. Set the **SelectedIndex** property of the **DataList** to the **ItemIndex** property of the **Item** property of the **DataListCommandEventArgs** parameter.

13. Call the **BindList** method.

14. Write an expression that uses the **FindControl** method of the current item, stored in the **Item** property of the **DataListCommandEventArgs** parameter, to find a control with an ID of "CustomerID." Store this value in a **ViewState** object named "CustomerID." Your code should resemble the following:

Visual Basic .NET

```
Dim cmd As String = CType(e.CommandSource, LinkButton).CommandName
If cmd = "select" Then
    CType(sender, DataList).SelectedIndex = e.Item.ItemIndex
End If
BindList()

ViewState("CustomerID") = CType(e.Item.FindControl("CustomerID"),
    Label).Text
```

C#

```
string cmd = ((LinkButton)e.CommandSource).CommandName;
if (cmd == "select")
    ((DataList)sender).SelectedIndex = e.Item.ItemIndex;

BindList();

ViewState["CustomerID"] =
    ((Label)e.Item.FindControl("CustomerID")).Text;
```

15. Locate the comment "TODO Implement the Orders DataList ItemCommand event handler."

16. Write an expression that retrieves the **CommandSource** property of the **DataListCommandEventArgs** parameter and converts it to a **LinkButton** type. Retrieve the **CommandName** property from the **LinkButton** and assign it to **cmd**.

17. Create a variable of type **DataList** named **dl**. Write an expression to convert the **sender** parameter to a **DataList** type. Assign the result of this conversion to **dl**.

18. Check to see if **cmd** holds the string "select." If so, set the **SelectedIndex** property of the **DataList dl** to the **ItemIndex** property of the **Item** property of the **DataListCommandEventArgs** parameter.

19. Create a variable of type **DrillDownReportCollection** named **orderList**. Write an expression that calls the **GetOrders** method, passing in the value of the **ViewState** object "CustomerID." Convert the parameter to a string type before passing it to the method.

20. Databind **dl** to **orderList**.

Visual Basic .NET

```
Dim cmd As String = CType(e.CommandSource, LinkButton).CommandName
Dim dl As DataList = CType(sender, DataList)
If cmd = "select" Then
    dl.SelectedIndex = e.Item.ItemIndex
End If

Dim orderList As DrillDownReportCollection = _
    GetOrders(CStr(ViewState("CustomerID")))
dl.DataSource = orderList
dl.DataBind()
```

C#

```
string cmd = ((LinkButton)e.CommandSource).CommandName;
DataList dl = (DataList)sender;
if (cmd == "select")
        dl.SelectedIndex = e.Item.ItemIndex;

DrillDownReportCollection orderList =
GetOrders((string)ViewState["CustomerID"]);
dl.DataSource = orderList;
dl.DataBind();
```

21. Locate the comment "TODO Call the SortGridData function."

22. Check the **orderList.Count** property. If it is greater than 0, call the **SortDataGrid** method, passing in three parameters: **orderList**, **SortField**, and **SortAscending**.

23. Return **orderList** from the function. Your code should resemble the following:

Visual Basic .NET

```
If orderList.Count > 0 Then
    SortGridData(orderList, SortField, SortAscending)
End If
Return orderList
```

C#

```
if (orderList.Count > 0)
    SortGridData(orderList, SortField, SortAscending);
return orderList;
```

24. Each time the page is reloaded, the Orders **DataList** re-binds to its DataSource by using this method. The call to **SortDataGrid** ensures that the data will be properly sorted.
25. Locate the comment "TODO Implement the Command event handler for the LinkButtons."
26. Write an expression that uses the **CommandEventArgs** parameter to retrieve the **CommandArgument** property. Convert the value to a string type. Assign the value to the **SortField** property.
27. Call the **BindList** method. Your code should resemble the following:

Visual Basic .NET

```
SortField = CStr(e.CommandArgument)
BindList()
```

C#

```
SortField = (string)e.CommandArgument;
BindList();
```

28. This method is called whenever the user clicks one of the **LinkButtons** at the top of the columns in the Orders **DataList**. Because **DataLists** do not have built-in sortability, this method allows you to add sorting to a **DataList** in an efficient way.

29. Build the project and correct any errors.

30. Load DrillDown.aspx in the browser and make sure it functions as expected.

Module 4: Building Custom Controls

- Understanding Controls
- Using Custom Controls

Overview

Although the standard Microsoft® ASP.NET Web controls offer a rich array of functionality, developers may find that none of these controls meet the needs of a particular application. In that case, developers may either derive from an existing control or create their own control by deriving it from the **Control** or **WebControl** classes. Custom controls are created as managed classes and are compiled before deployment.

In this module, you will learn how to implement custom controls to extend the user interface of your ASP.NET application.

Objectives

After completing this module, you will be able to:

- Describe the architecture of server controls.
- Create an object model for a custom control.
- Raise and use event handlers during control execution.
- Use rendering methods to create control content.
- Implement data-bound custom controls.

Lesson: Understanding Controls

> **Lesson: Understanding Controls**
>
> - Control Architecture
> - Elements of a Custom Control
> - Code Walkthrough: A Basic Custom Control

Overview

Web controls are an essential element of any ASP.NET Web application. In order to fully exploit the potential of Web controls in your application, it is important to understand their architecture and how they can be customized to enhance functionality.

In this lesson, you will learn about control architecture and how it can be customized to suit your business needs.

Lesson Objectives

After completing this module, you will be able to:

- Explain the differences between a user control and a custom control.
- Describe the elements of a basic custom control.

Control Architecture

> **Control Architecture**
>
> - System.Web.UI.Control
>   - Provides the functionality needed to participate in the page framework
>   - Implements the System.ComponentModel.IComponent interface
>   - Should be chosen as the base class for a custom control if it will not be rendering a user interface
> - System.Web.UI.WebControl
>   - Adds properties, methods, and events necessary to generate a visual interface
>   - Should be chosen as the base class for a custom control that will create a user interface

Introduction

A custom control is essentially a software component that renders Hypertext Markup Language (HTML), Extensible Markup Language (XML), Wireless markup Language (WML), or other markup languages to the client. By deriving from the **System.Web.UI.Control** or **System.Web.UI.WebControl** classes, the infrastructure necessary to interact with an ASP.NET page is automatically provided. Deriving from one of these base classes allows the control to be placed in the control tree of a page. The main task of the control developer is to create an object model to render the markup.

Unlike a user control, a custom control is a control authored as a managed class and compiled before deployment. It can be added to the Toolbox, dragged onto a Web Form, and declaratively programmed through selections in its property box. Custom controls are best suited to rendering dynamic content, such as a **TreeView** control with expandable nodes. User controls work best with static content in a fixed layout. User controls cannot be shared across applications, but since custom controls are compiled assemblies, they can be used by any application.

Two base classes can be used to create a custom control:

- **System.Web.UI.Control**: All ASP.NET controls derive from this class or one of its derived classes. It provides the functionality needed to participate in the page framework. It also implements the **System.ComponentModel.IComponent** interface, which allows a control to be represented visually on the client Web Form. This class should be chosen as the base class for a custom control if it will not be rendering a user interface. If the control were to be used to embed keywords in a metatag, this would be the appropriate base class.

- **System.Web.UI.WebControl**: This class derives from the **Control** class and adds properties, methods, and events necessary to generate a visual interface. This class contains properties such as **Font**, **BackColor**, and **Forecolor**. Custom controls that will create a user interface should derive from this class.

Elements of a Custom Control

> **Elements of a Custom Control**
>
> Major elements of a custom control
> - A class that derives from **Control**
> - The **Render** method implementation
> - The **HtmlTextWriter** class
>   - **WriteFullBeginTag**
>   - **Write**
>   - **WriteLine**
>   - **WriteEndTag**
>   - **WriteAttribute**

Introduction

A number of elements are common to custom Web controls. This section describes the most important of these elements.

Custom Control Elements

The major elements of a custom control are as follows:

- A class that derives from **Control**.

- The **Render** method implementation. The purpose of the **Render** method is to write text to the Hypertext Transfer Protocol (HTTP) Response stream. The **Control** class uses the **HtmlTextWriter** object to write the content of the control to the client.

- The **HtmlTextWriter** class. This class encapsulates the HTTP Response stream. The methods of this class simplify the writing and formatting of HTML tags and attributes. Some of its important methods are:
  - **WriteFullBeginTag**. Writes the opening tag of the specified HTML element and the closing character of the opening tag (>). You use this method for HTML elements that have no attributes.
  - **Write**. Writes literal text.
  - **WriteLine**. Writes text followed by a line terminator.
  - **WriteEndTag**: Writes the closing tag of the specified HTML element.
  - **WriteAttribute**: Writes an HTML attribute to the output stream.

Code Walkthrough: A Basic Custom Control

> **Code Walkthrough: A Basic Custom Control**
>
> **Key points:**
> - The **SimpleControl** class derives from the base **Control** class
> - The **Render** method outputs the content by using an **HtmlTextWriter** object
> - The **HtmlTextWriter** methods handle the details of HTML syntax

Introduction

In this code walkthrough, you will study the essential elements of a basic custom control. This topic examines the functionality that the following code sample represents. The Democode for this module contains a fully worked-out sample file in the CustomControlLibrary project in the Mod04 solution. The control code is in a file named SimpleControl.cs or SimpleControl.vb. The page that uses the control is named WebForm1.aspx, which is in a Web application project named TestControls.

Key Points

Emphasize the following points in the code sample:

- The **SimpleControl** class derives from the base **Control** class.
- The **Render** method outputs the content by using an **HtmlTextWriter** object.
- The **HtmlTextWriter** methods handle the details of HTML syntax.

Demonstrating the Control

Demonstrate how the control can be used by adding the control to the existing WebForm1.aspx page as follows:

1. Rebuild the **CustomControlLibrary** project.
2. Add the control to the Toolbox by right-clicking the Toolbox and then selecting **Add/Remove Items**.
3. Select the **.NET Framework Components** tab.
4. Click **Browse**, navigate to the bin directory on the CustomControlLibrary project, select the CustomControlLibrary.dll file, and then click **Open**.
5. Show the new icon on the Toolbox. Drag the SimpleControl control onto WebForm1. Open the Web Form and show the **Register** tag and how the control is sited on the form.
6. Open the code-behind file for the Web Form and show where the control is declared.
7. Select the WebForm1 and view it in the browser to show the control. The following code is from the SimpleControl.vb or SimpleControl.cs file.

Visual Basic .NET

```vbnet
Imports System
Imports System.Web.UI
Imports System.Drawing

Namespace BncWebWorks.ServerControls

Public Class SimpleControl
    Inherits Control '

    Private maxRows As Integer = 3
    Private maxCols As Integer = 5

    Protected Overrides Sub Render(writer As HtmlTextWriter)
        writer.WriteFullBeginTag("h1")
        writer.Write("Using the HtmlTextWriterClass")
        writer.WriteEndTag("h1")
        writer.WriteLine()

        ' Create the table
        writer.WriteBeginTag("table")
        writer.AddStyleAttribute(HtmlTextWriterStyle.FontWeight, "bold")
        writer.AddStyleAttribute(HtmlTextWriterStyle.FontFamily, "verdana")
        writer.AddStyleAttribute(HtmlTextWriterStyle.FontSize, "14pt")
        writer.WriteAttribute("border", "1")
        writer.Write(HtmlTextWriter.TagRightChar)
        writer.WriteLine()

        writer.Indent += 1
        Dim i As Integer
        For i = 0 To maxRows - 1

            writer.WriteFullBeginTag("tr")
            writer.WriteLine()

            writer.Indent += 1
            Dim j As Integer
            For j = 0 To maxCols - 1

                writer.WriteBeginTag("td")
                writer.WriteAttribute("valign", "top")
                writer.WriteAttribute("bgcolor", "lightblue")
                writer.Write(HtmlTextWriter.TagRightChar)

                writer.Write(("Cell (" + i.ToString() + "," + j.ToString() + ")"))

                writer.WriteEndTag("td")
                writer.WriteLine()
            Next j

            writer.Indent -= 1
            writer.WriteEndTag("tr")

            writer.WriteLine()
        Next i
        writer.Indent -= 1

        ' End the table
        writer.WriteEndTag("table")
        writer.WriteLine()
    End Sub 'Render
End Class 'SimpleControl
End Namespace 'BncWebWorks.ServerControls
```

C#

```csharp
using System;
using System.Web.UI;
using System.Drawing;

namespace BncWebWorks.ServerControls
{
    public class SimpleControl : Control
    {
        const int maxRows = 3;
        const int maxCols = 5;

        protected override void Render(HtmlTextWriter writer)
        {
            writer.WriteFullBeginTag("h1");
            writer.Write("Using the HtmlTextWriterClass");
            writer.WriteEndTag("h1");
            writer.WriteLine();

            // Create the table
            writer.WriteBeginTag("table");
            writer.AddStyleAttribute(HtmlTextWriterStyle.FontWeight,
                "bold");
            writer.AddStyleAttribute(HtmlTextWriterStyle.FontFamily,
                "verdana");
            writer.AddStyleAttribute(HtmlTextWriterStyle.FontSize, "14pt");
            writer.WriteAttribute("border","1");
            writer.Write(HtmlTextWriter.TagRightChar);
            writer.WriteLine();

            writer.Indent++;
            for (int i=0; i<maxRows; i++)
            {
                writer.WriteFullBeginTag("tr");
                writer.WriteLine();

                writer.Indent++;
                for (int j=0; j<maxCols; j++)
                {
                    writer.WriteBeginTag("td");
                    writer.WriteAttribute("valign","top");
                    writer.WriteAttribute("bgcolor","lightblue");
                    writer.Write(HtmlTextWriter.TagRightChar);

                    writer.Write("Cell (" + i.ToString() + "," +
                            j.ToString() + ")" );

                    writer.WriteEndTag("td");
                    writer.WriteLine();
                }
                writer.Indent--;
                writer.WriteEndTag("tr");
                writer.WriteLine();
            }
            writer.Indent--;

            // End the table
            writer.WriteEndTag("table");
            writer.WriteLine();
        }
    }
}
```

Lesson: Using Custom Controls

> **Lesson: Using Custom Controls**
> - Compiling and Deploying a Custom Control
> - Custom Control Interfaces
> - Creating the Control Object Model
> - Rendering Control Content
> - Using Data Binding in Custom Controls
> - Best Practices for Creating Custom Controls

Introduction

In the previous lesson, you learned about the architecture and essential elements of custom controls. In this lesson, you will learn how to use custom controls to enhance the functionality of your Web application.

Lesson Objectives

After completing this lesson, you will be able to:

- Describe the process of compiling and deploying a custom control.
- Understand the three most commonly used custom control interfaces.
- Identify the properties necessary to create a control's object model.
- Explain how to render control content.
- Describe how to use data-binding in custom controls.
- Understand recommended best practices for creating custom controls.

Compiling and Deploying a Custom Control

Compiling and Deploying the Control

- Compile a control by using:
  - The C# or Microsoft Visual Basic .NET command line compiler
  - The Microsoft Visual Studio Web Control Library project template
- Compiled controls
  - Should be moved to the application's bin directory
  - Must be registered
  - Can be modified by using the Properties box

Introduction

Unlike user controls, custom controls must be compiled into an assembly before they can be used. One way to compile the custom control is to use either the C# or Microsoft® Visual Basic® .NET command line compiler.

Compiling a Control

To compile the preceding code sample by using the C# compiler, you could open a command prompt and type:

```
csc /t:library /out:BncWebWorks.ServerControls.dll /r:System.dll
    /r:System.Web.dll SimpleControl.cs
```

Similar syntax could be used with the Visual Basic .NET compiler. After the control is compiled, you should move it to your application's bin directory, from which it can be deployed within the application by using a Registration directive on the pages where you wish to use the control.

As an alternative, Microsoft® Visual Studio® offers a Web Control Library project template. By authoring controls in this type of project, you can create several controls in the same project and allow clients to use them by making a project reference or by referencing the compiled assembly. In either case, you must have the compiled assembly in the bin directory of the application that requires the custom control.

Registering a Control

After the control is referenced, the page where it is to be used should implement a *Register* directive. To use the **SimpleControl** class compiled above, you could add the following code to the top of the page:

```
<%@ Register TagPrefix="ccl"
    Namespace="CustomControlLibraryVB.BncWebWorks.ServerControls"
    Assembly="CustomControlLibrary" %>
```

The control can be added to the Toolbox by right-clicking the Toolbox, selecting **Add/Replace Items**, locating the assembly, and then clicking the **Open** button. By dragging the control from the Toolbox onto the Web Form, the control is automatically registered. It is also represented in a form similar to how it will appear when the page is executed.

Setting Control Properties

The properties of the control can also be set by using the Properties box. The generated tags show the placement and attributes of the control:

```
<ccl:SimpleControl id=SimpleControl runat="server"></ccl:SimpleControl>
```

The developer will usually find it convenient to determine how the server tags that site the control on a Web Form are generated. By defining this, default values can be inserted into the tag, saving labor at design time. The **ToolboxData** attribute is normally used to accomplish this. It is placed immediately before the class declaration as follows:

Visual Basic .NET

```
<ToolboxData("<{0}:BarChartNoBind runat=server width=230px height=180px
    ChartTitle='Sample Chart'></{0}:BarChartNoBind>")> _
```

C#

```
[ToolboxData("<{0}:BarChartNoBind runat=server width=230px height=180px
    ChartTitle='Sample Chart'></{0}:BarChartNoBind>")]
```

In addition to automatically generating the Register directive and the server tags, default property values will be inserted when the control is sited on a form, such as the width and height properties illustrated below:

```
<cc1:BarChartNoBind id="BarChartNoBind1" runat="server" width="230px"
    height="180px" ChartTitle="Developing Web
    Services?"></cc1:BarChartNoBind>
```

Note that the name of the control – **BarChartNoBind** in this example – must match the name of the control class.

Custom Control Interfaces

> **Custom Control Interfaces**
>
> - **INamingContainer** – prevents naming conflicts
> - **IPostBackDataHandler** – allows controls to examine postback events
> - **IPostBackEventHandler** – allows controls to capture information submitted from the form

Introduction

It may be necessary to implement interface methods to gain control over the properties and postback behavior of the control. This section describes the three interfaces that are most commonly used for this purpose.

Common Custom Control Interfaces

The three interfaces most often used for custom controls are:

- **INamingContainer**. This interface is implemented by several data-bound controls such as **DataGrid**, **Repeater**, and **DataList**. Its purpose is to create a namespace in which all child control ID attributes (the **UniqueID** property) are guaranteed to be unique. This prevents naming conflicts from occurring on the pages that contain the control. This interface does not work by using a method but simply notifies ASP.NET that the control that implements it should be considered a naming container.

- **IPostBackDataHandler**. This interface is implemented by most of the standard Web controls. It allows controls to examine postback data, usually for the purpose of raising events. This is required in situations where the user can affect the state of a control, for instance by selecting an item from a drop-down list. Two methods are defined by this interface: **LoadPostData**, which allows controls to examine posted data, and **RaisePostDataChangedEvent**, which signals a state change.

- **IPostBackEventHandler**. This interface is used by Web controls that can raise a postback event. It allows the control to capture form submission information from the browser. When form information is submitted, the **RaisePostBackEvent** method is invoked for the server control that raised the event. This method allows the control to raise an event, such as a **Click** event for a button.

Creating the Control Object Model

Creating the Control Object Model

Options for persisting property values
- Explicitly set the properties when the page loads
- Use **ViewState** to persist the property values
- Use the **CreateChildControls** method to render control output

Introduction

When creating a control that produces a user interface, the developer should normally derive from the **WebControl** class. By doing so, a number of helpful properties are automatically inherited such as **Font**, **Height**, **Width**, and **BackColor**. These properties allow the control user to customize the control's appearance.

Other properties are necessary in order to create the control's object model. In the control built in this section, the bar chart's maximum value is exposed by using a **MaximumBarValue** property. After the object model is in place, it can be accessed by the control's rendering logic to output the content. To complete the control's its functionality, events can be exposed to the container, usually a **Page** object, so that the control's behavior can be customized.

Options for Persisting Property Values

The purpose of properties is to represent the state of the control. When defining properties, the developer needs to decide how they will be persisted. The three options for persisting property values are:

- Explicitly set the properties when the page loads. This frees the control from depending on **ViewState**, but requires that values must be reset and possibly recalculated or requeried from a database on each page load.

- Use **ViewState** to persist the property values. After postback, the page automatically restores the previous values of properties that use **ViewState** to store those values. An additional advantage of this option is that **ViewState** detects value modifications and only saves them when they change. This minimizes the size of the **ViewState**.

- Use the **CreateChildControls** method to render control output that allows controls to automatically preserve property values in **ViewState**.

Persisting Values in ViewState

The following code illustrates how a property can be defined so that its value will be persisted in **ViewState**.

Visual Basic .NET

```
Public Property ChartTitle() As String
    Get
        Return Convert.ToString(ViewState("ChartTitle"))
    End Get
    Set(ByVal Value As String)
        ViewState("ChartTitle") = Value
    End Set
End Property
```

C#

```
public string ChartTitle
    {
        get { return Convert.ToString(ViewState["ChartTitle"] );}
        set { ViewState["ChartTitle"] = value;}
    }
```

Note that the **DataSource** can also be persisted in the **ViewState**. This allows the data to be re-created on each page load without necessitating a roundtrip to the database if this is a data-bound control. Because bar charts do not typically hold large amounts of data, the approach adopted in the lab application is to persist the data in **ViewState**. To facilitate data-binding, it is convenient to have two locations for the data: one to store the initial data, which would not be persisted, and another to store and persist the processed data.

Only data types that can be serialized or have a type converter can be stored in **ViewState**. **ViewState** is optimized for the following data types: **Int32, Boolean, String, Unit, Color, Array, ArrayList**, and **Hashtable**. Other data types will incur more overhead, thereby degrading performance. Default property values can be set either in the constructor or in the get accessors of the property procedures.

When using **ViewState** to persist property values, the fundamental tradeoff is between the size of **ViewState** and the overhead of manually repopulating the values. The general rule is to use **ViewState** to set values for properties that incur significant overhead when they are restored, such as values that must be queried from a database. Large values (more than 2 kilobytes) should generally not be stored in **ViewState**.

Using Events

Many standard ASP.NET controls provide events that the developer can use to "hook into" the processing of a control element. To add a ToolTip to the header link in a **DataGrid** column, you can use the *ItemDataBound* event that occurs when the item is initially populated with data. The same model can be applied to custom controls.

In the charting example, custom events should be implemented to change the color of the bar whenever its value falls outside of a certain range. Events in controls follow the same pattern as events in other classes. You begin by declaring an event using a delegate. In the chart control, a delegate named **ChartEventHandler** will be declared as follows:

Visual Basic .NET

```
Public Delegate Sub ChartEventHandler(ByVal sender As Object, ByVal e As _
 ChartEventArgs)
```

C#

```
public delegate void ChartEventHandler(object sender, ChartEventArgs e);
```

After the delegate is declared, the events themselves can be declared as follows:

Visual Basic .NET

```
Public Event TableDrawn As ChartEventHandler
Public Event BarDrawn As ChartEventHandler
```

C#

```
public event ChartEventHandler TableDrawn;
public event ChartEventHandler BarDrawn;
```

When events are raised, it is often helpful to pass information about the event that took place so that the event processor can have ready access to useful values. In the case of the chart control, it would be beneficial to know whether the chart had been drawn yet, and to have access to the items that had been drawn such as the table, row, and bar items. An **EventArgs** class can hold this type of property, as shown in the following example:

Visual Basic .NET

```
Public Class ChartEventArgs
    Inherits EventArgs
    Public IsChartDrawn As Boolean
    Public ChartTable As Table
    Public ChartRow As TableRow
    Public Bar As SingleBar
End Class
```

C#

```
public class ChartEventArgs : EventArgs
{
    public bool IsChartDrawn;
    public Table ChartTable;
    public TableRow ChartRow;
    public SingleBar Bar;
}
```

After these elements are in place, you can raise the events at the appropriate point in the rendering of the output. This will take place at the end of the process of drawing the chart table.

Visual Basic .NET

```
Dim e As New ChartEventArgs
    e.IsChartDrawn = False
    e.ChartTable = outerTable
    e.ChartRow = Nothing
    RaiseEvent TableDrawn(Me, e)
```

C#

```
if (TableDrawn != null)
    {
        ChartEventArgs e = new ChartEventArgs();
        e.IsChartDrawn = false;
        e.ChartTable = outerTable;
        e.ChartRow = null;
        TableDrawn(this, e);
    }
```

After the event has been raised, the page hosting the control can react in whatever way is appropriate to the application. As the bar is being drawn, if its value falls below a particular amount, it will be drawn in red. To handle such events, the page uses an event handler method named **BarChartNoBind1_TableDrawn**:

Visual Basic .NET

```
Private Sub BarChartNoBind1_BarDrawn(ByVal sender As Object, ByVal e As _
ChartEventArgs) Handles BarChart1.BarDrawn
    If e.Bar.Value < 15 Then
        e.ChartRow.BackColor = Color.Red
    End If
End Sub
```

C#

```
private void BarChartNoBind1_BarDrawn(object sender, ChartEventArgs e)
  {
      if (e.Bar.Value < 15)
          e.ChartRow.BackColor = Color.Red;
  }
```

Rendering Control Content

Rendering Control Content

- **Render** method
  - Creates control content by using **HtmlTextWriter**
  - Requires that each part of the HTML be created separately, greatly increasing code size
  - Performs more quickly for small amounts of simple output
- **RenderControl** method
  - Instantiate server controls to represent content
  - Makes code easier to read and maintain
- **CreateChildControls** method
  - Causes the server control to create any contained controls
  - Preferred when user-entered values must be maintained between page refreshes

Introduction

The developer has two main choices for creating the control's output: The HTML can be rendered directly by using the **HtmlTextWriter** methods, or the output can be created by using server controls that recursively output their content to the **HtmlTextWriter** used by the page.

Render Method

The **Control** class supplies a **Render** method that can create the control content by using the **HtmlTextWriter** instance that is passed to the method. In the **SimpleControl** example above, the **HtmlTextWriter** used methods such as **WriteFullBeginTag** to directly create the output in the form of HTML tags. Although this method can be used for simple output, it causes several calls to be made to the writer. It also requires that each part of the HTML be created separately, which greatly increases the size of the code, as you can see from the code sample for the **SimpleControl**.

A variation on this method that is slightly more efficient is to write out HTML strings directly as in the following example. (Note that **output** is an instance of the **HtmlTextWriter**.)

Visual Basic .NET

```
output.Write("<table><tr><td>")
```

C#

```
output.Write("<table><tr><td>");
```

The main advantage of this approach is that it performs more quickly for small amounts of simple output. Using the tag-rendering methods of the **HtmlTextWriter** class simplifies formatting, reduces errors, and makes the code more readable. You should use the alternative method whenever several attributes must be rendered, or the structure of the HTML is complex.

RenderControl Method

The alternative approach is to instantiate server controls to represent the content you want to create. This makes the code easier to read and maintain when complex structures of nested HTML elements need to be produced. This technique uses server controls to build an in-memory representation of the HTML structures, and then transforms the object model into HTML format by using the **RenderControl** method of the individual controls.

RenderControl is the method invoked on each control by the **Page** class to create the output for each control in the control tree. The control tree is a representation of the child controls that the page contains. The derived Page class of the Web form is the root of this control tree. When the page is processed during a postback event, the **RenderControl** method is called on the page and then on each control in the control tree whose **Visible** property is set to true. The **RenderControl** method calls an overridden **Render** method on each control to actually produce the content.

The same method can be invoked in a custom control to create the output for its constituent controls. Although it might not be as efficient as generating HTML tags directly, this method results in more flexible and manageable code. It also allows the control to render different HTML depending on the browser.

In the bar chart control sample, the **Render** method creates the outer table that will contain the bar chart:

Visual Basic .NET

```
Protected Overrides Sub Render(ByVal output As HtmlTextWriter)
        // Draw the outer table
        Dim outerTable As Table = New Table
   ...
        // Draw the ChartTitle row
        Dim titleRow As TableRow = New TableRow
   ...
        outerTable.Rows.Add(titleRow)
   ...
// Draw the subtitle row
        Dim subtitleRow As TableRow = New TableRow
   ...
        outerTable.Rows.Add(subtitleRow)
            ...
// RenderControl
        outerTable.RenderControl(output)
```

C#

```csharp
protected override void Render(HtmlTextWriter output)
{
    // Draw the outer table
    Table outerTable = new Table();
    ...
    // Draw the ChartTitle row
    TableRow titleRow = new TableRow();
    ...
    outerTable.Rows.Add(titleRow);
    ...
    // Draw the subtitle row
    TableRow subtitleRow = new TableRow();
    ...
    outerTable.Rows.Add(subtitleRow);
        ...
    // RenderControl
    outerTable.RenderControl(output);
}
```

RenderControl creates the table by calling **Render** on each individual table control.

CreateChildControls Method

An alternative to the **Render** method for rendering control content is the **CreateChildControls** method, which causes the server control to create any contained controls. Because this method allows the child controls to automatically preserve **ViewState** for control properties, it is often preferred when user-entered values must be maintained between page refreshes.

In addition, this method avoids the need to manually implement postback event handling for child controls because control events are automatically raised. However, the **Render** method provides optimal performance. This performance advantage is lessened somewhat when using **RenderControl** as in the preceding example.

Using Data-Binding in Custom Controls

> ## Using Data Binding in Custom Controls
>
> - Data binding encapsulates the process of populating a control with data
> - The built-in ASP.NET server controls can be bound to any object that implements the **ICollection** or **IEnumerable** interface
>   - Any control that is bindable should have a **DataSource** property
>   - The bindable control also needs to override the **DataBind** method of the base **WebControl** class

Introduction

Some of the most frequently used controls in Microsoft® Windows® or Web applications are those associated with graphic display. A large number of third-party controls has arisen to serve the need to display information graphically. By using the HTML-rendering features of custom controls, many types of information can be represented graphically. Such controls can also take advantage of data-binding.

One of the new features of ASP.NET is the ability to generate graphics in response to user interaction by using the **System.Drawing** classes.

Binding Controls to Data

You have already seen how a chart can be graphically rendered by using a custom control. In real-world applications, binding controls to a data collection is essential to productivity. The built-in ASP.NET server controls can be bound to any object that implements the **ICollection** or **IEnumerable** interface. Any control that is bindable should have a **DataSource** property. It will also need to override the **DataBind** method of the base **WebControl** class. It is convenient to have a set of supporting properties to expose and format the data, such as **DataTextField**, **DataValueField**, and **DataValueFormatString**.

The previously created bar chart control populated its **DataSource** property by using an **Add** method. This **Add** method was called from an event handler from the page that was hosting the control. The control to be built in this section will retrieve data from a database at run time. Although data-binding encapsulates the process of populating a control with data, it is often advantageous to combine it with other techniques for adding data. You may want to bind a control to a data source and then add other items manually; for example, by adding an "All" item as the first item in a drop-down list.

.NET Framework Support for Data-Binding

In the .NET Framework, there are two sets of types that support data-binding:

- Types that implement **ICollection** or **IEnumerable**. These are collections and arrays, as well as the **DataView**.
- Types that implement **ITypedList** or **IListSource**. The types that support these interfaces are **DataSet** and **DataTable**.

If you have worked with data-bound controls, you are probably familiar with the **DataSource**, **DataTextField**, and **DataValueField** properties. The **DataSource** property represents the data source to be bound to the control. One of the first decisions the developer must make is whether to cache the data source in **ViewState**. When making this decision, the most important consideration is the amount of data expected to be cached. **ViewState** works best with small amounts of data, especially if the types do not require binary serialization. The **DataGrid** will often work with large amounts of data, so it does not store the data source object in **ViewState**. Instead it caches the data source in public properties. **DataTextField** and **DataValueField** will usually contain small amounts of text data, so they are good candidates for storing their values in **ViewState**. You can use the following code to store state for the properties:

Visual Basic .NET

```vbnet
Public Property DataTextField() As String
    Get
        Return Convert.ToString(ViewState("DataTextField"))
    End Get
    Set(ByVal Value As String)
        ViewState("DataTextField") = Value
    End Set
End Property
```

C#

```csharp
public string DataTextField
{
    get { return Convert.ToString(ViewState["DataTextField"]);}
    set { ViewState["DataTextField"] = value;}
}
```

Overriding the DataBind Method

When overriding the **DataBind** method, the first step is to call the **DataBind** method of the base class. By doing this, the handlers of the base class that evaluate data-binding expressions are invoked. Because the purpose of the **DataBind** method is to retrieve and render the data for binding, it should call a method that loads the data in a format suitable for binding. Using the example control for this section of the module, this method is illustrated with the following code:

Visual Basic .NET

```vbnet
Protected Overridable Sub LoadChartData()
    ' The method called puts data in enumerable form
    Dim rawData As IEnumerable = ResolveData(DataSource)
    If rawData Is Nothing Then
        Return
    End If
    ' Iterate through the rawData items
    Dim iterator As IEnumerator = rawData.GetEnumerator()
    While iterator.MoveNext()
        Dim rawDataItem As Object = iterator.Current
        Dim barLabel As String = CStr(DataBinder.Eval(rawDataItem, _
            DataTextField))
        Dim barValue As Single = _
            Convert.ToSingle(DataBinder.Eval(rawDataItem, _
                DataValueField))
        Add(barLabel, barValue)
    End While
End Sub 'LoadChartData
```

C#

```csharp
protected virtual void LoadChartData()
{
    IEnumerable rawData = ResolveData(DataSource);
    if (rawData == null)
        return;

    // Iterate through the rawData items
    IEnumerator iterator = rawData.GetEnumerator();
    while (iterator.MoveNext())
    {
        object rawDataItem = iterator.Current;
        string barLabel = (string) DataBinder.Eval(rawDataItem,
                DataTextField);
        float barValue =
                Convert.ToSingle(DataBinder.Eval(rawDataItem,
                    DataValueField));
        Add(barLabel, barValue);
    }
}
```

The **LoadChartData** method calls a **ResolveData** method that translates the data from the data source into an **IEnumerable** object. The method can then enumerate the data items and populate the **DataSource** (an **ArrayList**) by using the **Add** method. The key issue here is that **ResolveData** must return a collection of data items. These data items correspond to the items in the **DataTable**, **DataSet**, or **DataView** that the control binds to. The values from the data items are retrieved by using the **DataBinder.Eval** method, which extracts the value from the data item according to the current value of the **DataTextField** and **DataValueField** properties.

The purpose of the **ResolveData** method is to determine the type of the data source object and then return an enumerable collection of items. The following code accomplishes this task by checking to see if the object implements **IEnumerable**:

Visual Basic .NET

```
Private Function ResolveData(ByVal dataSource As Object) As _
    IEnumerable
      ' Check to see if the object implements IEnumerable (i.e.
      ' DataView)
    If Not (CType(dataSource, IEnumerable) Is Nothing) Then
        Return CType(dataSource, IEnumerable)
    End If
    Return Nothing
End Function 'ResolveData
```

C#

```
private IEnumerable ResolveData(object dataSource)
{
      // Check to see if the object implements IEnumerable (i.e.
      // DataView)
    if (dataSource as IEnumerable != null)
        return (IEnumerable) dataSource;
    return null;
}
```

After it is in this format, the **LoadChartData** method can read and extract the data.

The control must be registered by using a Register directive, and a declaration must be made for the control in the code-behind page. Because this control will be data-bound by using the **DataBind** method, a method to retrieve the data from the database should be supplied. After the data is retrieved, it can be assigned to the **DataSource** property of the control. The code in the client's code-behind file might resemble the following. (This code is from the code-behind file for the TestBoundBarChart.aspx page in the Democode for this module.)

Visual Basic .NET

```
Private Sub btnBind_Click(ByVal sender As System.Object, ByVal e As _
    System.EventArgs) Handles btnBind.Click
    Dim dt As DataTable = ExecuteQuery()
    BoundBarChart1.MaximumBarValue = 150000
    BoundBarChart1.DataValueFormatString = _
        "<span style=font-size:smaller>{0:c}</span>"
    BoundBarChart1.ChartTitle = "Category Sales"
    BoundBarChart1.SubTitle = "(Year 1997)"
    BoundBarChart1.DataSource = dt.DefaultView
    BoundBarChart1.DataTextField = "CategoryName"
    BoundBarChart1.DataValueField = "CategorySales"
    BoundBarChart1.DataBind()
End Sub
```

C#

```
private void btnBind_Click(object sender, System.EventArgs e)
{
    DataTable dt = ExecuteQuery();
    BoundBarChart1.MaximumBarValue = 150000;
    BoundBarChart1.DataValueFormatString = +
        "<span style=font-size:smaller>{0:c}</span>";
    BoundBarChart1.ChartTitle = "Category Sales";
    BoundBarChart1.SubTitle = "(Year 1997)";
    BoundBarChart1.DataSource = dt.DefaultView;
    BoundBarChart1.DataTextField = "CategoryName";
    BoundBarChart1.DataValueField = "CategorySales";
    BoundBarChart1.DataBind();
}
```

Best Practices for Creating Custom Controls

Best Practices for Creating Custom Controls

- Choose **System.Web.UI.WebControl** as the base class for a custom control if it will not be rendering a user interface
- Custom controls that will create a user interface should derive from **System.Web.UI.WebControl**
- Use **ViewState** to set values for properties that incur significant overhead when restored
- Use **RenderControl** to create HTML from controls to produce more flexible and manageable code

Introduction

This section describes a number of valuable practices to follow when creating custom Web controls.

Best Practices

Consider the following recommended best practices:

- Choose **System.Web.UI.WebControl** as the base class for a custom control if it will not be rendering a user interface; for example, when the control is to be used to embed keywords in a metatag.
- Custom controls that will create a user interface should derive from **System.Web.UI.WebControl**.
- As a general rule, use **ViewState** to set values for properties that incur significant overhead when they are restored, such as values that must be queried from a database.
- Although it might not be as efficient as generating HTML tags directly, using **RenderControl** to create HTML from controls results in more flexible and manageable code. It also allows the control to render different HTML depending on the browser.

Lab 4: Building Custom Controls

Lab 4: Building Custom Controls

- Exercise 1: Identifying Parts of a Data-bound Custom Control
- Exercise 2: Implementing a Data-bound Custom Control
- Exercise 3: Using a Data-bound Custom Control

Introduction

After completing this lab, you will have demonstrated your ability to:

- Define an object model for a custom control.
- Use render methods to create control output.
- Create events and event handlers to customize control appearance.
- Use the control on an ASP.NET page.

Prerequisites

Before working on this lab, you must have the knowledge and skills necessary to develop class files and Web Forms applications by using a Visual Studio .NET–compatible programming language. This lab also requires a strong grasp of class structure.

Estimated time to complete this lab: 45 minutes

Starting a Virtual Machine

1. On the student computer, on the **Start** menu, point to **All Programs**, and then click **Microsoft Virtual PC**. If the Virtual PC console window does not appear, then right-click the **Virtual PC icon** in the notification area (system tray), and click **Show Virtual PC Console**.

2. In the Virtual PC console window, select the virtual machine that you would like to open then click **Start**.

   NOTE: Depending on your time zone, the first time you start each of the virtual machines, you may receive an error message that the parent virtual hard disk appears to have been modified. You can ignore this message.

3. The virtual machine will start up in a new window.

Closing a Virtual Machine

1. On the student computer, in the virtual machine window, on the **Action** menu, click **Close**.

   NOTE: To avoid accidentally closing the virtual machine during the lab, the Close button in the top right corner of the virtual machine is disabled.

2. The virtual machine window will close. All changes to the virtual hard disk are discarded.

Exercise 1: Identifying Parts of a Data-Bound Custom Control

In this exercise, you will create two projects. One will be a Web Control Library named "ChartControlLibrary." The other will be a Web application that will contain a page to test the custom control. Starter files for each project are provided in the Labfiles folder for this module. You will add to the provided code to complete the exercise. Note that the Solution folder in each lab will contain the completed solution files.

■ Create the lab starter projects

1. Browse to D:\2311\Labfiles\Lab04\Starter\VB or D:\2311\Labfiles\Lab04\Starter\CS.

2. Double-click the Lab04.sln file. This solution contains a Web application named "UseChartControl" and a Web control library named "ChartControlLibrary."

- **Examine the Control Class Structure**

1. In the **ChartControlLibrary** project, open the code for the **BoundBarChart** class file.
2. Examine the following code:
    a. **ToolboxData Attribute**. This attribute defines how the control tags will be rendered on the aspx page. It can be used to set default values for control attributes.
    b. **Class Constructor**. The **Class Constructor** sets the default properties for the control. This task could also be done in the property get accessors.
    c. **Control Property Definitions**. After it is processed, the data is stored in **PersistedDataSource**.
    d. **Event Declarations**. Note the **BarDrawn** event declaration at the top of the class.
    e. **Add Method overloads**. Three **Add** method overloads allow data from the **DataSource** to be added to an **ArrayList**. Part of the main overload will be implemented.
    f. **CreateChildControls Method**. This method renders the HTML that defines the content of the control. At the end of the method, after all the child controls have been created, the **outputTable** is rendered when the control is added to the **Controls** collection.
    g. **DrawSingleBar**. Open the region for **Drawing Methods** if it is not already open. Examine the drawing methods. Identify the **DrawSingleBar** method. This method creates the output for a single bar in the bar chart table. You will implement part of this method.
    h. **Data Load Methods**. Open the region for **Data Load Methods**. There should be two sections of stub code: one for **LoadChartData**, the other for **ResolveData**. You will implement both of these methods.
    i. Study the **SingleBar** class, the delegate declaration, and the **EventArgs** classes at the end of the **BoundBarChart** class.

Exercise 2: Implementing a Data-Bound Custom Control

In this exercise, you will add code to the custom control to implement properties, raise events, add data, and resolve data sources. Data-binding makes controls much easier to populate. To make binding flexible, methods must be created to resolve the different types of data structures that might be used.

■ Add code to implement a persistent DataSource property

1. Open BoundBarChart.cs or BoundBarChart.vb and locate the code where the **DataSource** property is declared.

2. Immediately below this property procedure, create a protected overridable (virtual in C#) property procedure named **PersistedDataSource** that stores its value in an **ArrayList**. Your code should resemble the following:

Visual Basic .NET

```
Protected Overridable Property PersistedDataSource() As ArrayList
    Get
        Return mPersistedDataSource
    End Get
    Set(ByVal Value As ArrayList)
        mPersistedDataSource = Value
    End Set
End Property
```

C#

```
protected virtual ArrayList PersistedDataSource
{
    get { return mPersistedDataSource;}
    set { mPersistedDataSource = value;}
}
```

3. Locate the comment "TODO Add a DataBind method." Add a method named **DataBind** that overrides the base class's **DataBind** method.

4. In the **DataBind** method, call the **DataBind** method of the base class. This ensures that the handlers of the base class that evaluate data-binding expressions are invoked.

5. Call the **LoadChartData** method, which takes no parameters. This has not yet been implemented. You will implement it in the next exercise. Your code should resemble the following:

Visual Basic .NET

```
Public Overrides Sub DataBind()
    MyBase.DataBind()
    LoadChartData()
End Sub 'DataBind
```

C#

```
public override void DataBind()
{
    base.DataBind();
    LoadChartData();
}
```

6. Locate the comment "TODO Add each bar to the chartData object." First check to make sure that the **chartData** object (an ArrayList) is not null (Nothing in Visual Basic .NET). If not, add the **SingleBar** object to **chartData** by using the **Add** method. Store **chartData** in the **PersistedDataSource** property. Your code should resemble the following:

Visual Basic .NET

```
If Not (chartData Is Nothing) Then
    chartData.Add(sb)
End If
PersistedDataSource = chartData
```

C#

```
if (chartData != null)
    chartData.Add(sb);
PersistedDataSource = chartData;
```

7. Locate the comment "TODO Raise the BarDrawn event." In this section of the **DrawSingleBar** method, you will add code to raise the **BarDrawn** event. Populate each of the properties of the **BoundChartEventArgs** class:

   a. **IsChartCreated**: True

   b. **ContainerTable**: Nothing (null in C#)

   c. **CurrentRow**: **barArea**, which is the **TableRow** object that contains the bar

   d. **Bar**: the **Table** object that contains all the bar information

8. Your code should resemble the following:

Visual Basic .NET

```
Dim e As New BoundChartEventArgs
e.IsChartCreated = True
e.ContainerTable = Nothing
e.CurrentRow = barArea
e.Bar = sb
RaiseEvent BarDrawn(Me, e)
```

C#

```
if (BarDrawn != null)
{
    BoundChartEventArgs e = new BoundChartEventArgs();
    e.IsChartCreated = true;
    e.ContainerTable = null;
    e.CurrentRow = barArea;
    e.Bar = sb;
    BarDrawn(this, e);
}
```

9. Locate the comment "TODO Implement the LoadChartData method." The purpose of this method is to resolve the data source object into an enumerable object (an object that implements the **IEnumerable** interface).

10. Call the **ResolveData** method, passing in the **DataSource** object as the parameter. Assign the return value to object of type **IEnumerable**.

11. Check the return value. If it is empty, return from the procedure.

12. Use the **GetEnumerator** method of the **IEnumerable** object to retrieve an enumerator that can be used to iterate through the data items in the data object.

13. Use a **While** loop to iterate through the data items. In the loop, use the **Current** property of the enumerator to get the current data object. Assign the **barLabel** property the value of the current items property that corresponds to the **DataTextField**. Use the **DataBinder.Eval** method to extract this value.

14. Assign the **barValue** property the value of the **current items** property that corresponds to the **DataValueField**. Use the **DataBinder.Eval** method to extract this value.

15. Use the **Add** method to add the **barLabel** and **barValue**.

16. End the loop

17. Your code should resemble the following:

Visual Basic .NET

```
Protected Overridable Sub LoadChartData()
    ' The method called puts data in enumerable form
    Dim rawData As IEnumerable = ResolveData(DataSource)

    If rawData Is Nothing Then
        Return
    End If

    ' Iterate through the data items
    Dim iterator As IEnumerator = rawData.GetEnumerator()
    While iterator.MoveNext()
        Dim rawDataItem As Object = iterator.Current
        Dim barLabel As String = CStr(DataBinder.Eval(rawDataItem,
            DataTextField))
        Dim barValue As Single =
            Convert.ToSingle(DataBinder.Eval(rawDataItem, DataValueField))
        Add(barLabel, barValue)
    End While
End Sub
```

C#

```csharp
protected virtual void LoadChartData()
{
    // The method called puts data in enumerable form
    IEnumerable rawData = ResolveData(DataSource);
    if (rawData == null)
        return;

    // Iterate through the data items
    IEnumerator iterator = rawData.GetEnumerator();
    while (iterator.MoveNext())
    {
        object rawDataItem = iterator.Current;
        string barLabel = (string) DataBinder.Eval(rawDataItem,
            DataTextField);
        float barValue = Convert.ToSingle(DataBinder.Eval(rawDataItem,
            DataValueField));
        Add(barLabel, barValue);
    }
}
```

18. Locate the comment "TODO Implement the ResolveData method." The **ResolveData** method needs to determine what kind of data source object has been passed to the control so that it can be transformed into an object with a collection of enumerable data items.

19. Check to see if the data source implements the **IEnumerable** interface. If so, convert the **dataSource** object to an **IEnumerable** object and return it from the procedure.

20. If the object does not implement either interface, return **Nothing** (null in C#) from the procedure.

21. Your code should resemble the following:

Visual Basic .NET

```
Private Function ResolveData(ByVal dataSource As Object) As IEnumerable

    ' Check to see if the object implements IEnumerable (i.e. DataView)
    If Not (CType(dataSource, IEnumerable) Is Nothing) Then
        Return CType(dataSource, IEnumerable)
    End If
    Return Nothing
End Function 'ResolveData
```

C#

```
private IEnumerable ResolveData(object dataSource)
{
    // Check to see if the object implements IEnumerable (i.e. DataView)
    if (dataSource as IEnumerable != null)
        return (IEnumerable) dataSource;
    return null;
}
```

22. Build the project and correct any errors. You have now completed creating the custom control.

Exercise 3: Using a Data-Bound Custom Control

In this exercise, you will deploy the control and use it on an ASP.NET page. Custom controls can be added to the Toolbox and programmed visually. The fundament deployment steps will be practiced.

- **Deploying a Server Control**

1. Click the UseChartControl project name. Right-click and then select **Add Reference**. Add a project reference to the ChartControlLibrary project. Inspect the bin directory of the UseChartControl project to ensure that the ChartControlLibrary dll file has been added. The advantage of using a project reference is that changes in the project will be immediately reflected in the application that has the reference.

2. Add the control to the Toolbox. Right-click the Toolbox and then select **Add/Remove Items**. Click the **Browse** button and then navigate to the ChartControlLibrary folder. Open the bin\Debug (if C#) or bin folder (if Visual Basic .NET). Select the ChartControlLibrary.dll and then click **Open**. Confirm that the check box next to BoundBarChart is selected and click OK. The item will be added to the Toolbox.

3. Drag the **BoundBarChart** item onto the TestForm1.aspx page. Position it in the upper-left corner of the page. Resize the control to about 200 X 300 pixels.

4. Right-click the custom control and then select **Properties**. Note the properties that can be set in the properties box.

5. Open the code for the TestForm1.aspx page. Examine the **Register** directive at the top of the page. Note the assembly name and namespace attributes.

6. Examine the server control tags for the custom control. Note that the default name and property values have been set according to the attributes in the **ToolboxData** attribute in the **Control** class.

7. Drag a button control onto the form. Give it an ID of **btnBind** and set its **Text** property to **Bind**. Position it below the custom control.

8. Double-click the button to open stub code for the button's click event handler.

9. Add statements at the top of the code-behind file to import the **ChartControlLibrary.BncWebWorks** namespace (in Visual Basic .NET) or the **BncWebWorks** namespace (in C#) by using either Visual Basic .NET or C# syntax, as appropriate.

10. Use the following instructions to add code to the button click event handler to set properties for the **BoundBarChart** control. The default name for the control will be **BoundBarChart1**.

Advanced Web Application Development using Microsoft ASP .NET

11. Retrieve the **DataTable** that will be bound to the control by calling the function **ExecuteQuery**(). Assign the **DataTable** to a variable named "dt." This function executes a SQL statement that retrieves category names and sales from the Northwind database. Your code should resemble the following:

Visual Basic .NET

```
Dim dt As DataTable = ExecuteQuery()
```

C#

```
DataTable dt = ExecuteQuery();
```

12. Set the properties of BoundBarChart1 in the button click event handler according to the values in the following table:

Property	Value
MaximumBarValue	150000
DataValueFormatString	"{0:c}"
ChartTitle	"Category Sales"
ChartSubTitle	"(Year 1997)"
DataSource	dt.DefaultView
DataTextField	"CategoryName"
DataValueField	"CategorySales"

13. Call the **DataBind** method on the **BoundBarChart** control.

14. The complete code for the event handler should resemble the following:

Visual Basic .NET

```vb
Private Sub btnBind_Click(ByVal sender As System.Object, ByVal e As
    System.EventArgs) Handles btnBind.Click
        Dim dt As DataTable = ExecuteQuery()
        BoundBarChart1.MaximumBarValue = 150000
        BoundBarChart1.DataValueFormatString = "<span style=font-
            size:smaller>{0:c}</span>"
        BoundBarChart1.ChartTitle = "Category Sales"
        BoundBarChart1.ChartSubTitle = "(Year 1997)"
        BoundBarChart1.DataSource = dt.DefaultView
        BoundBarChart1.DataTextField = "CategoryName"
        BoundBarChart1.DataValueField = "CategorySales"
        BoundBarChart1.DataBind()
End Sub
```

C#

```csharp
private void btnBind_Click(object sender, System.EventArgs e)
{
    DataTable dt = ExecuteQuery();
    BoundBarChart1.MaximumBarValue = 150000;
    BoundBarChart1.DataValueFormatString = "<span style=font-
        size:smaller>{0:c}</span>";
    BoundBarChart1.ChartTitle = "Category Sales";
    BoundBarChart1.ChartSubTitle = "(Year 1997)";
    BoundBarChart1.DataSource = dt.DefaultView;
    BoundBarChart1.DataTextField = "CategoryName";
    BoundBarChart1.DataValueField = "CategorySales";
    BoundBarChart1.DataBind();
}
```

15. Implement an event handler for the **BarDrawn** event with the name **BoundBarChart1_BarDrawn** and two parameters: **sender** with the type **Object** and **e** with the type of **BoundBarChart.BoundChartEventArgs**. (You might have to add the **BncWebWorks** namespace.)

16. Add code to the method to check if **e.IsChartCreated** is true. If it is true, check whether **e.Item.Value** is greater that 80,000. If this is true, set the **e.CurrentRow.BackColor** property to **Color.Green**. Check whether **e.Item.Value** is less than 60,000. If this is true, set the **e.CurrentRow.BackColor** to **Color.Red**.

17. Connect the event handler to the event by using either Visual Basic .NET or C# syntax as appropriate.

18. The code for the BarDrawn event handler should resemble the following:

Visual Basic .NET

```
Private Sub BoundBarChart1_BarDrawn(ByVal sender As Object, ByVal e As
    BoundBarChart.BoundChartEventArgs) Handles BoundBarChart1.BarDrawn
    If (e.IsChartCreated) Then
        If (e.Bar.Value > 80000) Then
            e.CurrentRow.BackColor = Color.Green
        End If
        If (e.Bar.Value < 60000) Then
            e.CurrentRow.BackColor = Color.Red
        End If
    End If
End Sub
```

C#

```
private void BoundBarChart1_BarDrawn(object sender,
    BoundBarChart.BoundChartEventArgs e)
{
    if (e.IsChartCreated)
    {
        if (e.Bar.Value > 80000)
            e.CurrentRow.BackColor = Color.Green;
        if (e.Bar.Value < 60000)
            e.CurrentRow.BackColor = Color.Red;
    }
}
```

19. Compile the application and correct any errors.

20. Test the page by viewing it in the browser and clicking the **Bind** button. The bars with values less than $60,000 appear in red, while those with values greater than $80,000 appear in green. Bars with values between $60,000 and $80,000 appear in the default blue color.

Module 5: Using Graphics Classes to Generate Images

> **Module 5: Using Graphics Classes to Generate Images**
> - ASP.NET Graphical Tools
> - Creating and Modifying Images

Overview

This module describes how to use the classes in the **System.Drawing** namespace to generate images in Microsoft ASP.NET pages. It is often necessary to create images in response to user interaction. The classes included in Microsoft Windows Graphics Device Interface (GDI+) provide a powerful and flexible set of tools to produce such images. In many cases, the images will be populated by using data from a database. This module demonstrates best practices for implementing user data to populate such commonly used business graphics as bar charts and pie charts using three-dimensional (3-D) effects.

Objectives

After completing this module, you will be able to:

- Describe the major elements of the GDI+ object model.
- Use the main GDI+ methods to manipulate graphical images.
- Create an ASP.NET page that creates chart graphics by using data objects.

Lesson: ASP.NET Graphical Tools

Lesson: ASP.NET Graphical Tools

- **System.Drawing** Classes
- Using the Methods of the **Graphics** Object
- Demonstration: Using Graphics Methods on an ASP.NET Page

Overview

ASP.NET supports a number of useful tools and methods that you can use to manipulate graphical images in your Web application. This lesson introduces some of the most important of these tools of methods, and demonstrates their use on an ASP.NET page.

Lesson Objectives

After completing this module, you will be able to:

- Explain the uses of the **System.Drawing** classes.
- Describe the principal tools and methods used for drawing.
- Explain how graphics methods are used on an ASP.NET page.

Course Note

Module 4, "Building Custom Controls" and this module contain similar material. Due to the time constraints of this course, either module 4 or 5 can be skipped. If time permits, you can review the skipped module at the end of day 3.

System.Drawing Classes

> **System.Drawing Classes**
>
> - Major namespaces in GDI+
>   - **System.Drawing**: basic classes such as **Graphics** and **Bitmap**
>   - **System.Drawing.Imaging**: image formats such as GIF and JPEG
>   - **System.Drawing.Drawing2d**: advanced graphics functionality such as gradient brushes
> - The **Graphics** object
>   - Acts as a "canvas" for you to draw on
>   - **Bitmap** supplies the object you use to work with images

Introduction

Web sites often need to deliver information in graphical format. For example, on a financial site a user might want information about a particular stock. Along with information in text format, a graphical stock chart could be returned that presents data within a date range selected by the user. This type of graphical presentation is made possible by the graphics classes found in the **System.Drawing** namespace, which can generate images in response to user selections.

GDI+

The Windows Graphics Device Interface (GDI+) is the graphics engine for Microsoft Windows XP. For platforms other than Windows XP, the gdiplus.dll must be installed. This is done automatically when the Microsoft .NET Framework is installed. GDI+ is built into the .NET Framework and is available from any .NET application, including ASP.NET.

GDI+ comprises a set of managed classes. The major namespaces for GDI+ are the following:

- **System.Drawing**. This namespace provides basic graphics functionality and essential classes such as **Graphics**, **Pen**, **Brush**, and **Bitmap**. These classes allow line, rectangle, and shape drawing. The **Graphics** class also allows text string output. For more advanced text functions, the **System.Drawing.Text** namespace allows users to create collections of fonts.
- **System.Drawing.Imaging**. This namespace primarily contains classes for manipulating such image formats as *.gif and *.jpeg. The **ImageFormat** class is used to specify the format of an image such as GIF or PNG.
- **System.Drawing.Drawing2D**. This namespace provides advanced graphics functionality such as gradient brushes, transformations, and other special graphics effects.

The Graphics Object

In order to create images, an object of type **Graphics** is required. However, this object cannot be directly instantiated because it does not have a public constructor. To generate a **Bitmap** from an ASP.NET page, you will normally use the **FromImage** method of the **Graphics** class. This method returns an object of type **Graphics** and uses a **Bitmap** as the input parameter, as shown in following code example:

Microsoft Visual Basic .NET

```
bmAlpha = New Bitmap(300, 300)
    grCanvas = Graphics.FromImage(bmAlpha)
```

C#

```
bmAlpha = new Bitmap(300, 300);
grCanvas = Graphics.FromImage(bmAlpha);
```

The **Graphics** object plays the role of a canvas for you to draw on. The **Bitmap** class encapsulates pixel data, specifying properties such as the size of the canvas and the pixel format (the number of memory bits per pixel), also known as the "color depth". In other words, **Bitmap** supplies the object you use to work with images. It is a rectangular array of bits that correspond to the pixels to be rendered on the screen. It allows the developer to directly read and write individual pixel values.

Web developers may be confused by the **Bitmap** class name. An instance of a **Bitmap** class is *not* a *.bmp file. **Bitmaps** can encapsulate pixel data for any image type, including GIF-, JPEG-, or PNG-formatted images. The **FromImage** method of the **Graphics** class accepts a **Bitmap, Metafile,** or **Icon** object. You can manipulate the image by using the returned **Graphics** object. Any **Graphics** methods that are called will affect the **Bitmap** from which it was created.

The **Bitmap** object can be created from a pre-existing image, thereby allowing you to load that image and add new features to it. **Bitmap** constructors allow images to be created from files, streams, and resources. The files can be in any supported image format. The manipulated image can also be saved to any supported format including **BMP, GIF, JPEG, PNG, TIFF, WMF,** and **ICON**. The **Bitmap** also has a **RotateFlip** method that can be used to rotate or flip the image.

Using the Methods of the Graphics Object

> **Using the Methods of the Graphics Object**
>
> - Pen object
>   - Used to draw lines and curves
>   - Has the following methods:
>   - **DrawLine**
>   - **DrawRectangle**
>   - **DrawEllipse**
>   - **DrawPie & FillPie**
> - Brush object
>   - Fills areas enclosed by lines and curves with color
>   - Has the following classes:
>   - **SolidBrush**
>   - **TextureBrush**
>   - **HatchBrush**
>   - **LinearGradientBrush**
>   - **PathGradientBrush**

Introduction

In this topic, you will learn about the major drawing tools of the **Graphics** class, including the **Pen** and **Brush** objects, as well as methods for drawing lines and rectangles.

Pen Object

The **Pen** object is used to draw lines and curves. When creating a pen, you should specify the color in the **Pen** constructor. (The following code excerpts are contained in the code-behind page for the PaintImage.aspx page.)

Visual Basic .NET

```
penColor = Color.White
  webPen = New Pen(penColor)
```

C#

```
penColor = Color.White(drawColor);
  webPen = new Pen(penColor);
```

In addition, you can create a **Pen** with a specific color by using the **Pens** class, which has a **Pen** for all of the standard colors; for example, **Pens.HotPink**. To ensure that a **Pen** will use a color that will be visible against the background color chosen by a user, you use the **ForeColor** property as follows:

Visual Basic .NET
```
Dim pen As Pen = New Pen(ForeColor)
```

C#
```
Pen pen = new Pen(ForeColor);
```

Width Property

By default, pens have a pixel width of one pixel. To set the width to a different value, use the **Width** property or create the Pen by using a constructor that accepts a **Width** parameter. The following code creates a red pen with a width of 10 pixels:

Visual Basic .NET
```
Dim pen As Pen = New Pen(Color.Red, 10)
```

C#
```
Pen pen = new Pen(Color.Red, 10);
```

DrawLine Method

To draw a straight line, you use the **DrawLine** method of the **Graphics** object. All of the overloads for this method require the following elements: a starting point, an ending point, and a pen to draw the line. The following code draws a line from the coordinate point at (1,1) to the point at (6,6), making a line 5 pixels long. **dynImage** is a **Graphics** object:

Visual Basic .NET

```
dynImage.DrawLine(Pens.SeaGreen, 1, 1, 6, 6)
```

C#

```
dynImage.DrawLine(Pens.SeaGreen, 1, 1, 6, 6);
```

DrawRectangle Method

To create a rectangle, you use the **DrawRectangle** method of the **Graphics** object. To specify a rectangle, you need to supply the upper-left starting point with coordinate values, a width, a height, and a pen to draw the rectangle. The overloads to the method allow two ways to do this. In one, you specify the upper left coordinates, along with a width and height. In the other, you create a **Rectangle** object and pass it as the second parameter to the method.

To create a sea-green rectangle that starts at the point (5, 10) and has a width of 60 pixels and a height of 40 pixels (suitable for picture legends, as you will see later), use the following code:

Visual Basic .NET

```
dynImage.DrawRectangle(Pens.SeaGreen, 5, 10, 60, 40)
```

C#

```
dynImage.DrawRectangle(Pens.SeaGreen, 5, 10, 60, 40);
```

DrawEllipse Method

Drawing circles and ellipses makes use of a similar method: **DrawEllipse**. To use this method, you need to define a rectangle that will contain the circle or ellipse and an upper-left starting point for the rectangle. Although the rectangle is invisible, it defines the placement and shape of the ellipse it contains. A **Pen** must be furnished to draw the object. The following code creates a circle inside a rectangle with an upper-left coordinate point at (100, 200), a width of 200 pixels, and a height of 200 pixels, using a powder-blue colored **Pen**:

Visual Basic .NET

```
dynImage.DrawEllipse(Pens.PowderBlue, 100, 200, 200, 200)
```

C#

```
dynImage.DrawEllipse(Pens.PowderBlue, 100, 200, 200, 200);
```

DrawPie Method

Because the pie chart is considered a basic tool for business presentations, two methods are dedicated to producing the necessary shapes: **DrawPie** and **FillPie**. You will learn about the **FillPie** method after examining the **Brush** object. **DrawPie** allows you to describe an arc shape within a circle or ellipse.

To describe a part of an ellipse, you first describe the ellipse by using a rectangle with an upper-left coordinate point, a width, a height, and a **Pen** with the appropriate color. In addition, a pie is defined by using the starting point of an angle (with a vertical line defined as 0), and the sweep angle, which specifies how far the angle extends. The following code uses the same-size circle as that created above and defines a pie section with a sweep angle of 45 degrees:

Visual Basic .NET

```
dynImage.DrawEllipse(Pens.PowderBlue, 100, 200, 200, 200, 0, 45)
```

C#

```
dynImage.DrawEllipse(Pens.PowderBlue, 100, 200, 200, 200, 0, 45);
```

Brush Object

The **Brush** object fills areas enclosed by lines and curves with color. It is also used to draw text. Because **Brush** is an abstract class, it cannot be instantiated. The names of its derivative classes indicate the type of brushes available to work with:

- **SolidBrush**
- **TextureBrush**
- **HatchBrush**
- **LinearGradientBrush**
- **PathGradientBrush**

Of these, the type most-often used is **SolidBrush**, which fills its area with a solid color. The **LinearGradientBrush** is used to blend from one color to another over a rectangular area. You create a **SolidBrush** by passing a color to its constructor as follows:

Visual Basic .NET

```
Dim orangeBrush As Brush = New SolidBrush(Color.Orange)
```

C#

```
Brush orangeBrush = new SolidBrush(Color.Orange);
```

After a **Brush** object has been created, it can be used for the **Fill** methods of the **Graphics** object. For example, to fill a rectangle, you use one of the overloads of the **FillRectangle** method and pass in a **Brush** as the first parameter, as shown in the following code example:

Visual Basic .NET

```
dynImage.FillRectangle(New SolidBrush(DarkKhaki), 5, 10, 60, 40)
```

C#

```
dynImage.FillRectangle(new SolidBrush(DarkKhaki), 5, 10, 60, 40)
```

Note that the syntax is almost identical to the **DrawRectangle** method. The only difference is that a **Brush** is used rather than a **Pen**. The same idea applies to ellipses and pies.

FillPie Method

FillPie works in a similar way to **FillRectangle**, but just as **DrawPie** creates a shape proportional to the ellipse that describes the pie, **FillPie** fills the section of the pie according to the underlying shape of the ellipse. Because the purpose of **FillPie** is to fill part of an ellipse, you must designate the starting angle and the sweep, which are the last two parameters. **FillPie** fills the designated portion of the pie with the specified color as illustrated below:

Visual Basic .NET

```
dynImage.FillPie(New SolidBrush(penColor), previousX, previousY, currentX - previousX, currentY - previousY, 0, 45)
```

C#

```
dynImage.FillPie(new SolidBrush(penColor), previousX, previousY, currentX - previousX, currentY - previousY, 0, 45);
```

Demonstration: Using Graphics Methods on an ASP.NET Page

Introduction

This demonstration illustrates some of the major methods of the **Graphics** class that can be used to generate graphics on ASP.NET pages.

- **Using graphics methods on an ASP.NET page**

    1. In Windows Explorer, browse to D:\2311\Democode\Mod05*language*.

    2. Open the Mod05 project by double-clicking **Mod05.sln**.

    3. View the Painter.aspx page in the browser and demonstrate its functionality. Show the method names in the Draw list box and the colors in the Colors list box. Draw several lines and shapes with different colors.

    4. Open the code-behind for the page and examine the **ibtnCanvas_Click** event handler. Note how the querystring is built by using values from the Draw and Color list boxes.

    5. Open the code-behind page for the PaintImage.aspx page. This page generates the image that appears in the **ImageButton** on the Painter.aspx page.

6. In the **Page_Load** method, note where the **Bitmap** object is created and how it is used in the **FromImage** method of the **Graphics** class.

7. Examine how the **Pen** object is created.

8. Study the parameters called in each of the graphics methods used in the **Select** statement (**switch** if you use C#).

9. Note how the **Save** method of the **Bitmap** object can transform the format of an image.

Lesson: Creating and Modifying Images

Lesson: Creating and Modifying Images
- Modifying Images Dynamically
- Building Data-Driven Images
- Best Practices for Creating Graphics

Overview

After you have mastered the basic tools and techniques for manipulating graphical images in ASP.NET, you may find it advantageous to learn some of the more advanced techniques. This lesson introduces techniques for making in-memory modifications to images and for customizing image output based on database calls.

Lesson Objectives

After completing this module, you will be able to:

- Modify images dynamically by saving and manipulating them directly in memory.
- Create and manipulate data-driven images such as bar charts and pie charts.
- Describe the recommended best practices for creating images.

Modifying Images Dynamically

Modifying Images Dynamically

- Manipulating images in memory
  - Use the **Save** method of the **Bitmap** object to send an image into the response stream
- Adding and formatting text
  - Load images into a **Bitmap** object for manipulation
  - Use the **DrawString** method of the **Graphics** object to write text on an image
  - Use the **MeasureString** method to measure the size of text to be inserted into the image

Introduction

As an alternative to writing images to disk, you can modify the images directly in memory. This section explains how to modify images dynamically by using this approach.

Manipulating Images in Memory

You manipulate images in memory by using the **Save** method of the **Bitmap** object to send an image into the response stream. The relevant overload takes two parameters: a **Stream** object and an **ImageFormat**, as illustrated in the following example:

Visual Basic .NET

```
bmpProtectedImage.Save(Response.OutputStream, ImageFormat.Gif)
```

C#

```
bmpProtectedImage.Save(Response.OutputStream, ImageFormat.Gif);
```

The Stream parameter can be any stream object, such as a **MemoryStream** or a **NetworkStream** object. When working with an ASP.NET application, the stream will normally be the response stream.

Adding and Formatting Text

One common need among Web applications is to load an existing image and modify the output, such as by adding text. For example, you might want to add a copyright notice to discourage image theft. The most efficient way to load existing images for manipulation is to load them into a **Bitmap** object.

You use the **DrawString** method of the **Graphics** object to write text on an image. To call the method, you need to supply the string to write, a font, a brush to color it, and a rectangle to specify where to put it. The following code shows how the message could be written on the image:

Visual Basic .NET

```
Dim txtFormat As New StringFormat
 txtFormat.Alignment = StringAlignment.Near

Dim topColor As New SolidBrush(Color.Black)
Dim rectArea As New RectangleF(0, 0, bmpProtectedImage.Width, _
    bmpProtectedImage.Height)
 Dim topFont As New Font("Tahoma", 12, FontStyle.Bold)
 grpCanvas.DrawString(msg, topFont, topColor, rectArea, txtFormat)
```

C#

```
StringFormat txtFormat = new StringFormat();
 txtFormat.Alignment = StringAlignment.Near;

SolidBrush topColor = new SolidBrush(Color.Black);
 Rectangle rectArea = new RectangleF(0, 0, bmpProtectedImage.Width,
    bmpProtectedImage.Height);
 Font topFont = new Font("Tahoma", 12, FontStyle.Bold);
 grpCanvas.DrawString(msg, topFont, topColor, rectArea, txtFormat);
```

A **RectangleF** structure specifies the rectangle's dimensions by using floating point numbers. In the example shown here, the rectangle matches the width and height of the **Bitmap**. The text will be positioned in the upper-left corner according to the x and y coordinates selected. The last parameter of the **DrawString** method is an enumerated value of type **StringFormat**. These values allow you to specify how the text is formatted. For example, you can lay out the text vertically by using a **StringFormatFlags** value of **DirectionVertical**, or by using the **Alignment** property to specify **Near**, **Far**, or **Center** alignment. The **Dispose** method must be called on **Font** and **Brush** objects in order to release their resources.

It is usually necessary to measure the size of the text to be inserted into the image so that it can be correctly placed. The **MeasureString** method of the **Graphics** object measures string size in pixels by using a particular font and font size, and returns a **SizeF** structure. A **SizeF** structure represents the size of a rectangular region that contains the text string. It can be used to calculate how much space the text string will require so that it can be placed in a rectangular region.

After the textual information has been written to the image, it can be streamed into the browser client by saving to a **MemoryStream** object. This object represents a stream of data held in memory rather than on a disk file or through a network connection. Its data is stored as an unsigned byte array. The advantage of this approach is to reduce the need for temporary buffers and files, which can be particularly helpful in ASP.NET applications.

Calling the **Save** method of the **Bitmap** object can transform the image format. To use any format other than GIF or JPEG, use the **GetBuffer** method and the **Response.BinaryWrite** method to output the content.

Building Data-Driven Images

> **Building Data-Driven Images**
>
> - Creating Bar Charts
>   - Draw bars by using **FillRectangle** and **DrawRectangle**
>   - Use special **Brush** classes to create 3-D effects
>   - Use **HatchBrush** to create a shadow effect
>   - Use **LinearGradientBrush** to create the appearance of depth
> - Creating Pie Charts
>   - Use **FillPie** to create pie wedges
>   - Use an array of colors to ensure color contrast
>   - Use **FillRectangle** and **DrawString** to create legends for the chart

Introduction

One of the most valuable techniques for generating images is to customize image output based on database calls. For example, you can create charts of many different types in response to user choices without having to store static images. Two of the most popular chart types will be examined here: bar charts and pie charts.

Creating Bar Charts

A bar chart is made up of rectangles of various sizes. The developer's main job is to determine the size of each bar and format them attractively. The **FillRectangle** method of the **Graphics** object can be used to create the rectangles, while **DrawRectangle** can be used to create an outline around the rectangles. Different brush types can contribute special effects such as 3-D graphics.

Any graphics generation begins with the **Graphics** class. To set up the background color for the graphic, you use the **Clear** method to clear the drawing surface and fill it with the specified background color. For example, to create an ivory-colored background, you would use the following code:

Visual Basic .NET

```
grBarChart.Clear(Color.Ivory)
```

C#

```
grBarChart.Clear(Color.Ivory);
```

Next, you need to retrieve the data used to calculate the values for the graphic. Because this is ordinary ADO.NET code, the **DataSet** is likely to be the most appropriate object for populating charts since it allows the data to be reused as different parts of the output are drawn. For example, you might need to draw a legend, a series of captions, and the bars for the chart. Making repeated database calls for each operation would not be as efficient.

After the data has been retrieved, you need to determine the maximum value of the dimension that will be used to calculate the size of the bars. If the chart is to display sales numbers, the bar with the highest sales figure should be discovered. This can be used to measure the relative heights of the bars. The **Compute** method of the **DataTable** allows such values to be easily determined, as illustrated below:

Visual Basic .NET

```
Dim maxSales As Single = Convert.ToSingle(dt.Compute("Max(CategorySales)", ""))
```

C#

```
float maxSales = Convert.ToSingle(dt.Compute("Max(CategorySales)", ""));
```

Although creating bars with the appropriate height is a straightforward process, it will not result in a very attractive image. To give the chart a more striking appearance, examine some of the **Brush** classes that are members of the **System.Drawing.Drawing2D** namespace.

For example, creating a shadow behind the bar or pie can give the chart a 3-D effect. You can use **HatchBrush** to simulate color shading, which creates the appearance of a shadow. For the bar chart you will create in the lab, you will use a **HatchBrush** with a **HatchStyle** property of **Percent50**. The only way to create this effect is to repeatedly redraw the bar with a different offset each time. Because you are populating the bars in a loop, you will add another bar with an offset and use the **HatchBrush** to color this shaded area.

To calculate the right location for the offset, two nested loops will be created. The outer loop will create the shadow, and the inner loop will create the bars. The following code creates the bar and the shadow rectangle:

Visual Basic .NET

```
Dim solidBar As New Rectangle(x, barTop, barWidth - 10, barHeight)
Dim captionBar As New Rectangle(x, barBase + textAreaHeight, totalWidth, _
    textAreaHeight)
Dim barShadow As New Rectangle(solidBar.Location, solidBar.Size)
barShadow.Offset(j, -j)
grBarChart.FillRectangle(New HatchBrush(HatchStyle.Percent50, Color.Blue), _
    barShadow)
grBarChart.FillRectangle(New LinearGradientBrush(solidBar, Color.Blue, _
    Color.LightBlue, LinearGradientMode.Horizontal), solidBar)
```

C#

```
Rectangle solidBar = new Rectangle(x, barTop, barWidth-10, barHeight);
Rectangle captionBar = new Rectangle(x, barBase + textAreaHeight, totalWidth,
    textAreaHeight);
Rectangle barShadow = new Rectangle(solidBar.Location, solidBar.Size);
barShadow.Offset(j, -j);
grBarChart.FillRectangle(new HatchBrush(HatchStyle.Percent50, Color.Blue),
    barShadow);
grBarChart.FillRectangle(new LinearGradientBrush(solidBar, Color.Blue,
    Color.LightSkyBlue, LinearGradientMode.Horizontal), solidBar);
```

The **Offset** method adjusts the location of the rectangle by the specified amounts along the x and y axes.

The appearanace of depth can also be approximated by using a **LinearGradientBrush**. A *gradient* refers to a transition between two colors. A *linear gradient* is defined by a line that connects two points. Each point contains a color, and the gradient effect transitions from one color to the other. The final effect is a 3-D bulge effect applied to the bars in the bar chart. The effect is created by applying a **LinearGradientBrush** in the **FillRectangle** method and specifying a beginning and ending color, along with a type of transition. You can set the **LinearGradientMode** to make horizontal, vertical, or diagonal transitions.

Creating Pie Charts

The same data can also be used to create pie charts. When creating pie charts, the same outer and inner loops can be used as with bar charts. The outer loop is used to create the 3-D background effect by using the **Offset** method. The **FillPie** method of the **Graphics** class draws the wedges that correspond to the data.

Recall that when using **FillPie**, you must define a rectangle that will invisibly contain the ellipse or circle. For the example here, you will use the **FillPie** overload that takes four parameters: a **Brush**, a rectangle, a starting angle, and a sweep angle. The loop begins with a starting angle of 0 and adds a sweep angle corresponding to each new part of the data. The example here will retrieve sales figures for each product category in the Northwind database, so pie wedges will correspond to the total sales for each category. The **DrawEllipse** method can be used to draw a border around the ellipse.

As each pie wedge is drawn, it needs to have a color that distinguishes it from the wedge next to it. The easiest way to achieve an attractive effect is to create an array of colors larger than the number of wedges your data will produce. This ensures that the same colors will not appear side by side.

The 3-D effect for a pie chart calls for a technique similar to what was used in the bar chart. Instead of a rectangle, the wedges will be redrawn several times according to a varying offset value. As before, you will use a **HatchBrush** with a **HatchStyle.Percent50** to create the offset ellipse. The central code segment is as follows. (The following code snippets are from the DynamicPieChart.aspx page in the Democode for this module.)

Visual Basic .NET

```
Dim shadowSize As New Rectangle(pieArea.Location, pieArea.Size)
shadowSize.Offset(j, j)
grBarChart.FillPie(New HatchBrush(HatchStyle.Percent50, sliceColor), _
    shadowSize, startAngle, sweepAngle)
' Generate pie wedge
grBarChart.FillPie(New SolidBrush(sliceColor), pieArea, startAngle, _
    sweepAngle)
grBarChart.DrawEllipse(New Pen(Color.DarkGray, 1), pieArea)
startAngle += sweepAngle
```

C#

```
Rectangle shadowSize = new Rectangle(pieArea.Location, pieArea.Size);
shadowSize.Offset(j, j);
grBarChart.FillPie(new HatchBrush(HatchStyle.Percent50, sliceColor),
    shadowSize, startAngle, sweepAngle);
// Generate pie wedge
grBarChart.FillPie(new SolidBrush(sliceColor), pieArea, startAngle,
    sweepAngle);
grBarChart.DrawEllipse(new Pen(Color.DarkGray, 1), pieArea);
startAngle += sweepAngle;
```

Drawing a descriptive label on the wedges of the pie can present significant problems. Rather than performing the trigonometric calculations necessary to calculate the exact position of the labels for the wedges, you can create a legend. Inside a loop for each part of the data that corresponds to the wedges, you will use the **FillRectangle** and **DrawRectangle** methods to create colored rectangles with the colors of each wedge. Next to the colored rectangles, write the label by using the **DrawString** method. The code is illustrated below:

Visual Basic .NET

```vb
Dim rectLeg As New PointF(335, 20)
Dim labelLeg As New PointF(360, 16)

Dim rowCount As Integer = dt.Rows.Count
i = 0
For i = 0 To rowCount - 1
    grBarChart.FillRectangle(New SolidBrush(colors(i)), rectLeg.X, _
    rectLeg.Y, 20, 10)
    grBarChart.DrawRectangle(Pens.Black, rectLeg.X, rectLeg.Y, 20, 10)

    grBarChart.DrawString(dt.Rows(i)("CategoryName").ToString(), New _
        Font("Verdana", 10), Brushes.Black, labelLeg)
    rectLeg.Y += 15
    labelLeg.Y += 15
Next i
```

C#

```csharp
PointF rectLeg = new PointF(335, 20);
PointF labelLeg = new PointF(360, 16);

int rowCount = dt.Rows.Count;
for(int i = 0; i < rowCount; i++)
{
    grBarChart.FillRectangle(new SolidBrush(colors[i]), rectLeg.X,
    rectLeg.Y, 20, 10);
    grBarChart.DrawRectangle(Pens.Black, rectLeg.X, rectLeg.Y, 20,
    10);
grBarChart.DrawString(dt.Rows[i]["CategoryName"].ToString(), new
    Font("Verdana", 10), Brushes.Black, labelLeg);
    rectLeg.Y += 15;
    labelLeg.Y += 15;
}
```

Best Practices for Creating Graphics

> **Best Practices for Creating Graphics**
> - Use **MemoryStream** to create graphics in memory
> - Use **GetBuffer** and **Response.BinaryWrite** to output the content in any format other than GIF or JPEG
> - Use **LinearGradientBrush** to achieve a 3-D effect
> - Use **HatchBrush** to add offset effects

Introduction

A number of recommended best practices can help you achieve the best results with your graphical images.

Best Practices for Creating and Modifying Images

Consider the following best practices when creating or manipulating graphical images for your ASP.NET Web application:

- Creating graphics from existing images can increase response time.

- Use the **MemoryStream** object to create graphics in memory. This reduces the need for temporary buffers and files, which can be particularly helpful in ASP.NET applications.

- To use any format other than GIF or JPEG, you should use the **GetBuffer** method and the **Response.BinaryWrite** method to output the content.

- You can achieve a 3-D effect by using a **LinearGradientBrush**, and add offset effects with a **HatchBrush**.

Lab 5: Generating Data-Driven Graphics

> **Lab 5: Generating Data-Driven Graphics**
>
> - Exercise 1: Creating a Graphics Object
> - Exercise 2: Streaming the Image to the Browser

Introduction

After completing this lab, you will have demonstrated your ability to:

- Use major classes in the **System.Drawing** namespace.
- Create graphics by using data from a database.
- Use classes from the System.Drawing.Drawing2D namespace to create 3-D effects.
- Stream images to a browser.

Prerequisites

Before working on this lab, you must have the knowledge and skills necessary to develop class files and Web Forms applications by using a Visual Studio .NET–compatible programming language.

Estimated time to complete this lab: 45 minutes

Starting a Virtual Machine

1. On the student computer, on the **Start** menu, point to **All Programs**, and then click **Microsoft Virtual PC**. If the Virtual PC console window does not appear, then right-click the **Virtual PC icon** in the notification area (system tray), and click **Show Virtual PC Console**.

2. In the Virtual PC console window, select the virtual machine that you would like to open then click Start.

   NOTE: Depending on your time zone, the first time you start each of the virtual machines, you may receive an error message that the parent virtual hard disk appears to have been modified. You can ignore this message.

3. The virtual machine will start up in a new window.

Closing a Virtual Machine

1. On the student computer, in the virtual machine window, on the Action menu, click Close.

   NOTE: To avoid accidentally closing the virtual machine during the lab, the Close button in the top right corner of the virtual machine is disabled.

2. The virtual machine window will close. All changes to the virtual hard disk are discarded.

Exercise 1: Creating a Graphics Object

In this exercise, you will write code to create and populate a **Graphics** object. This object will contain a bar chart image that will be generated from a database call. Because this exercise is intended to build skills in generating graphics, all of the database code will be provided. The Solution folder in each lab will contain the completed solution files.

■ Create the lab starter project

1. Browse to D:\2311\Labfiles\Lab05\Starter\VB or D:\2311\Labfiles\Lab05\Starter\CS.

2. Open the Web application named UsingGraphics by double-clicking the **UsingGraphics.sln** file.

■ Examine the TestBarChart.aspx page

1. Open the code for the TestBarChart.aspx page. Note that it contains a server-side image control named **barChart**. This is where the generated bar chart image will be placed.

2. Open the code-behind file for the TestBarChart.aspx page. Examine the code in the **btnSend_Click** event handler. The first line makes the **barChart** control visible. The second line creates a **QueryString** that contains a year and passes it to the DynamicBarChart.aspx page. This page will create the bar chart image.

■ Add code to create a Graphics object

1. Identify the **Page_Load** method in the code-behind file for the DynamicBarChart.aspx page.

2. Locate the comment "TODO Create and populate a graphics object."

3. Write code to set the **ContentType** property of the **Response** object to **image/gif**. This allows the browser to identify the incoming content as an image in GIF format, thereby speeding the rendering process.

4. Create a new **Bitmap** object named **bmpChartSpace**. Set its size to 700 pixels wide and 200 pixels high.

5. Use the **FromImage** method of the **Graphics** class to create a **Graphics** object named **grBarChart**. Use **bmpChartSpace** as the input parameter to the **FromImage** method.

6. Call the **DrawBarChart** method and pass three parameters: **grBarChart**, **Color.Ivory**, and the value of the **Year** parameter of the **QueryString** of the **Request** object. (The syntax depends on whether you use C# or Visual Basic .NET). Your code should resemble the following:

Visual Basic .NET

```
Response.ContentType = "image/gif"
Dim bmpChartSpace As New Bitmap(700, 200)
Dim grBarChart As Graphics = Graphics.FromImage(bmpChartSpace)

DrawBarChart(grBarChart, Color.Ivory, Request.QueryString("Year"))
```

C#

```
Response.ContentType = "image/gif";
Bitmap bmpChartSpace = new Bitmap(700, 200);
Graphics grBarChart = Graphics.FromImage(bmpChartSpace);

DrawBarChart(grBarChart, Color.Ivory, Request.QueryString["Year"]);
```

- **Implement the DrawBarChart method**

1. In the **DrawBarChart** method, locate the comment "TODO Set the background color of the graphics object."

2. Write code to clear the background of the graphic and set the background color to the color passed into the method. Your code should resemble the following:

Visual Basic .NET

```
grBarChart.Clear(clrBackground)
```

C#

```
grBarChart.Clear(clrBackground);
```

3. Study the following data retrieval code. This code executes a SQL statement to retrieve summary sales information for each product category in the Northwind database. It populates a **DataTable** that has two columns: one for the **CategoryName** and the other for **CategorySales**. The bars in the bar chart will vary according to the value of **CategorySales**.

4. Locate the comment "TODO Get the maximum sales value." Write code that uses the **Compute** method of the **DataTable** object to retrieve the maximum value of the **CategorySales** column. This will be used to calculate the relative height of each bar. Your code should resemble the following:

Visual Basic .NET

```
Dim maxSales As Single = _
    Convert.ToSingle(dtSales.Compute("Max(CategorySales)", ""))
```

C#

```
float maxSales = Convert.ToSingle(dtSales.Compute("Max(CategorySales)", ""));
```

5. Locate the comment "TODO Calculate the position of bar and caption."
6. Begin by writing code to calculate the height of the bar. This will be the value of the **CategorySales** property divided by **maxSales** and then multiplied by **maxBarHeight**.
7. Write code to calculate the position of the base of the bar. This will be the sum of **topSpace** and **maxBarHeight**.
8. Convert the value of **barValue** to an integer and assign it to the **barHeight** variable.
9. Calculate the y position of the top of the bar by subtracting **barHeight** from **barBase** and assigning it to the variable **barTop**.
10. Calculate the y position of the caption at the top of the bar by subtracting the **shadowSize** from the **textHeight** of the **barHeight** of the **barBase** and assigning it to the variable **topCaptionPosition**.

11. Your code should resemble the following:

Visual Basic .NET

```
Dim barValue As Single = CSng(dtSales.Rows(i)("CategorySales")) / maxSales _
    * maxBarHeight
Dim barBase As Integer = topSpace + maxBarHeight
Dim barHeight As Integer = CInt(barValue)
Dim barTop As Integer = barBase - barHeight
Dim topCaptionPosition As Integer = barBase - barHeight - textAreaHeight - _
    shadowSize
```

C#

```
float barValue = Convert.ToSingle(dtSales.Rows[i]["CategorySales"])/maxSales *
    maxBarHeight;
int barBase = topSpace + maxBarHeight;
int barHeight = (int) barValue;
int barTop = barBase - barHeight;
int topCaptionPosition = barBase - barHeight - textAreaHeight - shadowSize;
```

12. Locate the comment "TODO Draw the caption at the top of the bar."
13. Write code to calculate the x position of the caption. Multiply the width of the bar by the current index of the loop.
14. Use the **DrawString** method of **grBarChart** to write the value of the **CategorySales** property by using a 7-point Tahoma font and a **SolidBrush** with a navy color at the position defined by the value of **x** and **topCaptionPosition**. Your code should resemble the following:

Visual Basic .NET

```
Dim x As Integer = i * barWidth
grBarChart.DrawString([String].Format("{0:c}", _
dtSales.Rows(i)("CategorySales")), New _
    Font("Tahoma", 7), New SolidBrush(Color.Navy), x, topCaptionPosition)
```

C#

```
int x = i * barWidth;
grBarChart.DrawString(String.Format("{0:c}", dtSales.Rows[i]["CategorySales"]),
new Font("Tahoma", 7), new SolidBrush(Color.Navy), x, topCaptionPosition);
```

15. Locate the comment "TODO Create the bar and the shadow effect."
16. Write code to create a new rectangle named **solidBar** with an x position of **x**, a y position of **barTop**, a width set to the value of **barWidth** minus 10 pixels, and a height set to **barHeight**.
17. Write code to create a new rectangle named **captionBar** with an x position of **x**, a y position calculated with the expression **barBase + textAreaHeight**, a width set to the value of **totalWidth**, and a height set to **textAreaHeight**.
18. Write code to create a new rectangle to hold the shadow bar named **barShadow**. Use the overloaded constructor of the Rectangle structure that accepts two parameters: Point and Size. Set the Point parameter to the **Location** property of the **solidBar** Rectangle. The **Location** property specifies the x and y coordinates of the Rectangle. Set the Size parameter to the **Size** property of the **solidBar** Rectangle. The **Size** property designates the width and height of the Rectangle.
19. Use the **Offset** method of **barShadow** to offset the location by an x coordinate of **j** (index of the outer loop) and **–j**.
20. Use the **FillRectangle** method of **grBarChart** to fill **barShadow**. Use the following table to assign the values of the parameters:

Parameter name	Value
Brush	New HatchBrush(HatchStyle.Percent50, Color.Blue)
Rectangle	barShadow

21. Use the **FillRectangle** method of **grBarChart** to fill the bar. Use the following table to assign the values of the parameters:

Parameter name	Value
Brush	New LinearGradientBrush(solidBar, Color.Blue, Color.LightSkyBlue, LinearGradientMode.Horizontal)
Rectangle	solidBar

22. Your code should resemble the following:

Visual Basic .NET

```
Dim solidBar As New Rectangle(x, barTop, barWidth - 10, barHeight)
Dim captionBar As New Rectangle(x, barBase + textAreaHeight, totalWidth,
    textAreaHeight)
Dim barShadow As New Rectangle(solidBar.Location, solidBar.Size)
barShadow.Offset(j, -j)
grBarChart.FillRectangle(New HatchBrush(HatchStyle.Percent50,
    Color.Blue), barShadow)
grBarChart.FillRectangle(New LinearGradientBrush(solidBar, Color.Blue,
    Color.LightSkyBlue, LinearGradientMode.Horizontal), solidBar)
```

C#

```
Rectangle solidBar = new Rectangle(x, barTop, barWidth-10, barHeight);
Rectangle captionBar = new Rectangle(x, barBase + textAreaHeight, totalWidth,
    textAreaHeight);
Rectangle barShadow = new Rectangle(solidBar.Location, solidBar.Size);
barShadow.Offset(j, -j);
grBarChart.FillRectangle(new HatchBrush(HatchStyle.Percent50, Color.Blue),
    barShadow);
grBarChart.FillRectangle(new LinearGradientBrush(solidBar, Color.Blue,
    Color.LightSkyBlue, LinearGradientMode.Horizontal), solidBar);
```

23. Locate the comment "TODO Draw the caption at the bottom of the bar."
24. Write code to create a Font with a FontFamily of "Tahoma", a size of 8 pixels, and a FontStyle of Bold.
25. Use the **FillRectangle** method of the **grBarChart** object to create a Rectangle with a **LightBlue** brush and a size using the **captionBar** Rectangle created above.
26. Use the **DrawString** method of **grBarChart** and set the parameters according to the parameter names and values in the following table:

Parameter name	Value
String	dt.Rows(i)("CategoryName").ToString()
Font	labelFont
Brush	New SolidBrush(Color.Navy)
X Coordinate	x
Y Coordinate	barBase + textHeight

27. Your code should resemble the following:

Visual Basic .NET

```
Dim labelFont As New Font("Tahoma", 8, FontStyle.Regular)
    grBarChart.FillRectangle(New SolidBrush(Color.LightBlue), captionBar)
    grBarChart.DrawString(dtSales.Rows(i)("CategoryName").ToString(),
labelFont, New SolidBrush(Color.Navy), x, barBase + textAreaHeight)
```

C#

```
Font labelFont = new Font("Tahoma", 8, FontStyle.Regular);
    grBarChart.FillRectangle(new SolidBrush(Color.LightBlue), captionBar);
    grBarChart.DrawString(dtSales.Rows[i]["CategoryName"].ToString(),
labelFont, new SolidBrush(Color.Navy), x, barBase + textAreaHeight);
```

Exercise 2: Stream the image to the browser

In this exercise, you will add code to stream the graphic created in the **DrawBarChart** method to the browser. You will then test the application.

■ Add code to implement a persistent DataSource property

1. Locate the comment "TODO Stream the contents of the graphics object to the client."
2. Declare and instantiate a new **MemoryStream** object named **ms**.
3. Use the **Save** method of **bmpChartSpace** to save the image to **MemoryStream** with the **ImageFormat** of GIF.
4. Use the **WriteTo** method of the **MemoryStream** object to stream the image to the **OutputStream** of the **Response** object.
5. Call **Dispose** on the **Bitmap** and **Graphics** objects. This is necessary to release the unmanaged resources consumed by these objects.
6. Your code should resemble the following:

Visual Basic .NET

```
Dim ms As New MemoryStream
bmpChartSpace.Save(ms, ImageFormat.Gif)
ms.WriteTo(Response.OutputStream)

bmpChartSpace.Dispose()
grBarChart.Dispose()
```

C#

```
MemoryStream ms = new MemoryStream();
 bmpChartSpace.Save(ms, ImageFormat.Gif);
 ms.WriteTo(Response.OutputStream);

bmpChartSpace.Dispose();
grBarChart.Dispose();
```

7. Build the project and correct any errors.
8. View TestBarChart.aspx in the browser. Ensure that the bar chart image appears correctly. Choose each year from the drop-down list and confirm that the bar chart for each year appears correctly.

Module 6: Creating a Secure Infrastructure

Module 6: Creating a Secure Infrastructure

- Authentication and Authorization in ASP.NET
- Security in ASP.NET

Overview

In today's computing environment, it is more important than ever to ensure the security of your Web applications. This module presents scenarios to help you identify the factors involved in effectively authenticating and authorizing clients to Microsoft ASP.NET Web applications. The module also examines how to build secure communication channels so that clients can interact without fear of privileged information being compromised. You will learn about some of the major risks and common pitfalls faced by developers when designing a security infrastructure. Finally, you will learn how a portal implements a flexible and extensible security system.

Objectives

After completing this module, you will be able to:

- Identify where and how you need to perform authentication in ASP.NET applications.
- Implement role-based authorization.
- Secure resources by using process identity.
- Identify where and how to secure communications by using encryption.

Lesson: Authentication and Authorization in ASP.NET

> **Lesson: Authentication and Authorization in ASP.NET**
> - Authentication and Authorization Strategies
> - Resource Access Models
> - ASP.NET Authentication Modes
> - Windows Authentication Scenarios
> - Forms Authentication
> - Configuring Forms Authentication

Overview

Authentication and authorization are critical elements of a Web application security strategy. *Authentication* is the process of identifying a user, typically based on a username and password. *Authorization* is the process of granting users access rights to system resources based on recognized credentials. In this lesson, you will learn about common authentication and authorization scenarios and strategies in the context of an ASP.NET Web application.

Lesson Objectives

After completing this module, you will be able to:

- Describe the principal ASP.NET and Microsoft Windows authentication and authorization strategies.
- Explain the concept of a resource access model.
- Understand how to configure Forms authentication.

Authentication and Authorization Strategies

> **Authentication and Authorization Strategies**
>
> - Role-based authorization
>   - Access to resources is based on a role assigned to the caller
>   - User base is segmented into major groups, with users assigned to one or more groups
>   - Usually preferred for Web applications
> - Resource-based authorization
>   - Caller is mapped to an identity contained in an ACL, which determines the permissions available to the caller
>   - Requires less code
>   - Tends to make the application's security code more complex and fragile

Introduction

Before you learn about the details of Windows authentication and Forms authentication, you need to consider the various authentication strategies that are available. Before deciding to use a particular mode, the developer should carefully examine:

- What resources need to be protected.
- What authentication options are available.
- Which identities should be used for resource access.
- What authorization methods can be used to validate identities.

In this section, you will learn about strategies that you can employ when making these decisions.

Protecting Resources

Before deciding on an authentication method, you will need to make an inventory of the resources to be protected. Web pages, user controls, and handlers with extensions recognized by ASP.NET (*.aspx, *.ascx, *.asmx, *.ashx) can be protected by the defined ASP.NET security modes: Windows, Forms, and Passport. Web resources such as Hypertext Markup Language (HTML) files and graphical images must use alternate means such as the access control lists (ACLs) maintained by Windows. Another way to protect these resources would be to configure the Internet Information Services (IIS) metabase to use the aspnet_isapi.dll as the handler for these types of files, but this would introduce performance overhead.

Database resources can be protected by using database accounts. To protect data, some mechanism for passing a user or group identity to the database security system needs to be enabled. The two fundamental approaches to this issue are discussed below. The approach you decide to take will have a direct influence on the ASP.NET security mode you choose.

Authorization Strategies

After you have determined which resources need protection, you must select an authorization strategy. There are two fundamental authorization strategies:

- **Role-based authorization**. The caller is assigned a role, and access to resources is based on that role. The user base is segmented into major groups and users are assigned to one or more groups. The groups take on a fixed identity, which is enforced by resource managers to allow or deny access to the resources under their protection.

- **Resource-based authorization** (also known as the Impersonation/Delegation Model). Each resource is protected by the Windows ACL. The caller is mapped to an identity contained in the control list that determines the permissions available to the caller. This approach has the advantage of requiring less code because it uses built-in operating system mechanisms. If database resources need to be protected, the advantages of connection pooling are lost when using this strategy. Connection pooling cannot be used effectively unless users share security contexts. The consequence is a negative impact on scalability. This strategy would only be appropriate in situations where protecting file resources is the main priority. If data needs to be obtained from several different sources and then consolidated, this approach is not suitable. Using ACLs requires the original caller's identity to flow through the application, which tends to make the application's security code more complex and fragile.

Because the priority for most Web applications is efficient and scalable database access, the role-based approach is usually preferred.

Role-Based Authorization Process

The pattern for role-based authorization, also known as the *trusted server model*, involves the following steps:

1. User are authenticated at the entry point into the Web application. This establishes a single point of trust where a fixed identity is determined for the caller. After this is done, individual resources can use that identity to apply whatever authorization rules they require.
2. The authenticated identity is used to choose the role or roles for the caller.
3. The role determines which operations the caller has access to.
4. The back-end resources then use the trusted identity to authorize access.

Identities in Role-Based Authorization

Two fundamental types of identities can be used as the starting point for this role-based mechanism:

- **Windows accounts**: Using Windows accounts as the basis for roles is a major decision point in the process of deciding what security mechanism to use. Doing so implies that all users need to have Windows accounts to access the protected resources. This scenario is only appropriate for internal Web applications, such as human resources applications for company employees. This method is impractical for externally facing applications, including most extranets. Creating network accounts for users outside the company can cause major security breaches. When using Windows accounts, there are two ways to establish identity:
    - **Original caller's identity**: The Windows account used by the caller is used at each point in the resource access process. In this case, the role used by the caller must be that of a Windows group.
    - **Process identity**: If ASP.NET is not impersonating the caller, the identity used for resource access is the identity of the default account used by the ASP.NET worker process. By default, this is a restricted account named "machine," but it can be changed. This account must have access to all of the resources that the application provides.

- **Generic and Custom identities**: An identification mechanism, usually database-driven, that is non–Windows-based, can be built by using the **GenericIdentity** and **GenericPrincipal** classes. These classes provide the ability to define identities and roles that can be used in conjunction with the roles defined in the Web.config file, as well as the declarative and imperative mechanisms defined in the permission classes. They are adequate for most authorization purposes. On occasion it is convenient to construct an entirely new system by using the **IIdentity** and **IPrincipal** interfaces. The reasons for creating such custom principals can be summarized as follows:
    - The role-checking mechanism must be extended to include conditions such as multiple roles. Methods such as **IsInMultipleRoles**("Supervisor," "Team Leader") or **IsInAnyRole** might be helpful to the logic of a program.
    - It might be useful to have a method that returns the roles for a user in an array, **ArrayList**, or other collection type. In the following example, **MyPrincipal** is an object that instantiates a custom principal class:

Visual Basic .NET

```
Dim roles As ArrayList = MyPrincipal.Roles
```

C#

```
ArrayList roles = MyPrincipal.Roles;
```

- Rather than having to check each role and make a lengthy series of comparisons between roles, it might be convenient to use hierarchical methods such as **IsInHigherRole** or **IsInLowerRole**, as in the following example:

Visual Basic .NET

```
MyPrincipal.IsInHigherRole("Team Leader")
MyPrincipal.IsInLowerRole("Supervisor")
```

C#

```
MyPrincipal.IsInHigherRole("Team Leader");
MyPrincipal.IsInLowerRole("Supervisor");
```

- The role-checking mechanism could be extended to provide additional features such as using certificates to validate roles. The **X509ClientCertificate** class could be used for this purpose.

Resource Access Models

Resource Access Models

- The Trusted Subsystem Model
  - Upstream Mechanism Supplies Downstream Components with an Identity
  - Advantages:
    - Connection Pooling
    - Smaller Set of Accounts
    - Less Vulnerability to Attack by Privileged Accounts
  - Disadvantage: Auditing Less Reliable
- The Impersonation/Delegation Model
  - Original Identity Flows Through the Application
  - Advantages
    - Auditing at the Time of Resource Requests
    - Minimal Code
  - Disadvantages:
    - Delegation Complexities
    - No Connection Pooling
    - ACLs Maintained for Each User

Introduction

The authorization approach determines which resource access model can be used by the ASP.NET application. The two major models are referred to as the trusted subsystem model and the impersonation/delegation model.

The Trusted Subsystem Model

This model matches the role-based authentication approach described previously. Downstream services, such as databases, are accessed using a fixed identity established at the entry point to the Web application. Unlike the resource-based approach, the operating system does not have access to the original caller's identity. The application might continue to track the original caller's identity for the purposes of personalization, auditing, or to offer identity-based access by using an application-based mechanism. In this scenario, downstream resources trust the upstream mechanism to supply them with a usable identity.

Though the original caller's identity is not passed on, Windows accounts can still be used as the role-enforcing mechanism. The middle tier can access resources such as Microsoft SQL Server™ by using a Windows account selected according to the role assigned to the caller. This security context will usually be assumed by a middle-tier component acting on behalf of the current client. These accounts may have different privileges such as read-only access or read/write access to particular data tables.

Advantages

- One of the prime benefits of this model is that because users share the same security context, connection pooling allows more scalable access to data.

- Managing ACLs, such as those used by SQL Server, is simpler when only a small set of accounts needs to be configured for access.

- Only middle tier-controlled roles have access to resources, not individual users. No direct user access means less vulnerability to attack by privileged accounts.

Disadvantages

- Auditing must be performed at the application level, which is considered less reliable than auditing by the process that accesses the resource.

- Though attackers cannot get access to resources through individual accounts, it might be possible to use one of the privileged roles defined by the middle tier.

The Impersonation/Delegation Model

In cases where the operating system must be used to protect resources, the caller's original identity may flow through the application. In Web applications, the ASP.NET worker process impersonates the caller and accesses resources using that identity. The main advantage of this approach is that the built-in features of the operating system such as auditing and access control lists can be used, thus reducing the size of the application's code base.

Advantages

- Auditing is performed at the exact time of resource access by the accessing process, which is considered the most authoritative type of auditing.

- Services such as auditing and resource permissions are provided directly by the operating system, requiring less code.

Disadvantages

- If resources need to be accessed in other Windows security domains, the application may need to duplicate user names and passwords for untrusted domains or use Kerberos-based authentication to support delegation.

- Connection pooling cannot be used effectively because the security context of each user is unique. This reduces the scalability of the application.

- ACLs must be maintained for each individual user that might need to access the application. This effort is multiplied by the number of resources that need to be safeguarded.

ASP.NET Authentication Modes

> **ASP.NET Authentication Modes**
> - Windows Authentication
>   - Basic with SSL
>   - Authorization Roles Define User Access
> - **UrlAuthorizationModule**
> - **FileAuthorizationModule**

Introduction

ASP.NET offers three authentication modes. The two used most often are Windows and Forms authentication. Microsoft Passport authentication is also available for those who download and install the Passport software development kit (SDK), but will not be considered here because it is not used as frequently as the other two. Both modes are appropriate to a role-based authorization model. We will first consider Windows authentication.

Windows Authentication

When resources need protection, and the users of the Web application all have Windows accounts, Windows authentication mode can be used. If the caller's security context needs to be passed to the middle tier or data tier to support per-user authorization, then ASP.NET impersonation should be enabled as well.

Each Windows-based IIS security mechanism is available when a user accesses a file with an extension handled by ASP.NET. Basic authentication is the least secure and sends the user's password over the network with base64 encoding. This mode should always be used in conjunction with Secure Sockets Layer (SSL) to encrypt traffic between the client and server or else passwords could be compromised. In this case, SSL should be used on all pages, not just the initial logon page, because credentials are passed on all requests.

No matter what the authentication mode (Anonymous, Basic, Digest, or Integrated Windows), IIS creates an authentication token for each logged on user. If anonymous access is enabled, the token for the anonymous Internet user account (IUSR_*machinename*) is assigned.

IIS passes this token to ASP.NET, which authenticates the user. ASP.NET will accept any token from IIS because only users with established Windows accounts can be issued tokens.

ASP.NET authorizes access to resources according to the authorization assertions defined in the Web.config's <authorization> elements:

```
<configuration>
   <system.web>
        <authentication mode="Windows" />
        <authorization>
            <allow users="domain1\user1, domain2\user2, domain1\user3" />
            <deny users="*" />
        </authorization>
    </system.web>
</configuration>
```

This mechanism is controlled by the **UrlAuthorizationModule**. The configuration above would allow specific user accounts access to the application as a whole, but would deny access to all other users. Windows authentication mode also makes use of the **FileAuthorizationModule** to check that a user's access token has specific permissions defined in the ACL for a resource. Note that this is a different process from impersonation. With impersonation, ASP.NET accesses resources using a specifically configured identity. With Windows-mode authorization, ASP.NET passes the token supplied by IIS to authorize access.

Windows Authentication Scenarios

> **Windows Authentication Scenarios**
>
> - Windows Authentication with Impersonation
>   - Uses Impersonation/Delegation Model
>   - Declarative Demands
>   - Imperative Demands
>   - HttpContext.User Object
> - Windows Authentication Without Impersonation
> - Windows Authentication Using a Fixed Identity
>   - Not Recommended
>   - Username and Password Are Stored in Clear Text in the Machine.Config File
>   - ASP.NET Must Act as Part of the Operating System

Introduction

Depending on the chosen authorization model, Windows authentication can be used in a number of different scenarios. For each scenario we will present the circumstances where it would apply, how it can be enabled, and summarize the advantages and disadvantages.

Windows Authentication with Impersonation

All of the Windows Authentication scenarios depend on users of the application having Windows accounts. If the application must support anonymous users from the Internet, this mode is not practical. It is primarily intended for internal applications with high-level security and auditing requirements, such as financial applications. By using ASP.NET impersonation, each user can have individual permissions and user-specific audit trails can be enforced.

In this scenario, resources are protected by Windows ACLs. Whenever a user attempts to access a resource, the FileAuthorizationModule checks the caller's access token and compares it to the permissions contained in the ACL for that resource. The **UrlAuthorizationModule** will perform checks against resources that have been configured in the Web.config file.

Windows Authentication Without Impersonation

If there is no need to flow caller-specific identity through the application, then resources can be secured using the "trusted subsystem" approach described previously. In this case, impersonation is turned off, but the **FileAuthorizationModule** performs access checks using the caller's access token which was passed to ASP.NET by IIS. When using explicit role checks, the Windows domain name for the group must be specified:

Visual Basic .NET

```
Dim inRole As Boolean = _
    HttpContext.User.IsInRole("DomainName\WindowsGroup")
```

C#

```
Boolean inRole = HttpContext.User.IsInRole("DomainName\WindowsGroup");
```

One of the primary advantages of this method is that connection pooling can be used because all users share the same security context.

Windows Authentication Using a Fixed Identity

ASP.NET can be configured to use a specific user account rather than the default "machine" or "System" identity. The default "machine" identity is an account with few privileges. This account is represented as "MachineName\ASPNET" on the network. It cannot write files or create registry entries. It is not recommended, in .NET Framework 1.0, to create a special account for ASP.NET, assign the necessary privileges, and configure the machine.config to use that account for the following reasons:

- userName and password attributes are stored in clear text in the machine.config file. Though we will see how to encrypt these values, it is preferable to avoid this overhead if possible.

- For ASP.NET to impersonate a specific account, it is necessary that it have the "Act as part of the operating system" privilege. This opens a serious security hole. If a hacker were to gain control of the ASP.NET worker process, this privilege would be available.

To address the encryption issue, we have suggested storing credentials in encrypted registry entries. (Also see the Knowledge Base article (Q329290) "HOW TO: Use the ASP.NET Utility to Encrypt Credentials and Session State Connection Strings" at http://support.microsoft.com/default.aspx?scid=kb;en-us;329290). In ASP.NET version 2, an encrypted <appSettings> section is planned. The second issue is addressed in .NET Framework 1.1, where IIS performs the logon so that ASP.NET no longer requires this privilege.

Declarative and Imperative Permissions

Each scenario described above allows specific classes and methods to be protected through declarative or imperative permission checks. Declarative permission checks make use of the **PrincipalPermissionAttribute**, as in the following code snippet:

Visual Basic .NET

```
<PrincipalPermissionAttribute(SecurityAction.Demand, _
      Name := "Richard")> Public Class SampleClass
```

C#

```
[ PrincipalPermissionAttribute(SecurityAction.Demand,
Name := "Richard")] public class SampleClass
```

When using declarative demands, the developer needs to be aware of its limitations. Declarative checks are static; they cannot be changed at run time. Moreover, they support OR logic only. The application can demand that a user be in one particular role, such as Supervisor, but cannot demand that a user be in two or more roles, such as Supervisor and Team Leader. To support these requirements, use imperative demands or create a custom principal class that implements the **IPrincipal** interface. To use a declarative demand to ensure that the current caller is in the Supervisor OR Team Leader role, the following attribute could be used:

Visual Basic .NET

```
<PrincipalPermissionAttribute(SecurityAction.Demand, Role="Supervisor"), _
PrincipalPermissionAttribute(SecurityAction.Demand, Role="Team Leader")>
Public Sub DoPrivilegedMethod()
...
End Sub
```

C#

```
[ PrincipalPermissionAttribute(SecurityAction.Demand, Role="Supervisor"),
PrincipalPermissionAttribute(SecurityAction.Demand, Role="Team Leader")]
public void DoPrivilegedMethod()
{
...
}
```

Imperative checks can demand that both conditions be present (AND logic):

Visual Basic .NET

```
Dim permCheckTellers As PrincipalPermission = _
    New PrincipalPermission(null,"Supervisor")
permCheckTellers.Demand()
Dim permCheckManagers As PrincipalPermission = New PrincipalPermission(null, _
    "Team Leader")
permCheckManagers.Demand()
```

C#

```
PrincipalPermission permCheckTellers As =
new PrincipalPermission(null,"Supervisor");
permCheckTellers.Demand();
PrincipalPermission permCheckManagers = new PrincipalPermission(null, "Team
Leader");
permCheckManagers.Demand();
```

The first parameter in this overloaded constructor of the **PrincipalPermission** object is the name of the user, which is null here. The second parameter is the role. Imperative checks can be made conditionally at run time. If the user is not in the specified role, a security exception will be thrown.

A third method can be used to check roles that supports both AND and OR logic. The **IsInRole** method of the **HttpContext.User** object can be used to enforce role checks against any **IPrinicipal** object:

Visual Basic .NET

```
If (User.IsInRole("Supervisor") AND User.IsInRole("Team Leader") Then
'Perform privileged operation
End If
```

C#

```
if ((User.IsInRole("Supervisor") && User.IsInRole("Team Leader"))
{
    // Perform privileged operation
}
```

The **System.Web** namespace must be imported into the code-behind file in order to make this check. Otherwise, the fully qualified name must be used: **HttpContext.Current.User.IsInRole** ("rolename"). This method has the advantage of requiring less code, but .NET handles these checks differently. The declarative or imperative demand will throw a security exception if it fails, but the **IsInRole** method simply returns a Boolean true or false.

The general rule is to use declarative checks to restrict access to methods. Use imperative checks to gain fine-grained control within methods. Using the **HttpContext** will often be preferred where roles may constrain the paths that users follow through a site. In this scenario, returning a Boolean value might be preferable to throwing a security exception.

Forms Authentication

> **Forms Authentication**
> - Steps in the Authentication Process
> - Using Active Directory for Authentication
>   - Optimized for Reading User Credentials
>   - .NET Class Support
>   - Steps to Allow ASP.NET to Use Active Directory
> - Creating Forms Authentication Ticket
> - Using Forms Authentication on a Web Farm
> - Guidelines for Forms Authentication

Introduction

If an application's users do not have Windows accounts, as is the case with most Internet applications, Forms authentication is the most likely security mode. This authentication mode makes no use of the built-in security features of the operating system. To enable Forms authentication, begin by enabling Anonymous Authentication for the application in the Internet Services Manager, and then set the mode attribute of the <authentication> element to Forms.

Authentication Process

Incoming requests will be processed using these steps:

- ASP.NET checks the <authorization> tags and reads the rules that have been configured.

- If the Web.config file requires authentication (contains a <deny users="?"> element), the user is redirected to the logon form specified in the logonUrl attribute in the <forms> element.

- The user enters credentials on the form which can then be validated against SQL Server or the Microsoft Active Directory® directory service.

- During the authentication process, the user's roles should be retrieved so that they can be used for role-based authorization.

- If the users' credentials are valid, an authentication cookie is created. User roles can be stored in this cookie to avoid requerying the data store each time roles are needed. Several methods of the **FormsAuthentication** class provide more fine-grained control over the authentication cookie than the **RedirectFromLoginPage** method.
- The user is redirected to the requested page. The page is not displayed until the **AuthenticateRequest** event has been handled.
- If role-based authorization is required, an **IPrincipal** object must be created and stored in the **HttpContext.User** property. The ideal location for this assignment is the **Application_AuthenticateRequest** event handler.
- ASP.NET checks the rules configured in Web.config. The user's name and role are checked against any deny or allow elements. If the designated conditions are met, the user is granted access.

Active Directory for Authentication

Active Directory is optimized for read access. With Active Directory, the directory is loaded into memory and optimized read algorithms are used, making it a natural repository for user credentials. The .NET Framework includes a set of classes for working with this information. The following code retrieves the list of groups that a user is a member of:

Visual Basic .NET

```vbnet
Public Function GetUserGroups() As String()
    Dim adSearch As New DirectorySearcher(_path)
    adSearch.Filter = _searchFilter
    adSearch.PropertiesToLoad.Add("memberOf")
    Dim groupNames As New StringBuilder()
    Try
        Dim adResult As SearchResult = adSearch.FindOne()
        Dim propertyCount As Integer = _
      adResult.Properties("memberOf").Count
        Dim groupName As [String]
        Dim equalsIndex, commaIndex As Integer
        Dim propertyCounter As Integer
        For propertyCounter = 0 To propertyCount - 1
            groupName = _
      CType(result.Properties("memberOf")(propertyCounter), [String])
            equalsIndex = groupName.IndexOf("=", 1)
            commaIndex = groupName.IndexOf(",", 1)
            If - 1 = equalsIndex Then
                Return Nothing
            End If
            groupNames.Append(groupName.Substring(equalsIndex + 1, _
      commaIndex - equalsIndex - 1))
            groupNames.Append("|")
        Next propertyCounter
    Catch ex As Exception
        Throw New Exception("Error obtaining group names. " + ex.Message)
    End Try
    Return groupNames.ToString()
End Function
```

C#

```csharp
public string GetUserGroups()
{
    DirectorySearcher adSearch = new DirectorySearcher(_path);
    adSearch.Filter = _searchFilter;
    adSearch.PropertiesToLoad.Add("memberOf")
        StringBuilder groupNames = new StringBuilder();
    try
    {
        SearchResult adResult = adSearch.FindOne();
        int propertyCount = adResult.Properties("memberOf").Count;
        string groupName;
        int equalsIndex;
        int commaIndex;
        int propertyCounter;

        for(i = 0; i < propertyCount - 1; i++)
        {
            groupName =
                (string)result.Properties("memberOf")(propertyCounter);
            equalsIndex = groupName.IndexOf("=", 1);
            commaIndex = groupName.IndexOf(",", 1);
            if(- 1 = equalsIndex)
            {
                return null;
            }

            groupNames.Append(groupName.Substring(equalsIndex + 1,
                commaIndex - equalsIndex - 1));
            groupNames.Append("|");
        }
    catch(Exception ex)
    {
        throw new Exception("Error obtaining group names. " + ex.Message);
    }

    return groupNames.ToString();
    }
}
```

The **DirectorySearcher** class is used to perform queries against an Active Directory hierarchy. In the code above, **_path** is a private variable used in the constructor to initialize the LDAP path, for example, "LDAP://MyServer."

Another private variable **_searchFilter** contains the search filter. An example of a search filter would be the following:

```
(&(objectClass=user)(lastName= Donaldson))
```

This filter matches all objects in the **user** class with a **lastName** property of "Donaldson."

The **DirectorySearcher** will return a collection of all objects that match the values specified in the Filter property. The **PropertiesToLoad** property is the set of properties to be retrieved during the search. The default is to retrieve all properties. In the code above, only the "memberOf" property will be retrieved. The **FindOne** method returns only the first **SearchResult** found. **SearchResults** correspond to nodes in the Active Directory hierarchy. In this case, the **SearchResult** will only contain the **memberOf** property. The rest of the code reads through the group names and adds them to a **StringBuilder** and returns the result as an array of strings.

The default IUSR_*machinename* account does not have permission to access Active Directory. Create a new least-privileged account and configure Anonymous Access to use this account. The account details can be changed as follows:

- Start the IIS Management utility.
- Open the **Properties** dialog box for the application.
- Click the **Directory Security** tab.
- Click the **Edit** button in the **Anonymous access and authentication control** group.
- Change the **Username** and **Password** fields to match those of the least-privileged account.
- All requests will now run under the configured anonymous account, which will have the privileges to access Active Directory.

Creating a Forms Authentication Ticket

The **RedirectFromLoginPage** method sets the authentication cookie and redirects the user to the original page requested. In many scenarios this may not be sufficient. This method does not allow roles to be stored in the cookie. To do this, use the **FormsAuthenticationTicket** which has a **UserData** property that can be used to store such information in a string. Consider the following code (this code is from the ASP.NET Starter Kit Portal application in the code-behind file for global.asax):

Visual Basic .NET

```vbnet
Dim roles As String = GetUserGroups(domainName, txtUserName.Text, _
     txtPassword.Text)
Dim authTicket As New FormsAuthenticationTicket( _
                1, _
                txtUserName.Text, _
                DateTime.Now, _
                DateTime.Now.AddMinutes(20), _
                False, _
                roles)

Dim encryptedTicket As String = FormsAuthentication.Encrypt(authTicket)
```

C#

```csharp
FormsAuthenticationTicket ticket = new FormsAuthenticationTicket(
            1,                              // version
            Context.User.Identity.Name,     // user name
            DateTime.Now,                   // issue time
            DateTime.Now.AddHours(1),       // expires every hour
            false,                          // don't persist cookie
            roleStr                         // roles
            );

// Encrypt the ticket
String encryptedTicket = FormsAuthentication.Encrypt(ticket);
```

In this example, **GetUserGroups** is a method that retrieves user roles stored in Active Directory. These roles along with other parameters are passed into the constructor for a **FormsAuthenticationTicket**, an object that allows the values of an authentication ticket to be created and retrieved. The constructor used here takes five parameters: **version, name, issueDate, expiration, isPersistent,** and **userData**. After the roles are stored in **userData**, the ticket can be encrypted using the **Encrypt** method of the **FormsAuthentication** class. Unlike **RedirectFromLoginPage**, which by default encrypts the cookie and verifies it using a Message Authentication Code (MAC), when creating the cookie using **FormsAuthenticationTicket** it must be explicitly encrypted.

If the application is served from a Web farm, the keys used for encryption must be fixed values. With the default settings, the keys used to perform this task are configured in the machine.config using the "AutoGenerate" value, which means that they are automatically generated machine by machine. On a Web farm, this means that forms authentication will quickly fail because the key from one machine will not match that of another. After the values of each key on each server in the Web farm are set to the same pair, forms authentication will work properly and cookies will be protected. The Framework provides a number of cryptographic classes that could be used to generate the key values, such as the **RNGCryptoServiceProvider**.

Guidelines for Forms Authentication

- The credentials that users enter on logon forms are passed in clear text to the Web server. To prevent passwords from being captured, SSL should be used whenever users access the form and submit their information. Sites can be partitioned so that some parts use SSL and other parts do not. Another reason for enabling this is to protect against cookie replay attacks. If a user's cookie is stolen, it can be reused by a hacker. If the cookie is temporary, the timeout value, 30 minutes by default, affords a certain degree of protection. Stolen persistent cookies present a more serious threat.

- Best practice recommends that data that is needed throughout the lifetime of an application should be quickly and easily retrievable. The **UserData** property of the **FormsAuthenticationTicket** is a suitable repository for role information which works well on a Web farm. In cases where user data might exceed the capacity of a cookie, 4096 bytes is the usual limit, the **Cache** object can be used.

- In order to protect against the danger of persistent cookies being stolen, cookies should be grouped by purpose. Authentication cookies should be separate from cookies used for personalization. The latter can be made persistent as long as they do not contain any information that could be used to access restricted areas of the site. Authentication cookies should be temporary with reasonably short expiration times in case they are compromised. Be aware that by default the forms authentication cookie is valid for 50 years. To limit its lifetime, the following code provides a sample of how it might be done:

Visual Basic .NET
```
Dim url As String = FormsAuthentication.GetRedirectUrl("Elmer", True)
FormsAuthentication.SetAuthCookie("Elmer", True)
Dim cookie As HttpCookie = _
    Response.Cookies(FormsAuthentication.FormsCookieName)
cookie.Expires = DateTime.Now + New TimeSpan(7, 0, 0, 0)
Response.Redirect(url)
```

C#
```
string url = FormsAuthentication.GetRedirectUrl("Elmer", True);
FormsAuthentication.SetAuthCookie("Elmer", True);
HttpCookie cookie =
    Response.Cookies(FormsAuthentication.FormsCookieName);
cookie.Expires = DateTime.Now + New TimeSpan(7, 0, 0, 0);
Response.Redirect(url);
```

- The **GetRedirectUrl** method obtains the URL of the original request that resulted in the redirect to the logon page. The first parameter is the name of the user and the second is a Boolean value that determines whether a persistent cookie is set. Next, the cookie name is used to set the cookie using the **Response** object. The expiration date for the cookie is set explicitly to seven days from now.

- The <forms> element has an attribute that can be used to set the cookie name. Use this attribute to create a different cookie name for each Web application. In this way, users authenticated in one application will not be able to reuse their cookie in another. This protection can be extended through the use of the **IsolateApps** modifier in the validationKey attribute of the <machineKey> element. When this value is set, ASP.NET generates a unique key for each application using the application ID. The cookies in one application will be encrypted using an application-specific ID and will be unavailable outside that application.

Though Forms authentication normally requires browser cookies to be enabled, it is possible to support this method of authentication without cookies by using the query string. This method can be used if the Mobile Internet Toolkit is installed. Details can be found in the Knowledge Base article "HOW TO: Use Mobile Forms Authentication with Microsoft Mobile Internet Toolkit" (http://support.microsoft.com/default.aspx?scid=kb;[LN];Q311568).

To enable role-based authentication, the **IPrincipal** object must be populated with roles. Then the roles can be programmatically checked using the **IsInRole** method of the **User** object.

Configuring Forms Authentication

> **Configuring Forms Authentication**
> - Securing Cookies
>   - Encryption Settings
>   - RequireSSL
> - Credentials Consideration
>   - Hashing Passwords
>   - Salted Hashes

Introduction

Before we examine the details of the portal authentication process, we will take a brief look at the significant features of the <forms> element. The attributes are illustrated in the following code:

```
<forms name="name"
       loginUrl="url"
       protection="All|None|Encryption|Validation"
       timeout="30"
       path="/"
       requireSSL="true|false"
       slidingExpiration="true|false">
   <credentials passwordFormat="format"/>
</forms>
```

The protection attribute refers to how cookies will be protected. The default is "All" which means that both data validation and encryption are used to protect the cookie. The validation algorithm is configured in the <machineKey> element which is usually set in the machine.config file. This element controls how encryption takes place both for view state and for authentication cookies. The validation attribute defaults to Triple DES, the most secure algorithm. If the protection element in the <forms> element is set to "All" or "Validation," then the **FormsAuthentication.Encrypt** method is called using the ticket value and the key set in the validationKey attribute of the <machineKey> element to calculate a Message Authentication Code (MAC), which is appended to the cookie. When the cookie is decrypted using the **FormsAuthentication.Decrypt** method, the MAC is recomputed and compared to the code appended to the cookie. If they do not match, the user is rerouted to the logon page. A similar process takes place when "Encryption" is specified in the protection attribute. The decryptionKey attribute is used to encrypt and decrypt the cookie using the **FormsAuthentication** methods. Details on how to generate the keys so that all the servers on a Web farm use the same key can be found in the Knowledge Base article "HOW TO: Create Keys by Using Visual C# .NET for Use in Forms Authentication" (Q312906) at http://support.microsoft.com/default.aspx?scid=kb;en-us;312906.

For increased security, the **requireSSL** value can be set. When this attribute is set to **true**, a secure connection is required to transmit the cookie. This protects against the cookie spoofing noted above. When this is set, compliant browsers will not return the cookie unless the connection is using SSL.

The timeout attribute specifies how long the session cookie will last. The default is 30 minutes. This value only applies to temporary cookies, not persistent cookies. If the slidingExpiration value is set to true, then the timeout value becomes a sliding value and expires according to when the last request was received.

The <credentials> subelement allows name and password credentials to be placed directly into the Web.config file. The **Authenticate** method of the **FormsAuthentication** class can be used to validate using the configured credentials. In most real-world applications, this method has a number of weaknesses. This method is not suitable for any reasonably sized application because user names and passwords are stored in a text file rather than a database or Active Directory. Passwords should be encrypted, yet storing encrypted passwords raises key management issues. The encryption key also needs to be stored. If a hacker compromises the key, then all the passwords are at risk. As an alternative, the following approaches are recommended:

- Use a one-way hashing algorithm on the password. The **HashPasswordForStoringInConfigFile** method is available for this purpose. When authenticating, the submitted password is hashed and compared with the stored value. If they match, the user is authenticated.

- To strengthen password protection, the hash value can be combined with a salt value. This protects against a dictionary attack, in which the hacker gains access to the hashed passwords and uses a dictionary of prehashed passwords to compare the resulting hash values with those of the hashed passwords. If any matches are found, the hacker has identified the passwords. A salt value is a cryptographically generated random number that is combined with the password prior to hashing. To create the salt, a function such as the following might be used:

Visual Basic .NET

```
Private Shared Function CreateSalt(size As Integer) As String
    Dim rngProvider As New RNGCryptoServiceProvider()
    Dim buff(size) As Byte
    rngProvider.GetBytes(buff)
    Return Convert.ToBase64String(buff)
End Function
```

C#

```
private static string CreateSalt(int size)
{
    RNGCryptoServiceProvider rngProvider = new
    RNGCryptoServiceProvider();
    byte[] buff = new buff[ size];
    rngProvider.GetBytes(buff);
    return Convert.ToBase64String(buff);
}
```

The **GetBytes** method of the **RNGCryptoServiceProvider** fills the byte array with a cryptographically strong series of random bytes. The byte array must be converted to a string in order to be concatenated with the password. Next, the combination is hashed:

Visual Basic .NET

```
Private Shared Function CreatePasswordHash(password As String, salt As _
    String) As String
    Dim saltAndPassword As String = [String].Concat(password, salt)
    Dim hashedPassword As String = _
    FormsAuthentication.HashPasswordForStoringInConfigFile( _
        saltAndPassword, _
        "SHA1")
    Return hashedPassword
End Function
```

C#

```
private static string CreatePasswordHash(string password, string salt)
{
    string saltAndPassword = String.Concat(password, salt);
    string hashedPassword =
        FormsAuthentication.HashPasswordForStoringInConfigFile(
            saltAndPassword,
            "SHA1");
    return hashedPassword;
}
```

Lesson: Security in ASP.NET

> **Lesson: Security in ASP.NET**
>
> - **Portal Security Infrastructure**
> - **Administering Security**
> - **Best Practices for Security**

Overview

Lesson Objectives

After completing this module, you will be able to:

- Explain the uses of the **System.Drawing** classes.
- Describe the principal tools and methods used for drawing.
- Explain how graphics methods are used on an ASP.NET page.

Portal Security Infrastructure

> **Portal Security Infrastructure**
> - Portal Security Process
>   - Check Request.IsAuthenticated
>   - SetAuthPassword
>   - Storing Roles in Cookies
>   - Create Generic Principal
> - PortalSecurity Class
>   - IsInRole
>   - IsInRoles

Introduction

In order to provide maximum flexibility, the portal supports both forms-based and windows-based authentication. Form-based authentication is the default because it allows security to be managed at the application-level. Rather than using location elements or protecting each individual section of the site with a separate Web.config file, a custom role-based security mechanism has been created to provide fine-grained control over access to resources.

Assigning Roles

In order to illustrate some of the best practices for Forms authentication, we will first describe the authentication process used by the ASP.NET Starter Kit Portal application. Then, in the lab, we will show how the Portal developed for this class implements a different method so that Windows and Forms authentication can both be supported through the use of a custom principal.

The process begins with the Web.config file in the root of the application. In the Starter Kit Portal application, the forms element contains no loginUrl attribute, so the value of the attribute defaults to default.aspx, which is the URL for the entry point page. The **Request.IsAuthenticated** is checked in the **Page_Init** event handler to see if the user has been authenticated yet. If not, the logon form contained in the user control SignIn.ascx is displayed so that the user can enter his or her credentials. When the user submits his or her credentials, email address and password, to this control, a **UserDB** object is created for that user. This class encapsulates all the logic needed to add new users, update user information, and query user data. This class is only used for Forms authentication.

In the Signin.ascx code-behind file, user credentials are passed to the **Logon** method of the **UserDB** class and a stored procedure is used to validate the user and return the user name. If the user is validated, the **SetAuthCookie** of the **FormsAuthentication** class sets the user's authentication cookie, and the user is redirected back to the default page by using the **ApplicationPath** property of the **Request** object:

Visual Basic .NET

```
FormsAuthentication.SetAuthCookie(email.Text, RememberCheckbox.Checked)
Response.Redirect(Request.ApplicationPath)
```

C#

```
FormsAuthentication.SetAuthCookie(email.Text, RememberCheckbox.Checked);
Response.Redirect(Request.ApplicationPath);
```

Using **SetAuthCookie** gives the developer control over where the user is sent after authentication. The second parameter of the method controls whether a persistent cookie is set.

As soon as the user has been authenticated, the **Application_AuthenticateRequest** event takes place which is handled in the global.asax file. Here the user's roles are determined by using the **GetRoles** method of the **UserDB** class and the **User.Identity.Name** property. This method uses a stored procedure to retrieve a list of roles which are returned as a String array. In accordance with the best practices described above, the roles are stored in the authentication cookie by using the **FormsAuthenticationTicket** class (this code is from the ASP.NET Starter Kit Portal application in the code-behind file for global.asax):

Visual Basic .NET

```
Dim ticket As New FormsAuthenticationTicket(1, _
                            Context.User.Identity.Name, _
                            DateTime.Now, _
                            DateTime.Now.AddHours(1), _
                            False, _
                            roleStr)

Dim cookieStr As String = FormsAuthentication.Encrypt(ticket)

Response.Cookies("portalroles").Value = cookieStr
Response.Cookies("portalroles").Path = "/"
Response.Cookies("portalroles").Expires = DateTime.Now.AddMinutes(1)
```

C#

```
FormsAuthenticationTicket ticket = new FormsAuthenticationTicket(
        1,                              // version
        Context.User.Identity.Name,     // user name
        DateTime.Now,                   // issue time
        DateTime.Now.AddHours(1),       // expires every hour
        false,                          // don't persist cookie
        roleStr                         // roles
        );

    String cookieStr = FormsAuthentication.Encrypt(ticket);

    Response.Cookies["portalroles"].Value = cookieStr;
    Response.Cookies["portalroles"].Path = "/";
    Response.Cookies["portalroles"].Expires =
        DateTime.Now.AddMinutes(1);
```

The String array of roles is transformed into a single string and stored in the **roleStr** variable. After the roles are stored, the cookie is encrypted and stored in the "portalroles" cookie for easy retrieval.

On subsequent executions of the **Application_AuthenticateRequest** event handler, the roles are extracted from this cookie after it has been decrypted, as shown below (this code is from the ASP.NET Starter Kit Portal application in the code-behind file for global.asax):

Visual Basic .NET

```
Dim ticket As FormsAuthenticationTicket = _
    FormsAuthentication.Decrypt(Context.Request.Cookies("portalroles").Value)
```

C#

```
FormsAuthenticationTicket ticket = _
    FormsAuthentication.Decrypt(Context.Request.Cookies["portalroles"].Value);
```

A new **GenericPrincipal** object is created and stored in the current User property so that the user role can be determined from the **IsInRole** method (this code is from the ASP.NET Starter Kit Portal application in the code-behind file for global.asax):

Visual Basic .NET

```
Context.User = New GenericPrincipal(Context.User.Identity, roles)
```

C#

```
Context.User = New GenericPrincipal(Context.User.Identity, roles);
```

Security Classes

The class that contains the methods used to check roles and other permissions is the **PortalSecurity** class. The two most frequently used methods are the shared **IsInRole** and **IsInRoles** methods, which check the role of the current client (this code is in the code-behind file for the DesktopDefault.aspx the lab portal application):

Visual Basic .NET

```
If PortalSecurity.IsInRoles(_portalSettings.ActiveTab.AuthorizedRoles) = _
    False Then
        Response.Redirect("~/Admin/AccessDenied.aspx")
End If
```

C#

```
if (PortalSecurity.IsInRoles(portalSettings.ActiveTab.AuthorizedRoles) ==
  false)
{
    Response.Redirect("~/Admin/AccessDenied.aspx");
}
```

In the DesktopDefault.aspx code-behind, the **AuthorizedRoles** are set from the **activeTab.AccessRoles** property which is retrieved from the sitewide configuration file. This constitutes a convenient method for checking user roles with minimal code. If the user is not in a role that has access to the current **ActiveTab**, which is identified by the tabId passed into the **Application_BeginRequest** method, the user is denied access. In this way, the same page can be reused for each tab that is clicked and protect tabs from unauthorized users.

Administering Security

Administering Security
- Administrative Modules
- Role of the RolesDB Class
- Security Roles Page

Introduction

The following module will fully describe the administrative infrastructure of the site. This topic will cover the design and class structure used to administer user roles and other portalwide security settings.

Administrative Modules

The Admin tab is used to configure Module Definitions, Site Settings, Tabs, Security Roles, and Users. We will describe how sitewide security roles are defined and how users are added to roles.

The process begins on the DesktopDefault.aspx page. When the tabId for the Admin tab is passed in, the modules defined for that tab are loaded into the page. Four of the modules are loaded into the Content Pane as specified in the configuration file. The configuration file also controls which roles have editing rights for a particular module. These roles are retrieved from the moduleSettings instance, which is populated when the **PortalSettings** object was initially created. This instance contains a member variable **AuthorizedEditRoles** that determines which roles are authorized to edit this module. The third module is used for managing security roles and the fourth is for managing users.

The Roles.ascx file supplies the functionality needed to manage roles. In the **Page_Load** event for this control, the role of the user is checked to make sure he or she is in the "Admin" role. Then, in the **BindData** method, an instance of the **RolesDB** object is created. This class encapsulates the logic necessary to manage users, roles, and security settings. The **GetPortalRoles** method retrieves a list of all the roles that have been defined for this portal. These roles are bound to a **DataList**. Next to each role name two buttons are added. One has the **CommandName** "edit" and the other "delete." When the "edit" button is clicked, two link buttons are displayed for each role, one set to the **CommandName** "apply" and the other to "members." Whenever the "apply" link button is clicked, the **UpdateRole** method of the **RolesDB** class is executed and invokes a stored procedure to update the **RoleName** field of the Roles table. If the "delete" link is clicked, the role is deleted with the "DeleteRole" stored procedure.

In the Manage Users section of the Admin tab, users can be added, deleted, edited, and assigned to roles. The module which allows this function is the Users.ascx control. This control uses the **GetUsers** method of the **RolesDB** object to retrieve a list of users and bind their names to a drop-down list. If the "Add New User" link is clicked, the user is redirected to the ManageUsers.aspx page. From this page, user information can be changed and users can be assigned to roles. The methods of the **RolesDB** and the **UsersDB** class are used to do this.

Best Practices for Security

> **Best Practices for Security**
>
> - Adopt the "Least Privilege" Principle
> - Store User Roles in the Authentication Ticket
> - Create an IPrincipal Object, and Store It in Context.User
> - Remember to Use SSL When Needed
> - Use the Trusted Subsystem Security Model
> - Use Declarative Checks to Restrict Access
> - Set the Cookie Name

Introduction

This module has explored many aspects of security in ASP.NET applications. The following principles summarize its key points:

- **Adopt the "Least Privilege" Principle**: Processes that execute code or run server-side script should execute under an account that includes only those privileges necessary for the operation. This limits the damage that can be done if the process is compromised. Code that requires additional permissions should be run in a separate process. An extension of the principle is to disable any application features or services that are not required. Reduce the points of vulnerability to a minimum and protect those points to the maximum. Do not run ASP.NET as System or grant it the "Act as part of the operating system" privilege so as to minimize the damage if the process is compromised.

- **Store User Roles in the Authentication Ticket**: Rather than using the **RedirectFromLoginPage** method, create a **FormsAuthenticationTicket** manually and store user roles in the cookie. This allows the roles to be retrieved quickly, thus minimizing trips to the database.

- **Create an IPrincipal Object and Store it in Context.User**: In order to enforce role-based security, an object that implements the **IPrincipal** interface must be conveniently stored. The **Application_AuthenticateRequest** event handler in the global.asax file is the best place to create the object because this event does not execute until the user has been authenticated. When using Forms authentication, a **GenericPrincipal** or a custom principal must be used. This is necessary so that the roles defined for that user can be conveniently accessed.

- **Remember to Use SSL When Needed**: The credentials that users enter on login forms are passed in clear text to the Web server. To prevent passwords from being captured, SSL should be used whenever users access the form and submit their information. Sites can be partitioned so that some parts use SSL, because they contain login functions, and other parts do not. Another reason for enabling this is to protect against cookie replay attacks. If a user's cookie is stolen, it can be reused by a hacker. If the cookie is temporary, the timeout value, 30 minutes by default, affords a certain degree of protection. Stolen persistent cookies present a more serious threat.

- **Use the Trusted Subsystem Security Model**: In the most common circumstances, the trusted subsystem model is preferred.

- Because users share the same security context, connection pooling allows more scalable access to data.

- Managing access control lists (ACLs), such as those used by SQL Server, is simpler when only a small set of accounts needs to be configured.

- Only middle-tier-controlled roles have access to resources, not individual users. No direct user access means less vulnerability to attack by privileged accounts.

- **Use Declarative Checks to Restrict Access:** The general rule is to use declarative checks to restrict access to methods. Use imperative checks to gain fine-grained control within methods. Using the **HttpContext** will often be preferred where roles may constrain the paths that users follow through a site. In this scenario, returning a Boolean value might be preferable to throwing a security exception.

- **Set the Cookie Name**: The <forms> element has an attribute that can be used to set the cookie name. Use this attribute to create a different cookie name for each Web application. Users authenticated in one application will not be able to reuse their cookie in another. This protection can be extended through the use of the IsolateApps modifier in the validateKey attribute.

Lab 6: Creating a Security Infrastructure

> **Lab 6: Creating a Security Infrastructure**
>
> - Exercise 1: Implementing the ICustomPrincipal Interface
> - Exercise 2: Creating Security Classes
> - Exercise 3: (Optional) Identifying User Roles

Introduction

After completing this lab, you will have demonstrated your ability to:

- Implement role-based security classes in a Web application.
- Use the ICustomPrincipal interface to add security features.
- Create a configuration infrastructure to control security modes.

Prerequisites

Before working on this lab, you must have the knowledge and skills to implement Forms and Windows authentication in a Web application. One of the most significant aspects of the portal is the defect tracking system. This system needs to ensure that only users with the appropriate privileges will be able to see all of the tasks. Other users should see only the tasks and defects which have been assigned to them. In order to enforce this security model, we will define a new interface named "ICustomPrincipal" which will contain methods and properties used to determine the user's project roles. We will define two classes that implement this interface, **CustomWindowsPrincipal** and **CustomFormsPrincipal**. We will initialize these objects in the global.asax file so as to assign roles to the user as soon as he or she has logged into the site. In addition to the sitewide role, we will also assign a project-specific role to the user. After these user roles have been set, we will check them at any point when the user needs access to project information or functions (such as adding a new defect) using static (Shared in Visual Basic .NET) methods of the **PortalSecurity** class. In the following exercises, you will implement a role-based authorization mechanism that will work with both Windows and Forms authentication.

Estimated time to complete this lab: 45 minutes for exercises 1 and 2

Starting a Virtual Machine

1. On the student computer, on the **Start** menu, point to **All Programs**, and then click **Microsoft Virtual PC**. If the Virtual PC console window does not appear, then right-click the **Virtual PC icon** in the notification area (system tray), and click **Show Virtual PC Console**.

2. In the Virtual PC console window, select the virtual machine that you would like to open then click Start.

NOTE: Depending on your time zone, the first time you start each of the virtual machines, you may receive an error message that the parent virtual hard disk appears to have been modified. You can ignore this message.

3. The virtual machine will start up in a new window.

Closing a Virtual Machine

1. On the student computer, in the virtual machine window, on the Action menu, click Close.

NOTE: To avoid accidentally closing the virtual machine during the lab, the Close button in the top right corner of the virtual machine is disabled.

2. The virtual machine window will close. All changes to the virtual hard disk are discarded.

Exercise 1: Implementing the ICustomPrincipal Interface

In order to determine the project roles for a particular user, we need to create objects which provide the methods and properties which allow access to this information.

■ Open the Lab Starter Project

1. Open the ASPProjectVB or ASPProjectCS project in Visual Studio .NET using the following instructions.

2. Browse to D:\2311\Labfiles\Lab06\Starter\VB or D:\2311\Labfiles\Lab06\Starter\CS.

3. Launch the project by double-clicking on the ASPProjectVB.sln or the ASPProjectCS.sln file in the lab starter folder.

■ Implement the ICustomPrincipal interface

1. Open the ASPProjectVB or ASPProjectCS project in Visual Studio .NET.
2. Open the CustomPrincipals.vb or CustomPrincipals.cs file in the Components\MainPortal folder.
3. Locate the comment "TODO Implement the ICustomPrincipal interface." This interface will contain methods to determine whether a user is in a project role and to get the project role for a particular user.
4. Declare a Public interface named "ICustomPrincipal" that inherits from IPrincipal. Any Principal object must implement this interface, which defines an IsInRole method and an Identity property.
5. Define two methods in the **ICustomPrincipal** interface according to the table following (Note: **EnumProjectRole** is an enumeration of project roles defined in the ProjectMember.vb or ProjectMember.cs file):

Method	Parameters	Return Value
IsInProjectRole	ByVal projectID As Integer	Boolean
	ByVal ParamArray roleArray As EnumProjectRole	
GetProjectRole	ByVal projectID As Integer	EnumProjectRole

6. Your code should resemble the following:

Visual Basic .NET

```vbnet
Public Interface ICustomPrincipal
    Inherits IPrincipal
    Function IsInProjectRole( _
        ByVal projectID As Integer, _
        ByVal ParamArray roleArray As EnumProjectRole()) As Boolean
    Function GetProjectRole( _
        ByVal projectID As Integer) As EnumProjectRole
End Interface
```

C#

```csharp
public interface ICustomPrincipal: IPrincipal
{
    bool IsInProjectRole(int projectID, params EnumProjectRole[] roleArray);
    EnumProjectRole GetProjectRole(int projectID);
}
```

- **Implement the CustomFormsPrincipal class**

1. Locate the comment "TODO Implement the CustomFormsPrincipal class." This class will contain implementations of methods used when the site is configured to use Forms authentication.
2. Inherit the **GenericPrincipal** class. Forms authentication uses the **GenericPrincipal**.
3. Implement the **ICustomPrincipal** interface.
4. Declare a Private variable "projectRoles" of type **HashTable**.
5. Create a constructor which accepts three parameters using the appropriate C# or VB syntax:
   a. name: **identity** type: **IIdentity.**
   b. name: **roles**() type: **String (array).**
   c. name: **projectRoles** type: **HashTable.**
6. In the first line of the constructor, call the constructor of the base class and pass the identity and roles parameters to it.
7. Set the **projectRoles** property of the class to the "projectRoles" parameter.
8. Create a Public function "IsInProjectRole" which implements the **ICustomPrincipal.IsInProjectRole** method using the following parameters:
   a. ByVal **projectID** As Integer.
   b. ByVal ParamArray **roleArray** As **EnumProjectRole**().
   c. Return value: Boolean.
9. Declare a variable "projectRole" of type **EnumProjectRole**.
10. Create a For Each loop and loop through each **projectRole** in the roleArray parameter.
11. In the loop, if one of the **projectRoles** for a specific project is equal to the **projectRole** that is being checked, return true. This indicates that the user has a role in the specific project.
12. Outside the loop, return false. The user has no role in the project whose **projectID** was passed to the **IsInProjectRole** method.
13. Create a **Public Function** (**public function** in C#) that implements the **ICustomPrincipal.GetProjectRole** method. It accepts one parameter "projectID" of type Integer and returns an **EnumProjectRole** value.
14. Declare a variable p of type **EnumProjectRole** and set it equal to the **projectRoles** for a particular **projectID**. Convert the **projectRole** to an **EnumProjectRole** before making the assignment.

15. Return p from the function. This retrieves the user's role in a specific project.
16. Your code should resemble the following:

Visual Basic .NET

```vbnet
Public Class CustomFormsPrincipal
      Inherits GenericPrincipal
      Implements ICustomPrincipal
      Private projectRoles As Hashtable

      Public Sub New( _
          ByVal identity As IIdentity, _
          ByVal roles() As String, _
          ByVal projectRoles As Hashtable)
          MyBase.New(identity, roles)
          Me.projectRoles = projectRoles
      End Sub

      Public Function IsInProjectRole( _
          ByVal projectID As Integer, _
          ByVal ParamArray roleArray As EnumProjectRole()) As Boolean _
              Implements ICustomPrincipal.IsInProjectRole
          Dim projectRole As EnumProjectRole
          For Each projectRole In roleArray
              If projectRoles(projectID).ToString() = _
                  projectRole.ToString() Then
                  Return True
              End If
          Next
          Return False
      End Function

      Public Function GetProjectRole( _
          ByVal projectID As Integer) As EnumProjectRole _
          Implements ICustomPrincipal.GetProjectRole
          Dim p As EnumProjectRole = _
              CType(projectRoles(projectID).ToString(), _
              EnumProjectRole)
          Return p
      End Function

End Class
```

C#

```csharp
public class CustomFormsPrincipal: GenericPrincipal, ICustomPrincipal
{
    private Hashtable projectRoles;

    public CustomFormsPrincipal(
     IIdentity identity,
     string[] roles,
     Hashtable projectRoles):base(identity, roles)
      {
         this.projectRoles = projectRoles;
      }
    public bool IsInProjectRole(
     int projectID,
     params EnumProjectRole[] roleArray)
    {
     foreach(EnumProjectRole EnumProjectRole in roleArray)
     {
       if ((string)projectRoles[projectID] == EnumProjectRole.ToString())
       {
          return true;
       }
     }
     return false;
    }

    public EnumProjectRole GetProjectRole(int projectID)
    {
    EnumProjectRole p = (EnumProjectRole)Enum.Parse(
        typeof(ASPProject.EnumProjectRole),
        projectRoles[projectID].ToString(), true);
    return p;
    }
}
```

- **Implement the CustomWindowsPrincipal class**

    1. Locate the comment "TODO Implement the CustomWindowsPrincipal class." This class will contain implementations of methods used when the site is configured to use Windows authentication.
    2. Inherit the **WindowsPrincipal** class.
    3. Implement the **ICustomPrincipal** interface.
    4. Declare a private variable "projectRoles" of type **HashTable**.

5. Create a constructor which accepts two parameters:
   a. ByVal identity As **WindowsIdentity.**
   b. ByVal projectRoles As **HashTable.**
6. In the first line of the constructor, call the constructor of the base class and pass the identity parameter to it. Set the projectRoles property of the class to the "projectRoles" parameter.
7. Create a Public function "IsInProjectRole" which implements the **ICustomPrincipal.IsInProjectRole** method using the following parameters:
   a. ByVal **projectID** As Integer.
   b. ByVal ParamArray **roleArray** As **EnumProjectRole**().
   c. Return value: Boolean.
8. Declare a variable "projectRole" of type **EnumProjectRole**.
9. Create a For Each loop and loop through each **projectRole** in the **roleArray** parameter.
10. In the loop, if one of the **projectRoles** for a specific project is equal to the projectRole that is being checked, then return true. This indicates that the user has a role in the specific project.
11. Outside the loop, return false. The user has no role in the project whose **projectID** was passed to the **IsInProjectRole** method.
12. Create a **Public Function** (**public function** in C#) that implements the **ICustomPrincipal.GetProjectRole** method. It accepts one parameter "projectID" of type **Integer** and returns an **EnumProjectRole** value.
13. Declare a variable p of type **EnumProjectRole** and set it equal to the **projectRoles** for a particular **projectID**. Convert the **projectRole** to an **EnumProjectRole** before making the assignment.
14. Return p from the function. This retrieves the user's role in a specific project.
15. You will test the code when you have added code for the next two exercises.

16. Your code should resemble the following:

Visual Basic .NET

```vb
Public Class CustomWindowsPrincipal
    Inherits WindowsPrincipal
    Implements ICustomPrincipal
    Private projectRoles As Hashtable

    Public Sub New( _
        ByVal identity As WindowsIdentity, _
        ByVal projectRoles As Hashtable)
        MyBase.New(identity)
        Me.projectRoles = projectRoles
    End Sub

    Public Function IsInProjectRole( _
        ByVal projectID As Integer, _
        ByVal ParamArray roleArray As EnumProjectRole()) As Boolean _
        Implements ICustomPrincipal.IsInProjectRole
        Dim projectRole As EnumProjectRole
        For Each projectRole In roleArray
            If CType(projectRoles(projectID), String) = _
                projectRole.ToString() Then
                Return True
            End If
        Next
        Return False
    End Function

    Public Function GetProjectRole( _
        ByVal projectID As Integer) As EnumProjectRole _
        Implements ICustomPrincipal.GetProjectRole
        Dim p As EnumProjectRole = CType( _
            projectRoles(projectID).ToString(), _
            EnumProjectRole)
        Return p
    End Function

End Class
```

C#

```csharp
public class CustomWindowsPrincipal: WindowsPrincipal,ICustomPrincipal
{
    private Hashtable projectRoles;
    public CustomWindowsPrincipal( _
        WindowsIdentity identity, _
        Hashtable projectRoles):base(identity)
    {
       this.projectRoles = projectRoles;
    }
    public bool IsInProjectRole( _
        int projectID,params EnumProjectRole[] roleArray)
    {
       foreach(EnumProjectRole EnumProjectRole in roleArray)
       {
       if ((string)projectRoles[ projectID] ==
              EnumProjectRole.ToString())
       {
           return true;
       }
       }
    return false;
}
public EnumProjectRole GetProjectRole(int projectID)
{
    EnumProjectRole p = (EnumProjectRole)Enum.Parse( _
        typeof(ASPProject.EnumProjectRole), _
        projectRoles[ projectID] .ToString(), true);
  return p;
}
```

Exercise 2: Creating Security Classes

In this exercise, you will implement methods necessary to retrieve project roles for users who are members of specific projects.

- **Implement the GetProjectRoles method of the ProjectMember class**

    1. Open the ProjectMember.vb or ProjectMember.cs file (found in the Components\Project folder) and locate the comment "TODO Implement the GetProjectRoles method."
    2. Declare and instantiate a **HashTable** named "ht."
    3. Declare a **SqlDataReader** named dr and initialize it to **Nothing**.
    4. Open a Try block.
    5. Call the **ExecuteReader** method of **SqlHelper** according to the parameter values in the following table:

Parameter Order	Parameter Value
1	ConfigurationSettings.AppSettings("ConnectionString")
2	"GetProjectRoles"
3	PortalSecurity.UserName

   6. **PortalSecurity** is the class that encapsulates methods and properties to access the security context of the current user. The **UserName** property returns the value of **HttpContext.Current.User.Identity.Name**.
   7. Create a While loop that calls the **Read** method of the **SqlDataReader** "dr." Inside the loop, add a key/value pair to the **HashTable** for each **ProjectID** and **ProjectRole**.
   8. Create a Finally block to end the Try block. In the **Finally** clause, call the **Close** method of the **SqlDataReader**.
   9. Return the **HashTable** "ht" from the function.

10. Your code should resemble the following:

Visual Basic .NET

```vb
Public Shared Function GetProjectRoles() As Hashtable
    Dim ht As Hashtable = New Hashtable()
    Dim dr As SqlDataReader = Nothing
    Try
        dr = SqlHelper.ExecuteReader( _
            ConfigurationSettings.AppSettings("connectionString"), _
            "GetProjectRoles", _
            PortalSecurity.UserName)
        While dr.Read()
            ht.Add(dr("ProjectID"), dr("ProjectRole"))
        End While
    Finally
        dr.Close()
    End Try
    Return ht
End Function
```

C#

```csharp
public static Hashtable GetProjectRoles()
{
    Hashtable ht = new Hashtable();
    SqlDataReader dr = null;
    try
    {
        dr = SqlHelper.ExecuteReader(
            ConfigurationSettings.AppSettings["connectionString"],
            "GetProjectRoles",
            PortalSecurity.UserName);
        while(dr.Read())
        {
            ht.Add(dr["ProjectID"], dr["ProjectRole"]);
        }
}
finally
    {
     dr.Close();
    }
    return ht;
}
```

- **Examine the Project role methods in the PortalSecurity class**

    1. Open the Security.vb or Security.cs file. Examine the properties and methods of the **PortalSecurity** class. Note particularly **UserName**, **IsInRole**, and **IsInRoles**. These methods allow the security roles of the user to be checked.

    2. Locate the comment "TODO Implement the IsInProjectRole method." Uncomment the code and note the following about this method:

        a. An **ICustomPrincipal** object is obtained from the **HttpContext.User** property.

        b. The **IsInProjectRole** method is called passing in the **projectId** and an array of roles to be checked.

    3. Locate the comment "TODO Implement the GetProjectRole method." Uncomment the code and note the following about this method:

        a. As before the **ICustomPrincipal** object is retrieved from the **User** property.

        b. The **GetProjectRole** method is called on the **ICustomPrincipal** object.

Exercise 3: (Optional) Identifying User Roles

In this exercise, you will implement a role-based authorization mechanism that will work with both Windows and Forms authentication in the global.asax file. This is an optional exercise, so feel free to copy the solution files into the project if time is running short.

- **Open the portal application project and study the global.asax file**

    1. Open the ASPProjectVB or ASPProjectCS project in Visual Studio .NET if it is not already open.

    2. Open the global.asax.vb or global.asax.cs file and locate the comment "TODO Get the user's project role." This comment is found in the **Global_AcquireRequestState** method. This method is invoked when Session state becomes available during the execution of the **HttpRuntime**. This event is chosen because it is first stage at which Session state can be used. The **ICustomPrincipal** object will be stored in a Session object so that it can be conveniently retrieved when needed.

    3. Uncomment the declaration of a variable named "custom" of type **ICustomPrincipal**.

    4. Write an If statement to check if the **CustomPrincipal** is available in the Session object. If the "CustomPrincipal" key of the **Session** object is not equal to Nothing, then set the **User** property of the **HttpContext.Current** object to the **CustomPrincipal** stored in the Session object.

    5. In the Else clause declare and instantiate an object of type **UsersDB** named "users."

    6. Set the **projectRoles** variable equal to the return value from a call to the static method **GetProjectRoles** of the **ProjectMember** class.

    7. Use an If statement to check the type of the current user's **Identity**. Use a **TypeOf** statement (**typeof** in C#) to check the **HttpContext.Current.User.Identity** to see whether it is a **WindowsIdentity** or a **FormsIdentity**.

8. If it is a **WindowsIdentity**, set the **ICustomPrincipal** object "custom" equal to a new **CustomWindowsPrincipal** using the current user identity and the "projectRoles" variable. Use the following table as a guide for assigning the parameters of the **CustomWindowsPrincipal**:

Parameter Name	Parameter Value
identity	CType(Context.User.Identity, WindowsIdentity)
projectRoles	projectRoles

9. In the Else clause, use the **GetRoles** method of the **UserDB** object "users" to return the roles for the current user. Assign this value to the "roles" array variable. This is required because Forms authentication provides access to user roles through a **GenericPrincipal** object that contains these roles. Recall that **CustomFormsPrincipal** inherits from **GenericPrincipal**. Note that these roles are site roles and have nothing to do with project roles.

10. Create a new **CustomFormsPrincipal** and set the parameters of the constructor according to the values in the following table:

Parameter Name	Parameter Value
identity	CType(Context.User.Identity, WindowsIdentity)
roles()	roles
projectRoles	projectRoles

11. End the If statement. Set the **User** property of **HttpContext.Current** equal to the "custom" variable. Store the "custom" variable in a **Session** object.

12. Your code should resemble the following:

Visual Basic .NET

```vb
If Not (Session("CustomPrincipal") Is Nothing) Then
    HttpContext.Current.User = CType(Session("CustomPrincipal"), _
    ICustomPrincipal)
Else

    Dim users As New UsersDB()
    projectRoles = ProjectMember.GetProjectRoles()
    If TypeOf HttpContext.Current.User.Identity Is WindowsIdentity Then
        custom = New CustomWindowsPrincipal(CType(Context.User.Identity, _
            WindowsIdentity), projectRoles)
    Else
        roles = users.GetRoles(User.Identity.Name)
        custom = New CustomFormsPrincipal( _
            Context.User.Identity, _
            roles, _
            projectRoles)
    End If


    HttpContext.Current.User = custom
    Session("CustomPrincipal") = custom
End If
```

C#

```csharp
if(Session["CustomPrincipal"] !=null)
{
    HttpContext.Current.User =
        (ICustomPrincipal)Session["CustomPrincipal"];
}
else
    {

    UsersDB users = new UsersDB();
    projectRoles = ProjectMember.GetProjectRoles();
    if(HttpContext.Current.User.Identity is WindowsIdentity)
    {
        custom = new
            CustomWindowsPrincipal((WindowsIdentity)Context.User.Identity,
            projectRoles);
    }
    else
    {
        roles = users.GetRoles(User.Identity.Name);
        custom  = new CustomFormsPrincipal(Context.User.Identity,roles,
            projectRoles);
    }
    HttpContext.Current.User =  custom;
    Session["CustomPrincipal"] = custom;
}
```

13. Build the project and view DesktopDefault.aspx in the browser.

14. Logon as administrator: **admin@contoso.com** and password of **P@ssw0rd** and click the **Admin** tab.

15. In the Security Roles section, add a **Tester** role if there is not one in the list.

16. Open the **TestProject** project for editing by clicking the pencil icon.

17. Change Project Member '**bob**" ProjectRole from **Developer** to **Tester**.

18. In order for this user to see the **Defect Tracking** tab, permissions must be configured so that the Tester role can see that tab.
    a. Click the **Admin** tab.
    b. Select **Defect Tracking** in the **Tabs** section of the **Admin** tab.
    c. Click the edit symbol (a pencil) to edit the tab.
    d. Click the checkbox for "Tester" to allow the tab to be visible to users in that role.
    e. Click **Apply Changes**.
19. Select the **Defect Tracking** tab, edit a defect and assign it to Bob.
20. Log off and log back in as **bob@contoso.com** with a password of **P@ssw0rd**.
21. Select the **Defect Tracking** tab and note the defect available for Bob.
22. Log off and log back in as **alice@contoso.com** with a password of **P@ssw0rd**. Note that the **Defect Tracking** tab is not available to Alice because she is not in the Tester role.

Module 7: Caching Patterns and Practices

> **Module 7: Caching Patterns and Practices**
> - **Understanding Caching**
> - **ASP.NET Caching Strategies**

Overview

One of the key innovations of Microsoft® ASP.NET over previous versions of Microsoft Active Server Pages (ASP) is its caching capability. In this module, you will learn how the cache object works and how it can be used with the portal module object model to optimize caching capabilities.

Objectives

After completing this module, you will be able to:

- Understand general considerations for the effective use of caching.
- Describe the features of the ASP.NET Cache application programming interface (API).
- Explain client-side caching options.

Lesson: Understanding Caching

> **Lesson: Understanding Caching**
>
> - **Basic Caching Considerations**
> - **Caching State Representation Types**

Overview

An effective caching strategy can increase the performance, scalability, and availability of a Web application. Performance increases because repetitive processing, data access, and transportation are avoided. Scalability grows because as the user base increases, demand for server resources remains constant. By keeping resources stored in a cache, the additional storage location can compensate for temporary connectivity losses or other interruptions in service.

Lesson Objectives

After completing this module, you will be able to:

- Understand basic caching considerations for Web applications.
- Identify the principal caching state representation types.

Basic Caching Considerations

> **Basic Caching Considerations**
>
> - Two caching options in ASP.NET
>   - **Output caching** allows you to cache entire pages or fragments of pages
>   - **Caching APIs** allow you to expire items from the cache based on time and other dependencies
> - The best candidates for caching are pages that are accessed frequently but change infrequently
> - Set expiration timeouts programmatically by using the **HttpCachePolicy** object

Introduction

ASP.NET provides two kinds of caching to allow faster page and data object retrieval: *output caching* (also referred to as *page caching*) and Caching APIs. This section describes output caching in detail.

Output Caching

Most developers who have had exposure to ASP.NET are familiar with output caching, which is the caching of entire pages or fragments of pages. This type of caching speeds page retrieval by serving the results of a previous execution of the page, thus preempting another execution. The cache can be configured to create different versions of the cached page according to the parameters passed to the page, as well as headers and server control values. In addition, the **OutputCache** directive allows control over the location of cached result, which can be kept in the client, on the proxy server, or on the Web server.

Rather than caching the entire output of a page, it is often more effective to cache only those portions that change infrequently, especially if they require calls to expensive resources to render. This is known as *fragment caching.* By encapsulating static portions of the page in user controls and then caching those controls, you can speed the retrieval of those portions without incurring the penalty entailed by caching an entire page that may change frequently. Good candidates for this type of caching include page fragments shared across multiple pages, such as dynamically populated menus. ASP.NET version 1.1 introduces the new **Shared** attribute for the **OutputCache** directive. This attribute allows multiple pages to share a single instance of a cached user control rather than having each page get its own instance of the cached fragment as with the current version.

Deciding Which Pages to Cache

The pages that make the best candidates for caching are ones that are accessed frequently but change infrequently. The benefits are even greater when the page requires database calls or other resource-intensive access the first time it is rendered. The main consideration in this type of decision is to balance the server memory allocated to the cached objects with the frequency with which those resources are likely to be requested. Although some optimization is provided automatically in that pages that are not frequently accessed will be scavenged (removed from the cache), caching pages or versions of pages that will be rarely accessed is a waste of memory.

This often becomes an issue when using the **VaryByParam** attribute of the **OutputCache** directive. A developer might suppose that setting **VaryByParam** = "*" would yield the best performance Because it would allow each version of the page to be automatically cached. It is likely that many versions of the page will only be accessed once, thus leading to a waste of memory for those pages. One way to compensate for this is to use a sliding expiration time for the pages that have this setting. Versions of the pages that are frequently accessed will be kept in the cache, while those that are not will be removed as their expiration time is reached.

Setting Expiration Timeouts

Be aware that this will entail varying expiration timeouts and thus varying degrees of staleness in the information cached. Sliding expirations must be set programmatically by using the properties of the **HttpCachePolicy** object, as shown in the following code example:

Microsoft® Visual Basic® .NET

```
Private Sub Page_Load(ByVal sender As System.Object, ByVal e As _
    System.EventArgs) Handles MyBase.Load
    'Put user code to initialize the page here
    Response.Cache.SetExpires(DateTime.Now.AddSeconds(3600))
    Response.Cache.SetCacheability(HttpCacheability.Public)
    Response.Cache.SetSlidingExpiration(True)
End Sub
```

C#

```
public void Page_Load(object sender, System.EventArgs e)
{   // Put user code to initialize the page here
    Response.Cache.SetExpires(DateTime.Now.AddSeconds(3600));
    Response.Cache.SetCacheability(HttpCacheability.Public);
    Response.Cache.SetSlidingExpiration(True);
}
```

This code segment sets a sliding expiration time of 60 minutes. The **SetCacheability** property is set by using the **HttpCacheability** enumeration to Public, which means that the response is cacheable by both the client browser and proxy servers. These settings will cause pages that are frequently accessed to be cached and infrequently accessed pages to be removed.

Unlike page caching, fragment caching does not support the **Location** or the **VaryByHeader** attributes. The fragment will be cached on the client and the server by using the default values. Because **VaryByHeader** is not allowed, there can be no language- or browser-specific caching of user controls.

Where to Cache Data

> **Where to Cache Data**
> - Cache data as close to the data source as possible
> - Cache raw (unprocessed) data in data access components to avoid further database retrieval
> - Cache transformed data in user interface components

Introduction

This section provides an overview of two important data caching considerations: where to cache your data, and use of the **Configuration** class to manage settings.

Where to Cache Data

The general rule for all data caching is to cache as close to the data source as possible. Raw data is data retrieved from a database but not yet processed by any business or user interface components. Such data should be cached in data access components to avoid further database retrieval. After data has been processed according to an application's business rules, it should be cached in business logic components to avoid the expense of reprocessing.

After data has been transformed into a rendering format such as Hypertext Markup Language (HTML), it should be cached in user interface components, especially where the display takes a large amount of output. This applies especially to dynamically rendered controls such as **TreeViews**, and other navigation controls that hold large amounts of rarely changed data. You should keep these options in mind as you consider the best strategy for caching data in your Web applications. Later in this module, you will use a user interface component to cache the output of the user controls from which the portal interface is created.

Configuration Class

In the portal, one of the main business components is the **Configuration** class, which encapsulates the logic necessary to manage tab configuration settings, module configuration settings, and module definition configuration settings that have been loaded from the PortalCfg.xml file.

The Caching API is used in this class to cache the **SiteConfiguration** object that corresponds to the settings in the PortalCfg.xml file. Not only does this allow fast access to these constantly used values, but a **CacheDependency** has been added so that any changes to the underlying Extensible Markup Language (XML) file invalidate the cache and cause the new settings to be loaded into the cache object. (This code is from the **Configuration** class in the lab portal application.)

Visual Basic .NET

```
HttpContext.Current.Cache.Insert("SiteSettings", siteSettings, New _
    CacheDependency(configFile))
```

C#

```
HttpContext.Current.Cache.Insert("SiteSettings", siteSettings, new
    CacheDependency(configFile));
```

Lesson: ASP.NET Caching Strategies

> **Lesson: ASP.NET Caching Strategies**
>
> - ASP.NET Data Caching
> - Summary: Using the Cache Object
> - Fragment Caching Strategies
> - Caching in the Data Layer
> - Managing Sessions
> - Determining What to Store in Session State
> - Client-Side Caching Options
> - Tradeoffs Between View State and Session State
> - Best Practices for Caching

Overview

Developers of ASP.NET Web applications can implement a number of different caching strategies to suit their specific business needs. This lesson describes several of the most useful data caching strategies and best practices.

Lesson Objectives

After completing this module, you will be able to:

- Understand data caching in the context of ASP.NET.
- Explain the use of the **Cache** object in a data caching scenario.
- Describe strategies for caching data fragments.
- Describe how to manage sessions.
- Identify the available client-side caching options.
- Contrast the advantages and disadvantages of Session state versus View state.

ASP.NET Data Caching

> **ASP.NET Data Caching**
>
> - **Cache** object
>   - Because objects can be removed, they must be checked every time the cache is accessed to ensure that they are still there
>   - Data contained in **Cache** objects can be corrupted unless a locking mechanism prevents it
>   - Has no **Lock** and **Unlock** methods but serializes access automatically
> - **Application** object
>   - Similar to **Cache** object, but items placed in the **Application** object are guaranteed to persist for the application's lifetime

Introduction

The traditional ASP approach to storing data that needs to be available to all users of an application is to use the **Application** object. In ASP.NET, the **Cache** object offers much the the same functionality, but enhances it in many ways to make it the preferred data repository.

Differences Between the Cache and Application Object

The major difference between the **Cache** and **Application** objects is that because objects placed in the **Cache** can be periodically removed, an object must be checked every time it is accessed to ensure that it is still there.

Also, similar to the **Application** object, the **Cache** object is scoped to the application domain within which the application is executing. The objects it stores can be simultaneously accessed by multiple users, and their data can be corrupted unless a locking mechanism prevents it.

In addition, unlike the **Application** object, the **Cache** object has no **Lock** and **Unlock** methods, but instead serializes access automatically.

Caching Tradeoffs

The only significant advantage that the **Application** object has over the **Cache** object is that items placed in the **Application** object are guaranteed to persist for the application's lifetime. As server resources diminish, objects placed in the **Cache** will be evicted according to the priority with which they have been configured. The lifetime of **Application** objects indicates the best practice for choosing **Application** or **Cache** objects to store data. **Cache** objects work best at page scope for objects that can be easily recreated.

Ensuring thread safety requires that objects can be accessed from multiple threads without unwanted interaction between them. Without thread safety, one user might read a value from a cache object while another is making changes to that same value. One thread might remove the item from the cache while another attempts to read that value. Fortunately, the **Cache** object provides an automatic locking mechanism that ensures that concurrent requests for an item cannot modify the object. This automatic locking mechanism protects in-process transactions when items are being updated.

This protection does not extend to accessing and modifying values stored in the cache, but only to placing and removing objects from the cache. If it is desirable to add a new row to a **DataTable** stored in the cache, it would be better to invalidate the cache, re-create the **DataTable** with the new row, and then store the new **DataTable** in the cache, rather than trying to modify it while it is in the cache. Concurrent access to the cache means that such a modification could easily lead to corruption.

Internally, the cache object uses a multi-reader, single writer object named **ReaderWriterLock** to enforce thread synchronization. If you need to enforce synchronization for multi-step updates, you can use the following code as a model:

Visual Basic .NET

```
Class Resource
    Private rwl As New ReaderWriterLock()
    Private mData As System.Object

    Public Sub SetData(ByVal data As System.Object)
        rwl.AcquireWriterLock(Timeout.Infinite)
        ' Update object data.
        rwl.ReleaseWriterLock()
    End Sub 'SetData

    Public Function GetData() As System.Object
        ' Thread locks if other thread has writer lock
        rwl.AcquireReaderLock(Timeout.Infinite)
        ' Get object data...
        rwl.ReleaseReaderLock()
        Return mData
    End Function 'GetData
End Class 'Resource
```

C#

```
public class Resource
{
    private ReaderWriterLock rwl = new ReaderWriterLock();
    private object mData;

    public void SetData(object data)
    {
        rwl.AcquireWriterLock(Timeout.Infinite);
        // Update object data.
        rwl.ReleaseWriterLock();
    }

    public object GetData()
    {
        // Thread locks if other thread has writer lock
        rwl.AcquireReaderLock(Timeout.Infinite);
        // Get object data...
        rwl.ReleaseReaderLock();
        return mData;
    }
}
```

Database Dependencies

One of the most convenient features of the **Cache** object is its ability to create dependencies between objects and files. Unfortunately, most data used in Web applications resides in databases rather than files. To create a cache dependency that works with a database, you can use a database trigger to modify a file when a row in a data table changes. The **CacheDependency** object can reference this file and invalidate the **Cache** when it changes. Objections can be raised to this technique.

The database server and the Web server are usually housed on different computers. For the **Cache** object to detect changes in the file, it must be able to access the file over the network. The **Cache** object uses Microsoft® Win32® file change notifications, which allow the use of Universal Naming Convention (UNC) path names. Therefore, a **CacheDependency** object can be created with the following code:

Visual Basic .NET

```
New CacheDependency ("\\DatabaseServerName\ASPDirectory\FileChange.txt")
```

C#

```
new CacheDependency ("\\DatabaseServerName\ASPDirectory\FileChange.txt");
```

Multiple Web servers could therefore access the file that signals the change, as this diagram illustrates:

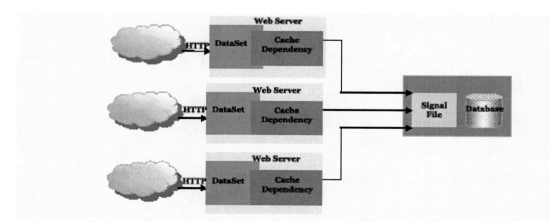

However, another obstacle arises at this point. Because the ASP.NET worker process runs in a local account, by default it cannot authenticate on remote servers. When it tries to access the file on the database server, an access denied error will be returned. One solution is to configure ASP.NET to use an account that can be authenticated on the remote server. The <processModel> section of the machine.config file has userName and password elements that define the account used by the ASP.NET worker process. This file could be modified on each Web server to reflect an appropriate account.

However, using passwords in plain text files opens up a security vulnerability, as you saw earlier, with connection strings stored in the web.config file. Version 1.1 of the .NET Framework allows these credentials to be encrypted and stored securely in the registry. A hotfix that allows this with Version 1.0 can be obtained at http://support.microsoft.com/?kbid=329250. After this hotfix is installed, the processModel can store the account used for the worker process in the following manner:

```
<processModel>
    enable="true"
    userName="registry:HKLM\Software\SomeKey,somevalue"
    password="registry:HKLM\Software\SomeKey,somevalue"
    ...
</processModel>
```

Caching Data Elements

One of the purposes of the **DataSet** object is to supply a data repository that can be easily serialized either for network transport or for storage. The structure of a **DataSet** is defined by a schema, which makes deserialization and reading the data by the client very straightforward. The **DataSet** is therefore the natural and preferred candidate for data caching.

DataReader objects should never be cached. The **DataReader** holds an open database connection, which will remain open while the object is in the cache, impacting other users of the application. As more **DataReaders** are added to the cache, all of the database connections will eventually be used up, making the database unusable until connections are closed. Not only is this a bad practice, but it also accomplishes none of the goals of caching. Because the **DataReader** is a forward-only stream of data, it is no longer available after it is read by the client, and therefore caching it achieves no purpose at all.

A recommendation that is sometimes found in books on ASP.NET is to cache **DataView** objects for reuse later in binding grids and other databound controls. This seems like an acceptable practice until one realizes what the **DataView** actually consists of: a nonserializable class that represents a view built on top of a **DataTable**. It does not contain data, but only caches the indexes of the rows in the underlying table that match the current filter and sorting rules that are being applied. Caching a **DataView** accomplishes no purpose without also caching the underlying data.

It is not a good practice to cache **DataAdapters** because they use **DataReaders** as the underlying means to fill **DataSets**. Of the classes in the data namespaces, only the **DataSet** is a suitable candidate for caching.

Summary: Using the Cache Object

> **Summary: Using the Cache Object**
> - Cache frequently used information that is relatively expensive to acquire
> - Keep the cache duration for the page shorter than the duration for the data objects placed in the cache
> - Set the time-out value according to a reasonable expectation of when the underlying data is likely to change
> - Use application performance counters to monitor the effectiveness of the caching strategy

Introduction

This section briefly summarizes some of the most important points to consider when using a **Cache** object.

Best Practices for Use of the Cache Object

The fundamental rule of caching is to cache frequently used information that is relatively expensive to acquire. When data caching, it is a good general rule to keep the cache duration for the page shorter than the duration for the data objects placed in the cache. This will ensure that the page does not get stale before the items in the cache. Recall that the default expiration time for cached items is no time-out. The time-out value should be set according to a reasonable expectation of when the underlying data is likely to change.

Several application performance counters can be used to monitor the effectiveness of the caching strategy. One of the most useful is the **Cache Total Turnover Rate**, which measures the total number of additions and removals from the cache each second. The higher this number, the more frequently items are being added and removed from the cache, and therefore the less effective the caching strategy is likely to be. **Cache Total Hit Ratio** measures the ratio of hits to misses for the cache – the higher this number, the better the strategy.

Fragment Caching Strategies

> **Fragment Caching Strategies**
>
> - The **PortalModuleControl** Class
>   - Defines a custom base class inherited by all modules in the portal
>   - Defines properties for the values that will be used to render the user controls Self-Caching Control
> - **CachedPortalModuleControl** wraps the output of a **PortalModuleControl** and stores the output in the **Cache** object

Introduction

Most ASP.NET developers are familiar with the practice of fragment caching, which is the use of an **OutputCache** directive on a user control to cache only a portion of a page. This practice does not address control caching when the controls are dynamically loaded, as is the case with the portal. For this purpose, you derive a custom control from the base **PortalModuleControl** class that will furnish an elegant, reusable, and scalable solution to this common problem.

The PortalModuleControl Class

To gain insight into one of the fundamental elements of portal functionality, you will first examine the class to be inherited. The **PortalModuleControl** defines a custom base class inherited by all modules in the portal. This base class derives from **UserControl**, which allows each module that inherits it to be treated as a user control at run time. The class defines properties for the values that will be used to render the user controls: **ModuleId**, **PortalId**, **Settings**, and **ModuleConfiguration**. The **Settings** property (a **HashTable** with name/value pairs) corresponds to the extra settings required by certain modules such as the Image Module, which needs a reference to one or more images, as shown in the following example:

```
<Settings>
    <Setting Name="src">~/data/nightvis.gif</Setting>
</Settings>
```

The **ModuleConfiguration** property contains a **ModuleSettings** object with detailed module settings for a specific module. The **IsEditable** property is a Boolean value that designates whether a module can be edited. Each user control, such as **Announcements**, inherits this class so that it has access to this base functionality.

CachedPortalModuleControl

To ensure that modules are retrieved from the cache rather than re-executed each time a new page is displayed, a class deriving from the **Control** class named **CachedPortalModuleControl** has been defined. In the **Page_Init** event of the DesktopDefault code-behind page, the _moduleSettings property for each module is checked to see if caching has been turned on for that module through the **CacheTime** property. If not, the user control instance is created and dynamically loaded into the page. If caching has been enabled for the module, a new **CachedPortalModuleControl** is instantiated, and the corresponding module is added to the designated pane for the page. (This code is from the code-behind file for the DesktopDefault.aspx page in the lab portal application.)

Visual Basic .NET

```vb
If _moduleSettings.CacheTime = 0 Then

    Dim portalModule As PortalModuleControl = _
        CType(Page.LoadControl(_moduleSettings.DesktopSrc), _
        PortalModuleControl)

    portalModule.PortalId = _portalSettings.PortalId
    portalModule.ModuleConfiguration = _moduleSettings

    parent.Controls.Add(portalModule)

Else

    Dim portalModule As New CachedPortalModuleControl()
    portalModule.PortalId = _portalSettings.PortalId
    portalModule.ModuleConfiguration = _moduleSettings

    parent.Controls.Add(portalModule)

End If
```

C#

```csharp
if ((_moduleSettings.CacheTime) == 0)
{
    PortalModuleControl portalModule = (PortalModuleControl)
        Page.LoadControl(_moduleSettings.DesktopSrc);

    portalModule.PortalId = portalSettings.PortalId;
    portalModule.ModuleConfiguration = _moduleSettings;

    parent.Controls.Add(portalModule);
} else {

    CachedPortalModuleControl portalModule = new
        CachedPortalModuleControl();

    portalModule.PortalId = portalSettings.PortalId;
    portalModule.ModuleConfiguration = _moduleSettings;

    parent.Controls.Add(portalModule);
}
```

The **CachedPortalModuleControl** wraps the output of a **PortalModuleControl** and stores the output in the **Cache** object. The **Render** method of the **Control** class is used to create the output from the user control into the page output stream. The **CachedPortalModuleControl** overrides this method so that, in addition to rendering the content to the client, it can also store the content in a **Cache** object.

The method also checks to see if content from a previous rendering of the control is available. The **CreateChildControls** method, which is normally used to signal to a control that it should create child controls, is overridden so that a check can be made for a previous rendering of the control. This is necessary because the check has to take place before the rendering process has begun. The method checks the cache for an item with the **CacheKey** corresponding to the particular module to be rendered. (This code is from the **CachedPortalModuleControl** class in the lab portal application.)

Visual Basic .NET

```vbnet
Protected Overrides Sub CreateChildControls()

    ' Attempt to resolve previously cached content from the ASP.NET Cache
    If _moduleConfiguration.CacheTime > 0 Then
        _cachedOutput = CStr(Context.Cache(CacheKey))
    End If

    ' If no cached content is found, then instantiate and add the portal
    ' module user control into the portal's page server control tree
    If _cachedOutput Is Nothing Then

        MyBase.CreateChildControls()
        Dim [module] As PortalModuleControl = _
            CType(Page.LoadControl(_moduleConfiguration.DesktopSrc), _
            PortalModuleControl)

        [module].ModuleConfiguration = Me.ModuleConfiguration
        [module].PortalId = Me.PortalId

        Me.Controls.Add([module])

    End If

End Sub
```

C#

```csharp
protected override void CreateChildControls()
{
    // Attempt to resolve previously cached content from the ASP.NET Cache

    if (_moduleConfiguration.CacheTime > 0)
    {
        _cachedOutput = (String) Context.Cache[CacheKey];
    }

    // If no cached content is found, then instantiate and add the portal
    // module user control into the portal's page server control tree

    if (_cachedOutput == null)
    {

        base.CreateChildControls();

        PortalModuleControl module = (PortalModuleControl)
            Page.LoadControl(_moduleConfiguration.DesktopSrc);

        module.ModuleConfiguration = this.ModuleConfiguration;
        module.PortalId = this.PortalId;

        this.Controls.Add(module);
    }
}
```

If the content does not exist in the cache, it is created and added to the control tree of the page. In the **Render** method, the _cachedOutput variable is checked for content, and if it is found empty, the content is rendered and stored in the **Cache** object. (This code is from the **CachedPortalModuleControl** class in the lab portal application.)

Visual Basic .NET

```vbnet
Protected Overrides Sub Render(ByVal output As HtmlTextWriter)

    ' If no caching is specified, render the child tree and return
    If _moduleConfiguration.CacheTime = 0 Then
        MyBase.Render(output)
        Return
    End If

    ' If no cached output was found from a previous request, render
    ' child controls into a TextWriter, and then cache the results
    ' in the ASP.NET Cache for future requests.
    If _cachedOutput Is Nothing Then

        Dim tempWriter = New StringWriter()
        MyBase.Render(New HtmlTextWriter(tempWriter))
        _cachedOutput = tempWriter.ToString()

        Context.Cache.Insert(CacheKey, _cachedOutput, Nothing, _
            DateTime.Now.AddSeconds(_moduleConfiguration.CacheTime), _
            TimeSpan.Zero)

    End If

    ' Output the user control's content
    output.Write(_cachedOutput)

End Sub
```

C#

```csharp
protected override void Render(HtmlTextWriter output)
{
    // If no caching is specified, render the child tree and return

    if (_moduleConfiguration.CacheTime == 0)
    {
        base.Render(output);
        return;
    }

    // If no cached output was found from a previous request, render
    // child controls into a TextWriter, and then cache the results
    // in the ASP.NET Cache for future requests.

    if (_cachedOutput == null)
    {
        TextWriter tempWriter = new StringWriter();
        base.Render(new HtmlTextWriter(tempWriter));
        _cachedOutput = tempWriter.ToString();

        Context.Cache.Insert(CacheKey, _cachedOutput, null,
            DateTime.Now.AddSeconds(_moduleConfiguration.CacheTime),
            TimeSpan.Zero);
    }

    // Output the user control's content
    output.Write(_cachedOutput);
}
```

Note that the **_moduleConfiguration** object's **CacheTime** property is used to control the expiration time for the cached content. This method allows controls to be cached for the designated time while still being rendered dynamically according to page requirements. In this way, you get optimal performance and cache management built into the standard module framework.

Caching in the Data Layer

Caching in the Data Layer

- Data caching strategies
  - Store parameter objects in **HashTables**
  - Repopulate and validate parameters by using the **CloneParameter** method
  - Use the **GetCachedParameterSet** method to retrieve arrays
- Alternatives to using the **Cache** object
  - Data abstraction layers
  - Static variables

Introduction

The data access layer is the central gateway used by all parts of an application to access and update data. It is the main location where a solid caching strategy can bring maximum performance and scalability benefits.

Data Caching Strategies

Earlier, you examined which layers of an application were appropriate for which types of cached data. The data access layer was found to be the best location for caching raw data. This layer was implemented by using the Data Access Application Block (DAAB) for optimized access to the data store and to consolidate common functionality into a single set of classes.

One of the most common operations for data access layer components is to execute stored procedures multiple times. Stored procedures usually require parameters to carry out their operations. In Microsoft® ActiveX® Directory Objects .NET (ADO.NET), each parameter must correspond to a **Parameter** object, and the DAAB includes flexible overloads to automate this process. Because parameters are used so frequently, they are prime candidates for caching. That way they do not have to be re-created every time the procedure is executed. The DAAB provides a **SqlHelper**

This caching must be implemented in such a way that both single values and arrays of **Parameter** objects are stored. When a method in the DAAB executes a stored procedure, it should be able to immediately retrieve the parameters or parameter array for that procedure. The two methods of the **SqlHelperParameterClass** used for this purpose are **CacheParameterSet**, which stores the parameters, and **GetCachedParameterSet**, which retrieves the parameters by using a static member variable. This private member variable stores the parameter objects in a **HashTable**, chosen for speedy access and type safety.

It would be convenient for the client to be able to make changes to the parameter values without necessarily affecting the cached parameter arrays. Parameters can be repopulated and validated without impacting the cached objects. To support this, a **CloneParameter** method is supplied.

When parameter arrays are inserted into the cache, they need a key so that they can be associated with a particular stored procedure. This key is the concatenated values of the connection string and the command text. The key is used by the **GetCachedParameterSet** method when the array needs to be retrieved. Because the key is matched by using simple string comparison, care must be taken when passing in the connection string that it is absolutely identical each time a call is made. Otherwise, the parameters will not be retrieved, thus incurring the overhead of regenerating the parameter objects.

In order to display a typical usage pattern for caching and retrieving parameter objects, as well as the quality of support a well-designed data abstraction layer supplies, consider the process of updating a **TimeEntry** in the TimeTracker application. Whenever the user needs to update entry information about a project that he or she is working on, an **EditItemTemplate** column in the **DataGrid** allows the grid to be edited. When the edits are complete, the user clicks the Update button and the following procedure is executed (note that some parts have been omitted for the sake of brevity). (This code is from the ASP.NET Starter Kit Time Tracker application in the code-behind file of TimeEntry.aspx.)

Visual Basic .NET

```vbnet
Protected Sub TimeEntryGrid_OnUpdate(ByVal sender As [Object], ByVal e As _
    DataGridCommandEventArgs) Handles TimeEntryGrid.UpdateCommand

    Dim item As DataGridItem = _
        TimeEntryGrid.Items(TimeEntryGrid.EditItemIndex)
...

    entryLogID = _
      Convert.ToInt32(TimeEntryGrid.DataKeys(CInt(e.Item.ItemIndex)))
    userID = Convert.ToInt32(UserList.SelectedItem.Value)

    projectID = _
      Convert.ToInt32(CType(e.Item.FindControl("EntryProjects"), _
      DropDownList).SelectedItem.Value)

    categoryID = _
      Convert.ToInt32(CType(e.Item.FindControl("EntryCategories"), _
      DropDownList).SelectedItem.Value)

    taskDate = Convert.ToDateTime(CType(e.Item.FindControl("EntryDays"), _
      DropDownList).SelectedItem.Value)

    description = _
      TTSecurity.CleanStringRegex(CType(e.Item.FindControl("EntryDescription") _
      , TextBox).Text)

    duration = Convert.ToDecimal(CType(e.Item.FindControl("EntryHours"), _
      TextBox).Text)

    ' Save the TimeEntry object.
    te = New BusinessLogicLayer.TimeEntry(entryLogID, userID, projectID, _
      categoryID, taskDate, description, duration)

    te.Save()
...

End Sub
```

C#

```csharp
DataGridItem item = TimeEntryGrid.Items[ TimeEntryGrid.EditItemIndex];
...
  entryLogID =
    Convert.ToInt32(TimeEntryGrid.DataKeys[ (int)e.Item.ItemIndex] );
          userID = Convert.ToInt32(UserList.SelectedItem.Value);

  projectID = Convert.ToInt32(((DropDownList)
      e.Item.FindControl("EntryProjects")).SelectedItem.Value);

  categoryID = Convert.ToInt32(((DropDownList)
      e.Item.FindControl("EntryCategories")).SelectedItem.Value);

  taskDate = Convert.ToDateTime(((DropDownList)
      e.Item.FindControl("EntryDays")).SelectedItem.Value);

  description = TTSecurity.CleanStringRegex(((TextBox)
      e.Item.FindControl("EntryDescription")).Text);

  duration = Convert.ToDecimal(((TextBox)
      e.Item.FindControl("EntryHours")).Text);

  // Save the TimeEntry object.
  te = new BusinessLogicLayer.TimeEntry(entryLogID, userID, projectID,
      categoryID, taskDate, description, duration);
  te.Save();
```

The user-entered data is first retrieved from the **DataGrid**, and then a **TimeEntry** object is instantiated. The **TimeEntry** class contains a **Save** method that uses the data access layer to persist the values. This method consists primarily of the following call. (This code is from the ASP.NET Starter Kit Time Tracker application in the **TimeEntry** class.)

Visual Basic .NET

```
SqlHelper.ExecuteNonQuery(ConfigurationSettings.AppSettings _
   (Web.Global.CfgKeyConnString), "UpdateTimeEntry", _entryLogID, _userID, _
   _projectID, _categoryID, _entryDate, _description, _duration)
```

C#

```csharp
SqlHelper.ExecuteNonQuery(ConfigurationSettings.AppSettings
    [ Web.Global.CfgKeyConnString], "UpdateTimeEntry", _entryLogID, _userID,
    _projectID, _categoryID, _entryDate, _description, _duration);
```

The overload for this version of **ExecuteNonQuery** requires three parameters: a connection string, the name of the stored procedure, and a parameter array, which will be matched by position to the parameters used in the stored procedure. (This code is from the **SqlHelper** class included with the Democode.)

Visual Basic .NET

```vbnet
Public Overloads Shared Function ExecuteNonQuery( _
    ByVal connectionString As String, _
    ByVal spName As String, _
    ByVal ParamArray parameterValues() As Object) As Integer

    Dim commandParameters As SqlParameter()
    If (connectionString Is Nothing OrElse connectionString.Length = 0) _
        Then
        Throw New ArgumentNullException("connectionString")
    If (spName Is Nothing OrElse spName.Length = 0) Then
        Throw New ArgumentNullException("spName")

    If Not (parameterValues Is Nothing) And parameterValues.Length > 0 Then

        commandParameters = _
            SqlHelperParameterCache.GetSpParameterSet(connectionString, _
                spName)
            AssignParameterValues(commandParameters, parameterValues)

        Return ExecuteNonQuery(connectionString, _
            CommandType.StoredProcedure, _
            spName, commandParameters)

    Else

        Return ExecuteNonQuery(connectionString, _
            CommandType.StoredProcedure, spName)
    End If

End Function 'ExecuteNonQuery
```

C#

```csharp
public static int ExecuteNonQuery(string connectionString, string spName,
    params object[] parameterValues)
{
    if( connectionString == null || connectionString.Length == 0 )
        throw new ArgumentNullException( "connectionString" );
    if( spName == null || spName.Length == 0 )
        throw new ArgumentNullException( "spName" );

    // If we receive parameter values, we need to figure out where they go
    if ((parameterValues != null) && (parameterValues.Length > 0))
    {
        // Pull the parameters for this stored procedure from the parameter
        //  cache (or discover them & populate the cache)
        SqlParameter[] commandParameters =
            SqlHelperParameterCache.GetSpParameterSet(
                connectionString,
                spName);

        // Assign the provided values to these parameters based on parameter
        // order
        AssignParameterValues(commandParameters, parameterValues);

        // Call the overload that takes an array of SqlParameters
        return ExecuteNonQuery(
            connectionString,
            CommandType.StoredProcedure,
            spName,
            commandParameters);
    }
    else
    {
        // Otherwise we can just call the SP without params
        return ExecuteNonQuery(
            connectionString,
            CommandType.StoredProcedure,
            spName);
    }
}
```

The process begins either by using the **GetSpParameterSet** method to pull an array of parameter objects out of the parameter cache, or by using the **SqlCommandBuilder DeriveParameters** method to discover them and populate the cache. **AssignParameterValues** then assigns the values to each element in the array of parameter objects, according to the order in which they were passed to the **GetSpParameterSet** method. It is critical that the developer knows the parameter order in the stored procedure. The DAAB does not look up parameters by name. Now that the parameter array has been populated, you can call the overload of **ExecuteNonQuery** that accepts a parameter array. This thread of the application process eventually leads to the execution of the stored procedure.

The following is the definition of the private member variable that will be used to hold the parameter array. (This code is from the **SqlHelper** class included with the Democode.)

Visual Basic .NET

```
Private Shared paramCache As Hashtable = Hashtable.Synchronized(New _
    Hashtable())
```

C#

```
private static Hashtable paramCache = Hashtable.Synchronized(new
    Hashtable());
```

Alternatives to Using the Cache Object

This module has gone into considerable detail about using the ASP.NET **Cache** object, but there are other alternatives that can be more attractive, particularly tools such as data abstraction layers that can be used by a number of different application types.

Static variables are often used to save object state and to create customized cache objects, as you can see in the **SqlHelperParameterCache** class of the DAAB in the above example. This is an easy-to-implement approach so long as no expirations, dependencies, or scavenging features are required. Because the class member is stored in-memory, the application has fast, direct access to the cached data. Its main disadvantage is that there is no built-in mechanism for invalidating the cache, as with the **Cache** object. It should be used with caution in Web applications that may be caching several sets of parameter arrays.

Note the use of the **Synchronized** method of the **HashTable**. Because read access tends to be more frequent than write access, the **HashTable** is built to support one writer and multiple readers concurrently. The **Synchronized** method returns a thread-safe wrapper for the **HashTable** so that it can support multiple write operations concurrently. Although using this method will aid thread safety, enumerating through a collection is inherently not a thread-safe procedure. Even if the collection as a whole is thread-safe, the items in the collection (in this case, the **Parameter** objects) could be modified by different threads. This will cause the enumerator to throw an exception. If the function enumerated the objects in the **HashTable**, you would have to apply a **SyncLock** statement before enumerating to ensure safe access. Because you are using a key to look up only one set of parameter objects at a time, you can dispense with this added code.

The **GetSpParameterSet** method retrieves the cached parameter array corresponding to a particular key as follows. (This code is from the **SqlHelper** class included with the Democode.)

Visual Basic .NET

```
Public Overloads Shared Function GetSpParameterSetInternal ( _
    ByVal connectionString As String, _
    ByVal spName As String, _
    ByVal includeReturnValueParameter As Boolean) As SqlParameter()

    Dim cachedParameters() As SqlParameter
    Dim hashKey As String

    hashKey = connectionString + ":" + spName + _
        IIf(includeReturnValueParameter = True, ":include
        ReturnValue Parameter", "")

    cachedParameters = CType(paramCache(hashKey), SqlParameter())

    If (cachedParameters Is Nothing) Then

        paramCache(hashKey) = _
            DiscoverSpParameterSet(connectionString, spName, _
                includeReturnValueParameter)
        cachedParameters = CType(paramCache(hashKey), _
            SqlParameter())

    End If

    Return CloneParameters(cachedParameters)

End Function 'GetSpParameterSet
```

C#

```csharp
private static SqlParameter[] GetSpParameterSetInternal(
    SqlConnection connection,
    string spName,
    bool includeReturnValueParameter)
{
    if( connection == null ) throw new ArgumentNullException( "connection" );
    if( spName == null || spName.Length == 0 ) throw new
    ArgumentNullException( "spName" );

    string hashKey = connection.ConnectionString + ":" + spName +
        (includeReturnValueParameter ? ":include ReturnValue Parameter":"");

    SqlParameter[] cachedParameters;

    cachedParameters = paramCache[hashKey] as SqlParameter[];
    if (cachedParameters == null)
    {
        SqlParameter[] spParameters = DiscoverSpParameterSet(
            connection,
            spName,
            includeReturnValueParameter);
        paramCache[hashKey] = spParameters;
        cachedParameters = spParameters;
    }

    return CloneParameters(cachedParameters);
}
```

The **hashKey** value optionally includes the Boolean **includeReturnValueParameter** in case the return value is required. The concatenated key is used to look up the correct parameter array in the **HashTable**. If the array is not found, the **DiscoverSpParameterSet** method is used to look up the parameters from the database. The array is stored in the **paramCache** member. The **CloneParameters** method is then used to return the values without affecting what is stored in the member.

One final item to note about the DAAB is that a new version (v. 2) was released in summer 2003 that contains several new features:

- Support for strongly typed **DataSets**.
- Support for committing updates back to the database.
- Support for **DataRow** parameters.

Managing Sessions

> **Managing Sessions**
>
> - Three ways to maintain client state
>   - Session state
>   - Cookie state
>   - View state
> - Session state is the most flexible and efficient
> - **StateServer** mode improved in ASP.NET 1.1
> - **SqlServer** mode
>   - Safest and most reliable mode
>   - Slowest mode because state must be serialized

Introduction

Most ASP.NET developers are familiar with the improved functionality of the **HttpSession** class over previous versions of the **Session** object. Of the three ways of maintaining client state—Session state, Cookie state, and View state—Session state is widely considered to be the most flexible and efficient. Many problems associated with previous versions of the Session object have been resolved in ASP.NET, but using it effectively requires awareness of a new range of issues.

Session Practices

Cache objects are effective within a single application, but when state needs to be persisted across a Web garden or Web farm, a more scalable repository needs to be considered. Session state can be configured in three modes: **InProc**, **StateServer**, and **SqlServer**. InProc stores state in the aspnet_wp.exe process and delivers the best performance because no cross-process calls are necessary. However, InProc cannot be used in a Web garden because Session state is held in independent instances of aspnet_wp.exe. For the same reason, it cannot be used in Web farms. Traditional ASP developers should be aware that only the **InProc** mode supports the **Session_End** event. The other modes cannot use this event to clean up resources used by the **Session** object.

The other modes allow cross-process state to be maintained, but entail certain limitations on the types of objects that can be stored. Any type that is stored by using **StateServer** or **SqlServer** mode must be serializable because these two modes work by serializing the object and storing it in a process outside the aspnet_wp.exe process. This limitation is important when developers attempt to store custom objects in Session variables. In such cases, the classes need to use the **Serializable** attribute to add serialization support.

Session State Improvements in ASP.NET 1.1

In ASP.NET version 1.1, **StateServer** mode has been improved to increase security., Because the state service was not restricted In ASP.NET version 1.0, any computer could access it. In ASP.NET 1.1, by default, only the local computer can retrieve values from the state service. A registry setting needs to be reset to grant any non-local computer the right to access the state service,.

There are additional configurations necessary if you intend to support Session State on a Web farm. Session state will not be accessible across servers unless the application path to the Web site is identical on all servers on the Web farm. For more information, see article Q325056, "PRB: Session State Is Lost in Web Farm If You Use **SqlServer** or **StateServer** Session Mode," in the Microsoft Knowledge Base.

Another critical consideration is failover support, because one of the main reasons for incurring the overhead of storing state out of process in the first place is to be able to recover in case of server failure. To store the Session state successfully in a failover cluster situation, the **<machineKey>** element must be set to the same value in the Machine.config file on all the Web servers on the farm. Backup servers will not be able to access the state that was stored by the failed server. For ore details, see article 323262, "INFO: ASP.NET Session State with SqlServer Mode in a Failover Cluster," in the Microsoft Knowledge Base.

SqlServer Mode

Although **SqlServer** mode is the safest and most reliable mode, it is also the slowest because state must be serialized, stored in a text column, and then retrieved whenever a page that is configured to use it loads. The larger and more complex the object, the more performance in this mode will be impeded. Serializing in this mode is efficient, especially when concurrent usage is low and small, easily serialized objects are being served, and has the added advantage over **StateServer** mode of durability.

Allowing Session state to be enabled with the default settings entails two round-trips to the database for every page load. With default Session state settings, ASP.NET assumes that the page requires Session state to be loaded during page initialization and then flushes the state back to the database before the page is disposed. A well-designed application will incur this overhead only when it is necessary. The session manager queries the current handler to determine its session requirements. By setting the **EnableSessionState** attribute to false, all the Session state overhead for that page is avoided. In cases where Session state is needed, the developer may find that the most frequent use of the **Session** object is for reading stored values. Pages that actually store values in a session tend to be relatively rare in most applications. In this case, **EnableSessionState** should be set to "readonly" to prevent the value from being unnecessarily flushed to the database server at the **ReleaseRequestState** event of page execution.

SqlServer mode entails consequences that may not be apparent. When using this mode, a connection string must be supplied in the web.config file to connect to the database that will store Session state. If this connection string uses integrated security, you cannot use impersonation in ASP.NET. For more information about this problem, see article Q324479, "FIX: ASP.NET SQL Server Session State Impersonation is Lost Under Load," in the Microsoft Knowledge Base.

This connection string does not require a database to be designated. By default, tempdb is used. Because this database is not fully logged, storing Session state here increases performance. Because tempdb is recreated whenever SqlServer reboots, all state is lost whenever the database server needs to be recycled. Microsoft provides scripts that can be used to persist state between reboots if this is a requirement. Full details can be found in article Q311209, "Configure ASP.NET for Persistent SQL Server Session State Management," in the Microsoft Knowledge Base. A high-traffic site can accumulate Session state rapidly, so a job is supplied with the default installation that cleans up expired Session state daily.

Determining What to Store in Session State

> **Determining What to Store in Session State**
>
> - Candidates for storage in Session state
>   - Complex types
>   - Custom collection types
>   - Large objects
> - Must be serialized, or response times will markedly degrade
>   - Use **BinaryFormatter**

Introduction

Basic types (numeric types, Boolean values, strings, etc.) are good candidates for storage using any mode because ASP.NET uses optimized serialization and deserialization methods for these data types when using out-of-process modes. When using complex types such as **SortedList** or custom collection types, the data must be serialized by using the **BinaryFormatter**. The overhead of serializing and deserializing these types, especially in **SqlServer** mode, can have a significant impact on performance. The same applies to large data objects. Though many variables are involved, response times on most Web servers will tend to markedly degrade when more than 200 kilobytes (KB) of data are stored in Session state.

Choosing Which Objects to Store in Session State

Choosing which objects to store in Session state is well illustrated in the TimeTracker's ProjectDetails.aspx page. This large and complex form allows users to enter information about a new project. When the Save button is clicked, the information the user entered for the project is validated, the properties for a new **Project** object are set, and the **Save** method of the **Project** object is called to persist the details for the new project.

Part of this process is to save and validate the categories that the user has selected for this project. These categories are bound to a **DataGrid**. The categories are stored in a custom collection class named **CategoriesCollection**, which inherits from **ArrayList**. Because **ArrayList** is marked with the **SerializableAttribute**, **CategoriesCollection** can be stored in a Session variable by using any of the modes. In the **Page_Load** event, the **CategoriesCollection** is initialized and stored in a Session variable. (This code is from the ASP.NET Starter Kit Time Tracker application in the code-behind file for the ProjectsDetails.aspx.)

Visual Basic .NET

```
Session("catArray") = New CategoriesCollection()
```

C#

```
Session["catArray"] = new CategoriesCollection();
```

The **AddButton_Click** event provides the logic necessary to add a category to the **CategoriesCollection**. After validations are complete, the current collection object is retrieved as follows. (This code is from the ASP.NET Starter Kit Time Tracker application in the code-behind file for the ProjectsDetails.aspx.)

Visual Basic .NET

```
Dim catArray As CategoriesCollection = CType(Session("catArray"), _
    CategoriesCollection)
If catArray Is Nothing Then
    catArray = New CategoriesCollection()
End If
```

C#

```
CategoriesCollection catArray = (CategoriesCollection)Session["catArray"];
if (catArray == null)
    catArray = new CategoriesCollection();
```

Notice that the object stored in the **Session** must be converted into the type needed in the procedure. Objects retrieved from **Session** variables are stored in a **HashTable** requiring conversion from **System.Object**. In order to populate the **CategoriesCollection**, a **Category** object must be populated and added to the **catArray** variable holding the current state of the collection. (This code is from the ASP.NET Starter Kit Time Tracker application in the code-behind file for the ProjectsDetails.aspx.)

Visual Basic .NET

```
Dim cat As New Category()
cat.CategoryID = catID
cat.Name = TTSecurity.CleanStringRegex(CategoryName.Text)
cat.Abbreviation = TTSecurity.CleanStringRegex(Abbrev.Text)

If CatDuration.Text.Length = 0 Then
    cat.EstDuration = 0
Else
    cat.EstDuration = Convert.ToDecimal(CatDuration.Text)
End If
catArray.Add(cat)
```

C#

```
Category cat = new Category();
cat.CategoryID = catID;
cat.Name = TTSecurity.CleanStringRegex(CategoryName.Text);
cat.Abbreviation = TTSecurity.CleanStringRegex(Abbrev.Text);
cat.EstDuration = (CatDuration.Text.Length==0) ? 0 :
    Convert.ToDecimal(CatDuration.Text);
    catArray.Add(cat);
```

Whenever the grid that displays the categories is re-bound in the **BindCategoriesGrid** method, the current set of categories overwrites the previous version stored in the **Session** object. (This code is from the ASP.NET Starter Kit Time Tracker application in the code-behind file for the ProjectsDetails.aspx.)

Visual Basic .NET

```
Session("catArray") = cats
```

C#

```
Session["catID"] = catID;
```

After the user is finished adding categories and clicks the **SaveButton**, the **SaveButton_Click** event retrieves the **CategoriesCollection** object from the **Session** and uses it to assign the **Categories** property of the **Project** object.

When editing the project details is complete, the user is redirected back to the ProjectList.aspx page and the **Session** is reinitialized to nothing. (This code is from the ASP.NET Starter Kit Time Tracker application in the code-behind file for the ProjectsDetails.aspx.)

Visual Basic .NET

```
Session("catArray") = Nothing
```

C#

```
Session["catArray"] = null;
```

Because this information is specific to a particular user for a particular project, Session state is the appropriate repository, though view state could also have been used.

Client-Side Caching Options

> **Client-Side Caching Options**
>
> - Benefits of View state
>   - Enables certain controls on a form to retain their state across page refreshes
>   - Increases scalability
>   - Security is limited
> - Limitations of View state
>   - Only objects that support binary serialization can be added
>   - Best used with the values held by controls, not the controls themselves
>   - Cannot be persisted between pages

Introduction

In most cases, applications will realize higher levels of scalability and performance by taking advantage of client-side resources. The more processing load can be shifted to the client, the more resources can be freed on the server to serve more clients. However, using resources that are not under complete application control is inherently less predictable than using resources that are.

Making Best Use of View State

In order for certain controls on a form to retain their state across page refreshes, ASP.NET includes a mechanism named View state. By default, the values stored in the hidden __VIEWSTATE field are base64 encoded and contain a Machine Authentication Check, which is a hash of the field's value to prevent tampering. The key in the <machineKey> element of the machine.config file is used to encrypt the hashed value. This process is configured by using the *EnableViewStateMac* Page directive. Because the data is kept in a hidden field, this mechanism works on Web farms. Scalability also increases because state is maintained with client resources. Because the values in the __VIEWSTATE field are directly accessible to the client, security is limited.

Server controls that display simple values such as short strings work well with View state, but databound controls such as the **DataGrid, DataList,** or **DropDownList** can store large amounts of data in the __VIEWSTATE field. This data must be passed back and forth from the client to the server each time the page is posted back. In addition, when using **DataSets** as the storage vehicle for databinding, some data must be serialized and encoded, then deserialized and decoded, if it is stored in View state. By default, **DataGrids** do not maintain their own View state. The **DataSource** property of databound controls must be persisted across page refreshes, but in most cases this is best achieved through the use of Session state rather than View state.

Only objects that support binary serialization can be added to View state. Serializable objects, such as the **ArrayList**, must be marked with the **SerializableAttribute**. If an object needs to control its serialization, it must implement the **ISerializable** interface. The class signature in the documentation will reveal which attributes mark the class and which interfaces a class implements.

Limitations of View State

View state is intended to be used with simple object types such as strings, numeric types, and Booleans, as well as collection types such as arrays, **HashTables**, and the **ArrayList**. View state is therefore best used with the values held by controls, and not the controls themselves, or objects that require more complex or resource-consuming serialization.

When a server control holds large amounts of data, it is usually best to disable View state for that control by setting its **EnableViewState** property to false. The most efficient way to handle View state is usually to enable View state for the page as a whole and disable it control by control as needed. Examples of controls that should have View state turned off include labels with fixed values, controls that are programmatically populated at each page request (such as a drop-down list that is populated from a cache), and controls that do not require event handlers (text boxes often require no event handling).

When making decisions about enabling or disabling View state, the decision should be guided by the main purposes of View state: convenience for the user and reduced server load. View state cost is measured in terms of the extra bytes it adds to the page plus the overhead of serialization and encryption. The Trace output can be used to determine how many bytes a particular control is using for View state.

Leaving *EnableViewStateMac* at true can cause problems when using **Server.Transfer** to move between pages because Transfer preserves the Request collections. The Form collection includes the __VIEWSTATE hidden field to which ASP.NET runtime has appended a hashcode to help verify the integrity of the View state contents. The message authentication check fails because the hashcode will be unique for each page. The hashcode for the calling page will not be the same as the hashcode for the page called.

This scenario arises particularly when developers try to use the Context.Items collection to pass values between pages. To do this effectively, you follow the pattern described in the .NET documentation "Passing Server Control Values Between Pages," which involves creating properties for each value that needs to be transferred. This method only works if **EnableViewStateMac** is set to false. There is a related issue when using view state on a server farm. For more information, see article 316920, "PRB: 'View State Is Invalid' Error Message When You Use Server.Transfer," in the Microsoft Knowledge Base.

Enabling View State Encryption

To enable View state encryption set the <machineKey> element in the web.config file as follows:

```
<machineKey
validationKey="AutoGenerate"
decryptionKey="AutoGenerate"
validation="3DES"
/>
```

The highest level of view state protection is provided by Triple DES encryption. The precise algorithm that is used is controlled by the validation attribute of the <machineKey> element. On Microsoft® Windows® 2000 servers, if the Windows 2000 High Encryption Pack has been installed, then Triple DES is used. Otherwise, DES encryption is the default.

Enabling View State on a Server Farm

When enabling View state on a server farm, the <machineKey> element must be set to the same encryption key for all the servers on the farm. As the request is transferred from one server to another, the second server will assume that View state has been corrupted and will throw a security exception with this message "The View State is invalid for this page and might be corrupted."

AutoGenerate cannot be used in this case because this specifies that ASP.NET will generate a random key and store it in the Local Security Authority. The developer must use a CryptoServiceProvider such as the RNGCryptoSecurityProvider to generate a key and copy it to the web.config, or machine.config file, for each server for every application where View state encryption is desired. This is a case where server farm management tools such as those furnished by Application Center 2000 would come in handy. By using these tools, changes to the machine.config could be easily replicated across the Web farm.

Using Cookies

Because **ViewState** cannot be persisted between pages, cookies are often used as an alternative. The advantages are similar because this mechanism takes some of the memory load off the Web servers. Also, unlike in View state, information can be persisted between pages. Cookies can also maintain information across browser sessions, and their time-out period is completely controlled by the developer. They are also subject to many of the same limitations as View state. The information stored is subject to tampering. Unlike View state, clients can turn off cookies, completely neutralizing this storage vehicle. They are also limited to 4096 bytes in most scenarios, though support for 8192 byte cookies is increasing.

Tradeoffs Between View State and Session State

> **Tradeoffs Between View State and Session State**
>
> - Session state
>   - Session variables can store any thread-safe object type
>   - Session variables last for the duration of a user's session
>   - Provides better privacy and security
> - View state
>   - Requires that the object support binary serialization
>   - Is accessible only from the page it was posted from
>   - Is directly accessible from the source code of the page posted to the browser

Introduction

Developers encountering View state functionality for the first time often see it as a more efficient alternative to Session variables. However, Session variables are recommended for use in ASP.NET for the reasons described below.

Session State vs. View State in ASP.NET

Classic ASP developers were trained to avoid Session variables because of performance and stability issues. Because View state works by posting information from the form in a well-defined manner, it is often perceived as an attractive alternative to Sessions. However, in ASP.NET, Session variables are preferred for the following reasons:

- Session variables, which use **InProc** mode, can store any thread-safe object type. View state requires that the object support binary serialization. However, if the Session mode is set to SqlServer or StateServer, Sessions have the same limitation.

- Session variables last for the duration of a user's session – 10 minutes by default on Microsoft Internet Information Server (IIS) 5.0. View state is only accessible from the page it was posted from.

- View state is directly accessible from the source code of the page posted to the browser, but Session objects are stored on the server. If privacy and security are requirements for the persisted information, Session state is the better choice.

View state is better in situations where security is not an issue and minimizing server load is an important priority. Because View state does not time out, it would be a better choice when a user is filling out a long, complicated (but single-page) form and the developer wants to ensure that the values will not time out. View state also entails fewer configurations on a server farm. In addition, on a server farm Session state mode must be SqlServer or StateServer, which will impact performance.

In low-traffic (single-server) environments where large or complex objects must be persisted between pages, Session variables using the **InProc** mode are likely to deliver superior performance. On server farms where easily serialized values must be persisted on single pages, View state is the better choice.

Best Practices for Caching

> **Best Practices for Caching**
>
> - Use a sliding expiration time for cached pages when using the **VaryByParam** attribute of the OutputCache directive
> - Cache data as close to the data source as possible
> - Cache raw data in in data access components to avoid further database retrieval
> - Never cache a **DataReader** object
> - Set **EnableSessionState** to "readonly" to prevent the value from being unnecessarily flushed to the database server
> - Disable View state for controls holding large amounts of data by setting its **EnableViewState** property to false

Introduction

A number of recommended best practices can help you achieve the best results with caching.

Best Practices

Consider the following best practices when determining how to implement caching in your Web application:

- Use a sliding expiration time for cached pages when using the **VaryByParam** attribute of the OutputCache directive. In this way, versions of the pages that are frequently accessed will be kept in the cache, while those that are not will be removed as their expiration time is reached.

- The general rule for all data caching is to cache data as close to the data source as possible. Raw data should be cached in data access components to avoid further database retrieval.

- Thread safety in the **Cache** object does not extend to accessing and modifying values stored in the cache, but only to placing and removing objects from the cache. If it were desirable to add a new row to a **DataTable** stored in the cache, it would be better to invalidate the cache, recreate the **DataTable** with the new row, and store the new **DataTable** in the cache, rather than trying to modify it while it was in the cache. Concurrent access to the cache means that such a modification could easily lead to corruption.

- **DataReader** objects should never be cached. The **DataReader** holds an open database connection, which will remain open while the object is in the cache, thereby impacting other users of the application. As more **DataReaders** are added to the cache, eventually all database connections will be used up, making the database unusable until connections are closed.

- The developer may find that the most frequent use of the Session object is for reading stored values. Pages that actually store values in a session tend to be relatively rare in most applications. In this case, **EnableSessionState** should be set to "readonly" to prevent the value from being unnecessarily flushed to the database server at the **ReleaseRequestState** event of page execution.

- When a server control holds large amounts of data, it is usually best to disable View state for that control by setting its **EnableViewState** property to false. The most efficient way to handle View state is usually to enable View state for the page as a whole and disable it control by control as needed. Examples of controls that should have View state turned off include labels with fixed values, controls that are programmatically populated at each page request (for example, a drop-down list that is populated from a cache), and controls that do not require event handlers.

Lab 7: Caching in the Portal Application

Lab 7: Caching in the Portal Application
- Exercise 1: Caching Site Configuration
- Exercise 2: Caching Dynamic Controls

Introduction

In most cases, the most effective tool for increasing the performance of Web applications is caching frequently used pages and data objects. The .NET Framework provides support for this in the **Cache** object. The portal uses custom controls to dynamically populate the user interface for each tab. Because most of the interface functionality is contained in these user controls, caching the controls will have a direct and significant impact on site performance. In order to minimize code duplication, this caching functionality should be placed into a custom control class that can be dynamically loaded. The student will implement this custom control class caching functionality in the second exercise.

After completing this lab, you will have demonstrated your ability to:

- Use the major properties and methods of the **Cache** object.
- Create custom controls by deriving from the **Control** class.
- Read configuration settings into a typed **DataSet**.
- Implement a caching strategy for dynamically loaded user controls.

Prerequisites

Before working on this lab, you must have the knowledge and skills necessary to manipulate **Cache** objects and create custom controls.

Estimated time to complete this lab: 45 minutes

Starting a Virtual Machine

1. On the student computer, on the **Start** menu, point to **All Programs**, and then click **Microsoft Virtual PC**. If the Virtual PC console window does not appear, right-click the **Virtual PC icon** in the notification area (system tray), and click **Show Virtual PC Console**.
2. In the Virtual PC console window, select the virtual machine that you would like to open then click **Start**.

   NOTE: Depending on your time zone, the first time you start each of the virtual machines, you may receive an error message that the parent virtual hard disk appears to have been modified. You can ignore this message.
3. The virtual machine will start up in a new window.

Closing a Virtual Machine

1. On the student computer, in the virtual machine window, on the Action menu, click Close.

   NOTE: To avoid accidentally closing the virtual machine during the lab, the **Close** button in the upper-right corner of the virtual machine is disabled.
2. The virtual machine window will close. All changes to the virtual hard disk are discarded.

Exercise 1: Caching Site Configuration

In order to minimize the time it takes to access site configuration settings, you need to cache the object that contains these settings. You will do this in the **GetSiteSettings** method of the **Configuration** class.

■ Open the lab starter project

1. Open the ASPProjectVB or ASPProjectCS project in Microsoft® Visual Studio® .NET by using the following instructions.
2. Browse to D:\2311\Labfiles\Lab07\Starter\VB or D:\2311\Labfiles\Lab07\Starter\CS.
3. Launch the project by double-clicking the ASPProjectVB.sln or ASPProjectCS.sln file in the lab starter folder.

■ Populate the typed SiteConfiguration DataSet

1. Open the ASPProjectVB or ASPProjectCS project in Visual Studio .NET.
2. Open the Configuration.vb or Configuration.cs file in the Components\MainPortal folder. Locate the comment "TODO Populate the typed DataSet SiteConfiguration and cache it."
3. Declare an object of type **SiteConfiguration** named **siteSettings**. Assign it the value of the SiteSettings key cached in the **Cache** object of the **HttpContext.Current** object. Convert the object to the type of **SiteConfiguration** before assigning it.
4. Use an **If** statement to check whether **siteSettings** contains a value. If it is Nothing (null in C#), the object needs to be regenerated and cached.
5. Set the **siteSettings** variable equal to a new **SiteConfiguration** object.
6. Declare a variable named **configFile** and assign it to the path stored in the configFile of the configuration file. This value can be retrieved by using the **ConfigurationSettings.AppSettings** property. Use the **Server.MapPath** method of the **HttpContext.Current** object to get a physical path as required by the **CacheDependency** object that will be created when the **SiteConfiguration** object is cached.

7. Before populating the **SiteConfiguration** object, you need to set some **AutoIncrement** properties so that the keys for the **Tab**, **_Module**, and **ModuleDefinition** objects will be be incremented as new rows are added. Set the properties of the **siteSettings** object according to the values in the following table:

Property	Value
Tab.TabIdColumn.AutoIncrement	True
_Module.ModuleIdColumn.AutoIncrement	True
ModuleDefinition.ModuleDefIdColumn.AutoIncrement	True

8. Use the **ReadXml** method of the **siteSettings** object to read the configuration file into the typed **DataSet**.

9. Use the **Insert** method of the **Cache** object (obtained from the **HttpContext.Current** object) to insert the **siteSettings** into the cache. Use the overload that accepts three parameters according to the following table:

Parameter	Value
key	"SiteSettings"
value	siteSettings
dependency	New CacheDependency(configFile)

10. Return the **siteSettings** object from the function.

11. Your code should resemble the following:

Visual Basic .NET

```vb
Public Shared Function GetSiteSettings() As SiteConfiguration
    Dim siteSettings As SiteConfiguration = CType( _
        HttpContext.Current.Cache("SiteSettings"), _
        SiteConfiguration)

    If siteSettings Is Nothing Then
        siteSettings = New SiteConfiguration()

        Dim configFile As String = _
            HttpContext.Current.Server.MapPath( _
            ConfigurationSettings.AppSettings("configFile"))

        siteSettings.Tab.TabIdColumn.AutoIncrement = True
        siteSettings.Module.ModuleIdColumn.AutoIncrement = True
        siteSettings.ModuleDefinition.ModuleDefIdColumn.AutoIncrement = True

        siteSettings.ReadXml(configFile)

        HttpContext.Current.Cache.Insert( _
      "SiteSettings", _
            siteSettings, _
            New CacheDependency(configFile))
    End If
    Return siteSettings
End Function
```

C#

```csharp
public static SiteConfiguration GetSiteSettings()
{
    SiteConfiguration siteSettings = (SiteConfiguration)
        HttpContext.Current.Cache["SiteSettings"];

    if(siteSettings == null)
    {
        siteSettings = new SiteConfiguration();

        string configFile =
            HttpContext.Current.Server.MapPath(
            ConfigurationSettings.AppSettings["configFile"]);

        siteSettings.Tab.TabIdColumn.AutoIncrement = true;
        siteSettings.Module.ModuleIdColumn.AutoIncrement = true;
        siteSettings.ModuleDefinition.ModuleDefIdColumn.AutoIncrement = true;

        siteSettings.ReadXml(configFile);

        HttpContext.Current.Cache.Insert(
            "SiteSettings",
            siteSettings,
            new CacheDependency(configFile));
    }

    return siteSettings;
}
```

12. Whenever changes are made to the configuration of the site, the configuration file must be rewritten and saved. This is accomplished by the **SaveSiteSettings** function that retrieves the **siteSettings** object from the cache by using the **GetSiteSettings** method. It then uses the **WriteXml** method to write out the new configuration file.

▪ Populate the ActiveTab by using the siteSettings object

1. Locate the comment "TODO Retrieve siteSettings from the Cache."

2. Declare a variable of type **SiteConfiguration** named **siteSettings**. Assign it to the return value from a call to the **GetSiteSettings** function of the **Configuration** class.

3. Your code should resemble the following:

Visual Basic .NET

```
Dim siteSettings As SiteConfiguration = Configuration.GetSiteSettings()
```

C#

```
SiteConfiguration siteSettings = Configuration.GetSiteSettings();
```

4. Locate the comment "TODO Retrieve the current (Active) Tab."

5. Declare a variable of type SiteConfiguration.TabRow named **activeTab**. Assign it to the return value from a call to the **FindByTabId** method of the **siteSettings.Tab** object. The parameter to this method is the tabId passed in from the **Application_BeginRequest** method of the global.asax.

6. Your code should resemble the following:

Visual Basic .NET

```
Dim activeTab As SiteConfiguration.TabRow = siteSettings.Tab.FindByTabId(tabId)
```

C#

```
SiteConfiguration.TabRow activeTab = siteSettings.Tab.FindByTabId(tabId);
```

7. Study the remainder of the constructor. Note how the **GetModuleRows** method of the **activeTab** object is used to retrieve the modules for the current Tab. For each module, a **ModuleSettings** object is created and added to the Controls collection of the current Tab. Therefore the user interface of the entire site is driven by the configuration settings cached in the **GetSiteSettings** method of the **Configuration** class.

Exercise 2: Caching Dynamic Controls

Because the site is built from dynamically loaded user controls, one of the most effective ways to increase performance is to cache those controls. In order to minimize code duplication, this caching is most efficiently implemented by creating the functionality in the control itself. For this purpose, you will create a **CachedPortalModuleControl** that derives from the **Control** class, and use it whenever a control needs to be cached. This class will make use of the **PortalModuleControl** to get user control functionality.

■ Implement the CreateChildControls method of the CachedPortalModuleControl

1. Open the DesktopControls.vb or DesktopControls.cs file in the MainPortal folder.

2. Locate the **CachedPortalModuleControl** class. Examine the properties defined at the beginning of this class.

3. Locate the comment "TODO Implement the **CacheKey** property." The **CacheKey** property is used as the key when the control is cached. The example uses a combination of the type, the module ID, and the authorized roles to guarantee key uniqueness.

4. Create a **ReadOnly** property named **CacheKey**.

5. In the get accessor, return a string that contains the following values:

Visual Basic .NET	C#
"Key:"	"Key:"
Me.GetType().ToString	this.GetType().ToString()
Me.ModuleId	this.ModuleId
PortalSecurity.IsInRoles(_ _moduleConfiguration.AuthorizedEditRoles)	PortalSecurity.IsInRoles(_moduleConfiguration.AuthorizedEditRoles)

6. Your code should resemble the following:

Visual Basic .NET

```
Public ReadOnly Property CacheKey() As String
    Get
        Return "Key:" & _
            Me.GetType().ToString() & _
            Me.ModuleId & _
            PortalSecurity.IsInRoles( _
                _moduleConfiguration.AuthorizedEditRoles)
    End Get
        End Property
```

C#

```
public String CacheKey{

    get
    {
        return "Key:" +
            this.GetType().ToString() +
            this.ModuleId +
            PortalSecurity.IsInRoles(
                _moduleConfiguration.AuthorizedEditRoles);
    }
}
```

7. Locate the comment "TODO Implement the CreateChildControls method." This method creates instances of the child controls and adds them to the Controls collection of this control. The output of the control is defined in the **CreateChildControls** method.

8. Check the **CacheTime** property of the **_moduleConfiguration** object with an **If** statement. If it is greater than 0, try to retrieve the control from the cache by using the **CacheKey**.

9. Use an **If** statement to see if the content has been successfully retrieved from the cache. If the content is Nothing (null in C#), call the **CreateChildControls** method of the base class (MyBase in Visual Basic .NET).

10. Declare a variable of type PortalModuleControl named "**_module** and assign it to the return value from the **LoadControl** method of the **Page** object. Pass the **_moduleConfiguration.DesktopSrc** property as the parameter to the **LoadControl** method. This parameter corresponds to the ascx file that contains the module to be loaded. Convert the loaded control to an object of type **PortalModuleControl**. Your code should resemble the following:

Visual Basic .NET

```
Dim _module As PortalModuleControl = CType( _
    Page.LoadControl(_moduleConfiguration.DesktopSrc), _
    PortalModuleControl)
```

C#

```
PortalModuleControl _module = (PortalModuleControl)
    Page.LoadControl(_moduleConfiguration.DesktopSrc);
```

11. Set the properties of the **_module** object according to the following table:

Property	Value
ModuleConfiguration	Me.ModuleConfiguration
PortalId	Me.PortalId

12. Add the **_module** object to the Controls collection of the **CachedPortalModuleControl**.

13. Your code should resemble the following:

Visual Basic .NET

```vb
Protected Overrides Sub CreateChildControls()

    If _moduleConfiguration.CacheTime > 0 Then
        _cachedOutput = CType(Context.Cache(CacheKey), String)
    End If

    If _cachedOutput Is Nothing Then

        MyBase.CreateChildControls()

        Dim _module As PortalModuleControl = CType( _
            Page.LoadControl(_moduleConfiguration.DesktopSrc), _
            PortalModuleControl)

        _module.ModuleConfiguration = Me.ModuleConfiguration
        _module.PortalId = Me.PortalId

        Me.Controls.Add(_module)
    End If
End Sub
```

C#

```csharp
protected override void CreateChildControls() {

    if (_moduleConfiguration.CacheTime > 0)
    {
        _cachedOutput = (String) Context.Cache[CacheKey];
    }

    if (_cachedOutput == null)
    {

        base.CreateChildControls();

        PortalModuleControl module = (PortalModuleControl)
            Page.LoadControl(_moduleConfiguration.DesktopSrc);

        module.ModuleConfiguration = this.ModuleConfiguration;
        module.PortalId = this.PortalId;

        this.Controls.Add(module);
    }
}
```

- **Implement the Render method of the CachedPortalModuleControl**

  1. Locate the comment "TODO Implement the Render method." The **Render** method is used to write markup text to the output stream. In this implementation, the output will be retrieved from the cache if it is available; otherwise it will be created and then cached.

  2. Use an **If** statement to check the **CacheTime** property of the **_moduleConfiguration** object. If it is equal to 0, call the **Render** method of the base object (**MyBase** in Visual Basic .NET) and pass the output to the method as a parameter. End the execution with a return statement. This will render the output without caching.

  3. Use another **If** statement to check the _cachedOutput field. If it is Nothing (null in C#), declare a variable of type TextWriter named **tempWriter**. Assign it to a new instance of **StringWriter**.

  4. Call the **Render** method of the base class (**MyBase** in Visual Basic .NET). Pass a new instance of **HtmlTextWriter** by using **tempWriter** as the input parameter.

  5. Set **_cachedOutput** to the return value of calling the **ToString** method on **tempWriter**. The effect of this and the previous instruction is to direct the output of the **Render** method, which is the markup to be rendered to the output stream, to the **tempWriter** object. The contents of this object are then cached.

  6. Use the **Insert** method of the **Context.Cache** object to insert **_cachedOutput** into the cache according to the properties and values in the following table:

Property	Value
key	CacheKey
value	_cachedOutput
dependencies	Nothing (null in C#)
absoluteExpiration	DateTime.Now.AddSeconds(_moduleConfiguration.CacheTime)
slidingExpiration	TimeSpan.Zero

  7. Output the control's content by calling the **Write** method of the output object and passing in _cachedOutput as the input parameter.

8. Your code should resemble the following:

Visual Basic .NET

```
Protected Overrides Sub Render(ByVal output As HtmlTextWriter)
    If _moduleConfiguration.CacheTime = 0 Then
        MyBase.Render(output)
        Return
    End If

    If _cachedOutput Is Nothing Then

        Dim tempWriter As TextWriter = New StringWriter()
        MyBase.Render(New HtmlTextWriter(tempWriter))
        _cachedOutput = tempWriter.ToString()

        Context.Cache.Insert( _
        CacheKey, _
        _cachedOutput, _
        Nothing, _
        DateTime.Now.AddSeconds(_moduleConfiguration.CacheTime), _
        TimeSpan.Zero)
    End If

        output.Write(_cachedOutput)
End Sub
```

C#

```csharp
protected override void Render(HtmlTextWriter output)
{
    if (_moduleConfiguration.CacheTime == 0)
    {
        base.Render(output);
        return;
    }

    if (_cachedOutput == null)
    {

        TextWriter tempWriter = new StringWriter();
        base.Render(new HtmlTextWriter(tempWriter));
        _cachedOutput = tempWriter.ToString();

        Context.Cache.Insert(
           CacheKey,
           _cachedOutput,
           null,
            DateTime.Now.AddSeconds(_moduleConfiguration.CacheTime),
           TimeSpan.Zero);
    }

    output.Write(_cachedOutput);
}
```

- **Use the CachedPortalModuleControl in the DesktopDefault.aspx page**

    1. Open the DesktopDefault.aspx.vb file in the application root.

    2. Locate the comment "TODO Create and populate a CachedPortalModuleControl." Note the **If** statement that contains this **Else** clause. It checks if the **CacheTime** property of **_moduleSettings** is equal to 0. If so, no caching is needed, so the module is loaded by using a **PortalModuleControl**. If **CacheTime** is not equal to 0, a **CachedPortalModuleControl** should be used.

    3. In the **Else** clause, declare and instantiate a **CachedPortalModuleControl** named **portalModule**.

4. Set the properties of the control according to the following table:

Property	Value
PortalId	portalSettings.PortalId
ModuleConfiguration	_moduleSettings

5. Add **portalModule** to the Controls collection of the parent object, which corresponds to the pane where the module will be inserted.
6. Your code should resemble the following:

Visual Basic .NET

```vbnet
Dim portalModule As New CachedPortalModuleControl()

portalModule.PortalId = portalSettings.PortalId
portalModule.ModuleConfiguration = _moduleSettings

parent.Controls.Add(portalModule)
```

C#

```csharp
CachedPortalModuleControl portalModule = new CachedPortalModuleControl();

portalModule.PortalId = portalSettings.PortalId;
portalModule.ModuleConfiguration = _moduleSettings;

parent.Controls.Add(portalModule);
```

7. Build the application.
8. Test the application by logging on as **admin@contoso.com** with a password of **P@ssw0rd**. Make sure that the appropriate tabs are displayed.
9. Click the **Admin** tab.
10. In the **Tabs** section, select the **Home** tab for editing.
11. On the Tab Name and Layout page, select the **Top Movers** module for editing.
12. On the Module Settings page, set the **Cache Timeout** to 60 seconds and then click **Apply Module Changes**.

13. Click **Apply Changes** on the Tab Name and Layout page.

14. Go to the "Data" folder and change the value for an item in the "sales.xml" file such as one of the "revenue" elements. Save the file.

15. Click on the **Home** tab and confirm that the content appears correctly. Any changes made to the page should now be cached for 60 seconds.

Module 8: Diagnostics and Exception Handling

> **Module 8: Diagnostics and Exception Handling**
>
> - Choosing Appropriate Exception Handling Techniques
> - Logging Exceptions
> - Using the Application Center Test Tool

Overview

Every application that requires maintenance and support must adopt a consistent and reliable strategy for exception management. Exceptions should be detected and logged, and should raise alerts, which can then be routed to the appropriate support personnel.

Objectives

After completing this module, you will be able to:

- Choose appropriate debugging techniques for Web applications.
- Implement an exception handling framework for logging and diagnostics.
- Use Application Center Test to stress-test Web applications.

Lesson: Choosing Appropriate Exception Handling Techniques

> **Lesson: Choosing Appropriate Exception Handling Techniques**
> - Understanding When to Use Exceptions
> - Logging Exceptions

Introduction

This lesson introduces the general principles of exception handling. An exception management system should be clearly separated from the business and data logic of the application so that it can be independently maintained. It should generate metrics for constant monitoring of the health and status of the application. Ordinary exceptions should be captured and severe problems should trigger alerts.

Lesson Objectives

After completing this lesson, you will be able to:
- Describe when and how to use exception handling.
- Explain alternative strategies for exception handling.
- Describe the Microsoft® Exception Handling Application Block.
- Explain the value of using custom exception classes.

Understanding When to Use Exceptions

> **Understanding When to Use Exceptions**
>
> - Handling Exceptions to:
>   - Log the Exception Data for Later Analysis
>   - Add the Exception Data to the Automatically Generated Exception Information
>   - Execute Cleanup Operations
>   - Attempt to Recover from The Exception
> - Propagating Exceptions
>   - Automatic Propagation
>   - Catch and Rethrow the Exception
>   - Catch, Wrap, and Rethrow the Wrapped Exception
> - Unhandled Exceptions
> - Custom Exceptions

Introduction

All exceptions in the .NET Framework derive from the **System.Exception** class. This class provides a consistent set of objects to support exception handling, and furnishes an extensible framework for developers to create their own custom exception classes. The base class for all application specific exceptions is the **ApplicationException** class, which should be used as the base for all custom exception classes.

Exceptions should be detected as soon as possible because unhandled exceptions in ASP.NET cause a default error-handling page to be displayed to the user. Exceptions can be handled within the function where they occur or passed up the call stack to the caller.

Handling Exceptions

Many developers believe that every function should have a *Try/Catch* block. Functions that exemplify this error can include catch blocks that are set to catch any exception and implicitly state that they are prepared to handle any exception. Instead of using this generalized approach, develop your code so that only certain exceptions are handled by a particular function. Other exceptions should be allowed to filter up the call stack to more general exception handling routines. Functions that violate this rule risk hiding exceptions that could cause the application to behave unpredictably.

Exceptions should be handled when the application needs to perform the following actions:

- Log the exception information for later analysis.
- Add information to the automatically generated exception information.
- Execute cleanup operations.
- Attempt to recover from the exception.

In other circumstances, it is not necessary to handle exceptions in the function itself. If the code raises an exception, it will be propagated up the call stack. An exception management layer than handles all exceptions and can record exceptions not handled lower in the call stack. Functions should only handle exceptions to which they are prepared to react.

Throwing exceptions is an expensive operation due to the amount of information that is passed and should be done when a condition outside of your code's assumptions occurs. Exceptions should not be used as part of the normal flow of application operations, nor should they be used as an ordinary means of communication between components.

Propagating Exceptions

There are three principal ways by which to propagate exceptions from the function where they were raised:

- **Automatic propagation**. With this approach, the exception is ignored and allowed to move up the call stack until it reaches a catch block that matches.
- **Catch and rethrow the exception**. The function either performs extra processing, such as adding information to the exception, or attempts to recover, and failing, throws the exception up the call stack.
- **Catch, wrap, and throw the wrapped exception**. This approach enhances the Catch-and-Rethrow approach. In this case, the exception is caught and any required processes are performed; the exception is then wrapped in a new exception with more relevant exception information, and passed to the caller. The original exception remains in the **InnerException** property of the **Exception** class.

Choose an approach based upon the exception type. Automatic propagation is best used for situations in which no additional processing is needed, because the exception is not one of the types to which the function is expected to react. For example, an **OutOfMemoryException** can be thrown at any point because of a garbage collection failure. This type of exception should be automatically propagated.

Select one of the other two exception propagation methods when the application can anticipate and react to a particular type of exception. For example, in the case of data access components, an **InvalidOperationException** thrown while opening a connection can indicate that a connection is already open. In that case, the application should quickly recover from the exception and resume operations. If it cannot recover, then it should rethrow the exception up the call stack for more generic handling. Before rethrowing, it should add information about its attempted recovery by reusing an existing connection and the results. This can be done by wrapping the exception in a custom exception class. In this scenario, the **InnerException** retains the original **InvalidOperationException**, which is then wrapped in a custom **UnrecoverableConnectionException** that includes a message about recovery attempts. This data would be much more valuable than the less relevant **InvalidOperationException**.

Unhandled Exceptions

The Web.config file is used to configure custom error-handling pages to react to errors with specific status codes, such as a 500: Internal Server Error, as shown in the following Web.config code segment:

```
<customErrors
    defaultredirect="http://localhost/defaulterror.aspx" mode="On">
    <error statuscode="500" redirect="/errorpages/servererror.aspx" />
    <error statuscode="404" redirect="/errorpages/filenotfound.htm" />
</customErrors>
```

This code ensures that any unhandled exceptions will cause well-designed custom error pages to be displayed to users, rather than system-generated pages containing detailed error information. Allowing detailed error pages to be viewed by users constitutes a serious security breach, because the user can view the complete call stack leading to the exception. There are three modes for the **customErrors** element:

1. **On**: All users are redirected to a custom error page. This setting is ordinarily used in production only.
2. **Off**: All users see the system error page. This mode is primarily used in development.
3. **RemoteOnly**: Users accessing the site on the local machine see the system error page. All other users see the custom error-handling pages. This setting is appropriate to production.

These applicationwide settings can be overridden by using the **ErrorPage** attribute of the **Page** directive:

```
<%@ Page ErrorPage="specialPageError.aspx" %>
```

When an exception reaches the last point at which the application can handle the exception, it is said to have reached the boundary of the application. After this point, the application can no longer recover from the exception and must perform the appropriate processing before the exception is communicated to the user. Two events are available in ASP.NET to handle these boundary events:

- **Page_Error:** This occurs when an error has not been handled in any of the functions on an individual page. A method to handle these pagewide errors can be wired to the event **Page.Error**.

- **Application_Error:** To create an applicationwide error handler, use this event in the Global.asax file. This event is raised whenever an exception is not handled by any page.

In both events, **Server.GetLastError** is used to reference the exception. If the error is being handled at the application level, the exception should be logged, any necessary notifications sent, and any final cleanup performed.

Developers should be careful not to use the **Server.ClearError** in the **Application_Error** event handler because when an error is cleared in this way, the user is not redirected to the error page configured in the Web.config file. **Server.ClearError** should be used only in the **Page_Error** event handler so that the exception is not filtered up to the **Application_Error** handler.

Custom Exceptions

Custom exceptions are primarily useful under three conditions:

1. No existing exception class in the .NET framework corresponds to the application condition needing detection. Meeting this condition requires careful research because the exception hierarchy is extensive.

2. The exception must be handled discretely. That is, it is more efficient to handle the exception through a custom exception class than to use a more generic exception with conditional logic.

3. The exception requires additional information that cannot be included in the **Exception** class properties.

To make custom exceptions most useful, they should derive from a single base class that inherits from **ApplicationException**. This base class should contain fields for all the additional information the exception should collect, such as date and time stamps, machine name, and any other information specific to the application. Placing this data in the base class makes it available to all the derived exception classes.

Beneath the base class, specific exception types should be grouped according to the specific classes of exceptions they represent. Using this structure makes code extensible because new exceptions will be interpreted by the catch blocks according to the object's base classes.

Logging Exceptions

> **Logging Exceptions**
> - Windows Event Log
> - Relational Databases
> - Custom Log Files
> - Notifying Support Staff of Exceptions

Introduction

To diagnose application problems, exception information must be reliably stored, or logged, in a consistent format. Monitoring applications can then read, filter, and analyze the log files to aid in troubleshooting.

Three options are available for logging exception information:

- **Windows event log**
- **Relational database**
- **Custom log file**

Windows Event Log

The Windows event log presents errors in a consistent format. It offers the following advantages and disadvantages:

Advantages
- Proven reliability.
- Available on all Microsoft Windows® platforms likely to be used as Web servers, including Windows NT, Windows 2000, Windows XP, and Windows Server™ 2003.
- Maximum log size and the number of days to retain records can be configured.
- Event Viewer can be used to view the information.
- The .NET **EventLog** class (in System.Diagnostics) makes it easy to log and maintain the information programmatically.
- Monitoring tools can use the event log as a source of event data.
- Can be used through Windows Management Instrumentation (WMI).
- System and application events write to the same event log, thereby simplifying comparisons.

Disadvantages
- On server farms, each application logs to the local server, so all logs must be collected to gain a complete picture of an application's exceptions. Logging can be done to a remote machine, but this introduces another area of risk.
- When the event log is full, it stops recording event information or overwrites earlier entries (depending on the log's settings in the Windows Event Viewer). The **EventLog.Clear** method can be used to clear the log so that it can begin recording again. By default, the Application, System, and Security logs are set to a maximum of 4996 kilobytes (KB). Custom logs are set to a maximum of 512 KB.

To write to the event log, use the **WriteEntry** method of the **EventLog** class. This method can add events to an application-specific log which usually has the same name as the application. The **DefaultPublisher** class of the Exception Handling Application Block has a **WriteToLog** method that illustrates the procedure (this code is from the **ExceptionManager** class in the Exception Management Application Block (EMAB), which is installed in the D:\2311\Microsoft Application Blocks for .NET\Exception Management\Code*language* folder):

Visual Basic .NET

```
Private Sub WriteToLog(ByVal entry As String, ByVal type As
    EventLogEntryType)
    Try
        EventLog.WriteEntry(applicationName, entry, type)
    Catch e As SecurityException
        Throw New
            SecurityException( _
                String.Format( _
                    m_resourceManager.GetString( _
                    "RES_DEFAULTPUBLISHER_EVENTLOG_DENIED"), _
                    applicationName), _
                e)
    End Try
End Sub 'WriteToLog
```

C#

```
private void WriteToLog(string entry, EventLogEntryType type)
{
    try
    {
        EventLog.WriteEntry(applicationName,entry,type);
    }
    catch(SecurityException e)
    {
        throw new
        SecurityException(String.Format(resourceManager.GetString(
            "RES_DEFAULTPUBLISHER_EVENTLOG_DENIED"),
            applicationName),
            e);
    }
}
```

The **applicationName** parameter determines the name of the log. By placing the call to **WriteEntry** in a Try/Catch block, any security exceptions caused by the absence of Write permissions to the event log can be captured. This is also a good example of how to add information to an exception before throwing it to the caller. The ASP.NET account has permission to write to an event log but does not have permission to create an event source. To add this permission, place an entry in the following registry hive:

```
HKEY_LOCAL_MACHINE\SYSTEM\CurrentControlSet\Services\Eventlog\<log>
```

You can avoid this problem by using Windows Installer to create the event source when the application is first installed.

Relational Databases

Relational databases are a common repository for logging exceptions. This option requires more code and customization than the Windows Event log. It offers the following advantages and disadvantages:

Advantages
- All the information is available centrally.
- Database tools for querying and reporting are available.
- The structure of the exception log data can be customized to reflect the needs of particular applications.

Disadvantages
- Just as with remote use of the event log, remote database access introduces an element of risk because data can be lost during transfer.
- Because the operating system events and the exception log are separate, determining the sequence of events leading to an exception can be more difficult.
- Custom tools must be created to read and analyze the data.
- Most monitoring systems will not interact directly with the database information.

Custom Log Files

The custom log file option incorporates some of the benefits of the database. The advantages and disadvantages are:

Advantages
- The log format can be customized according to application requirements.

Disadvantages
- Application instances that need to log exceptions can raise concurrency issues. Careful programming is required to ensure thread safety.
- You must create a process to manage the log file size.
- As with the database, tools must be developed to read and manage the data.
- Monitoring tools must be configured to read the custom format.

Notifying Support Staff of Exceptions

Notification provides an immediate warning that something has gone wrong with the application. Support staff should receive these warnings in a timely manner so they can react quickly. Just as with exception management services, notification processes should be decoupled from application code. The application should raise errors but rely on the monitoring system to notify the parties who will take the appropriate action.

There are several options for creating notifications through a custom monitoring system. The most common method is to send e-mail. The advantages and disadvantages are:

Advantages
- E-mail is quick and easy to implement. The .NET Framework provides a set of classes in **System.Web.Mail** to allow e-mail to be quickly constructed and sent using the CDOSYS (Collaboration Data Objects for Windows 2000) message component. A relay e-mail server can be used in place of the local server.

Disadvantages
- E-mail can fail.
- Large numbers of errors can result in a large amount of e-mail traffic, much of which would likely be redundant, because errors tend to be related. This could make tracking the sequence of errors and resolving the problem more difficult.

The Microsoft Exception Handling Application Block provides a demonstration of using **System.Web.Mail** classes for e-mail notification. In this example, a custom class which implements the **IExceptionPublisher** interface is used to supply the notification method. The following code sends exception information by e-mail (this code is from the **ExceptionPublisher** class in the lab portal project):

Visual Basic .NET

```
If m_OpMail.Length > 0 Then
    Dim subject As String = "Exception Notification"
    Dim body As String = strInfo.ToString()

    SmtpMail.Send("CustomPublisher@mycompany.com", m_OpMail, subject, body)
End If
```

C#

```
if (m_OpMail.Length > 0)
{
        string subject = "Exception Notification";
        string body = strInfo.ToString();

        SmtpMail.Send("brcoll@contoso.com", m_OpMail, subject, body);
        }
```

Lesson: Using the Application Center Test Tool

> **Lesson: Using the Application Center Test Tool**
>
> - Understanding the ACT Tool

Introduction

This lesson introduces the basic features of the Application Center Test (ACT) tool which is included with the Enterprise Architect version of Microsoft Visual Studio® .NET.

Developers who create Web sites that must operate under high stress loads often find that problems do not appear until realistic stress factors are applied. Visual Studio.Net Enterprise Architect and Developer Editions include a tool called Application Center Test (ACT). ACT allows developers to stress-test Web applications and analyze performance and scalability problems. Many ASP developers are familiar with the previous version of this tool, which was called the Web Application Stress Tool (WAST).

Lesson Objectives

After completing this lesson, you will be able to:

- Identify and use performance counters for application performance measurements.
- Use the ACT to stress-test Web applications.
- Create ACT performance reports.
- Script dynamic reports.

Understanding the ACT Tool

Understanding the Application Center Test Tool

- Using System Performance Counters to Identify Bottlenecks
- Using ASP.NET Counters to Identify Bottlenecks
- Creating Reports with ACT
- The ACT Graphing Tool
- Scripting Dynamic Tests

Introduction

Using the stand-alone ACT user interface provides more detailed reports than the version that is integrated into the Visual Studio.NET environment. The product documentation includes all the steps necessary to create and run reports. This course focuses on identifying the types of reports and counters that are generally useful.

ACT allows Web sites to be tested in the following ways:

- ACT simulates a configurable user load to isolate concurrency or other issues related to stress. ACT opens multiple simultaneous connections to the server and rapidly sends HTTP requests.

- ACT includes an object model for scripting dynamic tests that can be run repeatedly or scheduled. These tests can be recorded from an actual browser session and then replayed.

- Resultant ACT test data is stored for later analysis. Graphing tools aid in visual display, and Microsoft Office Web components can be used to create custom graphs.

- Tests can be carried out using Secure Socket Layers (SSL) and several Windows-based authentication schemes, including NT Lan Manager (NTLM), Kerberos version 5 protocol, Digest, and Basic.

- Cookie and user information can be managed to determine their effects on Web performance.
- ACT integrates performance counters into the test environment so that these metrics can be correlated with utilization and other measures.

Using System Performance Counters to Identify Bottlenecks

A major goal of monitoring Web applications is to target performance bottlenecks. The most important system counters for identifying bottlenecks are:

- **%Processor Time/_Total Instance**: Process use levels. This counter shows the amount of time spent in processing threads by all CPUs on the Web server. When this number rises above 85 percent, the maximum load level for this Web server has been reached.
- **Memory/Available Bytes**: The amount of physical memory available. Internet Informaton Systems (IIS) by itself uses 2.5 megabytes (MB) of memory and each additional connection consumes about 10 KB.
- **Network Interface/Bytes Total/Sec**: Network traffic from the client to the server. Values above 50 percent of the total available bandwidth typically indicate network bottlenecks.
- **System/Context Switches/Sec**: The combined rate at which all processors on the computer are switched from one thread to another. A high number in this counter can indicate a contention situation such as a deadlock.

Using ASP.NET Counters to Identify Bottlenecks

Several ASP.NET specific counters should also be measured:

- **ASP.NET/Requests Queued**: The number of requests waiting to be processed. This number should remain close to zero. The number will start to increase in a linear fashion when the server has reached the limit of the number of requests that it can process. The <processModel> element in Machine.config sets the default maximum of this value to 5000. When this value is exceeded, the worker process is recycled. If the value exceeds the IIS queue length, users receive a "Server Too Busy" message.
- **ASP.NET/Worker Process Restarts**: This counter records the number of times the worker process has been restarted during the Web server's lifetime. If this number increases without obvious cause, it can indicate deadlocks, memory allocation problems, and threading issues.

- **ASP.NET Applications/Errors Total**: The total number of errors that occurred. This number should be zero. It includes parser, compilation, and run-time errors. If errors occur, other counters such as throughput can become unreliable because of the different code paths for error recovery. This counter indicates bugs that should be fixed.

- **ASP.NET Applications/Requests/Sec**: The number of requests the application executes each second. This number represents the current throughput of the application and it should remain in a steady range so long as the load remains constant. Routine server processes such as garbage collection, cache cleanup, and similar tasks should be taken into account when observing this measure.

In addition, the reports produced by ACT include several counters that are not available in the Performance Monitor:

- **Web Application/Avg. Requests/Sec**: This number can be a better indicator than ASP.NET Applications/Requests/Sec because it is averaged over the length of the test.

- **Web Application/Avg. Time to First Byte (TTFB)**: The average time between sending the request to the server and receiving the first byte of the response.

- **Web Application/ Avg. Time to Last Byte (TTLB)**: The average time between sending the request to the server and receiving the last byte of the response.

- **Web Application/HTTP Errors**: Sum of all response with HTTP errors in the range from 400 to 499 and from 500 to 599. The error code results are broken out independently.

Application Center Test allows these performance counters to be integrated directly into the tests. They are automatically recorded and summarized in the results node.

Creating Reports with ACT

One of the key measurements of Web application performance is throughput versus user load. Throughput measures the amount of work done per unit of time. In Web applications, throughput tracks the rate at which requests can be serviced. This is usually measured as the number of GET or POST requests per second, represented as Requests Per Second (RPS). Throughput tends to increase in a linear fashion as user load increases, until a specific limit is reached. After this limit, more user load leads to decreasing throughput.

To determine the maximum number of RPS that a Web server can handle, several tests must be performed. Witheach iteration of the test, the number of simultaneous browser connections should be increased. A typical strategy is to double the number of browser connections for each iteration: for example, 15, 30, 60, 120, 240, and so on. The maximum number of connections depends on the traffic expected on the server.

The ACT Graphing Tool

ACT's graphing tool allows you to create custom graphs from the test data. Multiple reports resulting from a single test can be combined into a single graph, and you can combine reports from multiple tests. Any combination of measures can be used for the X and Y coordinates of the generated graphs. You can also generate detailed reports that combine the results of several tests.

You can create a graph that measures throughput versus user load. Such a graph combines the RPS measurement with the browser connections to determine at what point the RPS level becomes nonlinear as the user load increases and requests begin to be queued. The following graph shows the RPS versus connections on the portal site we are developing in this class. Stress levels of 15, 50, 100, and 250 were applied to the entry point page to determine the optimal throughput. With a **Processor/% Processor Time/_Total** count of over 85 percent, it is clear that optimal throughput was reached at 74 RPS. Above this level, the number of socket errors rose rapidly as Web server hardware became overloaded and began to reject page requests. The **average time to last byte** counter rose from its fastest reading of 176 milliseconds for 15 requests per second to 752 milliseconds with a user load of 250 requests per second. If the portal application needs to support more than 74 simultaneous connections, more hardware must be added to the server to support optimal response rates. The following graph measures RPS against the number of browser connections:

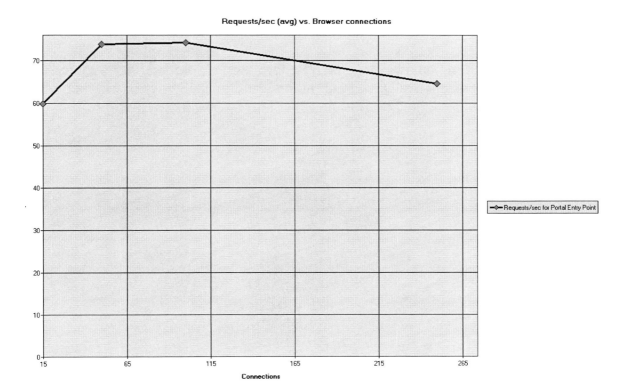

You can chart multiple values on the vertical axis. An important metric is Transmission Control Protocol (TCP) errors, referred to as **socket errors** in the Source list. As we see in the following graph, a rise in socket errors correlates exactly with a drop in RPS. This graph clearly indicates that the Web server's limits have been reached.

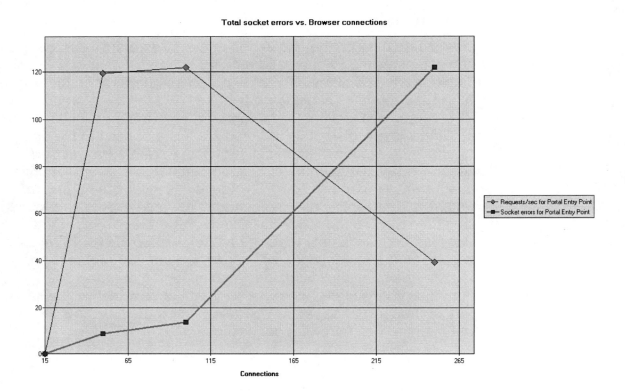

Since multiple values can be charted on the vertical axis, you can add TCP errors and view them along with the RPS values. The scale on the graph reflects the currently selected measurement in the **Source** list.

Another useful measurement examines how much performance decreases as the number of simultaneous connections increases. The following graph shows a linear increase in Time to Last Byte (TTLB) as the number of connections increases.

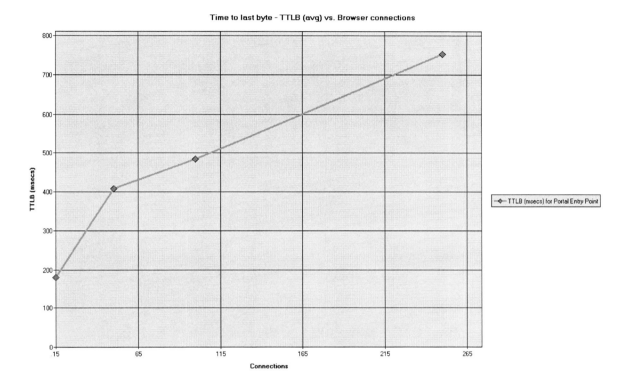

Scripting Dynamic Tests

Dynamic tests are scripts that send requests to the Web server during a test run. These are considered dynamic because the order of the requests, Uniform Resource Locators (URLs), and other properties can be configured at run time. The tests can also change conditionally depending, on the last response from the server. This capability allows the developer to create several different test scenarios within the scope of a single script. Almost any aspect of a Web request can be configured for a test.

Because all Web pages must be tested for functionality, ACT can help you automate this testing process by testing each page and recording the responses (including any error messages or other anomalies). You can configure a test script to iterate through a collection of pages in a text file. The Trace method of the Test object writes the results into the ACTTrace.log file, which displays the page, the time tested and the status code.

Lab 8: Using the Exception Manager

> **Lab 8: Using the Exception Manager**
>
> - Exercise 1: Implementing an Exception Handling Framework
> - Exercise 2: Creating and Handling a Custom Exception
> - Exercise 3: Using Application Center Test to Find Web Server Capacity (Optional)

Exercise 1: Implementing an Exception Handling Framework

Exercise 2: Creating and Handling a Custom Exception

Exercise 3: Using Application Center Test to Find Web Server Capacity (Optional)

After completing this lab, you will have demonstrated your ability to:

- Use the facilities of the Exception Management Application Block.
- Create and handle a custom exception.
- Create test projects in Application Center Test.

The Exception Management Application Block (EMAB) provides an extensible framework for handling exceptions. It provides the ability to publish exception information and provides a minimum level of contextual information for each exception. By encapsulating the details of logging, and reporting exceptions separately from an application's business logic, EMAB allows exception handling to be used with many application types. EMAB allows you to reduce the amount of custom error-handling code you need to maintain while making the application easier to debug.

Before working on this lab, you must have the knowledge and skills to raise and handle exceptions. You must also understand how and when to implement interfaces and derive from base classes. In Exercise 1, we will explore how the EMAB works. In Exercise 2, we will extend the framework by adding a new exception to track logon problems. In Exercise 3, you will learn how to use Application Center Test to measure the performance of a Web application.

Estimated time to complete this lab: 60 minutes

Starting a Virtual Machine

1. On the student computer, on the **Start** menu, point to **All Programs**, and then click **Microsoft Virtual PC**. If the Virtual PC console window does not appear, right-click the **Virtual PC icon** in the notification area (system tray), and click **Show Virtual PC Console**.

2. In the Virtual PC console window, select the virtual machine that you would like to open then click **Start**.

NOTE: Depending on your time zone, the first time you start each of the virtual machines, you may receive an error message that the parent virtual hard disk appears to have been modified. You can ignore this message.

3. The virtual machine will start up in a new window.

Closing a Virtual Machine

1. On the student computer, in the virtual machine window, on the Action menu, click Close.

NOTE: To avoid accidentally closing the virtual machine during the lab, the **Close** button in the upper-right corner of the virtual machine is disabled.

2. The virtual machine window will close. All changes to the virtual hard disk are discarded.

Exercise 1: Implementing an Exception Handling Framework

- **Open the Lab Starter Project**

    1. Open the ASPProjectVB or ASPProjectCS project in Visual Studio .NET using the following instructions.

    2. Browse to D:\2311\Labfiles\Lab08\Starter\VB or D:\2311\Labfiles\Lab08\Starter\CS.

    3. Launch the project by double-clicking on the ASPProjectVB.sln or the ASPProjectCS.sln file in the lab starter folder.

- **Examine the major features of the Exception Management Application Block**

    1. Note that you must have the ASPProjectVB.sln or the ASPProjectCS.sln file open to perform the following exercise.

    2. Open the Microsoft.ApplicationBlocks.ExceptionManagement project.

    3. Open the BaseApplicationException.vb or BaseApplicationException.cs file. This is the base exception class which is used to ensure that all exceptions provide a minimal level of contextual information about the exception. All custom exceptions will inherit from this class. Note the following features of this class:

        a. The class is marked with the **<Serializable>** attribute. This allows the state of the exception to be passed over remoting boundaries. Serialization of the class also requires the constructor with the signature: Protected Sub New (ByVal info As **SerializationInfo**, ByVal context As **StreamingContext**). Any fields added to the base **ApplicationException** class need to be persisted into the serialized data stream. The **GetObjectData** method accomplishes this purpose.

        b. The class inherits **ApplicationException**. This class serves as the base class for all application-specific exception classes.

        c. The **InitializeEnvironmentInformation** method gathers culture-specific strings to initialize key exception handling values and messages. These values allow access to the contextual information for the exception: machine name, timestamp, application domain name, thread identity, and windows identity.

4. Open the ExceptionManager.vb or ExceptionManager.cs file. This class contains static methods (shared in Microsoft Visual Basic® .NET) that publish exception information. Exceptions are published by using the publisher classes that have been configured in the config file. If no custom publisher is provided, the class uses the **DefaultPublisher** class that publishes exceptions to the Event Log. Custom publishers that implement the **IPublisher** interface can be implemented to exception details in a database, raise alerts through e-mail notification, or send notification messages using message queuing. Note the following features of this class:

   a. The main **Publish** method has the signature: Public Overloads Shared Sub Publish (ByVal exception As Exception, ByVal additionalInfo As NameValueCollection).

   b. The first part of the **Publish** method reads the contextual information and places it in a **NameValueCollection**.

   c. The **Publish** method checks for a configuration file. If a configuration file is available, it reads the configuration file. If none exists, it uses the **PublishToDefaultPublisher** method to write to an application-specific event log. The **Publish** method first checks for configured publishers, and if it finds them, it uses the **PublishToCustomPublisher** method to publish the exception with the logic defined in the custom publisher.

5. To allow dynamic exception handling modifications (without having to recompile the application), configuration settings control how exception handling works. A sample configuration file named App.config is included in the folder Components\ExceptionMgt folder. Note the following features of this file:

   a. The <configSections> declares a section of the configuration file that can be used to hold **ExceptionManagement** settings. Note the name of the section is "exceptionManagement." The **type** attribute defines the type that reads the configuration information. It is the class **ExceptionManagerSectionHandler**. This class is contained in the ExceptionManagerSectionHandler.vb or ExceptionManagerSectionHandler.cs file which is found in "D:\2311\Microsoft Application Blocks for .NET\Exception Management\Code*language*\Microsoft.ApplicationBlocks.ExceptionManagement."

   b. Below the <configSection> are several sample configurations of the **<exceptionManagment>** element which have been commented out. The comments can be removed to test the effect they have on exception handling. A Publisher Elements Quick Reference is included at the top of the file to describe the purpose of each attribute.

Exercise 2: Creating and Handling a Custom Exception

In this section, we will implement a custom exception for tracking logon problems. This exception is not intended to detect when the user types an incorrect user name or password, asthese are normal conditions and should be handled with a Boolean return value. The **LogonException** should be used for conditions such as a failure to connect to the database or file where credentials are stored. When deciding whether to create a new exception class, consider the following questions:

a. **Does an exception already exist for this condition?** Because logging on is application-specific, no generic **LogonException** exists.

b. **Does this exception require discrete handling?** Logon exceptions need more discrete handling than general data exceptions. You might be using the Microsoft ActiveDirectory® directory service for user lookup, or you might need to configure the credentials store according to the conditions for a particular installation. Having a record of specific logon exceptions enables specific error handling.

c. **Do you need specific behavior or additional information for a particular exception?** It can help debugging to know whether the credentials were stored in a SQL Server database or in Active Directory.

- **Create the custom exception class**

1. Create a class in the ExceptionMgt folder called LogonException.vb or LogonException.cs.

2. At the top of the file before the class declaration, create Imports or using clauses to bring in the following namespaces:

    - **Microsoft.ApplicationBlocks.ExceptionManagement**.
    - **System.Runtime.Serialization**.

3. Place a **Serialization** attribute before the class name using Visual Basic .NET or C# syntax as appropriate. This attribute allows the exception to pass remoting boundaries.

4. Inherit from the **BaseApplicationException** class. This class contains the following elements for tracking the context of the exception:
   a. The computer name where the exception occurred.
   b. The date and time of the exception.
   c. The name of the application domain hosting the application.
   d. The name of the thread and windows identities.
   e. Optional custom information that can be specified in configuration files.
5. The implementation will consist of constructors that match the constructors of the base class. This is necessary because constructors are not inherited.
6. Provide a constructor that accepts no parameters and calls the base class constructor.
7. Provide another constructor that accepts a **String** parameter named **message**. Call the base class constructor with the **message** parameter.
8. Provide another constructor that accepts a **String** parameter named **message** and one of type **Exception** named **inner**. Call the base class constructor with the message and inner parameters.

9. Your code should resemble the following:

Visual Basic .NET

```vbnet
Imports Microsoft.ApplicationBlocks.ExceptionManagement
Imports System.Runtime.Serialization

<Serializable()> Public Class LogonException
  Inherits BaseApplicationException

  Public Sub New()
    MyBase.New()
  End Sub

  Public Sub New(ByVal message As String)
    MyBase.New(message)
  End Sub

  Public Sub New(ByVal message As String, ByVal inner As Exception)
    MyBase.New(message, inner)
  End Sub

End Class
```

C#

```csharp
using System;
using System.Runtime.Serialization;
using Microsoft.ApplicationBlocks.ExceptionManagement;


[Serializable]
public class LogonException : BaseApplicationException
{

  public LogonException() : base()
  {
  }

  public LogonException(string message) : base(message)
  {
  }

  public LogonException(string message, Exception inner)
                     : base(message,inner)
  {
  }

}
```

- **Configure the application to publish the exception**

1. Open the Web.config file for the project. Identify the **<configSections>** element that defines the section named exceptionManagement. This defines the class which will handle the configuration settings in that section.

2. Identify the **<exceptionManagement>** element. Note the attributes of the publisher element. They are described as follows:

    a. **assembly**: The assembly which contains the publisher. In this case, the ASPProject assembly contains the **ExceptionManagement** class.

    b. **type**: The type name of the publisher class. This is used with the assembly name to instantiate the publisher.

    c. **exclude**: Designates which exceptions will not be published. An asterisk "*" excludes all exceptions. This value is overridden by the include attribute.

    d. **include**: Forces a particular exception type to be published. Note that the setting "+System.Exception" will allow any exception to be published since all exceptions derive from System.Exception. If you wanted to publish only LogonExceptions, the value of the attribute would be:

```
include="ASPProject.LogonException, ASPProject"
```

3. To test the default publisher, set the mode attribute of the **exceptionManager** element to ON:

```
<exceptionManagement mode="on" />
```

4. Next, place a Try/Catch block in the **Login** method of the **UsersDB** class in the Security.vb or Security.cs file. Open the Security.vb or Security.cs file in the MainPortal folder. Locate the comment "TODO Place a Try block around the data access code."

5. Begin a Try block using the **Try** keyword (**try** in C#). At the end of the code in the function, place two **catch** blocks (**Catch** in Visual Basic .NET) with the following exception types:
    - **InvalidOperationException**: This exception is thrown by the Open method of the **SqlConnection** object if the data source or server is incorrectly specified or if the connection is already open.
    - **SqlException**: This exception is thrown by the **Open** method of the **SqlConnection** object if the database is unavailable. This is the exception we will use to test the custom exception.
6. Inside each catch block, throw a new exception of type **LogonException**. Create the following messages for each exception type:
    - **InvalidOperationException**: "Connection problem – no database specified."
    - **SqlException**: "Sql Server not available."
7. The second parameter of the **LogonException** constructor should be the exception that was thrown.
8. Your code should resemble the following:

Visual Basic .NET

```
Try
    ' Method code
Catch e As InvalidOperationException
    Throw New LogonException( _
        "Connection problem - no database specified.", e)
Catch e As SqlException
    Throw New LogonException("SQL Server not available.", e)
End Try
```

C#

```csharp
try
{
    // Method code
}
catch (InvalidOperationException e)
{
    throw new LogonException(
        "Connection problem - no database specified.", e);
}
catch (SqlException e)
{
    throw new LogonException("SQL Server not available.", e);
}
```

9. Open the SignIn.ascx.vb or SignIn.ascx.cs in the Modules folder.

10. At the top of the file, before the Namespace declaration, import Microsoft.ApplicationBlocks.ExceptionManagement using the **using** keyword in C# or the **Imports** keyword in Visual Basic.NET

11. Add a Try block to the **LoginBtn_Click** method in the SignIn.ascx.vb or SignIn.ascx.cs file. Locate the comment 'TODO Add a Try…Catch block to capture LogonExceptions."

12. Begin a Try block using the **Try** keyword (**try** in C#). At the end of the code in the function, place a **catch** block (**Catch** in Visual Basic .NET) to catch a **LogonException**.

13. In the Catch block, make a call to the **static** (**Shared** in Visual Basic .NET) Publish method of the ExceptionManager. Pass the LogonException object as the input parameter.

14. Your code should resemble the following:

Visual Basic .NET

```vb
Try
    ' Method Code
Catch lex As LogonException
    ExceptionManager.Publish(lex)
    Response.Write(lex.Message)
End Try
```

C#

```csharp
try
{
    // Method code
}
catch (LogonException lex)
{
    ExceptionManager.Publish(lex);
    Response.Write(lex.Message);
}
```

15. To test your application, set a breakpoint on the Try block in the **Login** function in the **UsersDB** class and execute the application in Debug mode. Once the execution path has entered Try block in the Login method of the **UsersDB** class, double-click the **SQL Server icon** in the component tray and click the **Pause** button. Continue executing the function by pressing F5 to complete the execution, or continue following the execution path, pressing F11 if you want to see how the **ExceptionManager** handles the exception. Since the application cannot connect to SQL Server, it should throw a **SqlException** wrapped in a **LogonException**. The **LogonException** is then published in the Application section of the event log called ExceptionManagerPublishedException.

16. Restart the SQL Server service.

Exercise 3: Using Application Center Test to Find Web Server Capacity (Optional)

In this exercise, we will create a series of tests to determine the maximum capacity of a Web server executing the portal application. Throughput versus user load measures the amount of work done per unit of time, or the rate at which a server processes requests. To determine the maximum capacity of a server, we will increase the stress level until performance begins to fall off. By determining this point, we have a good starting point for estimating the size and numbers of servers needed to service a given user load.

- **Create a new test**

1. Start Application Center Test using Microsoft Visual Studio .NET 2003/Visual Studio .NET Enterprise Features/Application Center Test as the path.
2. Click **File/New Project**.
3. Set the name to **Test** and accept the default location of the new project.

- **Record a browser session**

1. Right-click the **Tests** node and select **New Test**.
2. Click **Next**.
3. Click **Record a new test** and click **Next**.
4. Accept the default script language and click **Next**.
5. Click the **Start Recording** button.
6. Type the start page of the portal solution (http://localhost/ASPProjectVB/DesktopDefault.aspx) into the location field for the instance of Internet Explorer that opens. If you want to use the portal version that you completed in this lab, you will need to change the security settings for the application in the Internet Information Services Manager to allow anonymous access for this application.
7. Load the URL.
8. Login as admin@contoso.com with a password of **P@ssw0rd**.
9. Click the **Defect Tracking** tab.
10. Select and edit a defect by changing its status. When finished, click **Stop Recording** and then click **Next**.

11. Enter the name **Portal Test** for the Test and click **Next**.
12. Click **Finish**.
13. You can examine the script by clicking the **Tests** node and the Portal Test you just created.

- ### Customizing the test
1. Right-click the **Portal Test** and click **Properties**.
2. Set the number of simultaneous browser connections to **15**.
3. Set the run time to 10 seconds.
4. Click the **Counters** tab and add the following counters:
    a. **Processor(_Total)/%Processor Time**: Primary indicator of processor activity.
    b. **Memory/Available Bytes**: Amount of physical memory available to processes.
    c. **ASP.NET/Requests Queued**: The number of requests waiting to be processed. Prime indicator of problems in ASP.NET.
5. Click **OK**.

- ### Run the test
1. Right-click the test script and click **Start Test**.
2. Click the **Show Details** button to watch the progress of the test.
3. When the status changes to "The test is no longer running", click the **Close** button.
4. Click the **Results** node and expand the **Portal Test** node.
5. Click the report labeled **report – Portal Test**. Examine the **Graph** and the **Summary** sections, especially the **Average requests per second** and **Average time to last byte**. Note any errors in the **Error Count** section and in the **Response Codes** at the bottom of the summary.
6. On the right side of the display under **Reports**, click **Performance Counters** (listed under **Summary**), and examine the values for the three counters.

- **Generate a throughput versus user load graph**

1. Run the test four more times, using load levels of 30, 60, 120, and 240 simultaneous users.

2. When all the tests are complete, select each test run by checking the check box next to the report node for that test.

3. Select **Graphs** from the **Reports** drop-down menu.

4. Select **Requests/sec (avg) on the y-axis** (next to Source).

5. Select **Test Runs** on the X-axis.

6. Observe the curves on the graph. Note the point at which performance begins to fall off. The point of maximum throughput should be fairly obvious. Study the performance counters for the test that produced the best results. Note particularly when the **%Processor Time** starts to average over 85 percent. This is typically considered the point of maximum capacity for the server. If the **%Processor Time** counter never gets close to 85 percent, you should increase the load. If the counters in the early tests are abnormally high compared to the later tests rerun the earlier tests to get more accurate numbers. Such effects are usually caused by interfering processes.

7. Note the **Error Counts** and the **Response Codes**, particularly any "403 Server Too Busy" errors. This error can indicate that the value for the **appRequestQueueLimit** attribute of the httpRuntime element in the machine.config file is set too low.

8. Click the **Summary** selection and note the maximum performance and the throughput at that stress load. This data can provide you with an idea of how much user load a server can handle.

Module 9: Interoperability with COM

> **Module 9: Interoperability with COM**
>
> - Understanding the Basics of COM Interop
> - Creating and Using a Runtime Callable Wrapper
> - Guidelines and Issues in COM Interop

Overview

Prior to .NET, developers who worked on the Microsoft platform often built their applications using COM components. COM provides a way for components to communicate with each other regardless of the language in which the components are written or on which platform they are running.

Given the large base of existing code written as COM components and the impracticality of rewriting everything in .NET, the interoperability features of .NET are essential for using COM components within .NET applications.

Objectives

At the end of this module, you will be able to

- Describe the basics of COM Interop
- Describe how to call COM components from .NET.
- Create and use a Runtime Callable Wrapper.
- Address common issues and pitfalls when working with COM Interop.
- Use COM Interop to export data into Microsoft Excel from ASP.NET.

Lesson: Understanding the Basics of COM Interop

> **Lesson: Understanding the Basics of COM Interop**
> - The Basic Components of COM Interop
> - COM Code vs. .NET Code

Introduction

This section explains some of the primary reasons for using COM components with .NET.

Lesson Objectives:

At the end of this lesson, the student should understand the basics of COM Interop and why this interoperability is important. The student should be able to describe each component of COM Interop.

The Basic Components of COM Interop

> **The Basic Components of COM Interop**
>
> Primary Reasons for Using COM Interop
> - Functions grouped into interfaces
> - Binary standard
> - Base interface implementation
> - Uniquely identifying components
> - COM infrastructure
> - Creating a Visual Basic COM object

Introduction

This section describes the basic structure of COM Interop and explains how this structure supports the use of COM components within .NET.

Primary Reasons for Using COM Interop

- **To Provide a Gradual Migration Path.** It cannot be expected that with the advent of .NET, all existing systems can be immediately rewritten to exploit the new development paradigm. The interoperability features allow for a gradual migration path in which ASP.NET pages can call out to existing COM components, while new components are written in .NET.

- **To Interface with Other Existing Components.** A huge base of existing software functionality is already written as COM components. For example, all Microsoft® Office components are written as COM components. The interoperability features of .NET allow us to continue using that functionality without having to immediately rewrite it into .NET components.

- **To Achieve Transparency.** The goal of interoperability is to access COM components from .NET applications seamlessly. This transparency is achieved through the use of proxy classes that hide integration details.

Functions Grouped into Interfaces

An interface is a related group of functions that can be considered a contract that a COM object implements. A COM object can implement multiple interfaces.

When a client accesses a COM object, it uses only an interface pointer to access the methods of the object. The pointer hides the internal implementation, thereby making COM access transparent.

Binary Standard

When an object is instantiated, it queries the COM infrastructure through a standard set of interfaces to retrieve an interface pointer for a specific interface. This interface is a pointer to a function table, or Vtable, which is an array of function pointers. Specifically, a Vtable is a data structure in the COM class that contains the memory addresses of the actual code associated with the properties and methods implemented in the interface.

For any platform, COM defines a standard way to lay out virtual function tables in memory, and a standard way to call functions through virtual tables. Any language that supports functions by way of pointers can be used.

Base Interface Implementation

All COM objects are required to provide a certain level of functionality and must support a standard interface called **IUnknown**. **IUnknown** has three methods: **QueryInterface**, **AddRef**, and **Release**.

- **QueryInterface** is used to query for or get references to other interfaces that an object supports.
- **AddRef** and **Release** are used to track how many clients are using an object so that it can destroy itself when no longer required.

Uniquely Identifying Components

In the COM environment, all elements are identified by 128-bit globally unique identifiers (GUIDs) to prevent the possibility of name clashes in multiple vendor component environments. User-friendly programmatic identifiers are resolved to class identifiers (CLSIDs). Interface identifiers (IIDs) and type library identifiers (LIBIDs) are also created.

Registry keys contain information on programmatic identifiers, class identifiers and type libraries. The registry keys are used to look up the COM components and their interfaces using the IDs.

COM Infrastructure

The Component Object Library is a system component that provides the underlying mechanics of COM, such as finding and launching components.

When an application creates a COM object, the application passes the CLSID to the library. The library looks up the registry and locates the component and, depending on whether it is an .exe or a .dll, the library uses the associated **class factory** to return an instance of the component.

If the component is a remote component, the libraries return a proxy and all cross-process communication is transparently handled by the remote libraries.

Creating a Visual Basic COM Object

The following is an overview of the steps involved in creating a Microsoft Visual Basic® COM object. Understanding these steps is necessary for Visual Basic developers, because the steps are performed behind the scenes when you call COM components from .NET.

Visual Basic 6

```
Dim obj as MyLib.Customer
Set obj = CreateObject("MyLib.Customer")
Obj.Foo()
```

1. **Call CLSIDFromProgID:** "MyLib.Customer" is a user-friendly programmatic identifier (ProgID). Visual Basic first calls the **CLSIDFromProgID** function provided in the COM library to look up associated values in the registry and retrieve the CLSID associated with that ProgID

2. **Call CoCreateInstance:** Visual Basic then calls the **CoCreateInstance** application programming interface (API) passing in the CLSID to retrieve the location of the DLL (dynamic link library) from the registry. The registry entry may also indicate the name of a remote machine on which the DLL resides.

3. **Launch the Server:** After the location is known, the component is launched. If it is a local DLL, it is launched in the address space of the client. If it is a remote .dll or .exe file, the libraries are contacted on the remote machine to launch it and the remote libraries handle the activation.

4. **Gets Pointer to IUnknown:** After the server is loaded, COM requests an instance of the desired object by instructing the class factory to create an instance of the object. A pointer to the object's **IUnknown** interface is returned.

5. **Queries for other interfaces:** **IUnknown** is used to query for the default interface or a specific interface.

6. **Assign the interface:** The interface pointer for this interface is assigned to the variable. Because the interface pointer points to a Vtable of method pointers, the methods can now be invoked.

COM Code vs. .NET Code

COM Code vs. .NET Code

- Unmanaged vs. Managed

Unmanaged	Managed
Binary Standard	Type Standard
Type Libraries	Assemblies & Metadata
Interface based	Object Based
Immutable Interfaces	Can Evolve
Type Unsafe	Type Safe
Reference Counting	Garbage Collector
HRESULTS	Exceptions
GUIDs	Strong Names

Introduction

The core differences between how COM code works versus how .NET code works are summarized in this section.

Types

.NET types are based on the Common Type System (CTS) and are defined as metadata in assemblies. The metadata contains the detailed type information emitted by the compiler.

COM components have type libraries that provide definitions of interfaces supported, as well as other helpful information. Type libraries are not mandatory and include only public types.

The .NET runtime uses metadata information to load and locate components. COM looks up an entry in the registry to locate components and returns an interface pointer after creating the object. The interface pointers are then used to work with the object.

Interfaces

In COM, you work only with interface pointers that refer to Vtables. You never access the object directly. In .NET, you refer to objects directly.

Interfaces are immutable in COM. If you want to add, delete, or modify a method signature you must create an interface. Once this is done, existing clients cannot reference the component until their references are updated. New interfaces can be created as a way to avoid breaking clients in this way. In .NET, interfaces may evolve.

Type Safety

Unmanaged code compilers provide no type checking on pointer types, whereas type safety is enforced by the .NET Common Language Runtime (CLR).

.NET can only work with pointer types by marking sections of code as "unsafe" and specifying trust levels through code access security (CAS).

Memory Management

The .NET runtime has a garbage collector algorithm that automatically manages memory by scanning the heap.

In COM, memory management is performed by maintaining a reference count through **AddRef** and **Release** methods.

Identity

In COM, identity is maintained through 128-bit GUIDs. CLSIDs have to be entered into the Microsoft Windows® registry so that components can be identified.

In .NET, classes use human readable names through namespaces. Identity can be enforced by signing components with strong names.

Lesson: Runtime Callable Wrapper

> **Lesson: Runtime Callable Wrapper**
> - Using the RCW
> - Using ADO
> - COM Threading Models

Overview

Runtime Callable Wrapper (RCW) is the term given to the .NET object that is used as a bridge to interact with the COM component. The RCW manages the data type conversions and memory management. To make .NET code work with COM code, you can build a proxy object to manage the differences between the managed and unmanaged types.

Objectives

At the end of this lesson, you will be able to

- Create and use the RCW.
- Use copying, pinning, and strings with the RCW.
- Use ADO.
- Explain COM Threading Models

Using the RCW

> **Using the RCW**
> - Creating the RCW
> - Role of the RCW
>   - Object binding
>   - Data marshaling and translation
>   - Object lifetime management
>   - Object identity
>   - Exception and error handling
> - Runtime Callable Wrapper Data Types
> - Copying and Pinning
> - Working with Strings

Introduction

The RCW is a .NET object and, like all .NET objects, it has metadata and is defined in an assembly.

Creating the RCW

To create the Interop assembly you can use the Type Library Importer (Tlbimp.exe). This command-line tool can create a .NET assembly based on the type library of the COM component. It is available with a Microsoft Visual Studio® or software development kit (SDK) installation. Adding a reference to a COM component in Visual Studio also creates an Interop assembly.

Once you have the .NET Interop assembly, the methods of the COM component are exposed through it and we can work with it in the same way as any other .NET object.

Role of the RCW

Object Binding

The RCW handles COM object creation. Based on attributes such as CLSIDs that are present in the Interop assembly, the RCW calls COM's CoCreateInstance API.

COM components that implement the **IDispatch** interface support late binding. *Late binding* is the practice of resolving method names at run time rather than compile time. This is done when type library information is not available at compile time. Less sophisticated clients, such as classic ASP, use late binding. With such clients, type information is not known until run time, impeding performance and preventing compile-time type checking. With ASP.NET, clients can use early binding through the RCW that extracts type information from COM type libraries.

Late binding is also supported by COM Interop for components that implement the **IDispatch** interface through the use of the standard reflection APIs in .NET. Once the COM component is registered, a generic RCW (_ComObject) is created. This can be activated using the **Activator** class from the reflection namespace.

Data Marshaling and Translation

The RCW handles the conversion of .NET types to unmanaged types. Method signatures are translated into the COM format and parameters are modified with **in** or **out** attributes.

Object Lifetime Management

The RCW is responsible for keeping the COM object alive while the RCW is being used. The RCW keeps track of references and internally calls the **IUnknown** interface's **AddRef** and **Release** methods. When the RCW itself is garbage-collected its finalizer calls the **Release** methods on any interface pointers it has cached.

Due to the nondeterministic nature of .NET garbage collection, it is often necessary to explicitly release resources. To explicitly release a .NET resource, call the **Marshal.ReleaseComObject** method. This will release the COM object immediately if there are no further references to it.

Object Identity

Every instance of a COM object has a single wrapper, no matter how many interfaces it implements. The RCW caches interfaces and pointers and maintains object identity.

Exception and Error Handling

If the COM server being wrapped returns an HRESULT error, the RCW will throw a corresponding **COMException** object. The details of the error can be examined by retrieving the properties of this object.

If the COM server supports additional error information by means of the **ISupportErrorInfo** interface, the extended error information will also be propagated to the exception object.

Runtime Callable Wrapper Data Types

Managed types may have different representations from unmanaged types. These types, referred to as nonisomorphic, might require conversion when moving between managed and unmanaged components.

Isomorphic types

The isomorphic types are System.Byte, System.SByte, System.Int16, System.Uint16, System.Int32, System.Uint32, System.Int64, System.IntPtr, System.UintPtr.

Nonisomorphic types

Boolean – Converted to COM as a 2- or 4-byte value with true as 1 or -1.

Char – Converted to COM as a Unicode or ANSI character.

String – Converted to COM as a Unicode or ANSI character array or a BSTR.

Object – Converted COM as a variant or interface.

Valuetype – Converted to a structure with fixed memory layout.

Arrays – Converted to either an interface or SafeArray.

Copying and Pinning

As data is marshaled, it might need to be copied or pinned. Pinning temporarily locks the data in its current memory location and keeps it from being relocated by the garbage collector. Copying copies the data from one location to another. Whether data is copied or pinned depends on the type of data and what **in** or **out** attribute it has.

Isomorphic types have a fixed layout and the same representation in managed and unmanaged components. When these types are marshaled, the recipient gets a pointer to the actual memory location and is free to change the contents.

Nonisomorphic types have a different representation in the managed and unmanaged components. When one of these types is marshaled by reference, the recipient receives a pointer to a copy of the data structure. If the **in** attribute is set, the copy is always initialized with the instance's state. If the **out** attribute is set, the state is always copied back into the instance on return. If both are set, both copies are required.

Working with Strings

When a **String** or **StringBuilder** is marshaled to unmanaged code, the marshaler, in most cases, copies data to a secondary buffer and passes a reference to the buffer on the recipient. However, as an optimization the recipient usually gets a direct pointer to a managed string unless the string is passed by reference or as a **StringBuilder**. This entails the risk that the immutable characteristics of a string can be corrupted. It is best to pass a string by reference or as a **StringBuilder** with a fixed size.

Using ADO

> **Using ADO**
> - ADO RecordSets
> - ADO.NET Data Set
> - Converting ADO RecordSets to ADO.NET DataSets
> - Converting DataSets to Recordsets

Introduction

Microsoft ActiveX® Data Objects (ADO) enable client applications to access and manipulate data from a variety of sources through an OLE DB provider. Its primary benefits are ease of use, high speed, low memory overhead, and a small disk footprint. ADO supports key features for building client/server and Web-based applications. In this section, you will learn about the use of ADO Recordsets and ADO.NET DataSets.

ADO Recordsets

.NET applications might need to use ADO recordsets to return data from the middle tier. Iterating through COM-based recordsets requires a significant number of Interop calls. Depending on the size of the recordset, performance will be impacted.

ADO.NET DataSet

The data-binding capabilities of ASP.NET server controls cannot be used with classic ADO. As a result, it can be useful to translate the recordset into a DataSet. For large volumes of data, converting to a DataSet is often the most efficient solution.

Converting ADO Recordsets to DataSets

The **System.Data.OleDb.OleDbDataAdapter** has an overloaded version of the **Fill** method that can fill a **DataSet** from a recordset. This is illustrated in the following code:

Visual Basic .NET

```
Dim myDataAdapter As OleDbDataAdapter = New OleDbDataAdapter()
Dim myDataSet As DataSet = New DataSet()

'Copies the contents of the ADODB.recordset rs into  the ADO.NET  DataSet

'myDataAdapter.Fill(myDataSet, rs)
```

C#

```
myDataAdapter = new OleDbDataAdapter();
myDataSet = new DataSet();

/*
Copies the contents of the ADODB.recordset rs into  the ADO.NET  DataSet
*/
myDataAdapter.Fill(myDataSet, rs);
```

Using this approach makes migration easier when you convert the entire application to .NET because you are already working with a DataSet.

Converting DataSets to Recordsets

There are several options for converting **DataSets** to recordsets:

- Work directly with a recordset using Interop and do not convert to a **DataSet**. This has a performance overhead but the impact is minimal for a small recordset.

- Save the **DataSet** as XML and use XSLT to convert the xml to the ADO XML format and load it back into a recordset.

- Manually iterate through the DataSet and populate a recordset.

- Write custom marshaling code that automatically translates between a DataSet and a recordset when a DataSet is returned as a parameter. This is the most elegant solution, but this requires skill in managed C++. Refer to the MSDN documentation for more details.

COM Threading Models

> **COM Threading Models**
> - Single- and Apartment-Threaded Components
> - ASP.NET and COM
> - ASPCompat Attribute
> - Internal Workings of ASPCompat

Introduction

The threading models used by COM components that can be called from ASP.NET are of two major types: those marked "Free" and those marked "Apartment."

Single and Apartment Threaded components

COM provided a solution to the concurrency problem in the form of *apartments*. An *apartment* is an operating system abstraction to group objects that share the same threading model. Every object resides in an apartment for its entire lifetime.

Versions of Visual Basic before Visual Basic.NET did not allow developers to create components marked "Free." "Apartment Threaded" and "Single Threaded" were the only choices available.

- **Apartment Threaded**: This setting ensures that instances of objects always reside in Single Threaded Apartments (STAs). COM serializes access to all objects within the STA. A process could contain multiple STAs with different objects in each one.

- **Single Threaded**: With this setting all objects resided in the primary STA but COM still serialized access to objects. This could affect performance for server-based applications.

- **Free Threaded:** The Multithreaded Apartment (MTA) model or free-threaded model allowed multiple threads to access objects in the MTA.

ASP.NET and COM

If the component is marked "Free," then the **Page** object and the component share the same thread pool. The threads in this pool are multithreaded apartment threads, so no thread switch is needed between the thread executing the page and the thread used by the COM component. This scenario yields the minimum performance penalty.

In most classic ASP applications, the components called from ASP pages were marked "Apartment Threaded." The single-threaded apartment model supported by such components is not compatible with the default threading model used by the MTA-based ASP.NET thread pool. As a consequence, when the page object calls a COM component that is marked as "Apartment," this will entail a thread switch and cross-apartment marshaling, with negative performance consequences. If the component has not been configured in COM+, then it issues a long running blocking call, which prevents other STA components from being instantiated, leading to further performance penalties.

Many fewer thread switches are required if the component has been configured in COM+, a behavior enforced when the **AspCompat** attribute is added.

AspCompat Attribute

The **AspCompat** attribute forces the page to execute in STA mode and causes the COM component to execute on a COM+ STA worker thread. This attribute is required when referencing an STA component from the page or else an exception will be thrown.

Using the **AspCompat** attribute also has an effect on security. When ASP.NET is impersonating, the thread switch caused from calling an STA object from an MTA object results in a lost impersonation token. The new thread will not be associated with the impersonation token. Using **AspCompat** prevents this thread switch and therefore allows the token to be retained.

Internal Workings of ASPCompat

When a page class marked with this attribute is compiled, the class implements the **IHttpAsyncHandler** interface and the constructor is modified to use **ASPCompatMode**. Two asynchronous methods are added to the page class to implement this interface: **BeginProcessRequest** and **EndProcessRequest**.

The **BeginProcessRequest** method determines what kind of threading model the **Page** object is using. If it is using the MTA model, as will usually be the case unless the **Page** class is marked with the **STAThreadAttribute**, then a call is made to the **ASPCompatProcessRequest()** function in the Aspnet_isapi.dll. This function creates a COM+ activity and binds the activity to an STA worker thread, which is used by the **Page** class from that point on. Wrappers are created for the ASP intrinsics, Request, Response, and so on, so there will be more overhead when working with these objects. When the page class finishes executing, the **EndProcessRequest** method is called to complete the request.

This process has an important consequence for how COM components should be instantiated for best performance. If the component is instantiated in the constructor or at any time before the Page_Load event takes place, the page will not yet execute on the COM+ STA thread. In this case, a considerable performance penalty will be incurred because of the cross-apartment marshaling. The following example will incur the penalty:

```
<%@ AspCompat="true" %>
<script runat="server" language="VB">
   ' The components is created at construction time.
   Dim comObj As MyComObject = New MyComObject()
   Public Sub Page_Load(sender As Object, e As EventArgs)
      ' The object is first used here.
      comObj.DoSomething()
   End Sub
</script>
```

In the next example, object instantiation is deferred until the page object is already executing on the STA thread:

```
<%@ AspCompat="true" %>
<script runat="server" language="VB">
Public Sub Page_Load(sender As Object, e As EventArgs)
   ' The component is created and used after the code is running
   ' on the STA thread pool.
   comObj = New MyObject()
   comObj.DoSomething()
End Sub
```

References for Further Reading

The article "Introduction to Production Debugging for .NET Framework Applications" on the Microsoft Patterns and Practices site (http://msdn.microsoft.com/library/default.asp?url=/library/en-us/dnbda/html/DBGch01.asp) provides samples and tools to help you deal with process terminations and other unexpected errors that could occur when working with COM components from .NET code.

Lesson: Interop Guidelines

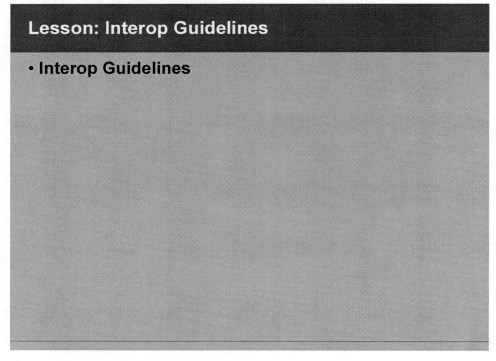

Overview

This section describes the basic guidelines you must follow to successfully run COM components with .NET.

Objectives

After completing this lesson, you will be familiar with:
- Try/catch error handling.
- Explictly freeing resources.
- Chunky calls
- Type libraries
- Isomorphic types
- Threading issues

Interop Guidelines

> **Interop Guidelines**
> - Error handling
> - Explicitly free resources
> - Use chunky calls
> - Provide and register type libraries
> - Use isomorphic types
> - Threading issues

Introduction

This section describes the basic guidelines you must follow to successfully run COM components with .NET.

Error Handling

Use try/catch error handling to catch COM Exceptions.

Explicitly Free Resources

Always release resources explicitly by using **Marshal.ReleaseCOMObject** when objects require cleanup. If this is not done, objects may remain in memory for an indeterminate amount of time locking up resources until the garbage collector runs.

Use Chunky Calls

For every Interop call there are approximately 20 to 30 processor-level instruction calls. Due to the overhead of Interop, it is important to make method calls wisely. Try to use methods that supply the maximum number of arguments rather than assigning properties one by one.

Provide and Register Type Libraries

Using type libraries allows metadata to be generated immediately. The Type Library Importer (Tlbimp.exe) uses the type library to generate the proxies. Without type library information, we would have to use late binding, and data types may not be correctly marshaled.

Use Isomorphic types

Isomorphic types have a common representation in the managed and unmanaged world and have the least overhead. The runtime marshaling service automatically supports all automation-compliant data types.

Threading Problems

The different threading models in COM and .NET can cause a number of problems. Use directives such as **ASPCompat** to make the models compatible.

References for Further Reading

COM Interop is an extensive topic. Creating custom wrappers and marshalers requires a high-level understanding of COM, C++ and .NET.

For further information refer to:

- Interoperating with Unmanaged Code at

http://msdn.microsoft.com/library/default.asp?url=/library/en-us/cpguide/html/cpconinteroperatingwithunmanagedcode.asp

- *COM and .NET Interoperability* by Andrew Troelsen, Apress Publishing (April, 2002).

Lab 9: Interoperability with COM

Lab 9: Interoperability with COM

- Exercise 1: Creating a COM Wrapper for Office Web Components
- Exercise 2: Exporting Data to Excel Using COM Interoperability

Introduction

After completing this lab, you will have demonstrated your ability to:

- Create a Runtime Callable Wrapper for a COM component.
- Use the Office Web Components to use Microsoft Office functionality in ASP.NET.
- Export data to Excel in different ways.

Estimated time to complete this lab: 30 minutes

Starting a Virtual Machine

1. On the student computer, on the **Start** menu, point to **All Programs**, and then click **Microsoft Virtual PC**. If the Virtual PC console window does not appear, then right-click the **Virtual PC icon** in the notification area (system tray), and click **Show Virtual PC Console**.

2. In the Virtual PC console window, select the virtual machine that you would like to open and then click **Start**.

NOTE: Depending on your time zone, the first time you start each of the virtual machines, you may receive an error message that the parent virtual hard disk appears to have been modified. You can ignore this message.

3. The virtual machine will start in a new window.

Closing a Virtual Machine

1. On the student computer, in the virtual machine window, on the **Action** menu, click **Close**.

NOTE: To avoid accidentally closing the virtual machine during the lab, the **Close** option in the upper-right corner of the virtual machine is disabled.

2. The virtual machine window will close. All changes to the virtual hard disk are discarded.

Exercise 1: Creating a COM wrapper for Office Web Components

In this exercise, we will create a wrapper for using the COM components that expose Microsoft Excel functionality. The Office Web Components are a version of the Microsoft Office components that are designed to meet the scalability and multithreaded requirements of Web applications. It is better to use this version than the actual Office components.

- **Create the Lab Starter Projects**

1. Browse to the D:\2311\Labfiles\Lab09\Starter\VB or D:\2311\Labfiles\Lab09\Starter\CS.

2. Open Lab9.sln in the appropriate folder depending on your language choice.

- **Create the COM wrapper for the OWC**

1. In Solution Explorer, right-click on the project and select **Add Reference**.

2. Select the **COM** tab, and select **Microsoft Office Web Components DLL**. (Microsoft Office Web Components 9.0)

3. Click **OK** and VS.NET will add the reference to your project and create the wrapper.

- **Open the COM wrapper using ILDASM**

1. Launch the Visual Studio Command Prompt from the start menu.

    a. Start>Programs>Microsoft Visual Studio .NET>Visual Studio Tools>

    b. Visual Studio Command Prompt

2. On the command line type **ILDASM**. This launches the Intermediate Language Disassembler, which is a tool for examining IL code.

3. On the **File** menu of **ILDASM**, click **Open** and navigate to the **bin** directory of your Web project and open the dll called **Interop.OWC.dll**.

- **Open the COM wrapper using ILDASM**

1. Open the node **OWC** and examine all the .NET types that have been generated based on the type library by the type library importer

2. Navigate to the node **WorkSheet**, which has a blue symbol with an "I" in it to indicate that it is an interface. It corresponds to an interface exposed by COM

3. Double-click the first item under the worksheet node and examine the IL code. Notice the GUID attributes that have been bought in from the Type Library

4. Double-click the method **Export** under the worksheet node. Examine the way the method signature has been translated and how the parameters are marshaled. The DispIDAttribute corresponds to the ID of the COM method and is used to identify methods.

Exercise 2: Populating an Excel Spreadsheet from a DataSet

■ Populating an Excel Spreadsheet from a DataSet

1. Open the Web page **Write2Excel.aspx**. In the codebehind, a method called BindDataGrid has been created to get data into a dataset and bind to a DataGrid. The **DataSet** variable has been declared globally so that its contents can also be written into a spreadsheet.
2. Create a private method **WriteData2Excel** and within it create an instance of a **SpreadSheetClass**. Your code should resemble the following:

Visual Basic .NET

```
Dim xlsheet as new SpreadsheetClass()
```

C#

```
SpreadsheetClass xlsheet = new SpreadsheetClass();
```

3. The **ActiveSheet** property of the **SpreadSheetClass** has a Cells collection. Populate the cells by iterating through the values in the DataSet. Your code should resemble the following:

Visual Basic .NET

```
Dim xlsheet As New SpreadsheetClass()

Dim rowIndex, colIndex As Integer
Dim row As DataRow, col As DataColumn

For Each row In ds.Tables(0).Rows
    rowIndex += 1
    colIndex = 0
    For Each col In ds.Tables(0).Columns
        colIndex += 1
        xlsheet.ActiveSheet.Cells(rowIndex, colIndex) = _
        row(col.ColumnName).ToString()
    Next
Next
```

C#

```
int rowIndex=0;
int colIndex=0;
foreach(DataRow row in ds.Tables[0].Rows)
{
    rowIndex++;
    colIndex=0;
    foreach(DataColumn col in ds.Tables[0].Columns)
    {
        colIndex++;
        xlsheet.ActiveSheet.Cells[rowIndex,colIndex] =
        row[col.ColumnName].ToString();
    }
}
```

4. After the spreadsheet class has been populated, we need to persist it. Use the **Export** method of the **ActiveSheet** property and pass in the name of a file as an argument. Your code should resemble the following:

Visual Basic .NET

```
xlsheet.ActiveSheet.Export(Server.MapPath("Products.xls"), _
         SheetExportActionEnum.ssExportActionNone)
```

C#

```
xlsheet.ActiveSheet.Export(Server.MapPath("Products.xls"),
     SheetExportActionEnum.ssExportActionNone);
```

5. A hyperlink control called lnkExcel has already been placed on the page. Set the **NavigateUrl** property of the link to the name of the file and set its **visible** property to **True**.

Visual Basic .NET

```
Me.lnkExcel.NavigateUrl = " Products.xls"
Me.lnkExcel.Visible = true
```

C#

```
this.lnkExcel.NavigateUrl = "Products.xls";
this.lnkExcel.Visible = true;
```

6. Test the page by viewing it in a browser. The DataGrid should display when the page loads. Click the button on the form to create and populate Excel. When the hyperlink becomes visible, click the hyperlink to view the Excel document.

Because Excel can interpret HTML, you can convert the contents of a DataGrid into an Excel spreadsheet without using any COM Interop. Simply set the response's content type to indicate that it is an Excel document and the HTML from the Grid will automatically be transformed into an Excel spreadsheet on the client. The page WithoutInterop.aspx illustrates this.

There are a few other ways to export Excel from ASP.NET. These include using XML/XSL transforms or client side scripts to manipulate Excel on the client.

Module 10: ASP.NET Configuration

> **Module 10: ASP.NET Configuration**
>
> - Configuration File Overview
> - Examples of Built-In Configuration Settings
> - Creating Custom Configuration Settings
> - Encrypting Configuration Settings
> - Using the Configuration Management Application Block (CMAB)
> - Lab 10: Configuration Management

Overview

With the advent of .NET came the ability to easily store configuration information in XML-based configuration files instead of in the Windows registry or ini files. The configuration information can be simple settings or complex settings that determine the entire layout and structure of your applications.

In this module, you will be exposed to the .NET configuration architecture, learn to read and write custom configuration sections, and learn to abstract configuration information so that it can be stored in different types of storage mediums.

Objectives

After completing this module, you will be able to:

- Create and modify configuration files.
- Take advantage of built-in ASP.NET configuration settings.
- Create custom configuration sections.
- Encrypt configuration sections for better security.
- Use the Configuration Management Application Block (CMAB) to abstract configurations management.

Lesson: Configuration File Overview

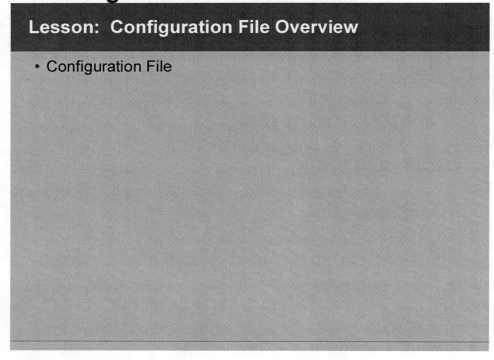

Introduction

Configuration files are well-formed Extensible Markup Language (XML) files that have a .config extension and the root element **<configuration>**. They can be modified using any text editor.

Lesson Objectives

After completing this lesson, you will be able to:

- Use Sections, Section Groups, and Section Handlers.
- Understand the hierarchical nature of configuration files.
- Target specific path locations.
- Prevent overriding.

Configuration File

Configuration File Overview

- Sections
- Section Groups
- Section Handlers
- Hierarchical Organization
- Targeting Specific Locations
- Preventing Overriding

The configuration file values are loaded into memory and cached for performance. However, every time the values in the configuration file are changed at runtime, the cache expires. This way the latest settings are available without explicitly recompiling. You should be aware that every change to the Web.config file at runtime causes the ASP.NET worker process to restart. This can adversely affect performance.

The .config extension is protected by IIS and not accessible via incoming http requests. This means you could give other XML files a .config extension and get the same level of protection as a Web.config file.

Configuration files contain section handler declarations, section groups and sections.

Sections

These are the XML sections that contain the configuration information.

```
<authorization>
    <allow roles = "Manager">
    <deny roles = "*"/>
</authorization>
```

Section Groups

Sometimes related sections can be organized into groups.

```
<System.Web>
   <authentication mode = "Windows"/>
   <authorization>
       <allow roles = "Manager">
   <deny roles = "*"/>
</authorization>
</System.Web>
```

Section Handlers

Section handlers are classes that handle the different sections. Every section has a section handler and they must be declared. For instance, the Machine.config file contains several section declarations.

```
<configSections>

<section name="appSettings"
type="System.Configuration.NameValueFileSectionHandler, System,
Version=1.0.5000.0, Culture=neutral,
PublicKeyToken=b77a5c561934e089" />

</configSections>
```

Above is the declaration of the class that handles the following section:

```
<appSettings file = "additionalSettings.xml" >
   < add key = "Tx" value = "Texas" />
</appSettings>
```

The <appSettings> section is used to store your key-value pairs.

Hierarchical Organization

Configuration files are hierarchically organized. The Machine.config file contains the settings that apply to the entire machine, and some base settings that are inherited by every application on the machine.

Some settings are available only in the Machine.config file (for example, the <processModel> section that is discussed later). Other settings can be placed in the both Machine.config and Web.config. An example of this is the <trace> section which is discussed later.

Subfolders or child applications in a Web application can each have their own Web.config file. Each Web.config file overrides the settings from the Machine.config file and Web.config file above it in the hierarchy. This means a single application can have multiple configuration settings based on which Uniform Resource Locator (URL) is used to access a resource.

Targeting Specific Locations

The location path can be used to target settings to a particular path, application or file. This allows a subfolder to have different settings from the rest of the application.

```
<system.web>
    <location path = "AdminFolder">
        <authorization>
            <allow roles = "Administrators">
            <deny roles = "*"/>
        </authorization>
    </location>
</system.web>
```

Preventing Overriding

The **allowOverride** attribute allows an administrator to force all users to have a specific setting and prevents individual applications or folders from overriding it.

```
<system.web>
    <trace enabled = "false" allowOverride = "false"/>
</system.web>
```

Lesson: Built-In Configuration Sections

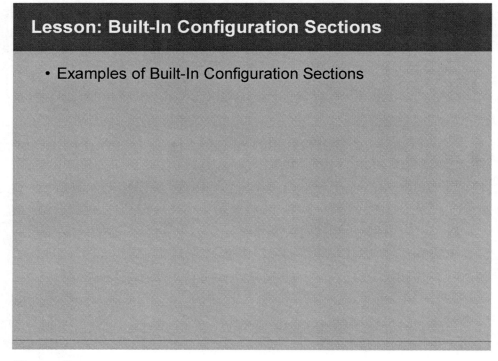

Overview

The <system.diagnostics> group provides a <trace> setting that allows you to write trace information to the Event Log, text files or a database.

Do not confuse this with the <trace> setting in <system.web>, which is used for page level tracing and can be used to write information out to a Web page only. Use the trace setting discussed in this example only if you want to write information out to a database or external source.

Objectives

After completing this lesson, you will be able to:

- Configure a listener.
- Configure switches.
- Use attribute settings of the <processModel> section in Machine.config
- Handle error messages.
- View and use account settings.
- Run ASP.NET on a domain controller.

Examples of Built-In Configuration Sections

> **Examples of Built-In Configuration Sections**
> - Configuring a Listener
> - Configuring Switches
> - Attribute Settings of the <processModel> Section in machine.config
> - Error Messages
> - Account Settings
> - Running ASP.NET on a domain controller
> - References and Downloads

Configuring a Listener

This example configures a file as a listener for trace information. Listeners can also be programmatically added to the **System.Diagnostics.Trace** class.

```
<trace autoflush="false" indentsize="4">
   <listeners>
   <add name="myListener"
        type="System.Diagnostics.TextWriterTraceListener.System"
        initializeData="c:\myListener.log" />
<remove type="System.Diagnostics.DefaultTraceListener.System"/>
   </listeners>
</trace>
```

Configuring Switches

Switches can be used to dynamically toggle the level of detail in the trace output.

```
<switches>
   <add name = "TraceLevel" value = "3">
</switches>
```

Trace switch values:

0	Off
1	Error
2	Warning
3	Info
4	Verbose

The following C# code is used to selectively write trace statements based on the level that is set in the config file.

```
TraceSwitch tSwitch = new TraceSwitch("TraceLevel", "Description goes here");
Trace.WriteLineIf(tSwitch.TraceWarning, "Warning Message");
Trace.WriteLineIf(tSwitch.TraceError, "Error Message");
```

Attribute Settings of the <processModel> Section in Machine.config

The process model section is used to configure settings pertaining to the ASP.NET process. It is set in the Machine.config file.

Microsoft Windows XP and **Windows 2000:** These settings are read directly by the ASP.NET ISAPI extension. Any changes to this section require a restart of IIS before the new settings take effect.

Microsoft Windows Server 2003: This section is ignored because you can modify these settings using the Administration tool.

idleTimeout: Specifies how long ASP.NET will wait before shutting down the worker process.

Timeout: Specifies the number of minutes until ASP.NET launches a new process to take the place of the current one. Pre-emptive recycling to take care of possible memory leaks, deadlocks, or other problems.

requestQueueLimit: The number of requests that are allowed in the queue before 503 Server Too Busy error start is returned. The default is 5,000.

requestLimit: The number of requests that ASP.NET will handle before launching a new worker process.

maxWorkerThreads: The maximum number of worker threads on each processor. This must be equal to or greater than the **minFreeThreads** value in the <httpRuntime> section. This value can range from 5 to 100.

maxIOThreads: The maximum number of IO threads per processor. Must be equal to or greater than the **minFreeThreads** value in the <httpRuntime> section. This number can range from 5 to 100.

memoryLimit: The maximum amount of memory a worker process can consume before a new process is launched and requests are reassigned. The default value is 60 percent of total memory.

webGarden: In a multiprocessor machine, this setting specifies whether individual worker processes should be assigned to each processor. If set to *true*, the user specifies the processors using the **cpuMask** property. If set to *false*, only one process is used and the OS manages the CPU use.

Error Messages

serverErrorMessageFile: Specifies the error file to use in place of the default "Server Unavailable" message.

Recommendation: Create a file that is not handled by the ASP.NET process and have a user-friendly error message such as "site is temporarily down, please try again later."

Account Settings

userName: Specifies the user name that should be used to run the ASP.NET process. The user name can be set to a pre-defined account, a specific domain, or a local user account. The following are possible values:

- **Machine** - This setting causes ASP.NET to run under a predefined account that has limited privileges for better security. This is the default.

- **System** - With this setting ASP.NET runs as an administrative account with maximum privileges. This was the default in the beta 2 version of the .NET Framework, but is no longer recommended.

- **Custom** - Specifies that the account should run under a custom account with the user name and password that are supplied in the .config file. These values can be stored in the registry.

Password: Used in conjunction with the above **userName** property.

Running ASP.NET on a domain controller

ASP.NET runs by default as a local system account and does not exist on domain controllers. There are two options for configuring ASP.NET to run on a domain controller.

- Configure ASP.NET to run as the system account by setting **userName** to **System**. This is not recommended because it now runs as Administrator and has full system rights.
- Configure ASP.NET to run as a weak domain account to log onto the domain and give it the most basic permissions. This is the better approach. The steps to assign such an account are:
    1. Create an account on the domain controller and add it to the users group.
    2. Grant the user the "Log on as a batch job" right.
    3. Give the user the necessary rights to the ASP.NET application directories and any other necessary directories.
    4. In the <processModel> section, set the **userName** and **password** properties to the correct values for that account

References and Downloads

There are several other settings such as **comImpersonationLevel** that are available within the **processModel** section. Other related sections include the <identity> section that can be used for impersonating accounts and the <httpRuntime> section that is used for configuring threads. More on this is available in the MSDN documentation.

More documentation about the above information is available from MSDN.

ASP.NET Setup and Configuration by James Avery from Microsoft Press (May, 2003) is a good pocket reference book on ASP.NET configuration settings.

Look up tracing and trace listeners in the MSDN documentation. These classes appear in the System.Diagnostics namespace. In addition, the Microsoft Enterprise Instrumentation Framework (EIF) contains a set of classes that .NET applications can use to instrument applications for manageability in a production environment. This framework provides an extensible event schema and unified API, which leverage existing event logging and tracing mechanisms built into Windows. These include WMI, the Windows Event Log and Windows Event Tracing and is available as a download from the Microsoft downloads.

NOTE

The Logging Application Block on the http://msdn.microsoft.com/practices Web site is another extensible block of code that can be used in applications to provide metering, logging, tracing, and exception reporting capabilities.

Lesson: Custom Configuration Settings

Lesson: Custom Configuration Settings

- Creating Custom Configuration Settings

Overview

In this lesson you will learn how to create a custom configuration section.

Objectives:

After completing this lesson, you will be able to:

- Create sections.
- Create a handler class and declare the handler.
- Read values.
- Use built-in section handlers.

Creating Custom Configuration Settings

- Creating the Sections
- Creating a Handler Class
- Reading Values
- Built-In Section Handlers
- References and Downloads

Creating the Sections

Example section:

```
<MyConfigSection homepage = "http://www.microsoft.com" />
```

Creating a Handler Class

Handler classes must implement the *IConfigurationSectionHandler* interface, which has a **Create** method.

Microsoft Visual Basic® .NET

```
Public Class MyConfigSectionHandler
    Implements IConfigurationSectionHandler
    Public Function Create(ByVal parent As Object, _
        ByVal configContext As Object, _
        ByVal section As XmlNode) As Object Implements _
        IConfigurationSectionHandler.Create

        Dim sHomePage As String = section.Attributes(0).Value
        Return sHomePage
    End Function
End Class
```

C#

```
public class MyConfigSectionHandler: IConfigurationSectionHandler
{
    public Object Create(Object parent, object configContext, XmlNode section)
    {
      String sHomePage = section.Attributes[ 0] .Value;
      return sHomePage;
    }
}
```

The **Create** method converts XML from the .config file into its object representation. In this example, we return a string, but it could be any kind of object.

Create method parameters:

- **System.Object – parent:** This parameter gives us a reference to any settings from a parent configuration section.

- **System.Object – configContext:** This parameter is useful to determine the virtual path used to access this resource.

- **System.Xml.XmlNode – section:** This parameter contains the XML that the handler interprets. We can traverse through the properties of this node and its child nodes using the XML classes in .NET to extract the XML and handle it.

Declaring the Handler

The handler must be declared in the <configSections> of the Web.config or Machine.config file. This step associates the handler with the section.

```xml
<configSections>
   <section name="MyConfigSection"
            type="MyConfigSectionHandler" />
</configSections>
```

Reading Values

When you call the **GetConfig** method of the **ConfigurationSettings** class, the **Create** method of the handler is called and an object is returned. This object is also added to an object tree and cached for performance.

Visual Basic .NET

```
Ctype(ConfigurationSettings.GetConfig("MyConfigSection"), string)
```

C#

```csharp
(string)ConfigurationSettings.GetConfig("MyConfigSection");
```

Using this method the object has to be cast back to the correct type. It would be easier to create a method in the Handler class that directly returns the correct representation.

Visual Basic .NET
```
Public Shared ReadOnly Property HomePage as String
    Get
        Ctype(ConfigurationSettings.GetConfig("MyConfigSection"), string)
    End Get
End Property
```

C#
```
public static string HomePage
{
    get
    {
        return (string)ConfigurationSettings.GetConfig("MyConfigSection");
    }
}
```

Now we can access it in the following manner:

Visual Basic.NET
```
Dim myHomePage = MyConfigurationSectionHandler.HomePage
```

C#
```
string myHomePage as String = MyConfigurationSectionHandler.HomePage;
```

Built-in Section Handlers

There are section handlers in the **System.Configuration** namespace used by the built-in sections that are not user-defined. For example, **NameValueFileSectionHandler** is used by the <appSettings> section. **DictionarySectionHandler** reads through the key-value pairs and adds them to a **Hashtable** object. **SingleTagSectionHandler** reads from a single tag that has multiple values.

Building Custom Sections Using Built-In Handlers

The handlers mentioned above can be used to read custom sections rather than building custom section handlers.

For example, here is a custom section to store key-value pairs.

```
<portalApplication>
    <databaseSettings>
        <add key = "connString" value = "server = localhost;...."/>
    </databaseSettings>
</portalApplication>
```

Declaring the Handler for Custom Sections

Because the section created above looks very similar to the built-in <appSettings> section, we can use the same handler class for both. The declaration of the section handler for our custom section would look like this:

```
<configSections>
    <sectionGroup name = "portalApplication">
        <section name="databaseSettings"
                 type="System.Configuration.NameValueFileSectionHandler,System,
                 Version=1.0.5000.0,Culture=neutral,
                 PublicKeyToken=b77a5c561934e089"/>
    </sectionGroup>
</configSections>
```

References and Downloads

ASP.NET Setup and Configuration by James Avery (Microsoft Press) (May, 2003).

Lesson: Encrypting Configuration Settings

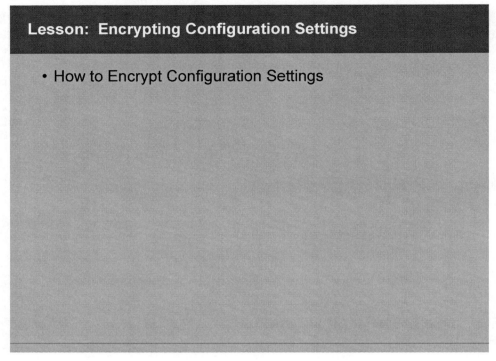

Overview

In this lesson, we will examine how to encrypt configuration settings. One-way encryption does not support decryption.

Objectives

After completing this lesson, you will understand:

- Hashing, symmetric and asymmetric encryption
- Popular symmetric algorithms supported in .NET.
- Architecture for symmetric algorithm classes in .NET.
- How to create a wrapper class to work with symmetric algorithms.
- How to create a handler class.
- How to manage keys.

How to Encrypt Configuration Settings

> **How to Encrypt Configuration Settings**
> - Hashing
> - Symmetric vs. Asymmetric Encryption
> - Popular Symmetric Algorithms Supported in .NET
> - Architecture for Symmetric Algorithm Classes in .NET
> - CryptoStreams
> - Creating a Wrapper Class to Work with Symmetric Algorithms
> - Creating a Handler Class
> - Key Management
> - References and Downloads

Hashing

Hashing is technically not encryption. Its primary use is to hide or protect data. Hashing is more appropriate than two-way encryption for password storage. Instead of decrypting and comparing password values, the application can compare password hashes.

Use salt values to reduce the possibility of dictionary attacks. A *salt* value is a bit of data that is appended to the end of the string to be hashed and is included with the string so that it can be used later when another string is compared with the hash.

Popular Hashing Algorithms

MD5: Provides 128-bit hashes.

SHA-1: Provides 160-bit hashes. SHA-1 is slower than MD5 but more secure. .NET also supports 256-, 384- and 512-bit versions of this algorithm.

The .NET Framework provides a number of classes (child classes of **HashAlgorithm**) to work with these algorithms.

One way to perform a hash is to use **HashPasswordForStoringInConfigFile** of the **FormsAuthentication** class.

Visual Basic .NET

```
Dim base64HashValue As String = 
    FormsAuthentication.HashPasswordForStoringInConfigFile( _
    "password", "sha1")
```

C#

```
string base64HashValue = 
    FormsAuthentication.HashPasswordForStoringInConfigFile(
    "password","sha1");
```

Example of Using the SHA-1 Class

Visual Basic .NET

```
Dim sh1 as SHA1 = SHA1.Create()
Dim hashValue() as byte = sh1.ComputeHash(message)
```

C#

```
SHA1 sha1 = SHA1.Create();
Byte[] hashValue = sha1.ComputeHash(message);
```

Symmetric vs. Asymmetric Encryption

Asymmetric encryption uses a public-key/private-key pair to encrypt data while symmetric encryption uses a single key both to encrypt and decrypt data. It is especially suitable for situations such as storing encrypted configuration settings on the back end, where there is no exchange of encrypted information between two parties. We will focus only on symmetric encryption in this module.

Asymmetric encryption uses a public key and a private key pair, and is best suited when encrypted information is to be transmitted between two parties, when keys have to be securely exchanged, and for digital data signing. Asymmetric encryption can cause performance degradation 1,000 times slower than symmetric encryption.

Popular Symmetric Algorithms Supported in .NET

Rijndael (Advanced Encryption Standard): This is the most secure algorithm. It supports 128-, 192- and 256-bit keys.

TripleDES: This algorithm is more secure than DES and supports 112- and 168-bit keys.

DES, RC2, RC4: These algorithms are less secure and should be avoided in most circumstances.

Architecture for Symmetric Algorithm Classes in .NET

. Net classes that support these algorithms include **TripleDESCryptoServiceProvider**, **DESCryptoServiceProvider**, and **RijndaelManaged**.

These classes are found in the **System.Security.Cryptography** namespace. Classes whose names end in **Managed** provide a fully managed version of the algorithm rather than making API calls to the operating system.

Visual Basic .NET

```
Dim _rijnDael As Rijndael = Rijndael.Create()
_rijnDael.Key = key    ' the encryption key
Dim rijnDaelEncryptor As ICryptoTransform = rijnDael.CreateEncryptor()
```

C#

```
Rijndael _rijnDael = Rijndael.Create();
_rijnDael.Key = key;   // the encryption key
ICryptoTransform rijnDaelEncryptor = rijnDael.CreateEncryptor();
```

The same key must be used for encryption and decryption, whether the key is automatically generated or created using the random classes. The key must be stored in a safe place.

CryptoStreams

Programmers frequently must read and write a stream of encrypted data to and from a source such as a file. This is where the **CryptoStream** class that works with streams is particularly useful. The following code snippet uses a CryptoStream with the specified encryptor and writes out to a FileStream. We could also use the **MemoryStream** class for in-memory transformations.

Visual Basic .NET

```
Dim cipherTextStream As New FileStream("c:\\ciphertext.bin", _
FileMode.Create)
    Dim _cryptoStream As New CryptoStream(cipherTextStream, _
        rijnDaelEncryptor, CryptoStreamMode.Write)
    _cryptoStream.Write(plainTextArray, 0, plainTextArray.Length)
    _cryptoStream.FlushFinalBlock()
    _cryptoStream.Close()
```

C#

```
FileStream cipherTextStream = new
    FileStream("c:\\ciphertext.bin", FileMode.Create);
CryptoStream _cryptoStream = new CryptoStream(cipherTextStream,
    rijnDaelEncryptor, CryptoStreamMode.Write);
    _cryptoStream.Write(plainTextArray, 0, plainTextArray.Length);
    _cryptoStream.FlushFinalBlock();
    _cryptoStream.Close();
```

Creating a Wrapper Class to Work with Symmetric Algorithms

The article "How to Create an Encryption Library" in the Microsoft Patterns and Practices Web site at http://msdn.microsoft.com/library/en-us/dnnetsec/html/SecNetHT10.asp?frame=true demonstrates how to create a library class to support the different encryption classes. It supports the TripleDES, DES, RC2 and Rijndael algorithms.

Creating a Handler Class

The section below shows how a simple handler class can be created to encrypt values. Notice a utility wrapper class called **DataProtector** is used to decrypt the values. The utility class depends on a key value that is either hard-coded or read from a file.

Visual Basic.NET

```
Public Class MyConfigSectionHandler
    Implements IConfigurationSectionHandler

    Private shared _connectString as String
    Public shared Readonly Property ConnectionString() As String
        Get
            Return _connectString
        End Get
    End Property

Public Function Create(parent as Object, configContext as Object, _
    section as XmlNode) as Object
    Implements IConfigurationSectionHandler.Create
        Dim nv as NameValueCollection
        Dim sh as new NameValueFileSectionHandler
        nv = Ctype(sh.Create(parent,configContext,section),NameValueCollection)
        If not nv is nothing Then
            _connectString = _
                DataProtector.DecryptString(nv.Item("ConnectionString"))
        End if
    End Function

    Private Sub New() 'the class cannot be instantiated
    End Sub
End Class
```

C#

```csharp
public class MyConfigSectionHandler:IConfigurationSectionHandler
{
    string _connectString;

    public string ConnectionString
    {
        get { return _connectString;}
    }

    public object Create(object parent, object configContext ,XmlNode section)
    {
        NameValueFileSectionHandler sh = new NameValueFileSectionHandler();
        NameValueCollection nv =
                (NameValueCollection)sh.Create(parent,configContext,section);
        if(nv!=null)
        {
            _connectString =
                    DataProtector.DecryptString(nv["connectionString"] );
        }
    }
    private MyConfigSectionHandler(){} //the class cannot be instantiated
}
```

Key Management

With symmetric encryption, the same key must be used to encrypt and decrypt the data. Protecting data by encrypting it requires that the key be protected. The cryptographic classes in .NET do not address the key management problem.

Keys can be managed in two ways, either by the user or by the operating system

Generating and managing keys yourself

- Use an implementation of the **System.Security.Cryptography.RandomNumberGenerator** class to generate keys or save the keys autogenerated by the classes that derive from **SymmetricAlgorithm**.

- Some ways of protecting the key:
    - Obscurity: By hiding it in Intermediate Language code. This is not recommended because Microsoft Intermediate Language (MSIL) code can be reverse-engineered.
    - Derivation: Keys are not stored, but the key can be derived using an unchangeable characteristic, such as a pass phrase.
    - File or Registry: The keys can be stored here and protected through access control lists (ACLs). However, this introduces maintenance considerations.

Using the operating system to generate and manage keys

Letting the operating system manage keys is a good way of solving the key management problem. There are two ways of doing this.

- **LSA:** Local Storage Authority policy functions, such as **LsaStorePrivateData** and **LsaRetrievePrivateData** can be used to secure keys but they are less secure than the DPAPI method. Because these methods use the registry, there is a limit to the size of the data and a risk of running out of disk space. For these reasons, LSA is not recommended.

- **DPAPI:** With Windows 2000, Microsoft introduced the Data Protection API, which we will consider next.

Data Protection API

The DPAPI includes two functions, **CryptProtectData** and **CryptUnProtectData**, either of which can be called by making unmanaged calls to Crypt32.dll of the win32 application programming interface (API).

DPAPI does not actually store keys but generates the same keys using some unchangeable characteristics, such as the machine identity, referred to as "machine store" or user identity, referred to as "user store."

- **Machine Store**: This is useful for applications that run under a single account and for Windows Service-type applications that run with a fixed user profile.
    - The disadvantage of this store is that any user on that machine can decrypt the values and that it is dependent on a specific machine.
    - If encrypted values are to be stored in a config file for an application that runs on a Web farm, the encrypted value must be computed on each machine separately.
    - An optional application-specific entropy value can be supplied to the API to create a more secure version. This requires the caller to know the additional entropy value. This presents the problem of storing the value.
- **User Store:** Although this is more secure, it does not work with some applications including ASP.NET applications that run under a fixed user account. In addition, this allows all applications that run under the same user profile to access each other's data. Entropies can be used with user stores as well.

References and Downloads

The article "How to Create a DPAPI Library" on the Microsoft Patterns and Practices Web site at http://msdn.microsoft.com/library/en-us/dnnetsec/html/SecNetHT08.asp?frame=true provides a managed library class to wrap the DPAPI. This class is used in the lab exercises and may be used to simplify access to DPAPI.

- Protect Private Data with the Cryptography Namespaces of the .NET Framework, by Dan Fox, MSDN magazine.
    - http://msdn.microsoft.com/msdnmag/issues/02/06/crypto
- Safeguard Database Connection Strings and Other Sensitive Setting in Your Code, by Alek Davis, MSDN magazine.
    - http://msdn.microsoft.com/msdnmag/issues/03/11/ProtectYourData/default.aspx
- .NET Framework Security, by Brian La Macchia, et al, Addison Wesley Publishing Company (April, 2002).

Lesson: Configuration Management Application Block (CMAB)

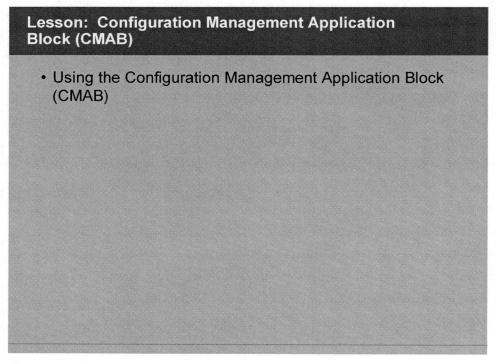

Overview

The Microsoft Configuration Management Application Block (CMAB) provides code that abstracts the logic required to store configuration information. CMAB can be directly plugged into your applications and extended if necessary. This is part of a larger set of application blocks available on the Microsoft Patterns & Practices Web site. CMAB is designed to provide developers with robust and tested frameworks for the configuration tasks they will often encounter.

Objectives

After completing this lesson, you will be able to:

- Understand the features of CMAB.
- Use the CMAB.

Using the Configuration Management Application Block (CMAB)

> **Using the Configuration Management Application Block (CMAB)**
> - Using the CMAB
> - Add a Reference to the CMAB
> - Declare the Section to be Used by the CMAB
> - Configure Providers to Store the User-Defined Sections
> - Declare Handlers to Interpret the XML from the Providers
> - Application Blocks

Features of the CMAB

CMAB is easy to use, as configuration information can be read from or written to using a single line of code.

```
ConfigurationManager.Write(data, section)
```

Or

```
ConfigurationManager.Read(data, section)
```

Where *data* is the data structure to be written out and *section* is the configuration section that it will be written to.

CMAB allows you to write configuration values without any data store dependencies. CMAB works with the registry, SQL Server, config files or external .xml files. If the data store changes later, simply modify a setting to specifying the new data store in the .config file.

Configuration data can be written out to data stores in the form of a Hashtable. As an alternative, the public properties of any object can be written out automatically using the **XmlSerializer** class. The CMAB can be modified to work with any custom data structure and is independent of memory structure. The CMAB supports encryption using the DPAPI for any data store that you use. The CMAB is extensible and allows you to create data storage locations.

Using the CMAB

The steps for using the CMAB are outlined. Detailed documentation is available with the download package.

Add a Reference to the CMAB

The Configuration Management Application Block can be downloaded from the following URL: http://msdn.microsoft.com/library/default.asp?url=/library/en-us/dnbda/html/cmab.asp.

The package includes the source code, Quick Start samples and documentation. To add its functionality to an application, you will need to add a reference to the compiled dll.

Declare the Section to be Used by the CMAB

Although the configuration manager can work with various data stores the settings for the CMAB itself are stored in the Web.config file. The section used by the CMAB for storing all its settings is called **applicationConfigurationManagement**. As with all sections, this section has to be declared in the <configSections> area of the .config file.

Configure Providers to Store the User Defined Sections

Users must tell the CMAB where they want their data stored. This is done by the CMAB using the <configSection> tags of the <applicationConfigurationManagement> section.

```
<configSection name = "UnencryptedXml">
    <configCache enabled = "true" refresh = "1 * * * *" />
    <configProvider
        assembly = "Microsoft.ApplicationBlocks.ConfigurationManagement,
                Version=1.0.0.0,Culture=neutral,PublicKeyToken=null"
        type = "Microsoft.ApplicationBlocks.ConfigurationManagement.Storage.XmlFileStorage"
        signed = "false"
        refreshOnChange = "false"
        encrypted = "false" />
</configSection>
```

The above section allows you to store your data into a configuration section called UnencryptedXml using the code shown below:

```
ConfigurationManager.Write(myData, "UnencryptedXml")
```

The **type** attribute of the configProvider is a class called **XmlFileStorage**. This class handles all the details of storing your section into the .config file.

Other classes available with the CMAB that you can use for the type attribute include **SqlStorage** and **RegistryStorage**.

Other settings for the provider specify caching and encryption.

Declare Handlers to Interpret the XML from the Providers

Providers are used to configure the data stores. Still, users must specify what kind of objects can be written out because each type is handled differently. This is done through the use of section handlers in the <configSections> area of the main Web.config file.

```
<section name = "UnencryptedXml"
type
="Microsoft.ApplicationBlocks.ConfigurationManagement.XmlHashtableSectionHandler,
         Microsoft.ApplicationBlocks.ConfigurationManagement,
   Version=1.0.0.0,Culture=neutral,PublicKeyToken=null"/>
```

- Notice the type attribute uses the **XmlHashTableSectionHandler** class. This indicates that our section called **UnencryptedXml** stores data in key-value pairs and this is done through a **Hashtable** object.
- Instead of using a **Hashtable**, we can use an object and have its public properties serialized using the **XmlSerializerSectionHandler** class.
- It is also possible to create our custom section handlers.

Application Blocks

The Configuration Management Application Block is just one of many Application Blocks made available as part of an effort by Microsoft to provide tested and robust frameworks for typical situations that developers encounter. More information is available on the Microsoft Patterns and Practices Web site.

Lab 10: Configuration Management

> **Lab 10: Configuration Management**
>
> - Exercise 1: Creating and Reading Custom Configuration Settings
> - Exercise 2: Working with Encrypted Configuration Sections
> - Exercise 3: Using the Microsoft Configuration Management Application Block

Exercise 1: Creating and reading custom configuration settings

Exercise 2: Working with encrypted configuration sections

Exercise 3: Using the Microsoft Configuration Management Application Block

Introduction

After completing this lab, you will have demonstrated your ability to:

- Place your own custom configuration information in the Web.config file.
- Write section handlers to interpret your custom sections.
- Encrypt connection string information by using classes that wrap the DPAPI.
- Use the Microsoft Configuration Management Application Block to store configuration information to different data stores.

Estimated time to complete this lab: 60 minutes

Starting a Virtual Machine

1. On the student computer, on the **Start** menu, point to **All Programs**, and then click **Microsoft Virtual PC**. If the Virtual PC console window does not appear, then right-click the **Virtual PC icon** in the notification area (system tray), and click **Show Virtual PC Console**.

2. In the Virtual PC console window, select the virtual machine that you would like to open and then click **Start**.

   NOTE: Depending on your time zone, the first time you start each of the virtual machines, you may receive an error message that the parent virtual hard disk appears to have been modified. You can ignore this message.

3. The virtual machine will start in a new window.

Closing a Virtual Machine

1. On the student computer, in the virtual machine window, on the **Action** menu, click **Close**.

   NOTE: To avoid accidentally closing the virtual machine during the lab, the **Close** option in the upper-right corner of the virtual machine is disabled.

2. The virtual machine window will close. All changes to the virtual hard disk are discarded.

Exercise 1: Creating and Reading Custom Configuration Settings

- **Create the Lab Starter Projects**

1. Browse to the D:\2311\Labfiles\Lab10\Starter\VB or

   D:\2311\Labfiles\Lab10\Starter\CS

2. Open Lab10.sln in the appropriate folder depending on your language choice.

- **Reviewing Built-In Functionality (<appSettings>)**

1. Open the **Web.config** file and under the **<appSettings>** node, notice the entry **<add key="TX" value="Texas"></add>**. This is a built-in feature allowing you to place your own key-value pairs in the .config file. The values can be read using the framework **ConfigurationSettings** class.

2. Open the CustomSection.aspx page in design view and double-click **Read values from AppSettings**. In the button_click event procedure you will notice the code to read the value associated with the key entered in the text box.

3. View the page in the browser and enter **TX** in the input box and the corresponding value from the config file will be placed in the label.

- **Adding Custom XML to the Web.config File**

1. Open the **BooksXmlSnippet.xml** file and locate the section beginning with the element **<books>**. This is a custom XML section that we have created to be added to the Web.config file.

2. Copy the entire books element – **<books>…. </books>** to the Web.config file and paste it after the **</appSettings>** tag. Do not copy the **<configSections>** element yet.

- **Creating a Configuration Handler Class**

1. *Configuration Handlers* are classes that are called to read XML from configuration files. These classes must implement the **IConfigurationSectionHandler** interface, which has a **Create** method.

2. Open the **BookSectionHandler.cs** (or .vb) file in the components folder of your solution. Study the **Create** method implementation. What does the **section** parameter of the **Create** method contain? Write your answer below.

   _____

   _____

   _____

   _____

   _____

   _____

3. In the same file, view the implementation of the **Book** class. Notice how the **Create** method interprets the XML and returns it as an array of **Book** objects

- **Registering the Configuration Handler**

1. We have to associate our custom XML snippet with its corresponding handler class. This registration is done in the Web.config file.

2. Open the **BooksXmlSnippet.xml** file and copy the entire **<configSections>…</configSections>** element and place it directly under the **<configuration>** tag of the Web.config file.

3. The above step allows the values from the XML file to be populated into in-memory objects based on our implementation. These objects are then cached and can be consumed from the application using code. In web applications, every time the Web.config file is changed the cache is deleted, thereby allowing users always to have the latest values.

- **Reading the Configuration Values**

1. Open the CustomSection.aspx page in design view and double-click **Read values from Custom Books Element**.

2. **Uncomment** the code in the button_click event procedure and notice the code to retrieve the custom element. The **GetConfig** method of the **ConfigurationSettings** class is used to retrieve the **Books** XML section and it is cast back to its object representation, which is a **Book Array** (returned from the **Create** method).

3. View the page in the browser once again and click the button on the form to display the values.

Exercise 2: Working With Encrypted Configuration Sections

In this exercise, we will encrypt a connection string using Symmetric Encryption. The encryption functions are written in a custom class called DataProtector. This class uses the operating system's Data Protection API (DPAPI) Libraries, which automatically generates the keys for encrypting and decrypting. The keys are constructed based on the identity of the machine (Machine Store)

- ### Examining the DPAPI Data Protection Class

    1. With Windows 2000 Microsoft introduced the Data Protection API which has two functions CryptProtectData and CryptUnProtectData implemented in Crypt32.dll. These functions can be wrapped in managed classes and we will use an implementation provided on the MSDN best practices site. This implementation has been further modified to work with strings and not just bytes.

    2. In the Components folder in Solution Explorer, examine the code in the DataProtector.cs (or DataProtector.vb) file. The Unmanaged APIs region contains the Win32 API function declarations. The Encrypt and Decrypt regions contain the methods that initialize the structures and make the unmanaged API calls. The Encrypt Strings region contains the modifications that we have made to get the methods to work directly with strings. This class may be used in your own applications.

- ### Encrypting and Decrypting Data on a Page

    1. Open the Encryption.aspx page. In the Encrypt button's click event, write code to encrypt the data in the **txtDataToEncrypt** text box and display the output in the **txtEncryptedData** text box.

        > **Hint**: Use the DataProtector.EncryptString method. Also use try/catch statements and write any exceptions to the lblError label.

    2. Write similar code in the Decrypt button's click event to decrypt the value in the **txtEncryptedData** text box and display the result in the **txtDecryptedData** text box.

▪ Reading Encrypted Values from the Web.config File

1. Open the **EncryptedSettings.xml** file and copy the **<atomicSettings>..</atomicSettings>** section and place it in the Web.config file after the </AppSettings> section. Notice the value attribute has an empty string. This is where we will place the encrypted value.

2. From the EncryptedSettings.xml file, copy the **<section>...</section>** section and paste it inside the **<configSection>** section of the Web.config file. This registers a handler.

3. Generate an encrypted string from the Encryption.aspx page created in the previous steps. Paste this string between the quotes of the value attribute of the **<atomicSettings>** element that you placed in the Web.config file.

   It is important to note that this process must be done separately on each machine if the application is deployed on multiple machines because the keys are machine-specific. A Windows or console application could be created for this purpose.

4. Locate the EncryptedSectionHandler.cs or EncryptedSectionHandler.vb file in the Components folder of the solution. This is the **Handler** class that is registered in Web.config to handle the **<atomicSettings>** section and decrypt its contents. Notice how the Create method takes advantage of the existing **NameValueSectionHandler** class, which is used by the built-in **<appSettings>** section.

5. In the Encryption.aspx page, write code in the click event of the btnGetConnString to display the encrypted value in the Web.config file. The value can be retrieved to the label below the button using the following code:

Visual Basic .NET

```
Me.lblDisplay.Text = Utils.ConnectionString
```

C#

```
this.lblDisplay.Text = Utils.ConnectionString;
```

Exercise 3: Using the Microsoft Configuration Management Application Block

In this exercise, you will first install the Configuration Management Application Block (CMAB). Next, you will configure various custom sections in the CMAB by specifying their data stores. Finally, you will test how the CMAB can work with various data stores.

- **Setting up the Application to use the CMAB**

1. Open the **CMABSettingsSnippet.xml** file and copy only the first **<section>** tag. This is the **<section name = "applicationConfigurationManagement"…./>** section. Paste this within the <configSections> section of the Web.config file.

2. From the CMABSettingsSnippet.xml file copy the entire **<applicationConfigurationManagement></applicationConfigurationManagement>** section and place it in the Web.config file under the **</books>** element. The step is used to declare and create the section used by the CMAB.

- **Using the CMAB**

1. Declaring your custom sections and their properties in the CMAB.

    a. Copy all the **configSection** elements:

    <configSection …>…</configSection>

    from the CMABSettingsSnippet.xml file and paste them within the **<applicationConfigurationManagement>** tags in the Web.config file. These custom sections can have any name, but we have chosen names that are descriptive for the purposes of the lab (for example, EncryptedXml).

    b. Study the **<configProvider>** element of each custom configSection.

    What does this element define? What are the **type** and **refreshOnChange** attributes are used for? Write your answers below:

    _____
    _____
    _____
    _____
    _____

2. Registering Section Handlers

   a. Copy all the **<section ..>** elements that were not copied earlier from the CMABSettingsSnippet.xml file and paste them within the **<configSections>** section of the Web.config file. These are the handlers that convert the XML nodes retrieved by the storage providers into their object representation.

   b. Note the **type** attribute of the various **<section..>** elements. The most frequently used **type** attributes are **XmlHashtableSectionHandler** and **XmlSerializerSectionHandler**. These handlers are used to read values into **Hashtables** and into the public properties of custom classes.

3. Testing the CMAB

   a. Open the CMAB.aspx page in **Design** view. The configuration sections that were declared earlier are shown in the drop-down list. You will save a hyperlink name and URL (as a key value pair) into the section chosen from the **Combo** box.

   b. Double-click the **Save Hyperlink** button and uncomment the code in the click event. Notice that three of the four sections stored the data as key-value pairs in a **Hashtable** using the single line of code: ConfigurationManager.Write. For the last section, a small object (Link) is created and saved. This is because the handler for this section uses the **XmlSerializerSectionHandler**, which can read and write out the public properties of the class.

   c. Uncomment the code in the Read HyperLink button's click event and uncomment the **imports** directive at the top of the page (**using** for C# developers).

   d. In the CMABSettingsSnippet.xml file, locate the comment "Please correct the path if the sample is not being run from VS.NET" and ensure the path is set to **D:\2311\Labfiles\Lab10\Starter\VB or CS\ OtherConfigFile.config**. Run the CMAB.aspx page and type **Microsoft** in the **Hyperlink Name** text box and www.microsoft.com in the **Hyperlink URL** text box. If the section chosen in the drop-down list is **Unencrypted Xml file (config)**, the values should be written out to the Web.config file when you click **Save Hyperlink**. Confirm that this is the case.

   e. If **Encrypted Xml file (config)** is selected, an encrypted value should be written out to the Web.config file. The values can be read back in by clicking **Read Hyperlink**.

   It is better to save settings to an external config file other than the Web.config file because every modification of the Web.config file causes the ASP worker process to restart.

f. If **Unencrypted Xml file (other)** is selected, the value should be written out to the OtherConfigFile.xml file in the application. Before you try it, go to the declarations in the Web.config file to the section called **<configSection name="OtherConfigFile">**. Verify that the **path** attribute of the **<configProvider >** section has the absolute path to the OtherConfigFile.xml file in your project. Confirm that the **refreshOnChange** attribute is set to **True**.

g. The **Unencrypted in Sql** option writes out the values to a database called CMAB that was declared earlier in the .config sections.

h. This is only a subset of the functionality available in the CMAB. It is also possible to write encrypted values to a SqlServer, external .config file, or even the Windows registry.

- **Adjusting Settings in the CMAB**

1. In the **<configSection name="OtherConfigFile">** the <configCache..> element is set to **True**. This enables caching for better performance. The **refresh** attribute is set to **1 * * * ***. This means the cache expires on the first minute of every hour. This value can be changed to other values including absolute dates and times.

2. Run the CMAB.aspx page in a browser window and save the information to the external OtherConfigFile.xml file. Without closing the browser window, go to the OtherConfigFile.xml file and manually change the URL that was just entered through the Web page. Now read the information from the Web page by clicking **Read Hyperlink**. You will notice that the latest value was read in despite enabling caching. This is because the **refreshOnChange** attribute was set to **True**.

Module 11: Administering and Extending the Portal

> **Module 11: Administering and Extending the Portal**
>
> - How to Administer and Extend the Portal
> - Lab 11: Extending the Portal with New Modules

Overview

This module presents an extensible administrative infrastructure for managing the portal application. This module explores the major features of the administrative interface and how they work. The module also presents the steps necessary for extending the portal by adding new modules.

Objectives

After completing this module, you will be able to:

- Describe the portal configuration file.
- Add modules and tab definitions to extend the portal.
- Create an extensible data layer and user control.
- Add modules to the framework.

Lesson: How to Administer and Extend the Portal

> **Lesson: How to Administer and Extend the Portal**
> - Portal Configuration
> - Adding New Module and Tab Definitions
> - Extending the Portal
> - Final Steps for Extending Portal Content

Introduction

This lesson explains how to administer and extend your portal using module and tab definitions, as well as adding modules.

Lesson Objectives

After completing this lesson, you will be able to:
- Describe the portal configuration file.
- Add modules and tab definitions.
- Extend the portal with an extensible data layer and user control.

Portal Configuration

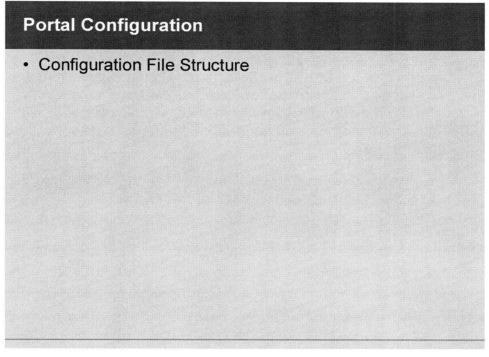

Introduction

The complete set of definitions and configurations for each tab and module displayed in the portal is contained in an .xml-formatted file, Portalcfg.xml. We will describe the parts of the file and how it can be changed. To add modules and tabs, settings in this file must be modified. Although this can be done manually, working manually with text files is prone to error and does not allow non-technical personnel to execute administrative tasks. The administrative infrastructure for the site depends on the programmatic reading and manipulating of file contents.

Configuration File Structure

The Portalcfg.xml file has a root element called **SiteConfiguration**. Because this element contains a reference to the schema for the configuration file, Portalcfg.xsd, the data is validated when it is loaded into the **DataSet**. Initializing the settings is performed in the **GetSiteSettings** method of the **Configuration** class. The **GetSiteSettings** method is called by the constructor of the **PortalSettings** object in the **Application_BeginRequest** method of the global.asax file. The data is read from the configuration file into the typed **DataSet** with the following line of code:

Microsoft Visual Basic® .NET

```
siteSettings.ReadXml(configFile)
```

C#

```
siteSettings.ReadXml(configFile);
```

As data is read into the **DataSet**, the schema used by the data is controlled by the **XmlReadMode** enumeration. The most significant values of this enumeration for the current purpose are:

- **Auto**: This is the default setting in the **GetSiteSettings** method. If the **DataSet** already has a schema, or if the document contains an inline schema, Auto sets the mode to **ReadSchema**. If the **DataSet** does not have a schema, and no in-line schema is found in the document, Auto sets the mode to **InferSchema**.

- **ReadSchema**: The data is loaded according to the inline schema. Because the typed **DataSet** was generated by using the schema referenced in the configuration file, the schema of the file and the **DataSet** are guaranteed to match. Any data in the file that does not conform to the schema will cause a validation exception to be thrown, thereby assuring data integrity.

- **InferSchema**: Reads the XML data and infers tables and columns from the data using a set of rules that can be referenced in the MSDN article, "Inferring DataSet Relational Structure from XML."

The **Global** element defines portalwide attributes such as the **PortalId**, **PortalName**, and **AlwaysShowEditButton**, which is a Boolean value that controls whether the **Edit** button is displayed. These values populate the **GlobalRow** object of **SiteConfiguration** when the **PortalSettings** object is initialized. This element allows the configuration of multiple portals. To extend the portal infrastructure to support this, the constructor of the **PortalSettings** class needs a new parameter corresponding to the **PortalId** of the portal to be displayed. The same basic set of components can be used to provide many different views and types of information according to the user group to be served.

The tabs are defined in a series of **Tab** elements. Each tab contains subelements corresponding to the modules to be displayed in that tab. The attributes of the **Tab** element control features such as which user roles have rights to view the tab and the order in which the tab will be sorted. These values are set in the constructor of the **PortalSettings** object when it is initialized. Each tab is populated using a **TabStripDetails** object which contains fields for **TabOrder** and **AccessRoles**. Each **TabStripDetails** object is then added to the **DesktopTabs** property so that it can be displayed by the Portalbanner.ascx control.

Each module element contains attributes that control its major features. Two ID fields are assigned to each module. **ModuleId** is the unique identifier for that module and **ModuleDefId** corresponds to one of the predefined module types, such as Announcements. In this way, module types can be reused throughout the portal while each retains its own unique features. On the **Home** tab, **News and Features** has a **ModuleDefId** of **1**, which means that the Announcements user control will be used, yet it keeps its own title, "News and Features." The **ModuleDefinition** elements contain the path for the source file of the user control.

Other attributes control other features of the module:

- **PaneName** controls in which table cell on the default page the module will be placed: Left, Content Pane, or Right.
- **EditRoles** determines which roles will be allowed to edit the content of the module. When the user is in a role contained in this attribute, the **Edit** button will appear next to each element of module content (such as an individual announcement) when the user is logged on. Clicking **Edit** will open the corresponding edit page for that type of content. We will examine this process in detail later in this module.

- **CacheTimeout** controls whether a module is cached. The process was described in Module 7. This property is checked in the default page. If the **CacheTime** value is other than 0, then the **CachedPortalModuleControl** is instantiated to control module caching.
- **ModuleOrder** controls the order of modules within the table cell where the module is rendered. The **Modules** collection of the **Tab** property is an **ArrayList** of **ModuleSettings** objects. Because the **ModuleSettings** class implements the **IComparable** interface, when the **Sort** method is called on the **Module** object, each **ModuleSettings** object is sorted according the rules defined in the **CompareTo** method implemented in that class.

The **Settings** element allows a module to have extended elements such as image files or .xml and .xsl files.

Adding Modules and Tab Definitions

Adding Module and Tab Definitions
- Editing Module Definitions
- Editing Tab Definitions

Introduction

Editing and adding modules involves several steps. Each module's properties are determined by the attributes in the **ModuleDefinition** elements. The first step is to specify these properties using the **ModuleDefinition** page (ModuleDefinitions.aspx). Once this is done, the user control for the module must be created and a page added for editing the information to be displayed. When defining a new tab, set the tab name, select the user roles that can edit the tab, and specify the modules to be displayed and where they appear. The **TabLayout** page (TabLayout.aspx) lets us make these selections.

Editing Module Definitions

Because each module uses the same configuration properties, the module definitions for each module can be edited using the same page. On the Admin tab page, a module to be edited can be selected from Module Definitions drop-down list or by clicking the **Add a New Module Type** link to access a form for adding a new module. Either action will call the ModuleDefinitions.aspx page and pass it three parameters: **ModuleDefId**, **tabId**, and **tabIndex**. The code-behind class for this page first checks to verify that user is an Admininistrator, then uses the **ModuleDefId** to fill the form with the appropriate values, which are either the values for the module definition selected or default values for a new module.

This page allows the user to update or delete the module type. When the user clicks **Update**, the **AddModuleDefinition** method of the **Configuration** class is called if a new module is to be added. If the module already exists, the **UpdateModuleDefinition** method is called to update the information for that module. The changes are made using the methods of the typed **DataSet SiteConfiguration**. The **WriteXml** method of the **DataSet** object rewrites the configuration file.

Editing Tab Definitions

A user control displayed on the **Admin** tab lists each tab that has been defined for the portal. This control, Tabs.ascx, is populated by using the cached **PortalSettings** object to retrieve a list of **TabStripDetails** objects and bind them into a listbox. The order of the tabs can be changed by clicking **Move selected tab up in list** or **Move selected tab down in list**. Clicking one of these buttons changes the **TabOrder** property for all the tabs, and saves the settings in the config file. Clicking the **Add** or **Edit** redirects the user to the TabLayout.aspx page, which is then populated with the tab's properties ready for editing. This page displays:

- **Tab Name**: This becomes the display name that appears on the tab.

- **Authorized Roles**: A listing of all the roles that have been defined for the site. Only users in one of the selected roles see the tab.

- **Listing of Module Types**: The **GetModuleDefinitions** method of the **SiteConfiguration** class is called to retrieve a list of all module definitions for this portal. The user can then select a module definition as the basis for a new module to be added to the site.

- **Module Name**: The name of the new module to be added.

- **Pane Locations for the Modules**: Clicking **Add to Organize Modules Below** invokes the **AddModule** method of the **Configuration** class, creating the new module with default properties and added to the "Content Pane." Note that this process requires that the updated settings must be reloaded. The **UpdateModuleOrder** method is called to preserve the new module order. The page is then reloaded to acquire the changes.

Once the new settings are saved, the newly defined module will appear in the designated location on its corresponding tab.

Extending the Portal

> **Extending the Portal**
>
> - Creating an Extensible Data Layer
> - Creating the User Control

Introduction

In the course of implementing an imaginary new module, which we will call ProjectStatus. Because it will be used to track a project's progress, we will demonstrate best practices for creating extensible Web applications. The pattern is sufficiently well defined so that a major part of the process of adding new modules can be easily automated.

Extending the Data Layer

Except in the case of administrative modules, which use the .config file for data storage, or modules with specialized purposes (for example, the XML module XmlModule.ascx), each module requires an underlying data store. Usually there is a one-to-one correspondence between a table in the portal database and the information needed by a particular module. The **Announcements** table contains all of the contents used by the Announcements user control. The first step in adding a new module is to create a table to hold its data:

Column Name	Data Type	Length	Allow Nulls
ItemId	int	4	
ModuleId	int	4	
CreatedByUser	nvarchar	100	✓
CreatedDate	datetime	8	✓
Title	nvarchar	100	✓
EstCompletionDate	datetime	8	✓
CurrentStatus	nvarchar	100	✓
PercentComplete	int	4	✓

Several fields are required because of how the portal is structured. Each module requires a **ModuleId**, which is used in the .config file to define which modules are displayed on a tab. It is also helpful to know which user created the module, which can help identify any unauthorized users who were adding modules. Most modules will also need a title, which, in this case, is the title of the project that we are tracking.

The data functionality for each module is handled through a set of stored procedures that encapsulate the major functions needed: adding, deleting, updating, and retrieving data for the module. Each module follows the same pattern:

- **AddProjectStatus**: A procedure that adds a new project status row and returns its ItemId.
- **DeleteProjectStatus**: Deletes a particular project status.
- **GetAllProjectStatus**: Retrieves status information for all projects.
- **GetProjectStatus**: Gets the status of a single project.
- **UpdateProjectStatus**: Updates all the fields for a particular project.

A primary purpose of this layer is to mediate access to the stored procedures that carry out the data functions. For each type of information provided by a module, a data access component is provided. The AnnouncementsDB.vb file contains the **AnnouncementsVB** class with all necessary data access methods. The ProjectStatusDB.vb file will contain a **ProjectStatusDB** class with the following methods:

- **AddProjectStatus**: Uses SqlHelper functions to add data for a new project status to the table.
- **DeleteProjectStatus**
- **UpdateProjectStatus**
- **GetProjectStatus**
- **GetAllProjectStatus**

The purpose of each method should be self-explanatory. As an example, and to illustrate how the use of the **SqlHelper** class can streamline the coding requirements, the **AddProjectStatus** code is shown below:

Visual Basic .NET

```vbnet
Public Function AddProjectStatus(ByVal moduleId As Integer, _
                                 ByVal CreatedByUser As String, _
                                 ByVal Title As String, _
                                 ByVal EstCompletionDate As DateTime, _
                                 ByVal CurrentStatus As String, _
                                 ByVal PercentComplete As Integer _
                                 ) As Integer

    If CreatedByUser.Length < 1 Then
        CreatedByUser = "unknown"
    End If


    Dim itemId As Integer = 0
    Dim arParms(6) As SqlParameter
    arParms(0) = New SqlParameter("@ModuleID", SqlDbType.Int)
    arParms(0).Value = moduleId
    arParms(1) = New SqlParameter("@UserName", SqlDbType.NVarChar, 100)
    arParms(1).Value = CreatedByUser
    arParms(2) = New SqlParameter("@Title", SqlDbType.NVarChar)
    arParms(2).Value = Title
    arParms(3) = New SqlParameter("@EstCompletionDate", SqlDbType.DateTime)
    arParms(3).Value = EstCompletionDate
    arParms(4) = New SqlParameter("@CurrentStatus", SqlDbType.NVarChar)
    arParms(4).Value = CurrentStatus
    arParms(5) = New SqlParameter("@PercentComplete", SqlDbType.Int)
    arParms(5).Value = PercentComplete
    arParms(6) = New SqlParameter("@ItemID", SqlDbType.Int)
    arParms(6).Value = itemId
    arParms(6).Direction = ParameterDirection.Output

    SqlHelper.ExecuteNonQuery( _
        ConfigurationSettings.AppSettings("connectionString"), _
        "AddProjectStatus", _
        arParms)

    Return CInt(arParms(6).Value)
End Function
```

C#

```csharp
public int AddProjectStatus(
    int moduleId,
    string CreatedByUser,
    string Title,
    DateTime EstCompletionDate,
    string CurrentStatus,
    int PercentComplete)
{

    if (userName.Length < 1)
    {
        userName = "unknown";
    }

    int itemId = 0;

    SqlParameter[] arParms = new SqlParameter[6];
    arParms[0] = new SqlParameter("@ModuleID", SqlDbType.Int);
    arParms[0].Value = moduleId;
    arParms[1] = new SqlParameter("@UserName", SqlDbType.NVarChar, 100);
    arParms[1].Value = userName;
    arParms[2] = new SqlParameter("@Title", SqlDbType.NVarChar);
    arParms[2].Value = title;
    arParms[3] = new SqlParameter(@EstCompletionDate", SqlDbType.DateTime);
    arParms[3].Value = estCompletionDate;
    arParms[4] = new SqlParameter "@CurrentStatus", SqlDbType.NVarChar);
    arParms[4].Value = currentStatus;
    arParms[5] = new SqlParameter("@PercentComplete", SqlDbType.Int);
    arParms[5].Value = percentComplete;
    arParms[6] = new SqlParameter ("@ItemID", SqlDbType.Int);
    arParms[6].Value = itemId;
    arParms[6].Direction = ParameterDirection.Output;

    SqlHelper.ExecuteNonQuery(
        ConfigurationSettings.AppSettings["connectionString"],
        "AddProjectStatus",
        arParms);
    return (int)(arParms[6].Value);
}
```

The pattern of the other methods should be clear from this example.

Creating the User Control

The fundamental definition of a portal module is a user control that inherits from **PortalModuleControl**. Because most of the modules display lists of information items, the main part of the user interface is a databound control. The Announcements.ascx user control interface contains a **DataList** that binds to the **Title** and **Description** properties for each announcement. A similar structural layout is adopted for the ProjectStatus user control. Status details are displayed using a **DataGrid** with **BoundColumns** to display each field:

```
<span class="ItemTitle">
    <%# DataBinder.Eval(Container.DataItem,"Title") %>
</span>
<br>
<span class="Normal">
    <%# DataBinder.Eval(Container.DataItem,"Description") %> 
    <asp:HyperLink id="moreLink" NavigateUrl='<%#
    DataBinder.Eval(Container.DataItem,"MoreLink") %>' Visible='<%#
    DataBinder.Eval(Container.DataItem,"MoreLink") <> String.Empty %>'
    runat="server">
    read more...</asp:HyperLink>
</span>
```

The data to populate the grid is retrieved using the **GetAllProjectStatus** method of the **ProjectStatus** class. This method requires a **ModuleId** as an input parameter. This parameter is supplied by the **PortalModuleControl** class, which is initialized when the module is loaded by the default page's code-behind class in the following line of code (this code is from the **PortalModuleControl** class in the lab portal application):

Visual Basic .NET

```
portalModule.ModuleConfiguration = _moduleSettings
```

C#

```
portalModule.ModuleConfiguration = _moduleSettings;
```

A user control for displaying module titles, DesktopModuleTitle.ascx, is shared by all the portal controls. This control contains an **EditUrl** property that establishes the **NavigateUrl** property for the **EditButton** which the user clicks to add a project status. The **HyperLink** control in the grid itself allows the user to edit the contents of the current project status using the EditProjectStatus.aspx page.

Final Steps for Extending Portal Content

> **Final Steps for Extending Portal Content**
> - Creating the Edit Page
> - Adding the Module to the Framework

Introduction

A page must be created to allow users to edit the content for a module. Due the consistent design of the site, adding a new edit page is as straightforward as the other parts of the extension process. The steps are:

- Create a form to display and validate content data.
- Create code-behind event handlers.
- Add the new module to the framework.

Creating the Edit Page

The edit page is a Web form that contains fields for each part of the content which is to be displayed. Each field has appropriate validation controls. A display area at the bottom of the form for content creator and creation date is automatically filled in according to the **Name** property of the current user and the current date and time.

Once the form has been created, event handlers are required for each type of user interaction. The **Page_Load** event populates the textboxes and drop-down list on the form using a **SqlDataReader**:

Visual Basic .NET

```
Dim statusDB As New ASPProject.ProjectStatusDB()
   Dim dr As SqlDataReader = statusDB.GetProjectStatus(itemId)

   dr.Read()

   TitleField.Text = CType(dr("Title"), String)
   EstCompletionField.Text = CType(dr("EstCompletionDate"), String)
   txtPercentComplete.Text = CType(dr("PercentComplete"), String)
   CreatedBy.Text = CType(dr("CreatedByUser"), String)
   CreatedDate.Text = CType(dr("CreatedDate"), _
   DateTime).ToShortDateString()

   ' Set the selected item to the value of Current Status
   Dim strCurrentStatus As String = dr("CurrentStatus")
   Dim intCurrentStatus = 0
   Select Case strCurrentStatus
       Case "Not Started"
       Case "Started"
           intCurrentStatus = 1
       Case "In Progress"
           intCurrentStatus = 2
       Case "Completed"
           intCurrentStatus = 3
       Case Else
           lblErrorMessage.Text = "Invalid status value retrieved."
   End Select

   ddCurrentStatus.SelectedIndex = intCurrentStatus

   dr.Close()
```

C#

```csharp
ASPProject.ProjectStatusDB statusDB = new ASPProject.ProjectStatusDB();
   SqlDataReader dr = statusDB.GetProjectStatus(itemId);

   dr.Read();

   TitleField.Text = (string) dr["Title"];
   EstCompletionField.Text = (string) dr["EstCompletionDate"];
   txtPercentComplete.Text = (string) dr["PercentComplete"];
   CreatedBy.Text = (string) dr["CreatedByUser"];
   CreatedDate.Text = (datetime) dr["CreatedDate"];
   // Set the selected item to the value of Current Status
   string strCurrentStatus = dr["CurrentStatus"]
   int intCurrentStatus = 0
   switch(strCurrentStatus)
   {
       case "Not Started":
       case "Started":
           intCurrentStatus = 1;
           break;

       case "In Progress":
           intCurrentStatus = 2;
       break;
   case "Completed":
       intCurrentStatus = 3;
       break;

       default:
           lblErrorMessage.Text = "Invalid status value retrieved.";
       break;
}

   ddCurrentStatus.SelectedIndex = intCurrentStatus;

     dr.Close();
```

When the user clicks the **Update** link, the user either adds a status item by using the **AddProjectStatus** method or updates with the **UpdateProjectStatus** method. The same **ProjectStatusDB** class is used when the user clicks **Delete**, invoking the **DeleteProjectStatus** method. When students build the portal extension in the final lab, it will become clear how easily extensible the design has been made.

Adding the Module to the Framework

The final step is to add the new module to the portal framework using the **Admin** tab. Because **ProjectStatus** is a new module type that will serve as the basis for an unlimited number of specific modules, it must be added using the **ModuleDefinitions** page. Once this has been done, a new entry is made in the **ModuleDefinitions** section of the .config file:

```
<ModuleDefinition FriendlyName="Project Status" MobileSourceFile=""
    DesktopSourceFile="DesktopModules/ProjectStatus.ascx" ModuleDefId="16" />
```

Now it can be added to one or more of the tabs by using the **Tabs** control of the **Admin** tab. **Project Status** now appears on the drop-down list for the TabLayout page so that it can be selected and added to one of the panes for the default page. Students can also use the **ModuleSettings** page to edit settings such as **CacheTimeout** and **Roles** for the new instance of the module. As soon as students click **Apply Changes**, the new content will be displayed on the next request to the site.

Lab 11: Extending the Portal with New Modules

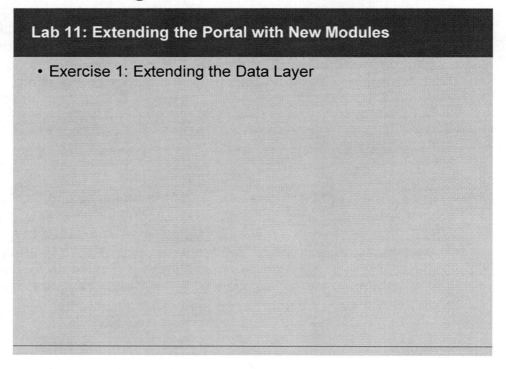

Exercise 1: Extending the Data Layer

After completing this lab, you will have demonstrated your ability to:
- Extend the data layer of a Web application.
- Create custom controls that extend base user controls.
- Create a Web form to edit a type of module content.

A primary design goal of the portal application is to create a framework that would allow new content types to be easily added. So long as the new content type follows a standard pattern, adding new content is very straightforward and can be automated. This final lab will lead the student through the steps necessary to add a new content module, which will be a module for adding FAQs. This lab requires knowledge of how to create tables and stored procedures in Microsoft SQL Server™, using ADO.NET to access data, and creating subclasses.

In the first exercise, students will extend the data structure of the site to add the new content type. This involves creating the underlying table and stored procedures, as well as the data class following the *Table Data Gateway* pattern.

Estimated time to complete this lab: 60 minutes

Starting a Virtual Machine

1. On the student computer, on the **Start** menu, point to **All Programs**, and then click **Microsoft Virtual PC**. If the Virtual PC console window does not appear, then right-click the **Virtual PC icon** in the notification area (system tray), and click **Show Virtual PC Console**.

2. In the Virtual PC console window, select the virtual machine that you would like to open and then click **Start**.

NOTE: Depending on your time zone, the first time you start each of the virtual machines, you may receive an error message that the parent virtual hard disk appears to have been modified. You can ignore this message.

3. The virtual machine will start in a new window.

Closing a Virtual Machine

1. On the student computer, in the virtual machine window, on the **Action** menu, click **Close**.

NOTE: To avoid accidentally closing the virtual machine during the lab, the **Close** option in the upper-right corner of the virtual machine is disabled.

2. The virtual machine window will close. All changes to the virtual hard disk are discarded.

Exercise 1: Extending the Data Layer

- **Open the Lab Starter Project**

    1. Open the ASPProjectVB or ASPProjectCS project in Visual Studio .NET using the following instructions.
    2. Browse to D:\2311\Labfiles\Lab11\Starter\VB or D:\2311\Labfiles\Lab11\Starter\CS.
    3. Launch the project by double-clicking on either the **ASPProjectVB.sln** or the **ASPProjectCS.sln** file in the lab starter folder.

- **Create a new table and stored procedure to handle the FAQ data type**

    1. In the Starter files for this lab, you will find a SQL script called FAQDataObjects.sql. Execute this script in the Portal database using the SQL Query Analyzer tool. The tool creates the table and stored procedures necessary to store and access data for this content type.
    2. Open SQL Server Enterprise Manager.
    3. Select **Tools/SQL Query Analyzer**.
    4. If prompted to log on, use "localhost" as the SQL Server name and select **Windows authentication**.
    5. At the top of the screen, select **Portal** as the database in the drop-down box.
    6. Click **Load SQL Script** or select **File/Open**.
    7. Navigate to **D:\2311\Labfiles\Lab11\Starter\FAQDataObjects.sql**.
    8. Click **Open**.
    9. Click **Execute Query** at the top of the screen (a green arrow).
    10. Confirm that the command completed successfully.

11. Close the SQL Query Analyzer and SQL Server Enterprise Manager.
12. This script will create the following tables and stored procedures:

    FAQs Table:

ItemID	int	4	
ModuleID	int	4	
CreatedByUser	nvarchar	100	✓
CreatedDate	datetime	8	✓
Question	text	16	✓
Answer	text	16	✓

    a. **AddFAQ**
    b. **DeleteFAQ**
    c. **GetFAQs**
    d. **GetSingleFAQ**
    e. **UpdateFAQ**

- ### Create a new data access layer component

1. In this section, students will create a new data access layer component using the *Table Data Gateway* pattern. The **AnnouncementsDB** class provides a good model from which to build in implementing this pattern. The methods in this class will serve as models for the methods in the **FAQsDB** class that we will create. Open the AnnouncementsDB.vb or AnnouncementsDB.cs file and study the following methods:

    a. **GetAnnouncements**
    b. **GetSingleAnnouncement**
    c. **DeleteAnnouncement**
    d. **AddAnnouncement**
    e. **UpdateAnnouncement**

2. Create a class file called FAQsDB.vb or FAQsDB.cs in the MainPortal folder. Reference the following namespaces with Imports or using clauses:

    a. **System.Configuration**
    b. **System.Data.SqlClient**
    c. **Microsoft.ApplicationBlocks.Data**

3. Start a namespace named **ASPProject**.
4. Create a public class named **FAQsDB**.

5. Create a public function named **GetFAQs**, which accepts a single parameter of type integer named **ModuleId** and returns a **SqlDataReader**.
6. Use the SqlHelper **ExecuteReader** method and pass in parameters according to the values in the following table:

Parameter Order	Parameter Value
1	ConfigurationSettings.AppSettings("connectionString")
2	GetFAQs
3	moduleId

7. Return a **SqlDataReader** named Reader from the function.
8. Your code should resemble the following:

Visual Basic .NET

```
Public Function GetFAQs(ByVal moduleId As Integer) As SqlDataReader

    Dim reader As SqlDataReader = SqlHelper.ExecuteReader( _
        ConfigurationSettings.AppSettings("connectionString"), _
        "GetFAQs", _
        moduleId)
    Return reader

End Function
```

C#

```
public SqlDataReader GetFAQs(int moduleId)
{
    SqlDataReader reader = SqlHelper.ExecuteReader(
        ConfigurationSettings.AppSettings.Get("connectionString"),
        "GetFAQs",
        moduleId);
    return reader;
}
```

9. Create a public function named **GetSingleFAQ**, which accepts a single parameter of type integer named **itemId** and returns a **SqlDataReader**.

10. Use the SqlHelper **ExecuteReader** method and pass in parameters according to the values in the following table:

Parameter Order	Parameter Value
1	ConfigurationSettings.AppSettings("connectionString")
2	GetSingleFAQ
3	itemId

11. Return a **SqlDataReader** named Reader from the function.

12. Your code should resemble the following:

Visual Basic .NET

```
Public Function GetSingleFAQ(ByVal itemId As Integer) As SqlDataReader

    Dim reader As SqlDataReader = SqlHelper.ExecuteReader( _
        ConfigurationSettings.AppSettings("connectionString"), _
        "GetSingleFAQ", _
        itemId)
    Return reader

End Function
```

C#

```
public SqlDataReader GetSingleFAQ (int itemId)
{
    SqlDataReader reader = SqlHelper.ExecuteReader(
        ConfigurationSettings.AppSettings.Get("connectionString"),
        "GetSingleFAQ",
        itemId);
    return reader;
}
```

13. Create a public function named **DeleteFAQ**, which accepts a single parameter of type integer named **itemId** and has no return value.

14. Use the SqlHelper **ExecuteNonQuery** method and pass in parameters according to the values in the following table:

Parameter Order	Parameter Value
1	ConfigurationSettings.AppSettings("connectionString")
2	**DeleteFAQ**
3	itemId

15. Your code should resemble the following:

Visual Basic .NET

```
Public Sub DeleteFAQ(ByVal itemId As Integer)
    SqlHelper.ExecuteNonQuery( _
        ConfigurationSettings.AppSettings("connectionString"), _
        "DeleteFAQ", _
        itemId)
End Sub
```

C#

```
public void DeleteFAQ (int itemId)
{
    SqlDataReader reader = SqlHelper.ExecuteReader(
        ConfigurationSettings.AppSettings.Get("connectionString"),
        "DeleteFAQ",
         itemId);
}
```

16. Create a public function named **AddFAQ**, which accepts four parameters: **moduleId** (integer), **userName** (string), **question** (string), and **answer** (string) and returns an integer. This procedure illustrates how to use the SqlHelper **ExecuteNonQuery** method to return an output parameter from a stored procedure.

17. Check to see if the **userName** parameter has a value. If not, set the value to **unknown**.

18. Declare and initialize a variable of type integer with a value of 0.

19. Declare an array named **arParams** which holds 5 elements of type **SqlParameter**.

20. Populate the array with **SqlParameter** objects according to the values in the following table:

Array Element	SqlParameter Object Values				
0	Name	SqlDbType	Value		
	@ModuleID	Int	moduleId		
1	Name	SqlDbType	Size	Value	
	@UserName	NVarChar	100	userName	
Array Element	SqlParameter Object Values				
Array Element	SqlParameter Object Values				
2	Name	SqlDbType	Value		
	@Question	Text	question		
3	Name	SqlDbType	Value		
	@Answer	Text	answer		
4	Name	SqlDbType	Value	ParameterDirection	
	@ItemID	Int	itemId	Output	

21. Use the SqlHelper **ExecuteNonQuery** method and pass in parameters according to the values in the following table:

Parameter Order	Parameter Value
1	ConfigurationSettings.AppSettings("connectionString")
2	AddFAQ
3	arParams

22. Return the output parameter **@ItemID** by referencing the fifth element in the array **arParams**, as shown below:

Visual Basic .NET
```
Return CInt(arParms(4).Value)
```

C#
```
return (int)(arParms[4].Value);
```

23. Your code should resemble the following:

Visual Basic .NET

```
Public Function AddFAQ( _
    ByVal moduleId As Integer, _
    ByVal userName As String, _
    ByVal question As String, _
    ByVal answer As String) As Integer

    If userName.Length < 1 Then
        userName = "unknown"
    End If

    Dim itemId As Integer = 0
    Dim arParms(4) As SqlParameter
    arParms(0) = New SqlParameter("@ModuleID", SqlDbType.Int)
    arParms(0).Value = moduleId
    arParms(1) = New SqlParameter("@UserName", SqlDbType.NVarChar, 100)
    arParms(1).Value = userName
    arParms(2) = New SqlParameter("@Question", SqlDbType.Text)
    arParms(2).Value = question
    arParms(3) = New SqlParameter("@Answer", SqlDbType.Text)
    arParms(3).Value = answer
    arParms(4) = New SqlParameter("@ItemID", SqlDbType.Int)
    arParms(4).Value = itemId
    arParms(4).Direction = ParameterDirection.Output

    SqlHelper.ExecuteNonQuery( _

    ConfigurationSettings.AppSettings("connectionString"), _
        "AddFAQ", _
        arParms)
    Return CInt(arParms(4).Value)

End Function
```

C#

```csharp
public int AddFAQ(
    int moduleId,
    String userName,
    String question,
    String answer)
{
    if(userName.Length < 1)
    {
        userName = "unknown";
    }

    int itemId = 0;
    SqlParameter [] arParms = new SqlParameter[ 5] ;
    arParms[ 0] = new SqlParameter("@ModuleID", SqlDbType.Int);
    arParms[ 0] .Value = moduleId;
    arParms[ 1] = new SqlParameter("@UserName", SqlDbType.NVarChar, 100);
    arParms[ 1] .Value = userName;
    arParms[ 2] = new SqlParameter("@Question", SqlDbType.Text);
    arParms[ 2] .Value = question;
    arParms[ 3] = new SqlParameter("@Answer", SqlDbType.Text);
    arParms[ 3] .Value = answer;
    arParms[ 4] = new SqlParameter("@ItemID", SqlDbType.Int);
    arParms[ 4] .Value = itemId;
    arParms[ 4] .Direction = ParameterDirection.Output;

    SqlHelper.ExecuteNonQuery(
        ConfigurationSettings.AppSettings.Get("connectionString"),
        "AddFAQ",
        arParms);
    return (int)(arParms[ 4] .Value);
}
```

24. Create a public function named **UpdateFAQ**, which accepts the parameters described in the following table:

Parameter Name	Parameter Type
itemId	Integer
userName	String
Question	String
Answer	String

25. Check to see if the **userName** parameter has a value. If not, set it to **unknown**.
26. Use the SqlHelper **ExecuteNonQuery** method and pass in parameters according to the values in the following table:

Parameter Order	Parameter Value
1	ConfigurationSettings.AppSettings("connectionString")
2	UpdateFAQ
3	itemId
4	userName
5	question
6	answer

27. Your code should resemble the following:

Visual Basic .NET

```vb
Public Sub UpdateFAQ( _
    ByVal itemId As Integer, _
    ByVal userName As String, _
    ByVal question As String, _
    ByVal answer As String)

    If userName.Length < 1 Then
        userName = "unknown"
    End If

    SqlHelper.ExecuteNonQuery( _
        ConfigurationSettings.AppSettings("connectionString"), _
        "UpdateFAQ", _
        itemId, _
        userName, _
        question, _
        answer)
End Sub
```

C#

```
public void UpdateFAQ(
    int itemId,
    String userName,
    String question,
    String answer)
{
    if(userName.Length < 1)
    {
        userName = "unknown";
    }

    SqlHelper.ExecuteNonQuery(
        ConfigurationSettings.AppSettings.Get("connectionString"),
        "UpdateFAQ",
        itemId,
        userName,
        question,
        answer);
}
```

- **Implement a new user control to display the new content type**

    1. Open the file FAQs.ascx in the Modules folder. Examine the code, noting the following:

        a. At the top of the page, the Title control has the attribute **EditText**. This attribute is set to **Add New FAQ** which will be displayed as the link text. The URL of the link will be the value of the **EditUrl** attribute. The logic to obtain the **ModuleId** so that it can be passed to the edit page is contained in the **DesktopModuleTitle** control. The code-behind for this control reads the **ModuleId** from its parent, which is the **PortalModuleControl** object which contains the current **DesktopModuleTitle** control.

        b. The edit hyperlink is displayed whenever a user with editing privileges accesses the control. The **ItemID** and **ModuleId** properties are passed to the EditFAQs.vb or EditFAQs.cs page through the databinding tags.

        c. The control contains a **DataList** named **lstFAQs**. An **ItemTemplate** contains the databinding tags to display the question and answer. The question is contained in a **LinkButton** so that the user can click it and see the answer. The answer is a label nested in a panel named pn1.

2. Open the code-behind page for this control, FAQs.ascx.vb or FAQs.ascx.cs. Note the following:

   a. The control inherits from **PortalModuleControl**. The base class contains properties such as **ModuleId** which are initialized when the control is loaded.

   b. In the Page_Load method, the **GetFAQs** method of the **FAQsDB** class is called to retrieve the FAQs for a particular module using the **ModuleId** property.

   c. The **SqlDataReader** that returns from the function populates the **DataList**.

3. Locate the comment **TODO Implement a handler for the DataList ItemCommand**.

4. In the **lst_FAQs_ItemCommand** method, declare a variable of type Panel named CurrentPanel. Use the Items collection of the **lstFAQs DataList** and the **FindControl** method of the Item object to retrieve a reference to pnl1.

5. Set the **Visible** property of **pnl** to **True**.

6. Your code should resemble the following:

Visual Basic .NET

```
Private Sub lstFAQs_ItemCommand(ByVal Sender As Object, ByVal e As
    DataListCommandEventArgs) Handles lstFAQs.ItemCommand

    Dim CurrentPanel As Panel
    Dim dtItem As DataListItem = lstFAQs.Items(e.Item.ItemIndex)
    CurrentPanel = CType(dtItem.FindControl("pnl"), Panel)
    CurrentPanel.Visible = True

End Sub
```

C#

```
private void lstFAQs_ItemCommand(object sender, DataListCommandEventArgs e)
{
    Panel CurrentPanel;
    DataListItem  dtItem = lstFAQs.Items[ e.Item.ItemIndex] ;
    CurrentPanel = (Panel)(dtItem.FindControl("pnl"));
    CurrentPanel.Visible = true;
}
```

■ Implement a new edit page for the new content type

1. Open the file EditFAQs.aspx in the Modules folder. Examine the code and note the following:

   a. The display for the question and answer consists of a nested table with a textbox named QuestionField and another textbox named AnswerField.

   b. Three linkbuttons at the bottom of the form are named **cmdUpdate, cmdCancel** and **cmdDelete**.

2. Open the code-behind for the EditFAQs.aspx page. Examine the code and note the following:

   a. In the **Page_Load** method, security is checked using the **HasEditPermissions** method of the **PortalSecurity** class.

   b. A client-side check is added to the **cmdDelete** button using the Attributes collection.

   c. If the FAQ item is being added for the first time, the **ItemId** property is set to -1.

   d. The **GetSingleFAQ** method of the **FAQsDB** object is used to retrieve a **SqlDataReader** and populate the fields of the Web form.

   e. A security check is inserted to make sure the user has not attempted to pass in an itemId for an unauthorized item.

3. Locate the **comment TODO Implement the cmdUpdate_Click method**. You will implement the logic to update an FAQ content item or insert a new one.

4. Check that the information has been validated using the **Page.IsValid** property.

5. Declare and instantiate a new object of type **FAQsDB** named **FAQs**.

6. Check the value of the ItemId property. If it is -1, the item should be inserted. Use the **AddFAQ** method of the FAQ object and pass in the parameters listed in the following table:

Parameter Order	Parameter Value
1	moduleId
2	Context.User.Identity.Name
3	QuestionField.Text
4	AnswerField.Text

7. In the **Else** clause, call the **UpdateFAQ** method of the **FAQs** object. Pass in the parameters listed in the following table:

Parameter Order	Parameter Value
1	ItemId
2	Context.User.Identity.Name
3	QuestionField.Text
4	AnswerField.Text

8. Note the **Response.Redirect** statement that redirects the user back to the portal home page.
9. Your code should resemble the following:

Visual Basic .NET

```vb
Protected Sub cmdUpdate_Click(ByVal sender As Object, ByVal e As EventArgs) _
    Handles cmdUpdate.Click

    If Page.IsValid = True Then

        Dim FAQs As New FAQsDB()

        If ItemId = -1 Then
            FAQs.AddFAQ( _
            moduleId, _
            Context.User.Identity.Name, _
            QuestionField.Text, _
            AnswerField.Text)
        Else

            FAQs.UpdateFAQ( _
            ItemId, _
            Context.User.Identity.Name, _
            QuestionField.Text, _
            AnswerField.Text)
        End If

        Response.Redirect(CType(ViewState("UrlReferrer"), String))

    End If

End Sub
```

C#

```csharp
protected void cmdUpdate_Click(Object sender, EventArgs e)
{
    if (Page.IsValid == true)
    {
        ASPProject.FAQsDB FAQs = new ASPProject.FAQsDB();

        if (itemId == -1)
        {
            FAQs.AddFAQ(
            moduleId,
            Context.User.Identity.Name,
            QuestionField.Text,
            AnswerField.Text);
        }
        else
        {
            FAQs.UpdateFAQ(
                itemId,
                Context.User.Identity.Name,
                QuestionField.Text,
                AnswerField.Text);
        }

    Response.Redirect((String) ViewState["UrlReferrer"] );
    }
}
```

- **Implement a new edit page for the new content type**
    1. The final step is to add the new portal module to the framework using the online administrator's Module Definition section. Log on with an account that has administrative privileges. Go to the **Admin** tab. Under the **Module Definition** title, select the link **Add New Module Type**. In the **Friendly Name** field, type **FAQs**. In the **Desktop Source** field, type **Modules/FAQs.ascx**. This adds a new **ModuleDefinition** element to the Portalcfg.xml file. Click **Update**.
    2. The module should be added to a tab for display. Select the **Home** tab from the **Tabs** list box on the Admin page. Click the **Edit icon** to edit the tab.
    3. In the Add Module section, select **FAQs** as the module type to add. Enter the name **Portal FAQs** in the **Module Name** field. Click **Add to Organize Modules Below** to add it to the Content Pane.
    4. Use the arrow to move the Portal FAQs module to the left pane.

5. Click **Apply Changes**. Navigate to the **Home** tab.
6. Use the **Add New FAQ** link to add a new FAQ. Confirm that it appears on the **Home** tab.
7. You have now completed the steps necessary to add a new content type to the portal.

Notes

Notes

Notes

Notes

Notes Decisions Crystal & web must be compiled otherwise before the application will go to the GAC for source. Otherwise it (the assembly) must be in the bin/ or production server.

ms corecof.

Notes

MSM2311ACP/C90-03610